1977

FRENCH
COMIC DRAMA
FROM THE SIXTEENTH
TO THE EIGHTEENTH
CENTURY

By the same author

A SHORT HISTORY OF FRENCH LITERATURE

AN INTRODUCTION TO THE FRENCH POETS

JEAN RACINE: A CRITICAL BIOGRAPHY

PRINCIPLES OF TRAGEDY

(Ed.) THE PENGUIN BOOK OF FRENCH VERSE, Part 2

FRENCH TRAGIC DRAMA IN THE SIXTEENTH AND
SEVENTEENTH CENTURIES

FRENCH
COMIC DRAMA

FROM THE SIXTEENTH TO THE EIGHTEENTH CENTURY

GEOFFREY BRERETON

LONDON
METHUEN & CO LTD
1977

First published in 1977
by Methuen & Co Ltd
11 New Fetter Lane, London EC4P 4EE
© 1977 Geoffrey Brereton
Printed in Great Britain
by Butler & Tanner Ltd, Frome and London

ISBN 0 416 78220 5 (*hardbound*)
ISBN 0 416 80710 0 (*paperback*)

Distributed in the USA by
HARPER & ROW PUBLISHERS, INC.
BARNES & NOBLE IMPORT DIVISION

CONTENTS

Preface vii

1 French Comedy before 1630 1

2 The Comedies of Pierre Corneille 12

3 Rotrou and Romantic Comedy 44

4 Scarron and Burlesque Comedy 51

5 Molière: Life and Theatrical Career 85

6 Molière's Comedy 102

7 The Shadow of Molière 150

8 The Cynical Generation: Dancourt, Regnard,
    Dufresny, Lesage 163

9 Marivaux 194

10 Bourgeois Comedy: Sentiment and Moralization 214

11 Beaumarchais 237

12 Conclusion 256

Notable Comedies 1552–1784 272

Complete List of Molière's Plays 275

Select Bibliography 277

Index 285

PREFACE

❦

This book is a companion to my *French Tragic Drama in the Sixteenth and Seventeenth Centuries*, but covering a longer period. The extension to the eighteenth century was made possible on grounds of space and desirable because of the nature of the material by the relative poverty of French comedy before 1630, requiring only an outline for the general reader and ordinary student, with a few pointers for intending specialists, whereas tragedy in the same period was a much more important genre. By the eighteenth century true tragedy had faded out and its attempted developments and variations demand a separate study, preferably linking or comparing it with the *drame*. Comedy continued to flourish through several decades of that century, reaching a late climax in Beaumarchais. Although a decline had begun in the 1730s, until then at least there were organic connections with earlier comedy. To sever these at the end of the Grand Siècle would be an act of amputation. In part prolonging a tradition, in part renewing or transforming it, the new comedies were vigorous and full of character in themselves.

Wherever one looks in this field of drama, Molière's pre-eminence is apparent. No attempt at reassessment could shake his position as France's greatest comic dramatist – and, one might as well say, the world's. Nor can his influence on later comedy be doubted. But, as with Corneille and Racine in tragedy, concentration on Molière has obscured somewhat lesser writers whose work presents features which are not in him. Disregarding the very different and fully recognized comic vein of Marivaux and the early comedies of Pierre Corneille which have been reinstated by scholarship if not on the stage,[1] one can point to Scarron and later to Dancourt and his generation as outstanding examples of unmerited neglect. All these particularly, with about a dozen others, make up the substance of this selective survey.

Individuality in drama is less common than in other kinds of writing. The author of an unusual novel or poem has more chance of having it published and eventually appreciated. The playwright in most periods must comply with the conditions of the theatre, its preconceptions and its production and acting techniques. Though the strongly original dramatist always breaks through in the end, it is against this background of theatrical practice which is only moderately flexible. I have therefore sketched it in wherever it seemed significant. Nevertheless the main stress falls on the major dramatists and their work (which can always be read but in many cases never seen acted), and from comparisons between them a coherent picture should emerge of the nature and development of the comedy of the time. This is the principal advantage of studying them in juxtaposition rather than in isolation. What it gives is not indeed a pattern but an interrelated series.

The guiding principle, as in my *French Tragic Drama*, is again 'descriptive'. This is sometimes thought to preclude 'criticism', though it is difficult to understand why. The criticism accompanies the description or is inherent in it. Admittedly it rarely results in one of those general theories which seem so illuminating but after a time, measured in no more than decades, have only the period charm of gaslight and can no longer be regarded as fully switched-on. If, as is sometimes the case, they happen to be based on an insufficient number of examples, they can be positively misleading.

Meanwhile the original works remain, inviting various interpretations, but permanently there for reappraisal. The theory that any work of art, particularly drama, exists only in virtue of the spectator's or reader's response to it, is at first sight very attractive. This two-way act of creation through participation does give life to works which might otherwise seem dead. But the theory contains a serious flaw. Supposing the artist were a genuis and the spectator an imbecile, or of course vice-versa, what a monster they would conceive between them. To describe the original works as objectively and accurately as possible

---

[1] A table of performances at the Comédie Française from 1680 to 1973 shows: *Le Menteur*, 835; *L'Illusion comique*, 50 (33 in 1931–40); all the other comedies, nil. (Sylvie Chevalley in *Europe*, special number, April–May 1974.)

while indicating their tone, context and the main problems they raise
seems the best service the ordinary critic can render both them and the
ordinary reader.

In this book, as in its predecessor, I have often drawn on H. C.
Lancaster's *History of Dramatic Literature in the Seventeenth Century*
and *Sunset*. That monumental work runs, with its extensions to
eighteenth-century tragedy, to thirteen volumes and well over 5000
pages. It describes and comments on every available play from 1610
to 1715 and every tragedy from then until 1792. The product of a
lifetime's dedicated scholarship, it is never likely to be superseded as
a storehouse of factual information; only very occasionally does it
require corrections on minor points. But it also contains critical
opinions and summings-up. One may agree or disagree with them and
they tend to get lost in the factual mass, but a careful reading of only
a few score pages shows that Lancaster was aware of nearly all the
points which interpretative critics have developed, even if he did not
do so himself. A typical scholar of his day, he was perhaps over-
preoccupied with 'sources' – important certainly in dramatic literature
but not always of great explanatory value.

The foundation of the present book is the direct reading or reconsideration of two or three hundred plays. In recent years excellent
collective editions of several of the major dramatists and of selected
plays by others have appeared. They have made more readily available
essential information on textual and allied matters and I have often
utilized them with gratitude. Where they are lacking or not comprehensive enough, further textual and historical research has been necessary (Rotrou and Scarron are cases in point). Critical interpretations
of the more general kind have been taken into account whenever
possible, if sometimes only to be rejected. The author has retained the
right to exercise his own judgement.

Comedy has a more obvious and immediate relationship with the
life of its time than tragedy. It reflects the ethos and *mores* of the social
scene very closely. That provides its main material, and the social
significance of the plays reviewed has been pointed out constantly, as
both interesting and highly relevant. Aesthetic and dramatic criteria
distinguish the good comedy from the weak comedy, but the theme or
subject is nearly always, in the widest sense of the word, 'manners',
and without a basis in them the most beautifully constructed play
would have a hollow centre.

A*

Although these comedies have been placed in their historical context, modern parallels suggest themselves so forcibly that it was impossible to avoid drawing them. This body of comedy was not only lively and amusing in its own day, but much of it still seems to be alive now. It can be studied, yet at the same time enjoyed with less specialized knowledge than tragedy demands. There should be no contradiction here. A first-year French student recently reported back from her university that she was greatly enjoying the books set in her course and felt rather guilty about it. 'Enjoyment' did not seem to go with 'work'. If this attitude ever became general in the academic study of literature, equating 'rigorousness' (with its unfortunate associations with *rigor mortis*) with boredom, it would be a sad day and a prediction of the end of this particular road.

FRENCH COMEDY
BEFORE 1630

The comic and comedy, meanings and types – French
Renaissance comedy: the Pléiade group and their models in
Latin and Italian literary comedy – later French comedy to 1630 –
the commedia dell'arte *– its type-characters – native French*
farce and the seventeenth-century farceurs *–*
forerunners of television – romantic
comedy and pastoral

Comedy is a broad term and, if extended to take in 'the comic', it becomes even broader. Far from being confined to drama it occurs throughout literature, in the epic, the novel, the poem and also, without benefit of art, in our diverse reactions to the ordinary incidents of life. 'A funny thing happened the other day, I (nearly) ran over my husband/boss/dog.' In its connection with theories of laughter the Comic Sense has been exhaustively analysed. It is unnecessary to go over this ground again beyond saying that, superficially at least, laughter is usually provoked by incongruity or surprise, by an unexpected departure from the normal. But what is thought 'funny' in this sense and what 'normal' may vary from individual to individual and also according to the time, place and circumstances. Some bystanders found the Crucifixion funny, others not. The response depends ultimately on the reigning psychological and social or communal assumptions and is therefore changeable. Even those simple jokes which appear basic because of their constant recurrence in known literature have not always amused everyone.

The comic is not necessarily even laughable, though it is hard to refuse it the element of surprise, either pleasant or unpleasant. In the second case the way may be open for 'bitter comedy', 'cruel comedy', 'black comedy', and so on. The comedy of the absurd, which seems based on the obvious, can be ranged in the familiar category of the surprisingly obvious and loaded with irony. These general theories, however, do not affect the description of most of the plays considered in this book, though they must enter into the analysis of some of them at a deeper level which will be indicated where relevant.

Our terms of reference are already laid down on general lines and our first concern is to characterize the successive phases of a plainly demarcated genre conceived as such by its authors and performed in the appropriate theatrical convention by actors specialized in representing it. Although they may have been mistaken, these knew what they meant and what they were aiming to offer to the public as stage comedy. Within the genre there were several variations and changes of emphasis which should emerge from this study. In its relationship to other genres – tragicomedy, *drame bourgeois*, and even tragedy – there was some interpenetration which also will be indicated where it seems significant. But on the whole French comedy over this long period can be surveyed as an independent genre, reflecting in its different facets qualities which are primarily its own and in which the external associations are of lesser importance. Even when, as in the comedy of intrigue, there is an obvious debt to Italian or Spanish originals which were not laughable, the French comic sense has usually taken over and adapted the material to its own purposes. A plot in itself is a mere convenience. It is the effects drawn from it which determine the nature of the play.

A distinction should no doubt be made between comedy (i.e. 'high comedy') and farce. These are the two opposite ends of the scale and it is not difficult to isolate the grosser forms of farce which have no ambition to be other than that. But farcical features are so persistent in every type of comedy that it is impossible to ignore them there or to detach them. How, for example, could one approach Molière without an awareness of his farces and near-farces and their overspill into his most serious plays? There are the peasants and Sganarelle in *Dom Juan* and why did he put Orgon under the table in *Tartuffe?*[1] Only *Le Misanthrope* is completely purged of the farcical.

---

[1] Because it was theatrically effective and convenient, it might be replied. Orgon must be able to get out easily in order to hide behind his wife. But Molière could certainly have devised some different overhearing-scene less reminiscent of the husband–wife–lover business of the traditional farce. Other

These two concrete examples only begin to suggest the importance of farce as both a stage influence and a habit of mind in the comedy of the whole period covered in this book.

༺ᏻᏻ༻

In the sixteenth and early seventeenth centuries, comedy certainly attempted to break free from farce and to acquire a higher status. For convenience we may call it literary comedy, though the term is descriptively inadequate. It was, however, still a poor relation to the more highly esteemed genre of tragedy, which claimed a direct ancestry from Seneca and the Greeks, and this inferior standing partly explains why so few comedies were printed (for the eighty years 1550–1630, about fifty, of which the majority are translations). There was no theatrical tradition and none grew up to compete seriously with the native farce and the work of the Italian comedians which will be described later. Though of considerable interest to specialists, French comedy in this period hardly constituted a live drama and produced no plays of outstanding quality.

The earliest attempt to create a new literary comedy must be credited to the Pléiade group of poet-dramatists. The same writers who had launched French tragedy in the 1550s, beginning with Jodelle's *Cléopâtre* (1552–3), produced in that and the following decade a handful of comedies which can be listed briefly:

Étienne Jodelle: *L'Eugène* (1552?) and a lost comedy, *La Rencontre* (1552–3), which seems to have been acted together with *Cléopâtre* at the first memorable performance of that tragedy before the king.

Jean de La Taille: *Le Négromant* (c. 1562) and *Les Corrivaux* (1562).

Jacques Grévin: *La Trésorière* (1558) and *Les Ébahis* (1561).

Rémy Belleau: *La Reconnue* (c. 1563).

Jean-Antoine de Baïf: *L'Eunuque* (1565) and *Le Brave* (1567).

These plays were performed by students in their colleges and occasionally in aristocratic houses or at Court. Though mainly

---

comic dramatists put their characters in clothes-closets or adjoining rooms. The characters of tragedy, of course, hid behind the arras or its equivalent.

written in the octosyllabic verse of the old farce (Jean de La Taille's were in prose), and containing similar passages of coarse humour, they were consciously intended as a departure from popular drama and designed to appeal to a more educated public. Their models and sources already point to the main influences that ran through French comedy for the rest of the sixteenth century.

Jodelle and his contemporaries could draw directly on the classic works of Latin comedy, which in its turn had derived from the Greek New Comedy.[1] The plays of Terence were familiar to every schoolboy as classroom texts. Those of Plautus, bawdier and linguistically more colloquial and exuberant, were less prized as examples of pure Latinity, but nevertheless widely read. The comedies of Belleau and de Baïf listed above were little more than translations or close adaptations of the Latin dramatists, whose influence is also perceptible in some of the others.

The more modern Italian influence already appeared in Grévin's *Les Ébahis* and in La Taille's two comedies (*Le Négromant* was a translation from Ariosto; *Les Corrivaux* had a plot taken from Boccaccio). It was soon to become very powerful in its two forms.

The so-called 'learned comedy' (*commedia erudita*) had flourished in Italy since the early years of the century. Based essentially on the Latin comedy, whose virtues as live theatre the Italian humanists had rediscovered, it produced both translations of the originals and adaptations showing varying degrees of inventiveness and transposing them to the contemporary Italian scene. In general, these became comedies of love intrigue with complicated plots and a strong element of bawdiness. Thus French writers could either borrow straight from Terence and Plautus or from the sometimes richer Italian versions. The results were predictably similar.[2]

---

[1] Principally Menander, whose original work was almost unknown to the sixteenth century. Some of his lost plays have been rediscovered, in whole or in part, in the twentieth century. The Greek Old Comedy of Aristophanes was available to sixteenth-century scholars, but was hardly utilized.

[2] In drama, and comedy in particular, one can go back and back for the themes, plots and characters. The question the critic will ask is less: 'Where did he get it from?' than: 'What did he make of it?' In 166 B.C. Terence, defending himself against a charge of plagiarism, wrote: '*The Flatterer* is a play of Menander's. One of the characters is a parasite, and there is a braggart captain. Our playwright does not deny that he has transposed these characters to his play from the Greek original . . . But if he is not allowed to introduce the same characters, how can it be more legitimate to introduce a servant on the run or a good old gentlewoman

For the remainder of the sixteenth century one can add to the plays of the Pléiade group the more or less original comedies of *Les Néapolitaines* (1584) by François d'Amboise, *Les Contents* (1584) by Odet de Turnèbe, *Les Écoliers* (1589) by François Perrin, and *Les Déguisés* (1594) by Jean Godard. (The dates are of publication and some of these plays must have been acted earlier.) The most prolific comic dramatist was Pierre de Larivey (*c.* 1540–1619), an Italian by birth who seems to have spent most or all of his life in France. He published six comedies in 1579 and three more as late as 1611. All were translations from Italian playwrights but were given French settings and character-names and written in lively colloquial French prose.

Apart from Larivey's last three comedies, probably written much earlier, very little survives from the early seventeenth century. Pierre Troterel published two highly vulgar 'comédies facétieuses', *Les Corrivaux* (1612) and *Gillette* (1620), but though of five-act length these were extended farces in their manner and material. Alexandre Hardy, most of whose extant plays are tragedies and tragicomedies, is known to have written one lost comedy in 1625, while the sole noteworthy comedy of the time, *Les Ramonneurs* (*c.* 1624), has also been attributed to him.

✦

In most of the Pléiade comedies the social background implied was that of an urban (Parisian) middle class, amoral and motivated almost exclusively by money and sex. The characters were merchants, their unfaithful wives, lawyers, the occasional priest (as in Jodelle's *L'Eugène*), the minor nobleman and the soldier. But these characters and their actions did not constitute a true social comedy. In that respect they projected the world of the older farce, going back to the fifteenth century and earlier, in spite of a more sophisticated treatment. Moreover the plays were too few and their impact too limited for it

---

or unprincipled courtesans or a greedy parasite or a braggart soldier or a suppositious child or an old gentleman tricked by a servant, or love or hate or jealousy? In fact nothing is said that has not been said before . . .' (Prologue to *The Eunuch*, Loeb translation.)

It will be noticed that Terence's list includes the basic elements of the majority of the French comedies described in this book. The principal exceptions are in P. Corneille and Marivaux.

to be possible to see them as a reflection of contemporary society. It was visibly very partial and founded more on convention than on observation.

The same can be said of the later sixteenth-century comedies. The down-to-earth middle-class background is again implied, though certain characters such as the braggart soldier, the student and the servants are more in evidence. Disguises and recognitions become more frequent and complicated as the Italian influence grows. But here also the small number of plays does not permit a valid generalization about their social basis. If not socially rootless they bring nothing new to a picture of the *mœurs* of the time, and this is truer still of the early seventeenth century.

The second Italian influence, more immediate than the *commedia erudita*, was that of the *commedia dell'arte*, which brings us back to the indefinite borderline between comedy and farce. There seem to have been several visits of Italian players to France – and French writers also visited Italy – before the almost permanent establishment of Italian companies in Paris which began in the 1570s with a royal invitation to the celebrated Gelosi. This was in the reigns of Charles IX and Henri III, whose mother was Catherine de Medici. It continued, with a few breaks, for about two hundred years.

The *commedia dell'arte* had sprung up in Italy towards the middle of the sixteenth century. Much of the basic material – plots, situations and characters – derived from the *commedia erudita* which the same players also performed at times, and through that once again from the Latins, but they transformed it for delighted audiences by their stage technique. This was physically lively and even acrobatic in what became the manner of the modern circus clown. Relying on mime, they improvised what dialogue was necessary in a jargon compounded of Italian, Spanish, French and mock-Latin, comic in itself and quite adequate to convey the meaning of their crude and simple situations to foreign audiences. Their performances were unscripted, or largely so. It seems unlikely that verbal scripts were used until the last quarter of the seventeenth century and none was published before 1691. By then French authors were writing for the Italians and scenes from their plays, in French, were published by Évariste Gherardi, the then

Harlequin of the troupe. Twenty-seven years later Luigi Riccoboni, a contemporary of Marivaux, published French and Italian versions of eight plays in his *Nouveau Théâtre Italien* (1718). Collections of outline scenarios appeared, however, much earlier, such as those of Flaminio Scala, who was in Paris with the Gelosi in 1577, and of Domenico Biancolelli (1640–88). The humour typical of the *commedia dell'arte* can be illustrated by an extract from Biancolelli's scenario for *Il convitato di pietra*, a Don Juan play a few years earlier than Molière's:

> In the shipwreck scene I am in the water in my shirt with ten or twelve bladders. I rise up and down as though I were swimming and I come out on the stage saying, 'No more water, no more water, but as much wine as you like.' My master recovers from his faint and while he is talking to the girl I do the trick [*lazzi*] of bursting one of the bladders by falling on my bum. It makes a noise and I say that is the cannon I am firing to celebrate our safe arrival.

The *commedia dell'arte* players usually acted in masks or made up their faces with powder and paint to create fixed character-types. In one or other of these their greatest actors would specialize throughout their careers, introducing their own modifications and becoming identified in the public mind with the character itself. Their strongest influence on French comedy was to be exerted through these types or 'masks'. The principal were these:

The Braggart Soldier or Captain (*Capitan, Capitano*), fantastically boastful about his impossible military exploits and also a Great Lover – irresistible, he believes, to women. Cowardly at heart, he is always deceived and deflated in the end. He was a development of Plautus' *Miles gloriosus*. Resenting the Spanish occupation of parts of Italy, the sixteenth-century Italians usually made him a Spaniard. Among his various names were Capitano Spavento di Valle Inferno, Terremoto, Matamoros, Rodomonte, Coccodrillo, Sangre y Fuego; in Germany, Horribilifibrax. He became naturalized in French comedy as *le fanfaron*.

Arlecchino (Harlequin), at first the Second Zanni or comic, reminiscent of the Parasite of Latin comedy, in which he had followed the Captain for what he could get out of him, generally a huge meal, since he is obsessively greedy for food. He often mocks and double-crosses his patron. The type was developed in a subtler direction in the seventeenth and eighteenth centuries.

Brighella, the First Zanni, the cunning servant, intriguing with great resource on his own or his master's behalf. He is related to such seventeenth-century French masks as Scapin, Turlupin, Sganarelle.

Pantalone, the First Old Man, with the comic features ascribed to his age. He was usually a rich and avaricious merchant, crafty yet easily taken in, wheezy but given to sudden leaps in the air which left him exhausted. He still fancied his chances with women and sometimes also had a scolding wife. As an authoritarian father he was in conflict with his children, attempting to thwart their love affairs or force undesirable marriages on them.

The Doctor, the Second Old Man, with various names such as Doctor Baloardo and Doctor Balanzone. Initially a comic-professor-type, perhaps invented by the students of Bologna, later he was more usually a lawyer or a physician. He remained pedantic and loquacious, given to long speeches full of mangled Greek and Latin phrases. Like Pantalone he had amorous inclinations but was always frustrated.

Pulcinella or Cetrulo was originally a ridiculous buffoon, also elderly, related to the traditional court jester. Developed by various Italian actors in the seventeenth century, be became, with his hunchback and his beaked nose, the Punch of the eighteenth-century puppet shows.

In contrast to these strongly caricatured types, the young characters were recognizably human and presented as attractively as possible, without masks or exaggerated make-up. As pairs of lovers they had various names. The quick-witted serving-maids with their ready tongues abetted them. These also played unmasked and were co-quettishly attractive. At first called Zagne and later Servette, giving the French *soubrettes*, they generally paired with the Zanni or menservants of the Brighella line. Colombina, a name first assumed by the famous actress Catarina Biancolelli round the turn of the seventeenth century, paired, however, with the developed Harlequin to form the now established couple.

Such were the main types which the *commedia dell'arte* placed before the French public for the best part of two centuries. Far from being merely 'popular', its chief exponents enjoyed the esteem and friendship of kings and princes. An excellent amateur interpreter of the Doctor's part was Prospero Lambertini, who remained proud of the fact after he became Pope Benedict XIV in 1740. It was to this Pope that Voltaire dedicated his tragedy *Le Fanatisme ou Mahomet* and received a warm letter of thanks in which Benedict gave his apostolic blessing to his 'dear son'.

Though much has been written on the subject, it is hardly possible to draw a clear line between the influence of the *commedia dell'arte* on the French theatre and that of Latin comedy and the *commedia erudita*. The only generalization to be made is that it was manifestly important and had a physical presence lacking in the other potential models. Its main weakness was the absence of idiosyncratic female masks: the Scolding Wife as a type-character, the Courtesan, the more novice Prostitute and the Procuress with her near-relation the Nurse.

❧

Though all these, except the Wife, disappeared in the more squeamish drama of the seventeenth century,[1] they had persisted until about 1630 in Parisian farce and in more ambitious plays, such as Alexandre Hardy's tragicomedies. The native farce might be seen as an alternative to the *commedia dell'arte*, but it also sometimes borrowed from the Italians and here again a precise distinction is unrealistic. To find the French farce in a pure state one has to look back to pre-Renaissance times and one can indeed look a long way – to the Latin writings of obscene-minded monks, to the *jongleurs*, to the *fabliaux*, to the clowning episodes which enlivened the Mysteries, to a number of precedents not necessarily meant for acting which composed the great medieval tradition that Rabelais inherited. In the sixteenth century the farce, together with the *moralité* and the *sotie*, continued this popular vein of broad clowning and bawdy which needed no foreign examples to sustain it. The tradition survived vigorously in the provinces until at least the 1650s (as Scarron's *Roman comique* testifies), and in Paris itself during the first two or three decades of the Grand Siècle.

It was then that the three celebrated *farceurs*, with the stage-names of Gros-Guillaume, Gaultier Garguille and Turlupin, performed at the Hôtel de Bourgogne, giving place sometimes to Italian companies

[1] The Procuress reappears in modified form in the Frosine of Molière's *L'Avare*. She inaugurates a long line of *femmes d'intrigue*, who are semi-respectable in that they do not keep brothels or tout for them but arrange chiefly marriages, together with other activities such as letting lodgings or money-lending. One can perceive a descendant of the Prostitute in the more mercenary of the coquettes of late seventeenth-century comedy, but these have risen above the humble professionals by their social standing and their methods.

and to shortlived attempts to present more serious drama by the actor-manager Valleran le Conte. In this period they offered the only kind of native comedy that the Parisian public knew, or apparently wanted. Their acts consisted of broadly humorous monologues and brightly smutty songs delivered solo, and they also had their feeds or combined together to present sketches inspired by topical and local events. A wife could not cheat her husband or a husband beat his wife without the risk of seeing the drama re-enacted amid laughter at the Hôtel de Bourgogne. They had much in common with the modern comics of television and the music-hall, each building up a personality which, once established, was a certain draw in itself. Outside this theatre other *farceurs* performed in the streets, notably Tabarin on his outdoor trestle stage on the Pont Neuf. He was a distant forerunner of commercial television since, continuing an earlier practice, he performed to attract customers to the shop next door. The object was to draw crowds who could then be sold quack medicines by a *charlatan* or *opérateur*, or be persuaded to undergo rudimentary surgery or dentistry. The performance itself had no open connection with the goods on sale.[1]

The acts of the Hôtel de Bourgogne *farceurs* were not printed, no doubt because, like those of the Italians, they were largely improvised. But they can be reconstructed with fair plausibility on the model of the numerous other farces which were printed[2] and with the help of other publications, the *Œuvres* of Tabarin,[3] the *Chansons* of Gaultier Garguille,[4] and the humorous monologues of the earlier *farceur* Bruscambille.[5]

❧

So in the eighty years following 1550 nearly all the elements of later comedy appeared, but were not seriously or consistently developed.

[1] There have never been more than four ways in which actors, musicians and other exponents of the non-plastic arts, who have nothing material to sell, can earn a living. They can charge admission fees, they can send round the hat (but this is notoriously chancy), they can draw subsidies from the State or other patrons, or they can rely on the kind of side-benefits that Tabarin enjoyed.

[2] Two collections appeared in the seventeenth century, one in 1612 and the other in 1619 (*Recueil Trepperel*, ed. E. Droz and H. Lewicka, 1935–61).

[3] Tabarin, *Œuvres* (1609), ed. G. Aventin, 2 vols (Paris, 1858).

[4] G. Garguille, *Chansons* (1631), ed. E. Fournier (Paris, 1858).

[5] Bruscambille, several publications, as *Facécieuses paradoxes et autres discours comiques* (1615), *Œuvres* (Rouen, 1629).

The four main streams, often intermingling, of Latin comedy, the *commedia erudita*, the *commedia dell'arte* and the farce flowed through this drama which lacked all the first requirements of success – an adequate theatre, a responsive and habituated public, and an outstanding author. The only type of play that was conspicuously absent was what in English terms is usually described as 'romantic comedy', the play concerned with lovers, with a complicated plot and a happy ending. It tends to be poetic and devoid of open cynicism.

In many such plays, whether they were Shakespearian or Spanish, there was no definable 'comic' element unless it was supplied by the Fool or *gracioso*, who was generally outside the main scheme of action and structurally dispensable. The germ of romantic comedy might be seen in some of the chaster love intrigues which stemmed particularly from the *commedia erudita*. In France, however, these were characteristic less of early comedy than of pastoral, which was classed and performed as a separate genre at the opposite pole to farce. Dramatic pastoral, again following the Italians, had appeared at the end of the sixteenth century and was to receive a new charge of energy from Honoré d'Urfé's pastoral novel *L'Astrée* (1607–27) and to enjoy a vogue which lasted well into the 1630s. After 1640 it virtually disappeared, but not without leaving perceptible marks on tragicomedy and comedy itself.

One of Rotrou's experiments in romantic comedy is considered in Chapter 3 below.

THE COMEDIES OF
PIERRE CORNEILLE

*Personal background and first plays –
outline of* Mélite *– La Veuve – La Galerie du Palais –
role of parents and servants in* La Galerie *– La Suivante –
the* vieillard amoureux *– La Place Royale – L'Illusion comique –
modern view of this 'caprice' – Le Menteur – La Suite du Menteur –
youthful atmosphere of the comedies – realism of dialogue –
of social background – higher bourgeoisie – ethos of
the comedies – characteriζation – the* Suivante *– Célidée –
Marivaux anticipated – Alidor – Alidor and Angélique –
a type-character, the* Menteur *– inadequacy of
classifications – Corneille's* Examens *and
his attitude towards the unities*

❦

Pierre Corneille was born at Rouen in 1606 of a family of provincial
lawyers and officials. He qualified for the bar and at the age of twenty-
two became the holder of two small Government posts[1] which his
father bought for him in the then usual way. These involved him in
the administration of the rivers and forests in his part of Normandy,
with the predominantly legal work which that required. He fulfilled his
duties conscientiously during the first twenty years of his literary career
and always retained his native connections after he had become the most
celebrated dramatist of France. His literary talent, which distinguished
him from the rest of his family, except for his younger brother Thomas,
was no doubt stimulated by his education at the Jesuit College of
Rouen which encouraged his early exercises in Latin and French verse.

Towards the end of 1629 his first play, *Mélite*, was performed,
apparently with great success, by a theatre company just establishing

[1] Those of *Avocat du Roi au siège des eaux et forêts* and *Premier avocat du Roi
en l'amirauté de France.*

itself in Paris, led by the actors Le Noir and Montdory. How this came about is not exactly known. It is supposed, with every appearance of probability, that the troupe were touring the provinces (after previous shortlived attempts to obtain a foothold in Paris), met Corneille while performing at Rouen, and went on to the capital taking his play with them. Writing some thirty years later in the *Examen* of *Mélite*, Corneille said that his comedy 'established a new company of players in Paris, notwithstanding the merit of the [other] company which had been in sole possession there. It equalled the best that had been produced until then and made me known at Court.'

This may be true in every particular. At least there is no doubt that Le Noir and Montdory successfully challenged the near-monopoly of the Hôtel de Bourgogne and presently founded the Théâtre du Marais, a second playhouse which at times almost eclipsed its rival. For some eighteen years Corneille remained with the Marais, which performed nearly all his most famous plays, both tragedies and comedies.[1] His success and that of the company were interdependent and grew together.

He wrote eight comedies in all. The first five formed a compact and homogeneous group extending over five years (1629–34) and broken only by a wildly experimental tragicomedy, *Clitandre* (1631). He then experimented with a tragedy, *Médée* (1635), followed by another comedy, *L'Illusion comique* (1635–6), which differed from the earlier group and might also be called experimental. After this there was the triumph of *Le Cid*, a tragicomedy (January 1637), and of his four 'Roman' tragedies, from *Horace* (1640) to *La Mort de Pompée* (1642–3). He returned to comedy with *Le Menteur* (1643) and *La Suite du Menteur* (1644), after which his comic book was closed.

It is interesting even if hypothetical to remark that if Corneille had continued in his early vein and if contemporary circumstances had been different one of France's greatest tragic dramatists might equally well be remembered as one of her great comic dramatists.

❦

What moved or enabled Corneille to write *Mélite*? The biographical explanation that he was inspired by an unhappy love affair is hardly

---

[1] The last for a long time was the tragedy of *Héraclius* (1647). He then transferred to the Hôtel with its new manager, Floridor, returning only once to the Marais to give his penultimate tragedy, *Pulchérie*, in 1672.

a sufficient answer, though verses which he wrote at the time and statements made after his death by his nephew Fontenelle and his brother Thomas can be quoted in support of it. The lived experience which may be incorporated in the comedy cannot account for its form and style, which give it its principal importance. Precedents or models for several of its features exist in earlier works which Corneille could have known. They are imperfectly digested and sometimes discordant, yet in spite of these weaknesses the comedy comes to life and, taken as a whole, was a kind of play new to the French stage. It reveals an original dramatist already at work on shaping material drawn from various sources in a mould he was making his own.

The plot depends on the relationships of two young women and three young men. This gives two potential couples and one unprovided male in the monogamous ethic which Corneille took for granted. Misunderstandings caused mainly by letters forged by one of the men, Éraste,[1] threaten the last-act marriages usual in this kind of comedy and when they come they are not entirely what a romantic temperament might wish for. The heroine, Mélite, is united to Tircis, these two having fallen in love during the play, and this is sentimentally satisfying. But her original suitor, the jealous and intriguing Éraste, is married to the second girl, Chloris, whom he has not courted and who accepts him on the advice of her brother Tircis and because of his 'merit'. The third male, Philandre, who was in love with Chloris from the beginning but turned temporarily to Mélite, errs by stupidity and inconstancy and is left out in the cold. The practical considerations of money and of socially suitable matches are of some importance. Realistic views on sex and marriage are expressed by the only stock character, Mélite's Nurse.[2] The uncompromising directness of some of her remarks was toned down in later editions of the play. In a final monologue, feeling insulted, she threatens to frustrate the arranged

[1] Original title *Mélite ou les Fausses Lettres*. The subtitle was dropped later.
[2] This favourite character in Renaissance and post-Renaissance drama was based on social reality. Well-to-do families gave their children to be breast-fed by a woman of peasant or equivalent stock. She brought up the infant and often remained with the family as a retainer long after her foster-child had grown up. Notable examples in drama range from the Nurse in Shakespeare's *Romeo and Juliet* (1594) to the Œnone of Racine's *Phèdre* (1677). The Nurse had a rustic mind and tongue. In comic drama particularly she was ready to take bribes to influence love affairs and sometimes acted as a procuress. In Corneille's time the part was taken by a man. The old Nurse, without her vices, reappears in some of Chekhov's plays (*Uncle Vanya, Three Sisters*). See also below, pp. 19–20.

marriages, though exactly how and whether her threat will be effective is not made clear.

The love intrigues and the implied emotional conventions had been paralleled in pastoral, as had the business of the false letters, a creaky device which becomes rather tedious but sets the plot moving and gives it the necessary twists. It had a long life in front of it in later comedy. The analysis of feeling in some of the dialogues and the long monologues also belonged to pastoral, which the young Corneille had ample opportunity to read and possibly to see acted without moving from Rouen. The scenes in which Éraste, believing that his intrigues have caused the deaths of Tircis and Mélite, goes temporarily mad and raves bombastically, had precedents in pastoral as well as in Garnier's old tragicomedy *Bradamante* (1582) and more recent tragicomedies. They might be explained here as burlesque or parody of the more nearly tragic examples and they certainly end on a comic note. But even if taken only half seriously they seem inappropriate to comedy,[1] as indeed is the violent distress or vindictiveness of some of the lovers as expressed in the course of the play. *Mélite* is in no sense funny, it is constructed from disparate material, and it is uneven in tone. The dialogue varies from the literary and pretentious to the colloquial and natural. Whenever naturalness obtains, as in the conversations between Tircis and his sister Chloris, the play shows a fresh and attractive face.

Where, however, it is most novel and deserving of Corneille's claim to have owed his success mainly to the use of 'a little common sense' is in its adaptation of the idealistic love ethic and some of the situations of pastoral to a modern urban social environment. If the realism of this is incomplete it is already apparent, sufficiently so to suggest a future line of development.

In his next four comedies Corneille retained the basic machinery of the love intrigue, always directed towards an appropriate marriage. In

---

[1] At least as comedy is usually conceived. In the *Examen* of the play Corneille has this to say of Éraste's madness: 'I condemned it even then in my heart, but as it was a theatrical highlight which never failed to please [probably because it gave actors an opportunity for a virtuoso display of emotionalism], I readily appropriated these bouts of frenzy and derived an effect from them of which I should still be proud today.' Corneille goes on to justify his mad scenes because they have a functional bearing on the plot.

their efforts to achieve this, or in some instances to avoid it, men deceive men and women, while women do the same, sometimes with the help of a subsidiary character. But the plays, though of similar type, are not repetitive. They contain variations and enrichments of incident and situation, a stronger element of social observation (possibly because Corneille was acquiring greater worldly experience) and above all an advance in characterization, which becomes subtler and deeper.

La Veuve has as its heroine a young and wealthy widow, Clarice, who is courted by a diffident lover, Philiste. She loves him also but wishes he would not be quite so modest and respectful. Too conscious of his inferiority in rank and fortune, he has been wooing her in troubadour fashion for some time and in Act I she is growing impatient:

> Il me sert en esclave et non pas en amant . . .
> Ah, que ne devient-il un peu plus téméraire!

There is no such diffidence in Philiste's supposed friend Alcidon who is attracted by the young widow's money but cannot declare himself openly because of loyalty to his friend, who was there first. Instead he pretends to be in love with Philiste's sister Doris, and meanwhile engages Clarice's Nurse to help him in his plotting. A third man, Célidan, is truly in love with Doris, but he is a friend of Alcidon's and here again male loyalty prevents him for a time from putting in his own claim. He takes part in Alcidon's plan to abduct the widow when she is walking in her garden one evening (a scene of some violence and excitement), and it is only later that he realizes that Alcidon has exploited his honest simplicity and double-crosses him in his turn. Finally Alcidon is exposed and exits ashamed. Clarice accepts the self-doubting Philiste after all but 'punishes' him by telling him to wait for four days – an exception to the comic convention of instant marriages. Doris is to marry her ardent suitor Célidan on the advice of her mother and her brother Philiste.

As in *Mélite* there are two females and three males, with an intriguing lover and an element of uncertainty in the final pairings. There are, however, additional complications and characters. The Nurse, only sketched in in *Mélite*, is treacherous and has an important role. The older generation appears and takes a hand. While the young widow is a free agent, the mother of Philiste and Doris[1] is an active

---

[1] In *Mélite* a mother had been briefly referred to as a person who ought to be consulted, but her consent to her children's decisions was taken for granted. The

matchmaker who has arranged independently a marriage for her daughter with an immature young man who does not appear (Florange) but is represented by his 'agent'. But she is quite ready to cancel this arrangement when informed of a more suitable match. There is a well-meant attempt at parental guidance but no parental tyranny. It is again the girl's brother who has the most decisive say.

In all this there is more substance than in *Mélite* and the plot has become more involved.

◆◆◆

The most immediately noticeable feature of the next comedy, *La Galerie du Palais*, was its stage-setting. The normal décor of comedy at this period was a street with houses fronting on to it, a convention which went right back to Roman comedy. Usually the characters met and conversed in the street, using the doors of the houses only for entrances and exits. The implausible situations to which this could lead, such as a private conversation or an emotional soliloquy delivered in the middle of the street, were sometimes circumvented by making the houses practicable. A side-curtain could be drawn to reveal an inner room in which monologues or conversations could take place more naturally. In certain scenes of this play the curtain was drawn aside to show the stalls of shopkeepers who set out their goods under the arcades of the Palais de Justice (the Law Courts), the whole being represented realistically. The stallkeepers themselves added to the effect. A bookseller, a draper and a haberdasher exchanged remarks on their best-selling lines and quarrelled in popular language if one took up space belonging to the other. This innovation on a stage where scenery was relatively unimportant might be regarded as a gimmick from a theoretical point of view and Corneille conceded as much in his *Examen*. But there is no doubt that it appealed to Parisian audiences

---

independence of the widow in French society at the time is made clear in Rotrou's *Les Ménechmes* (c. 1630–1):

ÉROTIE   [I will marry you]
        Quand j'aurai là-dessus consulté mes parents [relatives];
        Il est en mon pouvoir d'engager ma franchise,
        Je suis veuve, et ce titre à ce point m'autorise,
        Mais je dois ce respect à leur autorité.
                               (V. vii)

and contributed to the play's success. Its utility was to provide a place where the main characters could meet naturally while examining the goods on sale.

On a different level the play is constructed on the relationships of two women and two men only this time. The men are friends of each other, as are the women, and in the end the men marry the women of their first choice. Since there is no third lover to maintain the uncertainty, the plot seems potentially somewhat lean, but Corneille overcomes this by giving greater prominence to the reactions of his four main characters and by introducing a number of vicissitudes caused primarily by the hesitations of the leading female character, Célidée. This character will be discussed more fully later, but so far as the plot is concerned she has a rival in her friend Hippolyte, who is attracted by the same man, Lysandre. Lysandre's friend Dorimant falls in love at first sight with Hippolyte when he sees her at the merchants' stalls. He is presently introduced to her but snubbed in favour of Lysandre. It does appear possible in Act III that Hippolyte might capture Lysandre since the capricious Célidée has treated him coldly with the object, she says, of testing his affection, though at heart she is deeply in love with him. Lysandre, mutually in love with her, switches to Hippolyte to provoke her jealousy, but Hippolyte is rightly unconvinced of his sincerity. Eventually the two principal lovers are reconciled and Hippolyte settles for Dorimant, giving one love match and one marriage more or less of convenience, at least on the bride's part.

While the characterization enriches what otherwise would be yet another play based on rivalries and misunderstandings between lovers, there are further additions which distinguish it from the previous comedies. Corneille develops the role of parents beyond that first appearance in *La Veuve*. Hippolyte has a mother called Chrysante – the same name as that of the mother in *La Veuve* – who agrees to her daughter's union with Dorimant although, remembering an unhappy first marriage of her own, she refuses to force her into it. Corneille does not elaborate, but presumably she has been twice widowed, since divorce was unknown at the time in that social milieu. The father of Célidée (Pleirante), also widowed, is more interesting. Besides suggesting the Dorimant–Hippolyte match that ultimately takes place, he urges his daughter to marry her real love, Lysandre. But he does this just at the wrong moment, when the misunderstanding between the lovers is at its height (IV. x).

Corneille was already hinting that the older generation is never quite with the younger and, however good and reasonable their intentions, the best they can do is to keep out and rubber-stamp their children's arrangements if asked to. In the final curtain lines a cheeky *suivante*, Florice, suggests that the two poor old things should marry each other to round everything off. Chrysante shrugs this aside on the grounds of age, which she might not do in a more modern play:

CHRYSANTE Mon cœur est tout ravi de ce double hyménée.
FLORICE Mais afin que la joie soit égale à tous,
Faites encor celui de Monsieur et de vous.
CHRYSANTE Outre l'âge en tous deux un peu trop refroidie,
Cela sentirait trop sa fin de comédie.

The influence of the servants in *La Galerie du Palais* is developed in a way reminiscent of Roman comedy and also to become familiar in French comedy. Corneille's servants, whether he was then writing gropingly or deliberately, are of a superior type and could hardly be played by the professional comics. Both his young gallants have attendants he calls squires (*écuyers*), not valets, though their function is much the same. One of them plays an essential part in the intrigue and plots against his master in an attempt to make him marry the wrong woman. He is discovered, dismissed, but pardoned in the happy ending. His accomplice is Florice, the *suivante* of Hippolyte. She is a young follower or companion rather than a servant. Though witty, her wit is far from plebeian and she talks to her young mistress as an equal, as in the teasing scene in which Hippolyte is waiting impatiently for news of her lover's reactions:

HIPPOLYTE Dépêche. Ces discours font mourir Hippolyte.
FLORICE Mourez donc promptement, que je vous ressuscite.
HIPPOLYTE L'insupportable femme! Enfin diras-tu rien?
FLORICE L'impatiente fille! Enfin tout ira bien.
HIPPOLYTE Enfin tout ira bien? Ne saurai-je autre chose?

Corneille points out in his *Examen* of this play that his *suivante* is a successor of the Nurse of older comedy (a character he never used again) and that the part is taken by an actress playing unmasked:

Le personnage de nourrice, qui est de la vieille comédie et que le manque d'actrices sur nos théâtres y avait conservé jusqu'alors, afin qu'un homme le pût représenter sous le masque, se trouve ici métamorphosé en celui de suivante, qu'une femme représente sur son visage [with her natural face].

He seems to claim it as an innovation, though it was not completely so, since Rotrou had had a *suivante* in *La Bague de l'oubli*. She was a minor character (incidentally called Mélite) and spoke the unpolished language of the traditional Nurse.[1] In any case Corneille took up the *suivante*, even if she was not strictly his invention, modified her and made her the central character of his next play, to which she gave her name.

⁕ᠻᢒᠻᢒᠻ⁕

In *La Suivante* three young men, Florame, Clarimond and Théante, are all courting the same heiress, Daphnis, who loves only Florame. Though he is less rich than Clarimond, whom Daphnis dislikes, her marriage to him is favoured by her father for reasons which appear later. All might have been plain sailing but for the intrigues of Amarante,[2] Daphnis's *suivante*, a girl of good family but with no money. Both Florame and Théante pay court to Amarante whom they find attractive, but not sufficiently to divert them from the better match with Daphnis. While liking the maid, they really woo her to win the mistress. Amarante realizes this and intrigues against Daphnis, creating misunderstandings which nearly poison her relationship with the man she loves. Other misunderstandings are caused by Daphnis's father, Géraste. He insists that his daughter should marry a certain man whom he neglects to name. It is in fact the desirable Florame and Géraste's motive is to be accepted in marriage himself by Florame's sister (who does not appear) as part of the bargain. For the first time in Corneille's work a member of the older generation is in love with a young woman. His *vieillard amoureux* is unsympathetic but not treated as a figure of fun, as he had hitherto been in French and most other drama, certainly in comedy. In the end he gets his desire, his

---

[1] The word, in the general sense of 'follower' or 'attendant', is found much earlier. Montchrestien's *L'Écossaise* (1601) has a 'chœur des suivantes de la reine d'Écosse'.

[2] Amarante, like Célidée in *La Galerie du Palais*, is a name found in *L'Astrée*. Many of the confusingly identical or similar character-names in French seventeenth-century comedy derived primarily from pastoral and were then borrowed among the dramatists from play to play.

daughter marries Florame, and Amarante, deserted by everyone and deploring her poverty, calls down curses on the 'old man' in a long soliloquy which closes the play:

> ... Vieillard, qui de ta fille achètes une femme
> Dont peut-être aussitôt tu seras mécontent,
> Puisse le ciel aux soins qui te vont ronger l'âme
> Dénier le repos du tombeau qui t'attend!

These are strong words and hardly comic. Neither are other monologues in the play. Built though it is on similar lines to the preceding comedies, it is transformed by the prominence of these two characters, Amarante and Géraste, into something more nearly approaching the tragic and which at best could be classed as 'cruel comedy'.

In the same theatrical season (1634), so far as can be ascertained, Corneille produced his fifth comedy, *La Place Royale*. Until then he had been writing one play a year and it has been conjectured that he wrote this second play hurriedly to compete with a comedy of the same title by Claveret, now lost.[1] However that may be, there are no signs of haste in its composition. It rivals and indeed surpasses *La Suivante* in the seriousness of its psychological implications, relieved though they are by several scenes of true comedy. For his title and décor Corneille repeated the successful experiment of *La Galerie du Palais*, but this has no great significance and this time no local characters appear, though once again audiences must have been attracted by the scenic representation of an arcaded real square, then newly built in a fashionable quarter. It is still in existence as the Place des Vosges, near the eastern end of the Rue de Rivoli.

As the most interesting and sophisticated of Corneille's comedies and a development of his earlier ones, *La Place Royale* demands a fairly full description.

The cast pattern is the old one: two women and three men or, to be precise, three and a half, since there is a subsidiary lover (Lysis) who appears briefly in a few scenes and is not heard of again after Act III. There are no parts for parents, who are merely mentioned by one of the girls as people whom it would be desirable to consult

[1] See H. C. Lancaster, *History*, I, p. 582, footnote 2.

because of their greater experience. This is partly a pretext to save herself from accepting an offer of marriage unequivocally. Two of the men have followers, now called *domestiques*, who are inactive in the plot. The women are unattended; there are no *suivantes* or *soubrettes*, though some kind of confidante would have been useful to provide alternatives to the lonely soliloquies.

The love interest is focused on Angélique who has three admirers, Alidor, his friend Cléandre, and Doraste. Recognizing his friend's priority, Cléandre repeats the gambit of Alcidon in *La Veuve* and affects to be in love with Phylis, the sister of Doraste. The cynical Phylis, a new kind of character, is in love with no one. Her policy, she says, is to have lots of lovers (admirers) and at a critical moment for Angélique she offers her a choice of them:

> Choisis de mes amants, sans t'affliger si fort,
> Et n'appréhende pas de me faire grand tort.
> J'en pourrai au besoin fournir toute la ville,
> Qu'il m'en demeurerait plus de deux mille.
>
> (II. iv)

In a similar spirit, after several vicissitudes, she accepts Cléandre as a husband, finding him the best buy in a rather unexciting collection.

The strongly contrasted Angélique does not want just any man. She is passionately in love with Alidor. He is also in love with her but tormented by his obsession with independence, which conflicts with female domination and the chains of marriage. This complicated character will be returned to later with two or three others from the comedies. The immediate result is that he 'gives' Angélique to his eager friend Cléandre, but meanwhile Doraste slips in and wins Angélique at a moment when she is off-balance because of Alidor's apparent desertion of her. He then seems to return and she agrees to be 'abducted' by him at a ball given by Doraste to celebrate their engagement. This faked abduction again recalls *La Veuve*. It is an ingenious variation on the real one in that play and provides an admirable scene of comedy. Unknown to Angélique, she is really to be carried off by Cléandre, to whom Alidor has ceded his rights. A girl comes out from the ball and is seized by a gang of men and bundled rapidly away. Alidor, directing operations from the shadows, remains behind. He experiences some remorse and begins to doubt his own feelings but concludes resolutely in favour of independence.

At that precise moment Angélique appears at his elbow, saying: 'I'm sorry to have kept you waiting, but I was held up. We'd better go now, quickly.' Both soon realize that the wrong woman has been abducted – it proves to be Phylis, who had discovered Alidor's treachery and came out to warn Angélique. The latter also is enlightened now. If Alidor thought she was the abducted woman, why didn't he go with her? Alidor makes some unconvincing excuses, then gives up and sneaks away. Angélique tries to follow him, but is stopped by her fiancé Doraste coming out from the house to look for her. In an outburst of rage and frustration she tells him the whole truth: she still loves Alidor and not him. She now receives a further shock. Alidor had given her a letter promising marriage, as proof of his honourable intentions before the abduction. She was so sure of his sincerity that she had not bothered to read it, but had left it in her room for her father to see. There Doraste, looking for her, had found and read it. He now shows it to her. It is signed not by Alidor, but by Cléandre.

In the last act Phylis reappears, released by Cléandre. His earlier mock courting of her has changed to genuine feeling. He has been won over by her tears during the abduction (cf. a similar effect of tears in Racine's *Britannicus*, but on an altogether more ruthless character) and wants to marry her. He 'gives back' Angélique to Alidor. After all that has happened Doraste understandably rejects her also. Let her return to her beloved Alidor, and Alidor himself, in love yet not in love, begs her to have him. But she has been through too much. She will marry no one and will enter a convent. On this apparently firm decision and her words which recur in Racine's *Bérénice*, the play nearly ends:

Cherche une autre à trahir; et pour jamais adieu.

It is left for Alidor in a final soliloquy[1] to express his pride at having conquered love and escaped from the too attractive Angélique. It is best that she should become a nun, for then she will be beyond his reach. She will have no human husband to provoke his jealousy and

---

[1] Both *La Place Royale* and *La Suivante* end in soliloquies by what may be considered the principal characters, Alidor and Amarante. To finish with a soliloquy was quite exceptional, particularly in comedy, and marks the serious nature of the two plays. The soliloquies take the form of *stances*, in these cases cross-rhymed alexandrines in four-line stanzas.

will no longer endanger the freedom which he values above everything else.

This finally sombre play was the last of its kind that Corneille was to write.

✢✢✢

If any of the comedies was composed hurriedly it would be *L'Illusion comique*, an ingenious entertainment of great theatrical interest but lacking the depth and unity of the earlier plays and of an entirely different kind. It followed *La Place Royale* after the tragedy of *Médée* and appeared at a time when Corneille may already have been planning *Le Cid* and preparing to shift his work to the different register of tragi-comedy. At this date he was quite evidently beginning the serious exploration of Spanish literature which gave him his greatest popular triumph, for in *L'Illusion comique* there is an apt and open reference to several picaresque novels and this is the first trace of any kind of Spanish influence in his work.

L'Illusion contains a play within a play. In Act I the elderly Prida-mant, searching for his long-lost son Clindor, consults the magician Alcandre[1] in his enchanted cave. Alcandre waves his wand and reveals a collection of sumptuous clothes. They belong, he says, to the son, who must have become a highly important man to possess such garments. He explains that, after exercising various humble or disreputable trades, Clindor began his rise in the world by attaching himself to the braggart Gascon Captain Matamore and exploiting him as his follower. He then offers to show Pridamant the fortunes of his son from that time on, represented before his eyes by 'phantoms' which he will conjure up.

This gives Acts II to IV, which resemble a romantic tragicomedy with the insertion of the comic Captain. Clindor wins the beautiful Isabelle after spurning her servant Lyse (who betrays him for revenge, later repenting), kills a rival suitor Adraste, is imprisoned for this and sentenced to death, then released by the gaoler who has fallen in love

---

[1] This had been the name of the magician in Rotrou's *La Bague de l'oubli*, but before overemphasizing this fact it must be noted that Corneille himself had used the name twice already: for the King of Scotland in *Clitandre* and for Clarice's deceased husband in *La Veuve*. Rotrou also used it more than once for characters who were not magicians.

with Lyse. The two couples flee the town together. Matamore has already been shaken off. Defied and threatened by Clindor, he has refused to fight and has yielded Isabelle, whom he has been courting, to his ex-servant in a parodied gesture of 'generosity'.

In Act V two years are presumed to have passed. Clindor has become the right-hand man of a Prince and has clandestinely won the love of the Princess. Going to a midnight rendezvous with her he is surprised by his wife Isabelle and persuaded to remain faithful to her. Just then a squire of the Prince arrives and stabs Clindor mortally. Isabelle dies also, of grief.

Pridamant, watching this with the magician, is disconsolate. But there is another wave of the wand and the scene changes to show a company of actors counting their takings. These tragic deaths were part of a play they were performing and the real Clindor and Isabelle are now successful actors in Paris. The play ends with a eulogy by Alcandre of the theatre, today an honourable and lucrative profession.

L'Illusion shares one feature with Corneille's immediately preceding tragedy (his Médée was an enchantress with a magic wand) and several found in the works of other dramatists. Elements with which the public was familiar had been skilfully put together to provide a lively mixture in the vein of the more modern pantomime. Corneille claimed no more than this in his *Examen*, in which he called it a 'galanterie extravagante' and a 'caprice'. Though *L'Illusion* was a contemporary success, his point of view came to be shared by others and his 'étrange monstre' (Dedication) went totally unperformed until, in 1861, the Comédie Française presented an extraordinarily distorted version of it. Conventionally regular plays were preferred, even when they were comedies, and all too soon Corneille was consecrated as a classic author to the neglect of his remarkably varied gifts as a man of the theatre.

The twentieth century has seen *L'Illusion* with a different eye. An imaginative production by Louis Jouvet in 1937, giving full rein to scenic effects and transformations and stressing the play's 'magical' qualities, coincided in time with the new critical interest in the baroque – the anti-classical side of the seventeenth century. This gave rise to interpretations of the play as a masterpiece of illusionism, both aesthetic and psychological, which go much further than anything that Corneille or his generation intended or saw in it. Certainly a work can be interpreted on several levels and a creative writer may not realize what he has achieved, but it is doubtful whether *L'Illusion* really lends itself to this kind of appreciation in depth. *L'Illusion* is not another *Tempest.*

Seven years later and after his great Roman tragedies Corneille returned briefly to comedy and a Spanish source. *Le Menteur* was based on Alarcón's *La verdad sospechosa*, but transformed into a fine French play which was so appreciated that it has become almost over-familiar on the stage of the Comédie Française and in the classroom. The conditions in which it has been acted and studied might give the impression that it was the only comedy that Corneille wrote, whereas it has close and evident links with the earlier group and cannot be fully appreciated in isolation. The main differences are that the verse is more polished and the play more slickly constructed. There is unity of time (twenty-four hours), of place,[1] of action and certainly of interest, concentrated upon the protagonist, a congenital liar, whose prominence throughout makes this more obviously a comedy of character than *La Place Royale* or even *La Suivante*. At the same time, the love intrigue is more than a background device to animate the central character. It is ingenious and amusing in itself and it would be hard to imagine a different plot for this professionally integrated play. It depends, as in some of the previous comedies, on a misunderstanding caused, for the first time in Corneille, by a confusion over identities. This, however, though an innovation for him, was far from new in the theatre of the time. The parents seem rather more powerful than before, particularly the Liar's father, but this is because of his moneybags. The servants are conventionally lively, but restricted to the function of go-betweens. This applies even to the Liar's valet Cliton, who has many comments to make on his master's behaviour but is not a broadly comic character, although the original part was taken by the comedian Jodelet.[2] The cast is headed by two men and two women, giving two pairs or cross-pairs.

Dorante, newly arrived in Paris, whose wonderful new buildings are described, is determined to cut a figure by appearing to be a

---

[1] The scene is the town of Paris, which was considered enough in comedy at that date. The first act takes place in the Garden of the Tuileries, the rest in the Place Royale.

[2] See pp. 53–9 below.

gallant soldier, not the unworldly young law student that he is. The misunderstanding begins when he meets Clarice in the street and falls instantly in love with her (as Dorimant did with Hippolyte in *La Galerie du Palais*) but believes she is called Lucrèce, which in fact is the name of her more modest companion. Later the two girls trick him, Clarice at her window pretending to be Lucrèce and receiving his protestations of love for the person of that name. Before this Dorante's father Géronte had proposed to marry him to Clarice, the very woman he wanted. Mistaken in the name, Dorante wriggled out of the match by inventing a forced marriage to a girl he claimed to have met in Poitiers.

Clarice is attracted by Dorante and would have married him. She has been engaged for two years to Alcippe, the second leading man, and is tired of waiting. Hearing of a rival, Alcippe challenges Dorante to a duel, but is placated. Finally Dorante is unmasked – the two girls have never really believed him. He has invented other stories to justify himself in situations provoked by his confusion of Clarice with Lucrèce and has entangled himself more and more tightly in a net of lies. His ingenuity recoils on his own head. Alcippe marries the real Clarice and the Liar is to marry Lucrèce, who has already shown that she likes him. By indicating this beforehand Corneille did something to mitigate the impression of an over-brutal ending.

One feels considerably let down by *La Suite du Menteur*. No doubt the public was ready for a sequel and the theatre wanted a financial success, which it eventually had. But Corneille followed his sparkling comedy with a play which is nearer to tragicomedy and was suggested by Lope de Vega's serious cloak-and-sword drama, *Amar sin saber a quien*. The main relief is in the droll comments of the valet Cliton (again a part for Jodelet) and his conversations with the *soubrette* Lyse. Cliton and Dorante are carried over from *Le Menteur* together with Philiste, a subsidiary character in the first play. Dorante is presented as a reformed character (though Cliton cannot believe it) who only lies to help others and is now a thoroughly honourable man. In modern eyes this looks a little odd since, to link the two plays, it is explained that, fearing the chains of marriage, like Alidor in *La Place Royale*, he disappeared just before his wedding with Lucrèce, taking her money with him. His father married her in compensation, but died shortly after. However, two years have passed and Dorante is now in prison at Lyon, where the action takes place, under suspicion of having killed a man in a duel. Though innocent, he refuses to name the real killer on the principle of honour among gentlemen. The sister of this man, who dare not act openly, visits him in prison with her maid (a reminiscence of *L'Illusion comique*) and the two fall in love. She, however (her name is Mélisse), is engaged to Philiste, an old friend of Dorante's. Philiste, influential in Lyon, has him released, whereupon Dorante, discovering his friend's claim to Mélisse, nobly offers to renounce her and leave. With equal nobility Philiste refuses and Dorante and Mélisse are to marry.

The play is padded, though entertainingly, with topical references to Jodelet and *Le Menteur*, which tend to show, when one recalls the praises of the theatrical profession in *L'Illusion comique*, that Corneille composed it with his eye on the public rather than under any strong creative compulsion. It was in any case his farewell to comedy.

᠀᠀᠀᠀

Corneille's comedies introduce us to a world not hitherto represented in French drama, and hardly in French literature more generally. It is a young world, peopled by characters of whom most, if one had to guess their ages, would certainly not be out of their middle twenties. The women lead the dance with the help of their equally youthful followers who, from the third comedy on, are less servants than familiar companions. The men also are young and impetuous. They try to influence events and may think they are doing so, but with one or two exceptions they are manipulated by the women and their typical role and function is that of the handsome gallant who forms a necessary part of the women's emotional cosmogony and must be prepared to fight other males if circumstances demand it. Whether male or female, these characters are impelled by the feelings appropriate to their age. (In a few cases one could use the stronger word 'passions', which would underline the serious element in the plays. But it belongs more properly to tragedy, where the feelings are intensified to a point of total obsession.) They experience them with elation or depression. They are immensely active, lively, and on occasion gay; impulsive usually, though timid, sceptical or calculating if this happens to be their nature, but not in a mature manner. Calculation is called 'reason', the traditional counterpoise to emotion. It operates, however, not as a restraint, but to suggest some alternative line of action. The whole atmosphere is fast-moving and sometimes violent.

The older generation, as already indicated, remain in the background. There have to be parents and uncles to satisfy the marriage conventions of the time, but they are outsiders in this world of youth. The only one who seeks a sexual involvement in it (Géraste in *La Suivante*) is condemned by Amarante as much too old for such things.[1]

The characters do not exist in a social vacuum, unlike those in Rotrou's comedies. They belonged to a modern stratum of society, intended to be recognizable to contemporary audiences. Corneille was aiming at realism, a point which he stresses more than once in his critical comments and explicitly or implicitly in the plays themselves. It shows primarily in his language, which approximates closely to natural speech in numerous passages. In a few comedies (*Mélite, La Veuve, La Suivante*) he uses the old device of stichomythia, inherited from the previous century and soon to be confined to tragedy, but describes it, without giving it its name, as 'a rather pernicious affectation':

> L'entretien de Daphnis au troisième [acte] avec cet amant dédaigné a une affectation assez dangereuse, de ne dire que chacun un vers à la fois; cela sort tout à fait du vraisemblable, puisque naturellement on ne peut être si mesuré en ce qu'on s'entredit. Les exemples d'Euripide et de Sénèque pourraient autoriser cette affectation, qu'ils pratiquent si souvent qu'il semble que leurs acteurs ne viennent quelquefois sur la scène que pour s'y battre à coup de sentences; mais c'est une beauté qu'il ne leur faut pas envier. Elle est trop fardée pour donner un amour raisonnable à ceux qui ont de bons yeux . . .[2]

Soliloquies cast as *tirades* or in *stances* still occur, but these can be accepted as the inner thoughts of the speaker and therefore, according

---

[1] See pp. 20–1 above. Realistically, he was probably about fifty, but this was considered old at that period. One might perhaps add the father of Dorante, whose marriage to the deserted Lucrèce to fulfil an obligation of family honour is mentioned in *La Suite du Menteur*. The effort is too much for him and he dies after two months.

[2] *Examen de La Suivante*. The same preoccupation with naturalness inspires Corneille's dislike of *fardé* language (artificial, made-up) and the *fardés* stock characters of the *commedia dell'arte*.

to a principle not recognized until much later, legitimately cast in a special language. And even in them the terms are not extravagant or strikingly 'poetic'. Elsewhere the general difficulty of simulating natural dialogue in rhymed verse is largely overcome. The inevitable stylization gives them more point or humour than would be found in ordinary conversation but does not make them sound artificial. If totally naturalistic speech is hardly to be expected Corneille was evidently feeling his way towards it so far as the literary and theatrical conventions of the time would allow.

He was fully aware of his problems. The poetic expression of love, says Lysandre in *La Galerie du Palais* (I. vii), differs from the reality:

> Et je n'ai jamais vu de cervelles bien faites
> Qui traitassent l'amour à la façon des poètes.

And he goes on to deplore the unsuitable styles often used in comedy to deform its truth:

> O pauvre comédie, objet de tant de veines,
> Si tu n'es qu'un portrait des actions humaines,
> On te tire souvent sur un original
> A qui, pour dire vrai, tu ressembles fort mal.

A 'portrait of human actions' need not necessarily be 'a mirror held up to society', but on the overwhelming evidence of these comedies (always excepting *L'Illusion comique*) this formed an integral part of Corneille's conception of realism.

Commentators are agreed, and it is indeed obvious, that the social background was that of the Parisian middle class. It was upper rather than lower. M. Georges Couton, in some of his introductions to Corneille's plays,[1] has stressed the bourgeois aspect of the comedies. If this conjures up pictures of a comfortable housewife preoccupied with the *pot-au-feu* it would be gravely misleading. Money values, connected with marriage dowries, have a certain importance, but this business acumen was no monopoly of any particular class and the higher one looks in society the larger it looms. The aristocracy did

[1] *Théâtre complet de Corneille*, Vol. I (Paris, 1971).

not willingly marry off their children without a substantial *quid pro quo* in the form of income and estates. Corneille himself appears in a single passage to depreciate the social standing of his characters. He writes in the *Examen* of *La Galerie du Palais*: 'Célidée et Hippolyte sont deux voisines dont les demeures ne sont séparées que par le travers [width] d'une rue, et ne sont pas d'une condition trop élevée pour souffrir que leurs amants les entretiennent à leur porte.'

While it is true that the daughters of the higher bourgeoisie would not stand chatting to their admirers at the street-door but would have them ushered into the house by a servant – a fact which Corneille partly admits in his next sentence: 'Il est vrai que ce qu'elles disent serait mieux dit dans une chambre ou dans une salle' – the point which he is really discussing here, with hindsight, is the unity of place. Rigorously interpreted, this required a single scene – a street – and did not permit the actors to appear in interior rooms as well. Corneille is arguing that his staging observed this scenic convention and at the same time more or less fulfilled the requirements of realistic probability. 'Il sort un peu de l'exacte vraisemblance . . . mais il est presque impossible d'en user autrement.' He musters all the arguments he can find to support his contention and throws in among them a reference to the social standing of the two girls. This cannot be taken as conclusive either for this comedy or for the others in the group, and it is in fact contradicted in another *Examen*, that of *Mélite*: '[Cette comédie] faisait son effet par l'humeur enjouée de gens d'une condition au-dessus de ceux qu'on voit dans les comédies de Plaute et de Térence, qui n'étaient que des marchands.'

Characters in *La Place Royale* occupy houses whose modern equivalent would be a luxury flat in a select district. The women have nothing to do but pursue their love affairs and pay visits to each other. They go in their private coaches, the seventeenth-century equivalent of the chauffeur-driven car.[1] ('I need plenty of money to be able to run a coach [*rouler un carrosse*]' says a woman in one of Scarron's comedies, which have a similar social background.) The shoppers in *La Galerie*

---

[1] All coaches had to be 'chauffeur-driven', since no one would or could drive their own. There were grades of coaches, as of cars, but the upkeep of the plainest, with the coachman, horses and stabling, represented a considerable expense. See Molière's *L'Avare* (1668) for an attempt to run a coach over-economically. Coach-snobbery at a still later date, bearing on the type of vehicle and the number of horses and footmen, is stressed in Dancourt's *Le Chevalier à la mode* (1697).

du Palais are interested in the latest trends in literature and fashion. They choose with discrimination and send their servants to collect and pay for the goods they have ordered. On a bigger scale, Doraste in *La Place Royale* gives a ball in honour of his fiancée which would require the engagement of professional musicians, an expensive item. The magnificent fête on the Seine in *Le Menteur* (I. iv), with four boatloads of musicians, fireworks and an exquisite supper, was not given by Dorante, who claims it as his work with his usual powers of invention. But his friends, greatly impressed, do not question that he could have given it. The Liar adds to the effect by saying that he had only an hour or two to organize this costly 'bagatelle'. It was the best that could be managed in the short time given him. This particular throwaway tone, with its implications of good breeding, is often adopted in the comedies by more genuine speakers. *La Veuve* ends with an invitation to her friends by the young widow to come in that evening to eat 'un mauvais repas'. One can feel reasonably confident that the 'scratch meal' will consist of several beautifully served courses with the appropriate wines.

All this mirrors the higher bourgeoisie, cultivated and fairly rich, or aspiring to be. Some of its members are poorer than others, which is realistic, but all assume that they ought to have enough money to live with a certain *panache*. Somewhat surprisingly, the Court does not figure in Cornelian comedy, as it well might in a more romantic type of play. No comte or marquis appears or is even claimed as an acquaintance. Yet the young men could well be courtiers. They carry swords and are ready to fight duels. Some of them observe the courtly code of honour as it was then conceived – though it was beginning to be called in question concurrently with Richelieu's campaign to stamp out the duel as part of a wider attack on the old conception of personal and family honour which diverted loyalty from the State to the clan.

This gradual erosion of the old values is reflected in the comedies (notably in Alidor's opinions on love and friendship in *La Place Royale*) and here again Corneille's keen observation of contemporary trends is apparent. But on the whole the laws of chivalry are still observed. Respectful adoration of the lady is the weakest and the women themselves do little to encourage it. They will never remain on a pedestal if it interferes with their main interest, which is to get their man. Loyal friendship between males is more important and when it is betrayed it is considered scandalous. The necessary trust between fighting men in war, from which this ethic ultimately derived, is felt to have been undermined. The related idea that a brave man is sure to be honourable is asserted as late as *Le Menteur*. Since Dorante has offered to fight a duel he cannot, in the eyes of Alcippe, be deceitful:

> La valeur n'apprend pas la fourbe en son école:
> Tout homme de courage est homme de parole . . .

Philiste replies, sarcastically and rightly:

> Dorante, à ce que je présume,
> Est vaillant par nature et menteur par coutume.

The threatened duels in the comedies are all over women. There are two motives, either 'Keep away from my girl', or 'Since you've seduced my sister, you marry her – or else'.

This, with loyalty among friends and the class loyalty among gentlemen found in *La Suite du Menteur* (from a Spanish original) is what remains of the honour code in the comedies and forms their most clearly definable ethical background. Dented though it is by individual males and by the more pragmatic females and their servants, it is not openly mocked, as it was a little later in Scarron's comedies, but is subtly shown to be in a state of incipient decay.[1] Since Corneille's spirited young gallants respect or are aware of it, it is impossible to think of them as typically bourgeois. But one can reconcile this with their lack of titles by attaching them to an upper middle class which modelled its conduct on the aristocracy – a phenomenon no less usual then than in other periods. Its members are depicted as neither exceptional nor fantastic and never as subjects for caricature in the same way as the braggart captain.

---

[1] This position was strikingly reversed in *Le Cid*, in which the complete code of honour rules supreme and is never seriously questioned. If it were, the dilemmas of the play and the play itself would collapse. Like *La Suite du Menteur*, *Le Cid* had a Spanish source in which considerations of honour were more tenacious. It was also a tragicomedy, later restyled a tragedy, and therefore exempt from the realism of comedy. (See Molière's comments on this, p. 111 below.) In tragic drama the public were ready to applaud a representation of ideal conduct – what they would like to imagine themselves doing if they were greater or better people – without regard for everyday realities. This alternative formula, involving the 'heroic', has proved effective again and again. It ensured the success of the Roman tragedies which followed *Le Cid* and incorporated an even more demanding ethic.

Corneille's comedies are social comedies in that they reflect the ethos and customs of the time, though without insistence on them. But they cannot be classed as comedies of manners, in which social habits and peculiarities are satirized or caricatured for their own interest, as in several of Molière's plays, in Congreve, in Sheridan, to mention only some outstanding examples. They simply accept contemporary society with a minimum of direct comment or condemnation and use it as a background for situations and characters that appear naturally to belong to it.

They cannot be typified as comedies of character either, yet character plays too important a part in them to be overlooked.

In the *Examen* of his first play, *Mélite*, Corneille wrote:

> La nouveauté de ce genre de comédie, dont il n'y a point d'exemple en aucune langue, et le style naïf [natural] qui faisait une peinture de la conversation des honnêtes gens, furent sans doute cause de ce bonheur surprenant qui fit alors tant de bruit.

This reinforces the point we have already made about the realism of the dialogue, and Corneille continues:

> On n'avait jamais vu jusque-là que la comédie fît rire[1] sans personnages ridicules, tels que les valets bouffons, les parasites, les capitans, les docteurs, etc.

Corneille himself later introduced a *capitan* into *L'Illusion comique* who was a prize example of the type. But this play, as has been seen, was exceptional, and Corneille's theory and practice from the beginning was to avoid stock characters in favour of something subtler and observed more directly from life. In *La Galerie du Palais* another stock character, the Nurse, is discarded and replaced by the more modern servant-companion.[2] In his next comedy, *La Suivante*, she becomes the principal centre of interest, but she is not featured as an embryonic new type nor as a pleader in a case for social justice (which would be anachronistic at that date, though today it is possible to read such a plea into the comedy), but as an individual who happens to have been caught up in unfavourable circumstances. This is reflected in the characterization, which is primarily psychological. Necessity forces her to

---

[1] The term is revealing, since it shows that Corneille expected laughter for his own comedies.

[2] See pp. 19–20 above for Corneille's comment on this.

intrigue, given the kind of woman she is. She resents her lowly position and hopes to escape from it by marriage, but she is also in love and from this stems her jealousy of her mistress Daphnis, who she feels is only preferred to her because of her fortune. The second main object of her resentment, the old man whose passion for a girl definitely extinguishes her own hopes, is condemned, together with Daphnis and her calculating lovers, in the final soliloquy already referred to. Her bitterness here and throughout makes her an unsympathetic character, but that does not prevent her being fully drawn in by Corneille who gives her a much larger part and fuller opportunities for self-expression than mere plot necessitates. Without her, there is no play. With her, there is a play, partly of intrigue but based at least equally on the portrayal of a character – a simple but powerful one.

The character of Célidée in the immediately preceding comedy, *La Galerie du Palais*, is less simple at first sight. Her inconsistent treatment of her lover, it will be recalled, is the mainspring of the plot. She snubs Lysandre to see what his reactions will be, but also to discover how she herself will react: it will depend on him. In conversation with the second girl, Hippolyte, she begins confidently:

Je connais mon Lysandre, et sa flamme est trop forte
Pour tomber en soupçon qu'il m'aime de la sorte [superficially].

But still, I will test him, and that will decide the line I shall follow:

Toutefois un dédain éprouvera ses feux,
Ainsi, quoi qu'il en soit, j'aurai ce que je veux;
Il me rendra constante ou me fera volage:
S'il m'aime il me retient; s'il change il me dégage.
Suivant ce qu'il aura d'amour ou de froideur,
Je suivrai ma nouvelle ou ma première ardeur.
(II. vi)

A moment later, in a short soliloquy (II. vii), she almost abandons her plan. Even if, as she declares, her love has cooled somewhat, can she really bear to risk losing her still darling Lysandre? But once again, she will leave it to him. She will show him a 'forced disdain':

Pour régler sur ce point *mon esprit balancé*,
J'attends ses mouvements sur mon dédain forcé;
Ma feinte éprouvera si son amour est vrai . . .

Under the cover of testing Lysandre's feelings she is also testing her own. But can she carry it through? At least – making a new reservation – let her basic love for him be perceptible beneath her harsh words:

> Prépare-toi, mon cœur, et laisse à mes discours
> Assez de liberté pour trahir mes amours.

In the event she handles the dismissal so clumsily that Lysandre is convinced that she hates the sight of him (II. viii). Bewildered and heartbroken, he agrees reluctantly in the next act to the stratagem suggested by his deceitful squire. To provoke Célidée's jealousy, he will pretend to fall in love with Hippolyte.

The counter-stratagem works very well. After informing Hippolyte of her latest decision to keep Lysandre (since she is now convinced that he loves her), but to continue to torment him with 'disdain' till the last moment, when she will save him by confirming her love for him, Célidée is snubbed by Lysandre in her turn and leaves the stage hurriedly. Regretful and ashamed, she offers her love to Dorimant, Hippolyte's true admirer, and is refused (IV. iii).

Not long after this comes her father's intervention (IV. xii). He wishes to conclude her marriage to Lysandre who, he is sure, loves her and has demanded her hand. When Célidée refuses, her father is out of his depth. He can only ascribe her 'bizarre humeur', her 'inégalité', to some new love affair with 'quelque jeune étourdi qui vous flatte un peu mieux', and orders her to obey his wishes. Disbelieving her objection that Lysandre is courting Hippolyte, he can find only the logical explanation that if his daughter no longer wants Lysandre it must be because she has fallen in love with someone else.

A final scene (V. iv) clears up the whole misunderstanding. Shocked into reality by the beginning of a duel between Lysandre and Dorimant, in which either might have been killed and which her arrival stops, Célidée accepts her lover's explanation and confesses her own stratagem. Their love is genuine on both sides and they can be happily married.

Various words have been applied to Célidée, with the general effect of classing her as a 'coquette', which would make her the first notable example of a standard type in sophisticated comedy. M. Couton describes her as 'une enfant gâtée', and even 'une petite peste'. An impatient male character might well apply harder and grosser words to a female who will not make up her mind and seemingly prevaricates with tricks – though Lysandre never does this. But 'coquette' is a blanket term inadequate to cover the subtlety of the character. One finds in Célidée (and to a lesser degree in Hippolyte) a perceptive study of a young girl hesitating before the prospect of marriage and the resulting sexual intercourse (never mentioned, but surely not absent from the minds of any audience[1]). She is uncertain of the nature of love, of herself, and of her lover.[2] In an attempt to make sense of all this she experiments wilfully and perhaps irresponsibly with her own feelings and those of others. This makes her appear infuriating and even objectionable, but before a male commentator utters the platitude of 'souvent femme varie, bien fol est qui s'y fie' he must stop to consider the psychology of the young female and admit that Corneille has rendered it in very convincing terms.

La Galerie du Palais acquires an added though probably fortuitous interest when it is compared with Marivaux's *Jeu de l'amour et du hasard* and his two *Surprises de l'amour*. The doubts and hesitations of Marivaux's women characters and the 'test' to which Silvia subjects her lover in *Le Jeu de l'amour*[3] resemble Célidée's behaviour towards Lysandre. The part Célidée's well-meaning father plays is also not dissimilar, though he is blunter and less understanding than in Marivaux. Some of Corneille's young men in his other comedies are also troubled by the same doubts and self-doubts and it is easy to recognize this as an incipient stage of the Marivaudian psychology of love which remained undeveloped for nearly a century. It could hardly have been otherwise, since the circumstances and conventions which ruled Marivaux's comedies were entirely different, but the fact that Corneille could suggest the same thing in his less 'delicate' theatrical idiom with almost no stimulus outside his own creative imagination is a further sign of the fertility of this diversely gifted dramatist.

---

[1] The literal-minded Nurse referred to it crudely in the first version of *La Veuve*. Characters in Rotrou's comedies do the same.
[2] After 'mon esprit balancé' (II. vii) she speaks of 'mon esprit flottant' (III. iv). In the latter scene she is discussing love and lovers with the equally virginal Hippolyte. When the *suivante* Florice, who has evidently had some love affair, joins in, Hippolyte refers to 'l'avantage qu'elle a d'un peu d'expérience'.
[3] See below, pp. 203–5.

One can approach Alidor of *La Place Royale* as a male counterpart to
Célidée. He also could be described as inconstant, as the summary of
the play will have shown.[1] But there is another side to him: a fierce
determination not to be dominated by love or 'an object of love', in
this case Angélique:

> Il ne faut point servir d'objet qui nous possède;
> Il ne faut point nourrir d'amour qui ne nous cède;
> Je le hais s'il me force, et quand j'aime je veux
> Que de ma volonté dépendent tous mes vœux.
>
> (I. iv)

Quoting this and similar speeches, certain critics have discerned in
Alidor a forerunner of the stoically 'virtuous' heroes of the great
Roman tragedies, exercising their will to conquer their desires. This
interpretation of the ethical and psychological motivation in Cornelian
tragedy has a long history and is still valid in part, but it can no
longer be maintained as the principal motivation, and if it is not that
in the plainly heroic characters it becomes less significant in Alidor.
The speech just quoted from continues:

> Que mon feu m'obéisse, au lieu de me contraindre,
> Que je puisse à mon gré l'enflammer et l'éteindre,
> Et toujours en état de disposer de moi,
> Donner, quand il me plaît, et retirer ma foi . . .

and concludes:

> A tel prix que ce soit, il faut rompre mes chaînes,
> De crainte qu'un hymen, m'en ôtant le pouvoir,
> Fît d'un amour par force un amour par devoir.[2]

If one could forget for a moment all that has been said of the
triumph of duty over passion, of will over inclination in Corneille, one
would see this as a perfectly coherent picture of a young man determined to preserve his freedom of action and, to put it in slightly
different terms, his emotional virginity, at all costs. This is certainly
not a conflict between duty and desire, since the two are aligned and

---

[1] See pp. 21–4 above.

[2] In eighteenth-century bourgeois comedy, 'amour par devoir' is held up as
the highest ideal. See e.g. La Chaussée's *Mélanide*, p. 224 below. From that point
of view Alidor would be an unmitigated scoundrel, like the protagonist of
Gresset's *Le Méchant*.

his only perceptible duty is to marry the girl who attracts him. But that, he feels, would not be 'me' and one can legitimately invoke the Cornelian *moi* to explain his inner debates. When almost moved to compassion by Angélique's distress, he pulls himself back with the remark:

> Suis-je encore Alidor après ces sentiments?
> Et ne pourrai-je enfin régler mes mouvements?

and goes on more firmly:

> Ne me présume pas tout-à-fait succombé.
> Je sais trop[1] maintenir ce que je me propose,
> Et souverain sur moi, rien que moi n'en dispose.
> (IV. v)

Even after this he almost 'succumbs' to love (V. iii). But braced by Angélique's refusal of him, he confirms in his final soliloquy the assertion of personality which he has been moving towards throughout:

> Je cesse d'espérer et commence de vivre,
> Je vis dorénavant puisque je vis à moi;
> Et quelques doux assauts qu'un autre objet[2] me livre,
> C'est de moi seulement que je prendrai la loi.

In the process of asserting his independence he has treated Angélique cruelly, even abominably, but moral judgements are beside the point. The complete selfishness with which he has behaved – though he sees it in another light – is the core of his true character, which he has come triumphantly to recognize. He is not presented as a pattern of conduct, good or bad,[3] but as a young man of a certain type, not all that uncommon. As much as Célidée, he is seeking for himself. But whereas Célidée's search ended in a natural surrender to emotion, Alidor's led to the opposite. His nature, he concluded, was to be hard and free, and on that note the play ends.

---

[1] *Trop: très bien.*
[2] I.e. some possible new love.
[3] That is, in the play. In his *Examen* of 1660 Corneille more than half condemns Alidor. It should also be conceded that the original title was *La Place Royale ou l'Amoureux extravagant*. Morality so easily creeps in through the back door.

One can also analyse this differently. Instead of considering Alidor in isolation, one might couple him with his victim or would-be partner Angélique and admire Corneille's handling of this interacting pair. Instinctively in love with each other yet incompatible, temperament rather than situation brings about their definitive separation. They will not and cannot remain together. In the classic example of lovers separating, Racine's *Bérénice*, situation provides the decisive and only factor. They part reluctantly because of external pressures. The divisive situations in *La Place Royale* (Alidor's subterfuge, Angélique's acceptance of Doraste) are manufactured by the characters themselves and can be overcome; their reluctance is a deeper and more complicated matter which finally proves to be psychologically irreducible.

Taken separately, Angélique is a less interesting character than Alidor. For most of the play she is indeed his pathetic victim whose actions and emotions are dictated by his attitude towards her. They ring true and are not superficial, but leave little scope for variation or surprise. It is only by her late decision to refuse Alidor and take the veil that the depth of this relatively simple character is established. A potentially 'comic' dénouement is sacrificed to the logic of characterization. It might be added that only once, in *Le Misanthrope*, did Molière clearly do the same thing.

❦

In *Le Menteur*, written after an interval, Corneille at last centred a play on a type-character, but a new type and not one from the old gallery of the *commedia dell'arte* which he had already condemned. The title is revelatory. The plot and idea of the play came from Alarcón's *La verdad sospechosa*, which is almost a proverb or a moral statement: 'Even truth is suspect'. Not this for Corneille, but a title defining in a generalized word the quality of his main character, different from *La Suivante*, who was an individual reacting to a particular condition, and standing near[1] the beginning of a long line of similarly titled 'portrait' comedies running through Molière to Regnard and others in the eighteenth century.

[1] There had been one or two earlier examples: Mareschal's *Le Railleur* (1635), Desmarets's *Les Visionnaires* (1637) which was not, however, centred on one protagonist.

Dorante differs from Corneille's earlier important characters. He is certainly not groping for self-realization and there is little to say about him beyond what the title implies. He is a chronic liar throughout, an impulsively imaginative man who cannot resist improvising a tall story on the slightest provocation. He leaps, like some inexperienced journalist, at the first hint of a story with no thought of its context, then fills it out with circumstantial detail like an inventive novelist. In the end he is 'unmasked' by the machinery of the plot, but neither altered nor fulfilled as a person, since he has always been like that and always will be.[1] Since real life is full of such persons one need not conclude that Corneille had entirely abandoned realism in favour of caricature, but one must perceive the stronger element of generalization which distinguishes this play from the psychological point of view. It also explains its success in a century which gravitated more and more towards the outline portrait, found in its perfection in La Bruyère's *Caractères*.

Had he gone on, Corneille could no doubt have written classic comedies of character built, like this one, on comedies of intrigue. But he had what he considered bigger and better things to do, among them the absorption of his comic technique into tragedy.

It is difficult to place Cornelian comedy under any of the accepted headings. Disregarding *L'Illusion comique* and *Le Menteur*, it is not primarily, as has been indicated, comedy of manners, comedy of character or comedy of intrigue, though features of all these enter into it. Since the plays are all concerned with love affairs, with no farcical and few humorous elements, they might seem to fall into the class of romantic comedy, but the realism of the settings and the modernity of the characterization and language is non-romantic. They are plays about the emotional adventures of characters like, or not unlike, contemporary people, and the consequences of those adventures. In the nineteenth and twentieth centuries they would find a natural place among numerous other plays of similar conception. In their own time, when distinctions were more rigid and theatrical conventions more absolute, they were certainly not tragedy, pastoral, nor even tragicomedy. Neither, in spite of their frequent seriousness, were they forerunners of the eighteenth-century *drame*, whose moral heaviness they avoid. One has to take them as they were, forgetting the categories,

---

[1] The reformed Dorante of *La Suite du Menteur* must be regarded as a different character, and even he lies on occasion.

and conceding broadly their author's claim to have invented something new but which was also too original to be imitated by other dramatists.

❧❧

A word should be said on Corneille's *Examens*, quoted several times in this chapter. Published in 1660 with three more general essays (the *Discours du poème dramatique, de la tragédie*, and *des trois unités*), these writings together constitute one of the most interesting bodies of critical theory and self-criticism ever produced by a practising dramatist, and certainly in seventeenth-century France. The *Examens* of individual plays do not express the more immediate reactions to be found in various prefaces and dedications, but have the advantage of representing the author's considered judgements on plays whose success or failure might go back as much as thirty years and which he discusses in the light of a long experience of the theatre.

Even in 1660, however, he is far from recollecting in tranquillity. He is still involved in polemics and has eight plays yet to write. This explains some of his reasoning and his preoccupation with questions of dramatic technique. He is at pains to admit or to justify lapses in verisimilitude or propriety, faults in the linking of scenes or the tardy appearance of an important character or the inadequate preparation of the dénouement – in short the whole technical streamlining of the classically regular play. This entailed observance of the unities, of the 'rules' which had become much more rigid since he began to write. For *Mélite* he confesses that he had never heard of them, which was not surprising since they had not yet been formulated;[1] for *La Suivante* (1634) he could not plead this and in fact from that play on he observed the unities, with a liberal interpretation of the unity of place, as the stage conventions of the period allowed. Of his three earlier comedies, *Mélite* was irregular in several respects and violated propriety in its original version which Corneille later toned down. The five acts of *La Veuve* occur on five consecutive days, the unity of place is stretched to the limit of the permissible, and several scenes are not logically linked. The action of *La Galerie du Palais* also occupies five days; the

[1] The debate on the unities extended over a number of years. Though the principle had been recommended by earlier critics or could be deduced from them, a positive starting-point for Corneille's generation was Chapelain's *Lettre à Godeau sur la règle des vingt-quatre heures* (1630), followed by the preface to Mairet's *Silvanire* (1631).

partial scene-change showing the merchants' stalls is defended because of the pleasure it gave audiences, but Corneille admits that it infringed the unity of place. After that he came to heel and did his best to observe the rules which had so troubled him.

These are old quarrels, largely on points of detail long since irrelevant in drama. But for Corneille, as both a writer of plays and a commentator on them, they were very actual and absorbed what may seem a disproportionate share of his attention.

ROTROU AND
ROMANTIC COMEDY

*Rotrou's varied production – uncertainty as to
nature of comedy – influence of pastoral and the Spanish* comedia *–
approach to romantic comedy –* La Belle Alphrède *– staging and
style – absorption of romantic comedy into tragicomedy –
Rotrou's general influence*

While Corneille was writing comedies for the Théâtre du Marais, his contemporary Jean Rotrou (1609–50) was also producing comedies, or plays so styled, for the rival company of the Hôtel de Bourgogne. Rotrou had succeeded Alexandre Hardy as the *poète à gages* or 'salaried poet' of the Hôtel on the production of his first play, *L'Hypocondriaque*, in 1628. This tragicomedy was followed, almost certainly in the next year, by a 'comedy', *La Bague de l'oubli*, concerning a magic ring which makes its wearer forget what he has just decided and the people he knows. Rotrou went on to compose a dozen or more comedies, of which some have been lost, in the decade of the 1630s. He returned briefly to the genre in the 1640s with *Clarice* (*c.* 1641) and *La Sœur* (*c.* 1645), the second of which may have been intended as a reply by the Hôtel de Bourgogne to Corneille's recent *Le Menteur* and its *Suite*.

By then, however, Rotrou had practically abandoned comedy to exploit the vein of tragicomedy and tragedy which was soon to lead to his three most memorable plays, *Saint Genest* (1645), *Venceslas* (1647) and *Cosroès* (1648). In quality and importance these three tragedies have completely overshadowed his comedies, and understandably so. Although he was in the field a little before Corneille, was more prolific, and may even have influenced him slightly, his significance in the history of French comedy in no way reaches the same level.

Towards 1630 there was considerable doubt as to what a modern comedy should be. The few earlier comedies mentioned in Chapter 1 were disregarded. There were Italian, and soon Spanish, examples of comedy for dramatists to look to, but at first they did so uncertainly. Plautus and Terence were always known and admired, but in themselves they could not inspire the new comedy that was being sought for. Corneille's solution and his great achievement were to base a body of comic drama on the social life of the time, connecting it inextricably with contemporary manners and settings. Rotrou never attempted this. He moved about erratically, always shunning realism, and taking now one model, now another, which he adapted rather than transformed to satisfy the continuous requirements of the theatre company which employed him. In this he was Alexandre Hardy's true successor.

His work reflects the general uncertainty about the nature of comedy. It inclines sometimes to pastoral, sometimes to tragicomedy, and in several cases to the two combined. But for the minor character of the jester Fabrice, *La Bague de l'oubli* could equally well be a tragicomedy or almost a tragedy. A major character is condemned to execution – a scaffold is shown on the stage – and only saved by the last-minute intervention of his king. The love dilemmas, jealousies and rivalries prominent here and in other plays are treated seriously and debated in monologues which could easily lead to suicide or murder if the situations were not eventually cleared up in the somewhat artificial happy endings. If the final outcome belongs to comedy, the plots and the general tone certainly do not.

The influence of pastoral, particularly of d'Urfé's *L'Astrée*, is most apparent in the love-casuistry of Rotrou's dialogues and in his situations. *La Diane* (c. 1633), though adapted from a play by Lope de Vega (as was *La Bague de l'oubli*), contains most of the pastoral features and ends with the recognition of the heroine, hitherto believed to have been a shepherdess, by her long-lost brother whom she is impersonating. The similar *Célimène*, of about the same date, was at first planned as a pastoral play, then changed to a 'comedy', and later readapted as a pastoral by Tristan L'Hermite under the new name of *Amarillis* (1652). On the other hand, *Les Deux Pucelles* (1636–7), based on a short story in Cervantes's *Novelas Ejemplares*, was presented reasonably enough as a tragicomedy but adapted later by Quinault as a comedy (*Les Rivales*, 1653). All that Quinault had to do, while preserving the plot and the main situations, was to introduce a comic valet in the first and final scenes and to develop the humorous side of two secondary characters, an innkeeper and his flighty wife.

Quinault suppressed Rotrou's scenes in a wood frequented by robbers, who have tied one of the two heroines (disguised as a young man) to a tree. In Rotrou this assumes some importance because, after being freed, the disguised girl, wishing for death, pretends to be a robber herself and confesses falsely to several murders. This was not in Cervantes's story, Rotrou's source, but there was a situation so similar in Hardy's *Gésippe* that it seems highly probable that the episode was suggested by the old French dramatist.[1]

Rotrou was the first Frenchman to borrow from the Spanish *comedia*, as distinct from the Spanish novel and short story, on which Hardy had drawn before him. The *comedia*, and Lope de Vega in particular, gave him his cloak-and-sword features of seductions, duels and the preoccupation with family honour – either neat or mingled with the influence of pastoral. Quite separately from this Rotrou went back to Latin comedy for his three adaptations of Plautus,[2] which he made no serious attempt to transpose to contemporary French settings.

In his other comedies the borderlines between comedy, tragicomedy and pastoral are imprecise or fluctuating. A dramatist with greater powers of assimilation might have erased them to create a unified type of drama in which fantasy and unreality can exist convincingly in a world of their own. Rotrou's work in comedy lacks the consistency of imagination necessary to achieve such an end. Nevertheless a certain number of his plays approach the idea of romantic comedy which, as remarked earlier, had not appeared in France until then. If anyone put it on the stage it was Rotrou and, though one cannot consider him as a master of it, one can at least give him credit for introducing it and also bring the category into service to characterize part of his work.

A typical example is *La Belle Alphrède*, produced around 1636 and apparently a largely original composition, since no definite source has been found for it.[3]

The play opens on the coast of Algeria, with a wrecked ship in the

---

[1] Hardy in turn took it from Boccaccio (*Decameron*, Tenth Day, VIII). Rotrou does not seem to have used the *Decameron* directly.

[2] *Les Ménechmes* (1630–1), *Les Sosies* (1637) from the *Amphitruo*, and *Les Captifs* (1638?). Rotrou does not appear to have used Terence.

[3] Lope de Vega's similarly titled *Hermosa Alfreda* was not the source, since Rotrou borrowed nothing from it, as H. C. Lancaster points out (*History*, II, p. 106).

background. Alphrède, in male disguise, has escaped from the wreck with her follower, Cléandre. Pregnant and deserted by her lover Rodolphe, she has set out in pursuit of him. Enter Rodolphe and his follower, pursued by Arab pirates. He kills one of them and drives the others off, aided by Alphrède, who then attacks him with her sword. She quickly makes him recognize her. He offers to let her kill him, but explains that he has given his word to marry another girl, Isabelle, who lives in London. He was on his way there when he too was shipwrecked. While they are engaged in conversation the pirates return and capture them all.

In Act II Alphrède is brought before the chief pirate, who soon turns out to be her father, cast up in an earlier shipwreck and now a powerful man through having won the heart of a great lady of the country. With him is his son Acaste, shipwrecked with him when small and of about the same age as his sister Alphrède. The family are brought to recognize each other and there is an affectionate reunion. It is decided that Alphrède shall go on to London, accompanied by her brother. She hopes to win back Rodolphe by *douceur* rather than force. Rodolphe, who does not appear in this act and is kept uninformed of its revelations, is to be allowed to follow in another ship.

In Act III Rodolphe is shown in prison, where he has lain incommunicado for fifteen days. He is given an entirely false account of Alphrède's death at the hands of the pirate chief. On finding that Alphrède was a woman he fell in love with her and, when she resisted him through faithfulness to Rodolphe, stabbed her fatally. Rodolphe, racked by remorse, is freed, after a scene in which he insults Alphrède's father as a filthy old murderer. Told that the pirate chief's son is off to London to court Isabelle and supplant himself, Rodolphe decides to follow. He no longer wishes to marry Isabelle, but to avenge Alphrède by killing Acaste, since the father is too well guarded. The scene changes to a wood near London. Here Alphrède, still in male clothes, and her brother, rescue an old man from a villainous 'ravisher' and two soldiers, killing all three on stage. They also rescue two girls, the old man's daughters. The older is Isabelle, as Alphrède soon discovers, without disclosing her own identity. She falsely tells Isabelle that Rodolphe, whom she says she knows, is dead.

In Act IV Acaste tells his sister that he has fallen passionately in love with Isabelle. He understands why Rodolphe preferred her to Alphrède – she is irresistibly more beautiful. Alphrède very readily agrees to help him. At this point there is a further complication. Isabelle's younger sister Orante has fallen in love with Alphrède in her male disguise. She is depicted as a touchingly sentimental adolescent. She promises to help persuade her sister to marry Acaste in return for Alphrède's love. The marriage is arranged and Alphrède manages to put off Orante's suggestion that they should get married at the same time.

In Act V the wedding of Acaste and Isabelle is being celebrated. A short ballet is danced to entertain the guests. Outside the house Rodolphe, who has now reached London and still believes Alphrède to be dead, waits to kill Acaste in a duel. Acaste comes out in response to his challenge and even offers to yield Isabelle to him, since he obtained her by a trick.[1] But Isabelle, deeply in love with Acaste and impatiently waiting for the wedding night, will have none of this. Neither will Rodolphe. He adores Alphrède, even though she is now a corpse rotting in the grave. At this point Alphrède, who has come out in her woman's dress and is far from corpselike, persuades him to look at her and all ends happily for them. The young Orante does not reappear and, whether carelessly or intentionally, is not mentioned in the dénouement.

※⟨⟩※

This play contains nearly all the ingredients used by writers of comedy and tragicomedy, and also by novelists, over several decades. There is the resourceful heroine in male disguise, the tricks to win her lover, the misunderstanding caused by a false report, the long-lost father and brother, the shipwrecks and the capture by pirates, the reported threat to virtue by the old tyrant, the attempted abduction of Isabelle in the London wood, the role of the valets or squires which, of secondary importance in the plot, would be prominent on the stage. Above all, there is the dominant motivation of love, exclusive except for the closely related motivation of revenge.

In the theatre an audience, already gripped by the numerous in-

[1] The pretence that Rodolphe was dead. It is his feeling of guilt which prevents Acaste from accepting the challenge and fighting to keep his bride. To underline this and save him from the suspicion of cowardice, Rotrou shows him on the point of confessing his 'fraud' to Isabelle in an earlier scene before he knew that Rodolphe was in London (V. iii). Before he can explain he is interrupted by a page who calls them in to the wedding celebrations.

cidents and coincidences, would be further interested by the staging.
There are fights and killings, music and ballet. In Act IV the lovesick
Orante throws flowers into a pool after comparing them unfavourably
to the flowers of her own body which she hopes that Cléomède – the
name by which she knows Alphrède – will one day touch and save
from withering. There are several important scene-changes,[1] in contrast to the restrained décors of Corneille's social comedies. The unity
of place, not yet generally observed in the drama and optional in comedy
for a long time to come, is ignored, as is the unity of time. The action
occupies several weeks, if not longer. Rodolphe is held prisoner in
Oran for fifteen days, while the further time taken by the voyage to
London and the events which followed is left unspecified.

The play thus escapes the classical conventions to provide a spectacle
full of movement and life which could more than compensate for its
implausibility. But *La Belle Alphrède* is far from a masterpiece in any
genre. Apart from the over-richness of the incidents, which appears
wasteful, there is a distressing unevenness of tone in the dialogue.
Some is excellent and lyrically or dialectically effective, but other
passages are conventional, using the classical allusions of an earlier age
(as in Hardy) or the well-worn clichés of *galanterie* to fill out scenes,
particularly monologues, which Rotrou seems to have written with
his eyes half-shut. He was probably pressed for time and why do better
if this was good enough?

Other plays of the same kind, less action-packed but sometimes with
even more complicated imbroglios in which the misunderstandings
may stem from concealed identities, figure in Rotrou's comic drama.
They are plays full of vicissitudes and surprises in which romantic love
always reigns supreme and is fulfilled at the dénouement. Humour is
inconspicuous or incidental and never presented as the principal
attraction. This comedy hardly established itself as a major type. Other
dramatists practised it occasionally, sometimes in dilution. The clearest
case is that of Thomas Corneille, Pierre's younger brother, who

---

[1] Everything that is known of the fixed sets of the Hôtel de Bourgogne at this
date would preclude *complete* scene-changes, yet *La Belle Alphrède* seems to
require something approaching them. The ballet of Act V in particular could
hardly be hidden and revealed unless a curtain was drawn across the width of
the stage. This could be at any point in the décor provided it gave the dancers
enough room to move around. The stage-direction in the first edition (1639) is:
'La chambre s'ouvre et une pantalonnade déjà commencée se danse'. Other
directions in this text are brief and unilluminating.

began to write in the year before Rotrou's death and, like him, was a great adapter of Spanish models. Because of its later date his work contains less physical violence and scenic exuberance. It is more regular and comes nearer to observing the unities. But in several plays the cloak-and-sword element is recognizably strong, while the romantic element conditions the ingenious complications of the plots.

Later, following dramatic fashion, Thomas Corneille turned more and more to tragicomedies and so-called tragedies, yet retained in these different genres many of the features found in his own and Rotrou's comedies. So in Thomas Corneille the wheel came full-circle. What Rotrou had taken from pastoral and tragicomedy and called comedy returned to tragicomedy which, in French seventeenth-century drama at least, appears to be its most natural place.

❧

Rotrou, experimenting or improvising prolifically, should not be despised for this. Though he produced only a small number of well-finished plays and failed to naturalize much of his material, his work – though more particularly in tragedy and tragicomedy – was extensively drawn on by later dramatists as far forward in time as Racine. These used his subjects and situations to make plays which were indeed thoroughly native. He thus served as a fertile source of ideas and as an intermediary between foreign and French drama. Molière used his *Les Sosies* rather than Plautus as the main basis of his *Amphitryon* and numerous other borrowings can be found in his work. He copied the mock-Turkish jargon of *Le Bourgeois Gentilhomme* from Rotrou's *La Sœur*, an involved comedy dependent on hidden identities and disguises which was in turn imitated, down to the nonsensical 'Turkish', from an Italian play. But whereas Molière was a creative writer Rotrou hardly was, at least in comedy, and it remained for others to cultivate the fields he had opened up for them.

SCARRON AND
BURLESQUE COMEDY

*Features of burlesque – Scarron's work
in general – Spanish influences – influence and career
of the actor Jodelet – Philipin –* Jodelet ou le Maître-Valet *–*
Jodelet duelliste *–* Don Japhet d'Arménie *–* L'Héritier ridicule *–
pointers to Molière –* Le Marquis ridicule *– farcical elements –
verbal fantasy – 'metaphorization' – references to
contemporary literature – galanterie mocked – the honour
code and duelling – satire in Scarron – burlesque
tendencies in P. Corneille – the* blason *– the heroic
braggart – other notable* fanfarons *– Desmarets's*
Les Visionnaires *– literary parody –* Les Académistes *–
T. Corneille's* Le Berger extravagant

The starting-point of burlesque is parody of existing literary or
dramatic works, which are mocked or depreciated by transposition to a
different key, usually lower. To have a topical force the parody must
be of works which are popular, or at least respected at the time, and so
it glances at contemporary cultural fashions and often by a logical
extension at those who follow them. By parodying some established
work one is in effect making fun of those who admire it. If this is
stressed and the laughter is directed at a particular group of people
there will be an element of social satire, weaker or stronger according
to the author's intentions, as in Desmarets's *Les Visionnaires* or
Molière's *Les Femmes savantes*, which will be considered in their place.
But while parody easily leads to satire this cannot be considered as one
of its inherent features. The satirical potential may be so faint or so
general that it hardly emerges, but merely awaits deduction by some
interested critic. Two great examples, which were the principal forerunners of French seventeenth-century burlesque, were Rabelais's
Gargantua and *Pantagruel* (1532–52) and Cervantes's *Don Quijote*

(1605–12). Though both were developed by their highly creative authors into something larger, the first began as a parody of the popular adventure epics, the second as a parody of the romances of chivalry. In so far as both are satirical, Rabelais satirizes ideas and religious beliefs while the less intellectual Cervantes satirizes idealistic social values. Other writers, Italian and Spanish, parodied or 'travestied' more narrowly the epic and the romance before the French caught the infection from them.

French seventeenth-century burlesque can be seen as a particular class of parody distinguised by hyperbole and by a preoccupation with language which sometimes carries its authors a long distance away from their models and acquires an imaginative life of its own – again as had happened in Rabelais. It allows and almost requires the exercise of fantasy (the seventeenth-century synonym for imagination), and when this is sustained it has a high literary value in itself. When it falls flat it is very flat. It is typical of burlesque to know no middle way.

Paul Scarron (1610–60) became famous as a leading writer of burlesque with his *Virgile travesti*, published during the last decade of his life. This parody of Books I–VIII of the *Aeneid*, written in octosyllabic verse – a metre associated with popular or comic poetry – depends on a single basic joke, the rendering of the seriously heroic in ridiculously familiar terms. The earlier and shorter *Typhon ou la Gigantomachie* (1644) is similar. It describes the mythical war between the gods and the gigantic sons of earth, which breaks out when their leader Typhon, losing his temper over a game of *boules*, flings the huge rocks which serve as balls heavenwards and disturbs a feast which the gods are enjoying, breaking their wine-bottles. It was for these bluffly humorous poems and his novel, *Le Roman comique* (1651–7), concerning a troupe of travelling actors and containing incidentally much interesting information about the contemporary theatre, that Scarron was chiefly known. His work represented a brave defiance of ill-health. Crippled by arthritis from an early age, he underwent much physical suffering. He left a widow who, as Madame de Maintenon, became the consort of Louis XIV and was still sometimes referred to behind her back as 'la veuve Scarron'. She is unlikely to have been amused by her first husband's writings.

The best of these, his plays, have been almost completely forgotten with the exception of two, *Jodelet ou le Maître-Valet* (1643?) and *Don Japhet d'Arménie* (1647), which were preserved from neglect by being included in the repertory of the Comédie Française and acted frequently until the end of the eighteenth century, after which they virtually disappeared. His three other true comedies were *Les Trois Dorothées ou Jodelet souffleté* (1645), recast in a new version as *Jodelet duelliste* (1651), *L'Héritier ridicule* (1648-9) and *Le Marquis ridicule* (1655). These, though hardly inferior to the first two mentioned, were not saved by adoption by the national theatre and can be found only with difficulty today.

To complete the record, Scarron turned late in his career to romantic tragicomedy and wrote four more plays: *L'Écolier de Salamanque* (1654-5), *Le Gardien de soi-même* (c. 1655), *La Fausse Apparence* (1657-8) and *Le Prince corsaire* (probably 1658). In these the comic element is small or non-existent and we are not concerned with them here. A few fragments and scenes published in the seventh volume of the complete *Œuvres de Scarron* (Paris, 1786) show that Scarron worked on other tragicomedies and comedies which apparently were never completed. The most interesting might have been *Le Faux Alexandre* which seems to have resemblances with *Les Visionnaires* of Desmarets.

Nearly all these plays, whether comedies or tragicomedies, were freely based on Spanish originals, and no attempt was made to conceal the debt. The settings remain Spanish as do the character-names, with one outstanding exception. Yet Scarron succeeded in naturalizing his material to produce something that was new and highly effective on the French stage.

He wrote, seemingly *ad hoc*, for the Théâtre du Marais, moving later to the Hôtel de Bourgogne, and his first two plays were conceived as vehicles for the comic actor Jodelet, though Jodelet does not dominate them. This was one of those perfect marriages between an actor and an inventive author who could write with enthusiasm the kind of script that entirely suited his performer's style. Marivaux did it later as of course did Molière, but then he was both author and actor, writing for himself and his close companions. And in none of these cases can one say that the plays collapse when performed by other interpreters. Nevertheless it is highly probable that without Jodelet Scarron's plays would have been different, as might those of other dramatists who used the comedian's name in their titles or cast-lists. To appreciate his influence on a period of comedy based on the

requirements of a living theatre it is necessary to outline his career
before turning back to the printed texts.

Jodelet was the stage-name of Julien Bedeau (*c.* 1600–60), who is
first mentioned in a lease of the Marais in March 1634. He was 'certainly
more than thirty then and had no doubt acted for years in the provinces'.[1] He was a comic of the same line as the old *farceurs* such as
Turlupin, good at slapstick and a musician. He was famous for his
nasal voice and his hound-like nose, said to have been deformed by
smallpox.[2] After some nine months at the Marais he was transferred by
royal order to the Hôtel de Bourgogne, as part of an attempt to inject
new blood into the senior theatre, but returned to the Marais in 1641.
There he seems to have remained, with perhaps some short inter-
ruptions, until he joined Molière's company at Easter 1659. He died
almost exactly a year later.

His known parts were always those of the comic valet, ingenious
and humorous but rarely a complete buffoon, whose name gradually
became a draw in itself for Parisian audiences. Besides Scarron's two
Jodelet plays there were comedies entitled *Jodelet astrologue* (1645) by
d'Ouville, *Le Geôlier de soi-même ou Jodelet prince* (*c.* 1655) by Thomas
Corneille, and *La Feinte Mort de Jodelet* by Brécourt (before 1659). He
took the relatively restrained part of the valet Cliton in Pierre
Corneille's *Le Menteur* and its *Suite* and appeared as a named character
in such plays as Quinault's *Comédie sans comédie* (1654), finishing as
Le Vicomte de Jodelet in Molière's *Précieuses ridicules* (November
1659). After his return to the Marais the Hôtel had looked for a similar
comic for their productions and found one in 'Philipin' or Claude de
Villiers, a much younger man who lived until 1701 and who seems to
have imitated Jodelet closely and successfully. When Scarron wrote
for the Hôtel with no Jodelet available, it was this actor who played
his main comic parts, in *Don Japhet d'Arménie* and *L'Héritier ridicule*.
With Jodelet and Philipin went a *suivante*. In Scarron's Jodelet plays
and *L'Héritier ridicule* her name is Béatrix and she is a well-filled-in
character. Jodelet flirts with her but will not marry her, though he
would not mind sleeping with her, as she complains to his master:

> Votre grand fainéant, votre chien de valet,
> Enfin ce mal bâti, ce maudit Jodelet,

---

[1] S. W. Deierkauf-Holsboer, *Le Théâtre de l'Hôtel de Bourgogne*, I, p. 10.
[2] Tallemant de Réaux, *Historiettes*.

Depuis deux ou trois jours m'a prise pour une autre . . .
Il me va tourmentant de ses affections,
Il me va proposant des fornications . . .

(Jodelet duelliste, II. iv)

The recurrence of the name Béatrix (there are other less important *soubrettes*, called Marine, Louise, Lise, Paquette) suggests that one actress specialized in the part, but it is uncertain who she was.

❧

The story of Scarron's first comedy, *Jodelet ou le Maître-Valet*, was taken from a play by Rojas Zorilla, *Donde hay agravios no hay zelos y amo criado*.[1] Don Juan d'Alvarade has contracted to marry Isabelle de Rochas, a Madrilenian girl whom he has never seen, though they have exchanged portraits. On his way to Madrid from the army in Flanders he is delayed in Burgos by a family tragedy. An unknown man has killed his brother and seduced his sister who has disappeared, while their father has died of grief. The killer proves later to be Don Louis, the cousin of Isabelle de Rochas and in love with her, though she is not so with him. Don Juan sees Don Louis – unidentified – coming down by a rope-ladder apparently from Isabelle's bedroom and grows suspicious of her character and intentions. To test her out he changes places with his valet Jodelet. The substitution is made easier by a mix-up over the portraits. A picture of Jodelet with his 'badger's snout' has been sent by mistake to Isabelle, who is repelled by the prospect of marrying such a man, and even more when he begins his boorish wooing. But she falls in love with the real Don Juan, the supposed valet.

Meanwhile his sister Lucrèce arrives independently (improbable though this seems) and entreats Isabelle's father, Don Fernand, who was an old friend of her own father, to help her to find her seducer and avenge her.

The various characters become aware in time of the others' identities, though Don Juan's is not disclosed until near the end, except to his sister. This mettlesome 'valet' crosses swords with Don Louis, the fight is stopped by Don Fernand, and a formal duel is arranged between Don Louis and the supposed Don Juan, in other words the

---

[1] 'Where there is offence there is no jealousy and [or] the Master-Servant.'

c

protesting Jodelet. It takes place by candlelight in a darkened room, with Jodelet doing his best to defend himself and Don Juan popping out from an alcove just in time to save him and wound Don Louis. More lights are brought and the truth is revealed. Don Louis apologizes: he killed Don Juan's brother in Burgos by a mistake which he greatly regrets. He will make amends by marrying the deserted Lucrèce, since Isabelle, whom he has loved throughout, will not have him. Isabelle marries Don Juan as originally arranged. Jodelet asks to have his portrait back 'pour en favouriser ma chère Béatrix', Isabelle's maid, who has played an important part in the action as intriguer and go-between.

The basic plot of *Jodelet maître* could make it a serious cloak-and-sword play, and even the exchange of roles between master and valet[1] might, with more difficulty, be treated in a serious tone. But when the valet was Jodelet and the portrait complication was introduced the way was wide open for broad comedy. Theoretically the two modes appear incompatible, yet Scarron succeeds in blending them, with the humorous element overlaying the seduction-revenge theme and minimizing the wrong done to Lucrèce and the rough justice of her final loveless marriage. Need it be said that neither here nor elsewhere in the seventeenth century does one expect to find sentimental comedy?

There is an equal lack of pathos in *Jodelet duelliste*, the revised version of *Les Trois Dorothées ou Jodelet souffleté*. The general treatment is somewhat lighter, though here again there are potentially unpleasant situations, left undeveloped. In this play (also adapted from a Spanish source, Tirso de Molina's *No hay peor sordo*), the comedian is considering fighting a duel on his own account. He has been slapped and knocked about in front of Béatrix by a more aggressive valet, Alphonse. But, though he practises fencing assiduously, he cannot screw up his courage to the point of fighting. When Alphonse appears he apologizes abjectly and is beaten up again.

There is now no master–valet exchange to help him out. His master, Don Félix de Fonsèque, is a cynical example of what was later to become famous as the Don Juan type. He will make love to any female, 'la fille de dix ans et la sexagénaire', and, if she already has a lover,

---

[1] This was the first known example in French comedy of such an exchange and certainly the first notable one. As already seen, it stems from a Spanish original. It differs from the more familiar device of well-born characters or women posing as valets or pages, generally derived from the Italian.

enjoys butting in to wreck their relationship. Jodelet disapproves, but his moral comments are shrugged off. Don Félix is now courting Lucie, the younger of two sisters, though he has promised marriage to a certain Dorothée, who does not appear. He is said to have had two children by her. 'But', he says, 'I can buy her off. Money arranges everything.' He has two rivals in his present enterprise: Don Diègue, the sympathetic hero, engaged to marry Lucie's sister Hélène, but preferring the younger girl, and Don Gaspard de Padrille, a modified *capitano* type. Though martially boastful and an easy butt (Don Félix has infuriated him by imitating all his actions during the past six months, down to his coughs when he caught cold) he is no coward. Don Diègue, his cousin, who has served with him in the wars, sums him up: 'Not a bad sort and quite brave, though too loud-mouthed and completely mad.' True to form, he is doing the two sisters the honour of courting them both.

Both of them want Don Diègue. There is a bitter competition between them which Lucie, represented as sympathetic, wins. She is helped by their *suivante* Béatrix and invents various tricks to get her man, engaged though he was to her sister. Hélène, hating her for it,[1] has to be content with Don Gaspard, who offers to fight anyone with whom his future father-in-law, Don Pedro, may have a disagreement. He has rid him of Don Félix by impersonating a police official, cutting off his ear in the street, and getting him arrested. The Dorothée complication has already caused Don Pedro to have second thoughts about marrying his daughter to Don Félix. It is never completely cleared up, but causes some laughable confusion and explains the play's first title. After his abortive duel with Alphonse, Jodelet disappears from the action (V. i and ii).

This comedy and its predecessor belong as nearly as possible to the Spanish category of the *comedia de gracioso*, in which the *gracioso* (fool, jester) plays the leading part. Another recognized category is the *comedia de figurón*, in which the protagonist is a grotesquely ridiculous character. *Don Japhet d'Arménie* belongs to the second type, though there are evident relationships between the two and the protagonist happens to be a retired court jester; but he has no master to serve, unlike the Fool in *King Lear*. The theme is the mocking of this Don

---

[1] Rivalry and hatred between sisters occurs frequently in French comedy from this date on. In tragedy there was of course the classic Ariadne–Phaedra rivalry. See e.g. Hardy's *Ariadne ravie* (c. 1620), T. Corneille's *Ariane* (1672).

Japhet d'Arménie, the grandiose title taken by a former fool of the Emperor Charles V, now pensioned off and seeking to create an impression of high importance in the provincial town of Orgaz. He summons the *Bailli* (in modern terms, the Mayor) and requires him to find him servants. Four are produced, of whom one is Don Alfonce Enriquez, a young nobleman who is courting Léonore, apparently a village girl who soon proves to be of noble birth also. Don Alfonce accepts the post of secretary to Don Japhet in order to remain near her and avoid discovery of his whereabouts by his mother who has arranged an unwanted marriage for him in Seville. This background love interest ends happily in the marriage of Don Alfonce and Léonore.

Earlier Don Japhet had been attracted by her and wished to make her his mistress, then to marry her. Like everyone else she mocks him. He is encouraged to climb up to her room by a ladder but is surprised by her uncle and forced to come down and undress in the street. A duenna then empties a chamberpot over him. Don Alfonce takes his place and spends the night with Léonore. Her uncle is the Commander of Consuegra, a neighbouring town to which the characters move in Act III. He arranges various 'rewards' for the credulous Don Japhet, which are said to come from the Emperor. He is to be given a marquis-ate containing a rich town, reminiscent of the island given to Sancho Panza by the Duke and Duchess in *Don Quijote*. A mock oration is delivered in his honour by a *Harangueur* who can be seen as a fore-runner of Racine's l'Intimé in *Les Plaideurs*. A coaching horn is blown in his ear. Finally he is told that the Emperor has found him an Indian princess for a bride, with a splendid dowry of exotic treasures. He accepts after being forced to take part in a bullfight as a knightly exercise in which the bull comes off best. In all his failures he remains undeflatable, though slightly suspicious that his leg is being pulled.

This comedy, with its strong element of farce, was Scarron's greatest stage success. Modelled on Castillo y Solorzano's *El Marqués de Cigarral*, but considerably enriched, it is the most fantastic of the comedies and distinguished by the most sustained flights of verbal exuberance and invention.

Scarron's last two comedies, though separated by an interval of some seven years, are similar in conception and can be treated as a pair. They differ somewhat from the earlier comedies. Jodelet had not appeared in *Don Japhet*, no doubt because it was produced at the rival theatre, and the name-part had been taken by his opposite number Philipin. *L'Héritier ridicule* contains a part which might have been specially written for Jodelet but in fact was played by Philipin, who gives his name to the character, indicating that he too was now famous enough for this. In their influence on Scarron's plays Jodelet and Philipin now merge as comedians of identical type for whom the author can write similar lines. Béatrix also is prominent. None of these actors appears in *Le Marquis ridicule*, though there are reminders of them in two pert *soubrettes* and two enterprising valets. But their roles are relatively minor.

The foreground of *L'Héritier ridicule* is occupied by the love affair of the serious characters. The play opens with the heroine, Léonor, hurrying along a street in Madrid followed by a breathless Béatrix, who begs her to stop for a moment:

BÉATRIX Pour moi, je ne vais plus quasi que d'une fesse,
Car vous ne parlez point et vous rêvez sans cesse.
Madame, encor un coup, je ne puis tant aller
Si je n'ai quelquefois le plaisir de parler.
LÉONOR Oui, Béatrix, un peu de conversation;
J'y consens, et t'écoute avec attention.

For four days, says Béatrix, you've been rushing about Madrid without coach or sedan-chair. What will people say if they recognize you? Her mistress explains that she is looking for a man with whom she fell in love when he rescued her from a fire in her country cottage and left without giving his name. After this partial exposition she sees that she is being followed by an importunate admirer, Don Juan de Bracamont, and takes refuge in the nearest house. It belongs to the second leading female character, Hélène, who welcomes her in and vainly tries to send Don Juan away. He is another *capitano* type, resembling Don Gaspard in *Jodelet duelliste*, without his bravery, and is extremely persistent. He is eventually persuaded to leave by Don Diègue, the desirable unknown man whom Léonor was seeking, who arrives to visit Hélène. He wishes to marry her but Hélène does not want him because he has no money, as she explains to Léonor after he has left:

> Je veux vivre à la cour, sans bien [wealth] je ne le puis...
> Don Diègue est aimable et son nom est Mendoce,
> Mais cela ne fait pas bien rouler un carrosse.[1]

He says he has a rich uncle in Peru (an early example of the 'American uncle') but so far nothing has materialized from that quarter.

In Act II Don Diègue begins to suspect Hélène's mercenary motives. Léonor calls on him and – treacherously, though this is never stressed – strengthens his suspicions by recounting her conversation with Hélène. She knows a lady of higher rank who has an income of 6000 écus and loves him. 'I'll visit you to learn her name,' says Don Diègue. He then hears that his uncle has died and left him his fortune. He decides to give Hélène a final test. His valet Philipin, who first appears in this act, suggests that she should be told that Don Diègue has been disinherited in favour of another nephew whom he will impersonate.

Shown a faked letter containing this news, Hélène rejects Don Diègue in Act III but is ready to receive his moneyed cousin. Philipin, under the name of Don Pedro de Buffalos, is shown in and conducts a comically rustic wooing exactly in the vein of Jodelet's in *Jodelet maître*. It does not appear to put her off.

In Act IV Don Diègue offers his love to Léonor. While he is in her house Hélène calls and catches sight of him. The conversation between the two women degenerates from ironical politeness to open offensiveness, foreshadowing the exchanges between Célimène and Arsinoé in *Le Misanthrope*, though it is rather blunter. After Hélène has left in fury, the boastful Don Juan informs Don Diègue that he is transferring his affections from Léonor to Hélène. He will get rid of Don Pedro de Buffalos (Philipin) by attacking him that evening in the street. Don Diègue decides to intervene – he cannot allow his servant to be hurt – and calls for a sword. Vainly begging him not to put himself in danger, Léonor declares her love for him openly.

The night attack proves bloodless. Interrupted in a mock serenade of Hélène, the trembling Philipin makes a thrust at Don Juan, who begs for mercy. Philipin is doing the same when Don Diègue steps between them:

---

[1] See above p. 31.

D. DIÈGUE   Cavaliers, qu'est ceci?
       Vous vous entr'assommez!

PHILIPIN   Hélas, tout au contraire,
       Nous nous entre-sauvons.

Let off the hook, both the heroes boast. Don Juan goes off to look for another fight – this one was just a joke. But he can never sleep properly at night unless he has killed a man first.

In Act V Hélène is preparing for an immediate marriage with the rich cousin. She is choosing colours for the wedding and correcting Philipin's rustic choices when Don Diègue enters and suggests the *fanfaron* Don Juan as a better husband. The attempted rescue fails and she refuses to listen, whereupon Don Diègue leaves and returns with Don Juan and Léonor. Before them all she is told that Don Pedro de Buffalos is only a lackey. Each in turn, Don Juan, Don Diègue and then Philipin, repudiates her in short speeches containing similar lines:

> Moi, vous épouser? Vous, une intéressée . . .
> Madame, je serais le plus sot des humains;
> Je ne veux point de vous et vous baise les mains.

She is left utterly humiliated after a scene which foreshadows *Le Misanthrope* even more strongly.[1]

But Célimène at least had Alceste in reserve to turn to if she could have accepted his conditions. Scarron's ending is cruder and crueller. His Hélène has no one and she can only hope for 'vengeance or death' before the day is out. As though to lighten this, Scarron repeats the rejection in a comic key in a closing scene between Béatrix and Philipin:

BÉATRIX   Mon âme,
       Si tu voulais . . .

PHILIPIN   Et quoi?

BÉATRIX   Prendre . . .

PHILIPIN   Parle.

BÉATRIX   Une femme.

---

[1] H. C. Lancaster (*History*, II, pp. 729 ff.) finds rather less striking parallels between *L'Héritier ridicule* and *Les Précieuses ridicules*. It is not surprising that Molière should have taken hints from *L'Héritier*, since his own company acted the play frequently from 1659 on. The same applies to *Jodelet maître* and *Don Japhet* but not, for some reason, to *Jodelet duelliste* and *Le Marquis ridicule*. See La Grange's *Registre*.

PHILIPIN La prendre? A quel dessein?
BÉATRIX   Pour épouse.
PHILIPIN   Ha, ma foi,
       Le conseil est fort bon, la connais-je?
BÉATRIX   C'est moi.
PHILIPIN *Vade, vade retro Satanas*,[1] qui me tente! . . .

He is not going to be captured in marriage and perhaps have an endless
family of mewling and puking infants and he ends by saying:

    Si mes yeux t'ont fait mal, va te faire panser.

Béatrix hits back, illogically but very realistically. What, marry a man
like Philipin! She is besieged by admirers offering marriage, or something like it:

                        . . . gros vilain, va te faire
        Cent fois plus honnête homme, et lors j'aviserai,
        Par pitié seulement, si je t'épouserai.
        J'ai reçu depuis peu deux gros poulets [love-letters] d'un
            comte;
        Un duc me couche en joue,[2] et j'en fais peu de compte;
        Un jeune abbé qui n'est ni prêtre ni demi
        S'offre de m'épouser ou d'être mon ami,
        Il me fit l'autre jour don d'une porcelaine . . .

She exits, leaving Philipin standing there in some bewilderment:

    M'a-t-elle ainsi quitté par dépit ou par ruse?

Oh well, he finally decides, I'll write a rondeau about this and let her
have it.

                        ❧❧

This little-known comedy, which we have therefore described in some
detail, is reproduced on a more farcical level in *Le Marquis ridicule*,
with some echoes also of the earlier comedies. One cannot take the
feelings of any of the characters very seriously, except those of the
sympathetic pair of lovers, who are becoming little more than a
conventional concession to romance. The woman who is eventually

---

[1] 'Get thee behind me, Satan'.   [2] 'Is taking aim at me', 'is after me'

discarded is a comic adventuress, a Portuguese lady called Stéfanie. In a near-repetition of *L'Héritier ridicule* the opening scene shows her walking about in the blazing sun with her *suivante* Louise. She is searching for Don Sanche who, she believes wrongly, has made advances to her. In fact he is in love with the heroine, Blanche, whom he has saved, in this case from a runaway coach. Like the hero of *L'Héritier ridicule*, he was a stranger, but *he* tries to find *her*, discovers her name and calls on her. He is told to keep away because she is engaged to be married and is hurriedly hidden by a second *suivante*, Blanche's Lizette.

The prospective husband is his own elder brother, Don Blaize Pol, Marquis de la Victoire, a backwoods nobleman as unpolished as Don Sanche is courtly and possessing some of the features of Don Japhet d'Arménie. While not a full-blooded grotesque or *figurón* he introduces with Stéfanie a note of broad caricature which the previous comedy lacked. Morbidly jealous of every other man, he comes to accept his brother in Blanche's house and even suggests that he should court her to test her loyalty towards himself. Stéfanie does not remain inactive. Having transferred her pursuit to Blaize, she snatches Blanche's portrait from him through a window and visits Blanche. She makes up the story that she has had two children by Blaize. In order to avoid Blaize and Blanche's father Don Cosme (whom Blaize finds unlikeable) she is hidden with her two attendants in Blanche's room. They grow tired of waiting and in a later scene the three file across the stage with their heads heavily veiled in the crazy hope of getting away unnoticed, or at least unrecognized. 'Who are these people in your house?' asks the always suspicious Marquis de la Victoire, 'Connaissez-vous quelqu'un de cette noire bande?' 'Never seen them before,' replies the equally astonished Don Cosme.

The whole comic imbroglio comes to a head in Act V. In a burlesque of the traditional recognition scene Stéfanie claims to be a long-lost daughter of Don Cosme, who, she discovers, had an affair in Portugal many years ago. She entreats her 'father' to force her 'seducer' to honour his obligation towards her, then bursts into tears. One after another, the others do the same, for the only reason that the example is contagious. The last to break down is the bewildered Don Blaize:

D. BLAIZE [*snivelling*] Belle qui pleurez tant, inconnue à mes yeux,
    Voudriez-vous pleurer moins, ou vous expliquer mieux?

STÉFANIE [*leaping at him*] Tu ne me connais pas, ingrat! Ha! Tout
    à l'heure
    Il faut que je t'étrangle, ou qu'un de nous deux meure.
D. BLAIZE [*calling on his valets and his brother*] Ay, ay, ay, Ordugno!
    mon cher frère! Merlin!
    Venez me délivrer de cet esprit malin.
STÉFANIE Perfide! Scélérat!
D. BLAIZE   Seigneur en qui j'espère,
    N'était-ce pas assez de ce maudit beau-père,
    Sans lâcher contre moi la dame d'Angola?
STÉFANIE Dis d'Alcalca, méchant! auprès de Malaca.
D. BLAIZE D'Angola, d'Alcalca, Malaca! que m'importe
    De bien dire son nom? Que le diable m'emporte
    Si je t'ai jamais vue et si je crois jamais
    Te voir!

Stéfanie does not get Blaize, who decides to return to the safety of
his backwoods and leave Blanche, evidently a dangerous minx, to his
younger brother. He offers to share his estate with him.

⁂

The element of farce, so prominent in this last comedy, can be found
in all the others in varying degrees. Where there is a Jodelet or a
Philipin it depends mainly on them. Where there is not, other characters are promoted in absurdity. As the summaries will have shown,
Scarron re-uses the same situations to yield different effects. Don
Louis's descent from the balcony in *Jodelet maître* is not farcical; Don
Japhet's, with the uncle waiting for him with an arquebus and the
duenna with a chamberpot (O Romeo, O Juliet!) is. Of Jodelet's two
duels the second, which ends in a beating-up, is more farcical than the
first, while other duels are threatened which are not funny at all.
Scarron never reaches the tragic point at which discovery would mean
death for the man and a convent for the woman, but the concealments
of Lucrèce and Don Louis in *Jodelet maître* could have graver consequences than those in *Le Marquis ridicule*.
    The device of characters popping in and out of bedroom and other
doors and the related confusion about which door? which character?
might seem to be typical of modern farce. In fact it was used extensively

in French seventeenth-century comedy: in Scarron, as just remarked; in several of T. Corneille's comedies; and by other dramatists occasionally. It could be traced right back to the *Miles gloriosus* of Plautus, in which a girl, pretending to be her own twin sister, appears alternately at the doors of two neighbouring houses connected by a secret passage.

The stage-effects, dependent on physical movements and settings, range from plain knockabout (usually when Jodelet or Philipin gets beaten) to more sophisticated touches. Though the indecencies of the old farce are generally avoided and the caperings of the contemporary Italian comedians and the more modern circus clown are not much in evidence, these effects are still physical. They could not be admitted to 'high' or polished comedy and would have been unthinkable in Pierre Corneille. What upgrades them in Scarron and makes it impossible to establish a clear distinction between farce and comedy in his work is their association with a dialogue which is sometimes very witty, the two together creating an atmosphere of humorous fantasy going beyond realism. The sense of humour has taken some hard knocks over the centuries up till today, when grimness is often identified with efficiency, but one cannot read Scarron without finding that he possessed it. In *L'Héritier ridicule*, Philipin rushes on stage and nearly bumps into the beautiful Hélène. He has been hurrying through several rooms of this large house and expected to go through several more before finding the object of his wooing. His first words, in a speech which must be returned to later, are (my italics):

> Ha! pardon, *bel objet!*
> Je pensais bien encor faire un plus long trajet.

He pretends almost to faint at the sight of her beauty, and no doubt the actor would stagger about the stage:

> Tiens-moi bien, je palpite,
> O dangereuse vue! O fatale visite!
> . . . Hélas, je ne la vois que depuis un moment,
> Et je me sens déjà tout je ne sais comment.[1]

---

[1] Such exaggerations of the effects of love were typical of burlesque. In Saint-Amant's *Le Melon* even the taste of fruit almost causes the poet to swoon with ecstasy: 'Ha! soutenez-moi, je me pâme! / Ce morceau me chatouille l'âme.'

Another humorous touch, this time unphysical and muted enough to pass unperceived, occurs in the closing scenes of *L'Héritier*. The *suivante* Paquette has just announced Don Diègue, Léonor and Don Juan – quite a crowd to arrive together. Philipin, ironic, asks:

> N'ont-ils pas amené quelques autres encor?

Paquette, completely missing the irony, replies woodenly:

> Je ne le pense pas.

The verbally comic, sometimes integrated with the physically laughable, sometimes independent of it, is Scarron's strongest point. No French dramatist before him approached his mastery of dialogue, humorous in itself. Few after him, except Molière and perhaps Racine in *Les Plaideurs*, did better. Where Scarron differs from Molière is in his exuberant passages, which overshadow his subtler effects and are characteristic of him:

JODELET [*To Béatrix, whom he thinks has criticized him before her mistress*]
> Ah, louve! ah, porque! ah, chienne! ah, braque! ah, loup!
> Puisses-tu te briser bras, main, pied, chef, cul, cou!
> Que toujours quelque chien contre ta jupe pisse!
> Qu'avec ses trois gosiers Cerbérus t'engloutisse!
> Le grand chien Cerbérus, Cerbérus le grand chien,
> Plus beau que toi cent fois, et plus homme de bien.
>   (*Jodelet maître*, III. viii)

An accumulation of nouns or adjectives for comic effect is Rabelaisian, as also is the third line in this quotation (*Gargantua and Pantagruel*, Bk II, Ch. 22), though Scarron was quite capable of thinking of it for himself. Comic listings are found also in Plautus,[1] whose verbal inventiveness often prefigures Scarron's, but whether there was influence here or not, Jodelet's confused invective in the last three lines is Scarron's own. There is excellent nonsense in the three-headed hound of hell – a hundred times more beautiful and 'more of a gentleman' than the *soubrette* Béatrix.

---

[1] See e.g. *Bacchides*, 114–16: 'Quis istic habet?' / 'Amor, Voluptas, Venus, Venustas, Gaudium, / Jocus, Ludus, Sermo, Suavisaviatio.' Translated in Loeb Classics as: 'Who lives here?' / 'Love, Delight, Venus, Grace, Joy, / Jest, Jollity, Chitchat, Kissykissysweetkins.'

Jodelet's inapt comparisons are part of his persona. In the next scene he approaches Isabelle with:

> Ne pourrai-je savoir, ô beauté succulante,
> Que j'aime autant qu'un oncle et bien plus qu'une tante,
> Comment dans votre cœur Don Juan est logé?

Sometimes a character, carried away by words, reflects that they may not be suitable and stops to consider the point. This time it is Philipin paying his court to Hélène in the speech from which we have already quoted on p. 65:

> Ha, petite civette! Ha, chatte! Ha, petit chien!
> Petit chien, ce mot-là pour femme est ridicule.
> Ah pardon, je voulais vous nommer canicule,
> Mais vous avez bon sens et vous savez fort bien
> Qu'on nomme également femelle et mâle un chien.
> (*L'Héritier ridicule*, III. iii)

His excuse is rather lame, but only a verbalist would have thought of making it.

The most extravagant verbal gymnastics occur in *Don Japhet d'Arménie*, most of them in the mouth of the hero. He is conscious of his superior language when talking to the rustic *Bailli* of Orgaz:

> DON JAPHET L'Empereur Charles Quint, ce héros redoutable,
> Mon cousin au deux mille huitantième degré,
> Trouvant avec raison mon esprit à son gré,
> M'a promené longtemps par les villes d'Espagne,
> Et depuis m'a prié de quitter la campagne,[1]
> Parce que deux Soleils en un lieu trop étroit
> Rendraient trop excessif le contraire du froid.
> La façon de parler est obscure au village.
> Entendez-vous, Bailli, mon sublime langage?
> LE BAILLI Monsieur, je n'entends pas la langue de la cour.
> DON JAPHET Vous ne m'entendez pas? Je vous aime autant sourd,
> Car assez rarement mon discours j'humanise;
> Mais pour vous aujourd'hui je démétaphorise
> (Démétaphoriser, c'est parler bassement).

---

[1] The royal tour of the country.

Si mon discours pour vous n'est que de l'allemand,
Vous aurez avec moi disette de loquelle.[1]
L'Empereur donc, de qui je suis le parallèle . . .
M'entendez-vous, Bailli?

LE BAILLI   Nenny.

DON JAPHET   Le parangon?

LE BAILLI Encore moins.

DON JAPHET   Comment! Altérer mon jargon,
Ce serait déroger à ma noblesse antique.
Tâchons pourtant d'user de quelque terme oblique
Pour nous accomoder à cet homme des champs . . .

                              (*Don Japhet*, I. ii)

Don Japhet is using and abusing the kind of language on which
préciosité was based: principally on the far-fetched metaphor, incompre-
hensible to profane ears. 'Démétaphoriser, c'est parler bassement.' One
perceives already in his 'courtly' discourse the superior attitude and
the linguistic contortions derided in Molière's *Précieuses ridicules*
twelve years later, as in the famous:

MAGDELON Vite, venez nous tendre ici le conseiller des grâces.

MAROTTE Par ma foi, je ne sais point quelle bête c'est là; il faut
parler chrétien si vous voulez que je vous entende.

CATHOS Apportez-nous le miroir, ignorante que vous êtes . . .

This comes near to parody, but of a general kind best described as
mockery by exaggerated imitation, and not directed at any particular
work of literature. In the Jodelet comedies some of the references are
more precise, though still only distantly parodic. In a scene in *Jodelet
maître* (II. vii) of which the general drift is serious, the seduced and
deserted Lucrèce flings herself at the feet of Don Fernand to implore
his protection:

LUCRÈCE Et vous, mes faibles bras, embrassez ses genoux.
Vous ne me verrez point lever de devant vous
Que je n'aie obtenu le secours que j'espère.

D. FERNAND Ce style est de roman, et je vous en révère.
[*Helping her up*] Ma sotte d'Isabeau n'a jamais lu
roman.
Quant est de moi, j'estime *Amadis* grandement.

[1] 'Dearth of loquacity'. *Loquelle* was an archaic word, used here comically.

Lucrèce, who is not an object of burlesque, continues to unfold her pitiful story:

> Il faut donc, ô Fernand, que je vous importune
> Du récit de ma race et de mon infortune.
> Pour ma race bientôt vous en serez savant,
> Car mon père défunt m'a dit assez souvent
> Qu'il avait avec vous fait amitié dans Rome
> Et qu'il vous connaissait pour brave gentilhomme.

Don Fernand, moved though he is, replies:

> Ces vers sont de Mairet; je les sais bien par cœur.
> Ils sont très à propos, et d'un très bon auteur.[1]

Elsewhere contemporary plays are mentioned in less ambiguously comic contexts, in these cases by Jodelet. The comedian, posing as his master, is reproached by Don Fernand for his cowardice in trying to avoid the duel with Don Louis. He retorts:

> Que vous eussiez aimé pour votre gendre un Cid,
> Qui vous eût assommé, puis épousé Chimène.
> (*Jodelet maître*, IV. vii)

This certainly sums up Corneille's great tragicomedy from a new angle. The following exchange in *Jodelet duelliste* (I. i) does the same for another serious story. Don Félix, exasperated by Jodelet's moralizing, beats him and is compared by his valet to Nero:

JODELET Néron qui fit mourir feu sa mère Agrippine . . .
          Paraissait être bon et il ne valait rien . . .
D. FELIX De la part de Néron, sache, Monsieur Sénèque,
          Qu'un valet qui conseille, au lieu d'être écouté
          Mérite bien souvent de se voir bien frotté.

The allusion is obscure. The story was of course in Tacitus and other historians, but a playwright would hardly evoke it on the stage if there were no better reasons than that for his audiences to recognize it. If unrecognized there would be no point in it. Since nothing else seems to fit, the allusion may have been to Tristan L'Hermite's recent *La*

---

[1] If they are by Mairet we have not succeeded in tracing them.

Mort de Sénèque (1643 or 1644), though in that tragedy Agrippine does not figure and the role of Seneca is not so much that of a moralizing 'valet' as of a suspected conspirator.

Literature and drama are thus mentioned in a tone not developed into sustained parody but pointing in that direction.[1] The most conspicuous mockery is general and directed at the language and procedures of courtly love expressed through the twin conventions of *galanterie* and *préciosité*. Our quotations from the rustic wooings of Jodelet and Philipin have already illustrated this. *Galanterie* is guyed by them, either by misapplication or by contrast with their natural earthiness. The wooing of the grotesques, Don Japhet and Don Blaize Pol of *Le Marquis ridicule*, gives the same effect. Between the servants the mockery is open and deliberate. The valet Merlin thus addresses the *soubrette* Louise:

> Beau magasin d'attraits,
> Mon maître est déjà loin, il faut que j'aille après.
> Sans cela, croyez-moi, ma chère impératrice,
> Qu'il n'est rien ici-bas que pour vous je ne fisse . . .
> Adieu, moule adorable à faire des enfants.
> *(Le Marquis ridicule, I. iii)*

Though the 'adorable mould for producing children' is certainly an ingenious metaphor, it would hardly have been to the taste of the salons.

The braggarts or *fanfarons* are not totally comic. They are intermediate between the buffoon and the serious well-bred character. One at least, the Don Juan of *L'Héritier ridicule*, obeys the courtly love code the moment he is reminded of it. He has been besieging Hélène's door in his pursuit of Léonor and is persuaded to go away by Don Diègue, whose clinching argument is:

> Don Juan, en amour le vœu d'obéissance
> Va devant tous les serments. Allons.

His respect for 'good form' shows again in his later decision to transfer his attentions from Léonor to Hélène. Like a knight of old

---

[1] Cf. the allusions to well-known plays in Regnard and Dufresny, pp. 179–81 and 186–7 below.

he will find a highborn lady to serve and will win her by his fidelity
and merit:

> J'ai résolu d'aimer quelque dame bien née
> Et qui reconnaîtra la constance et la foi
> D'un homme de mérite, enfin fait comme moi.
> (*L'Héritier ridicule*, IV. iii)

None of the more serious and 'modern' characters entertains such
ideas. Their love is either passionate or mercenary. The lady waiting
passively for her perfect prince belongs to a different world.

As in Corneille's comedies,[1] the practice and idiom of courtly love
are shown to be passing out of fashion, but Scarron takes the decline a
step further. The honour code, from which his women have been
completely emancipated, is now serious˙ y questioned in its application
to men. Disregarding one or two examples of 'caddish' behaviour in
other fields (again as in Corneille) the obvious test-point is Scarron's
treatment of the duel. According to the traditional code, a gentleman
who had been insulted or wronged was obliged to fight a duel, or at
least to propose one, if he was not to be despised socially. Jodelet, the
comic, has considerable doubts about this. In *Jodelet maître* (IV. ii)
he speaks his long monologue in *stances* (the form itself parodies the
monologues in more serious plays in which characters debate their
dilemmas, e.g. Rodrigue in *Le Cid*), when he believes he may have to
fight a duel in his master's place. He stands in the middle of the stage
picking and polishing his teeth:

> Soyez nettes, mes dents; l'honneur vous le commande:
> Perdre les dents est tout le mal que j'appréhende.
> > L'ail, ma foi, vaut mieux qu'un oignon.
> > Quand je trouve quelque mignon,
> > Sitôt qu'il sent l'ail que je mange,
> > Il fait une grimace étrange
> > Et dit, la main sur le rognon:
> > Fi, cela n'est point honorable.
> > Que béni soyez-vous, Seigneur,
> > Qui m'avez fait un misérable
> > Qui préfère l'ail à l'honneur.
> Soyez nettes, mes dents; l'honneur vous le commande, etc.

---

[1] See above, pp. 32–3.

Honour consists in keeping his teeth clean. Apart from that, garlic is a
better thing than honour. And, he goes on, it is better to be a despised
lackey than to lose one's life for a mere slap on the face:

> Quand je me mets à discourir
> Que le corps enfin doit pourrir,
> Le corps humain, où la prudence
> Et l'honneur font leur résidence,
> Je m'afflige jusqu'au mourir.
> Quoi! cinq doigts mis sur une face
> Doivent-ils être un affront tel
> Qu'il faille pour cela qu'on fasse
> Appeler un homme en duel?

He concludes:

> Puisque soufflets les déshonorent,
> Ou les hommes sont insensés,
> Ou messieurs les vivants ignorent
> Quels sont messieurs les trépassés.

This seventeenth-century version of 'better red than dead' is confirmed in action in Jodelet's second non-duel in the next play, with its
successive titles of *Jodelet souffleté* and *Jodelet duelliste*. Here the
comedian's monologue as he practises for his duel with Alphonse is
preceded by:

> Oh! qu'être homme d'honneur est une sotte chose,
> Et qu'un simple soufflet de grands ennuis nous cause;

With some misgivings he begins his fencing exercises (he has obtained
all the necessary equipment) and, warming up, defeats his imaginary
opponent and refuses to spare his life:

> 'Ah, pardon, Jodelet.' 'Non, non, il faut mourir.'
> 'Ah, de grâce, pardon.' 'Meurs, sans plus discourir.'

At this point Alphonse enters in the flesh:

> Eh bien, le fanfaron, qui voulez-vous qui meure?

Jodelet protests that he was just acting a comedy but receives another
beating and is left totally humiliated, if he is capable of humiliation.
    The true *fanfarons* deflate also, notably Don Juan in *L'Héritier
ridicule*, but this had less significance because they were seen as de-

scendants of the *capitano*, who deflated traditionally. The attitude of the higher-type characters varies. One or two stand their ground. The caddish Don Félix in *Jodelet duelliste*, warned by his valet that his behaviour is likely to earn him a beating-up or a duel, replies contemptuously:

> Deux choses à la cour ont été condamnées:
> Pour les femmes se battre . . . et porter
> Le pourpoint boutonné.

This sly reference to the edicts against duelling is apparently contradicted in the closing lines of the play, in which Don Gaspard has just spoken of the duel as an obligation of honour:

> D. PEDRO Laissons là le duel, puisqu'il est défendu.
> D. GASPARD Dites-vous? Sans duel un état est perdu.
> C'est le seul métier noble où la vertu s'exerce,
> Et rien n'est comparable à la quarte ou la tierce.

But Don Gaspard is a modified *fanfaron* – a brave one – who has appeared slightly ridiculous earlier in the play. It seems obvious that by ending his comedy with these lines Scarron intended to finish with a laugh rather than with a sudden affirmation of the aristocratic values. The lines were not in the first version of the play and the probability is that they were written for the second to strengthen the impression of lightheartedness. The last line of all, in the mouth of a rapier-happy fanatic, does not suggest a very serious message. If one made an old-style foxhunter observe 'There's nothin' like huntin'. View hallo! Gone away!' it would be caricature of the same order.

❧

These ultimately social considerations have a bearing on the intention and nature of Scarron's plays. Entertainments? Yes, and good ones. Laughable entertainments? Preponderantly yes, but why laugh and at whom?

H. C. Lancaster, whose knowledge of this field of drama was so thorough and extensive that his conclusions cannot be lightly disregarded, wrote of *Jodelet maître*:

> As his hero, with whom we are in sympathy, is distinctly a man of honour, it is a mistake to suppose that Scarron was primarily

criticizing the code of his aristocratic contemporaries rather than seeking to create amusing situations by contrasting the feelings of Jodelet and Béatrix with those of their betters under similar circumstances.[1]

Lancaster's word 'primarily' is a partial qualification, but his general sense overrides this. He is evidently thinking of the well-tried comic formula by which lower-order characters attempt to imitate their 'betters' and, failing ludicrously, are funny *in themselves* but no more. The superior laughter which greets their efforts was a familiar product of English Victorian and Edwardian humour, as the pages of *Punch* show. But this will not do for Scarron. His 'low' characters are too prominent; one can sympathize with them; and, though there is 'contrast', there are also suggestions of affinity. One cannot make fun on this scale of an ethic or an attitude without at least beginning to call the ethic itself into question. The Shakespearian fool and the Spanish *gracioso* may often be supernumeraries whose function is to underline the superiority of the serious characters, though in several cases this reading is hardly tenable. Integrated in the plot in Scarron's way they assume a different significance and when the infection spreads to characters who are only half comic some criticism of the social code appears inevitable.

So were Scarron's comedies satirical? This is where any commentator must hesitate and return to the theoretical position stated at the beginning of this chapter before attempting a judgement. Scarron wrote burlesque, which began as an imitation, usually with conspicuous exaggeration, of serious literature and verbal habits themselves derived ultimately from literature. Burlesque is one form of parody. Some parody is inspired by disrespect of the original, on which it sheds an incongruous light. Other parody springs less from disrespect than from a new look at old works, encouraging a reinterpretation. Though 'literary' in either case it is not confined to literature. It involves the culture which literature both belongs to and helps to form. Since every society necessarily has a culture, from the rudimentary to the sophisticated, a questioning of the second can become a challenge to the first and lead, perhaps imperceptibly, to a reassessment of the whole.

The kind of questioning which parody initiates is often mild and

[1] H. C. Lancaster, *History*, II, pp. 444-5.

superficial, easily laughed off. No doubt it can be more aggressive and its aggression will be expressed in satire, though it is not the best medium for this. The satirical content of burlesque parody in particular is not very strong because it is swamped by exuberance and blunted by the general impression of good humour. One cannot say that Scarron's main object in writing was to satirize aspects of his society, yet one must admit some elements of satire into his comedies. His treatment of honour is too direct to be written off as incidental or explained solely as part of the Jodelet persona. But with this he seems to have stopped. To invoke the dog which keeps appearing in his dialogue, he showed his teeth and at the same time wagged his tail. The tail then wagged the dog – on the whole an amusingly amiable creature, if not to be trusted absolutely.

This same question of satire or satirical intention recurs for Molière in acuter form, for Beaumarchais and other dramatists. It must be reconsidered in each case. For Scarron the matter might be put in perspective by a comparison with Pascal's *Lettres provinciales* (1656–7 and so one year after *Le Marquis ridicule*), the sharpest satire of the century, not excluding Boileau. In these there is indeed a bite, achieved by a literary technique which is the opposite of broad-humoured burlesque.

While Scarron was easily the most prolific and accomplished exponent of the burlesque in comic drama, he was not isolated. Burlesque tendencies which could be developed naturally into literary parody occur incidentally in Corneille's earlier comedies. We have already seen how in *La Veuve* the realistically cynical Alcidon mocks both Philiste for his theory of courtship from a respectful distance and Célidan for his obsession with loyalty between friends. He does not parody their words, but simply thinks them fools and goes on to exploit them. More open and pointed is the scene in the same play (I. iv) in which the 'agent' Géron is trying to sell his client, the inexperienced and provincial Florange, to the worldly minded Chrysante as a husband for her daughter:

CHRYSANTE Que dit-il de ma fille?
    GÉRON   Ah, madame, il l'adore!

Il n'a point encor vu de miracles pareils!
Ses yeux, à son avis, sont autant de soleils;
L'enflure de son sein un double petit monde;
C'est le seul ornement de la machine ronde.
L'Amour à ses regards allume son flambeau,
Et souvent pour la voir il ôte son bandeau;
Diane n'eut jamais une si belle taille;
Auprès d'elle Vénus ne serait rien qui vaille;
Ce ne sont rien que lis et roses que son teint;
Enfin de ses beautés il est si fort atteint . . .

Chrysante finds this so affected that she thinks it must be mockery:

CHRYSANTE Atteint? Ah, mon ami, tant de badinerie
Ne témoigne que trop qu'il en fait raillerie.
GÉRON Madame, je vous jure, il pèche innocemment,
Et s'il savait mieux dire, il dirait autrement.
C'est un homme tout neuf: que voulez-vous qu'il fasse?
Il dit ce qu'il a lu [my italics].

Reassured on this point, the fond mother shows her readiness to talk money.

The young suitor's description of his beloved contains all the clichés of novelesque love-language and of related poetry, distantly Petrarchan, going back to the sixteenth century, when it had emerged in specific form in the *blason*, or description of the lady's charms, and was parodied in the *contre-blason* (yellow complexion, black teeth, etc.). Shakespeare was already holding it up to ridicule in the 1590s:

Speak, speak. Quite dumb?
Dead, dead? A tomb
Must cover thy sweet eyes.
These lily lips,
This cherry nose,
These yellow cowslip cheeks,
Are gone, are gone.
Lovers, make moan:
His eyes were green as leeks.
(*A Midsummer Night's Dream*, V. i)

In French romanesque literature comparisons with goddesses, 'miracles of beauty', 'lilies and roses', and 'eyes like suns', often outshining the sun itself, persisted into the 1630s and were fair game for Corneille. Some ten years later Scarron takes them on to the point of absurdity:

PHILIPIN Que dites-vous de moi, d'oser sans parasol
        Visiter un soleil? C'est un acte de fol.
                        (*L'Héritier ridicule*, III. iii)

Béatrix, having learnt this fine language from a young author she met at her cousin the bookseller's, advises Don Louis:

        Employez hardiment votre meilleure prose;
        N'oubliez pas le lis, n'oubliez pas la rose.
                    (*Jodelet maître*, III. ii)

After *galanterie*, the heroic was travestied, again by Corneille, in *L'Illusion comique*. His Matamore was an openly burlesque creation. He was the first notable example of the *fanfaron* in French original literary comedy, though familiar in earlier farce, in translations and in Italian comedy. His speech is hyperbolic in the highest degree:

    Le seul bruit de mon nom renverse les murailles,
    Défait les escadrons et gagne les batailles.
    Mon courage invaincu contre les empereurs
    N'arme que la moitié de ses moindres fureurs;
    D'un seul commandement que je fais aux trois Parques
    Je dépeuple l'état des plus heureux monarques;
    La foudre est mon canon, les Destins mes soldats;
    Je couche d'un revers mille ennemis à bas;
    D'un souffle je réduis leurs projets en fumée . . .
                    (*L'Illusion comique*, II. ii)

The stupendous warrior was irresistible to women:

    Quand je veux, j'épouvante, et quand je veux, je charme;
    Et, selon qu'il me plaît, je remplis tour à tour
    Les hommes de terreur et les femmes d'amour.
      Du temps que ma beauté m'était inséparable
    Leurs persécutions me rendaient misérable;

Je ne pouvais sortir sans les faire pâmer;
Mille mouraient par jour à force de m'aimer.
J'avais d ; rendez-vous de toutes les princesses . . .

(ibid.)

I had to stop that, continues Matamore, because it was interfering with my military activities and, besides, I was getting a bit tired of it. So I sent Fate to tell Jupiter to find some way of quenching the importunate passions I aroused in the ladies,

Et depuis, je suis beau quand je veux seulement.

In the play Matamore hides trembling in the attic of Isabelle's house for four days on the pretext of guarding her, but in fact for fear of her father's valets.

No parody of any specific work can have been intended though, as has often been pointed out, this could almost be a burlesque before the letter of Corneille's own *Le Cid*. The hero of that play is a literal *matamoros* (killer of Moors) and, toned down though his boasting is, his language sometimes comes near to the braggart captain's. There is no reason why an author should not develop a comic creation into a heroic one, or vice-versa, but this has only a marginal significance. The most one can see are certain embryonic resemblances between Matamore and Rodrigue, with the all-important difference that the latter was genuinely brave.

A cynical eye will discern traces of the comic *capitano* in many serious works, with little implication of a direct relationship. More than the pedant doctor or the foolish old man, he is the burlesque character *par excellence*. He parodies in one persona the hero of epic and the hero of romance, blowing them up to elephantine proportions, then subsiding in a ridiculous whimper. The spectacle is invariably effective because it satisfies the wishful beliefs that bullies are always cowards and masculine charm always a veneer.

Around the date of *L'Illusion* there was an outburst of *capitanos*, not set off by Corneille but no doubt encouraged by his example. An earlier play by Mareschal entitled *Le Railleur* (1635) contained a partly developed braggart who became the main character in the same author's *Le Véritable Capitan Matamore ou le Fanfaron*, produced in 1637–8 after *L'Illusion*. Both of Mareschal's plays were free adaptations of Plautus and the second competed with an anonymous adaptation of the same date, *Le Capitan ou le Miles gloriosus*. Also at that time a *capitano* of equal stature to Corneille's appeared in *Les Visionnaires* of Desmarets de Saint-Sorlin, a prime example of literary burlesque some six years earlier than Scarron's first comedy.[1]

◈◈◈

Produced at the Marais between 15 February and 6 March 1637, *Les Visionnaires* must have followed immediately after *Le Cid* on the same stage. A first version was read at the Hôtel de Rambouillet before production and amended to avoid giving offence. It may well have contained disrespectful references to *Le Cid* and to a play by de Scudéry, but it is impossible to know what they were since they do not figure in the surviving text.

Desmarets presents a number of 'visionary' or hallucinated characters, each suffering from a crazy obsession carried well into the realm of caricature. His *capitano*, Artabaze, runs true to type ('Je suis l'amour du ciel et l'effroi de la terre') with the addition of his terror of the frenzied poet Amidor whom he fears as a sorcerer (the joke wears rather thin), mistaking his technical literary terms for some kind of witchcraft. There is a lovesick swain of pastoral in Filidan, who is oversensitive to every beauty and even to the description of one. Amidor's nonsensical love verses overwhelm him. A fourth male eccentric, Phalante, comes out less clearly in modern eyes. His illusion is that he is rich and he is interested in building a grandiose house set in superb landscaped gardens. His description of these paralleled a contemporary literary fashion which had a longish life (see La Fontaine's *Le Songe de Vaux*, c. 1660).

A fifth character is Alcidon, an elderly man who has three daughters. His peculiarity is to be so impressed by each of the younger men that he immediately promises him one of his daughters in marriage – it hardly matters which. He eventually realizes, counting on his fingers,

---

[1] The last notable Matamore, so named and a fine specimen, appeared tardily in Tristan L'Hermite's *Le Parasite* (1654). He is somewhat overshadowed by his valet Fripesauces, an intriguing and exaggeratedly gluttonous character. The plot entails a capture by Turkish pirates and impersonation scenes by characters posing as Turks. The comedy has great verve and a farcical coarseness in places. It belongs to the burlesque tradition, though a late example of its type in the theatre.

that he has committed himself to four different men but has only three daughters. His long soliloquy (V. i) burlesques the dilemma monologues of serious drama and ends:

> A quoi suis-je réduit? Quel conseil dois-je prendre?
> Tout me plaît et me nuit; mais j'aperçois Lysandre.

Lysandre is a first sketch of the 'reasonable man', living in a practical world contrasted to that of the eccentrics, whom Molière was to utilize later.

The three daughters are if anything more fantastic than the men. Hespérie imagines that every man who sees her or even hears of her falls madly in love with her. She caricatures in a general way the 'ideal beauty' of pastoral and of Petrarchan-précieux love poetry. (For her and her counterpart Filidan compare Scarron's lines quoted on p. 65 above, 'Hélas, je ne la vois que depuis un moment,' etc.) Her sister Mélisse is crazy about Alexander the Great, about whom she has read in history and novels and whom she longs to meet. No other man will do for her, and certainly not Artabaze who, for his part, thinks he is greater than Alexander. The third sister, Sestiane, a relatively minor part, is mad on the theatre, and this opens the way for a discussion on drama and the unities with the poet Amidor.

The play is a structural mess, but this did not matter, as its success through the rest of the seventeenth century shows.[1] The first two acts are a parade of the characters just described, presented in successive scenes which establish them. There is a plot, which begins to move in Act III and ends with the four suitors withdrawing from marriage on their side and the three women on theirs. All prefer to remain in their happy imaginary worlds, and Lysandre comments:

> Doncques peu d'entre vous veulent le mariage:
> Vous n'êtes pas si fous, car fol est qui s'engage.
> . . . Enfants, jouissez tous de vos douces folies;
> Ne changez point d'humeur: plus heureux mille fois
> Que les sages du temps, les princes ni les rois.

---

[1] See H. Gaston Hall's edition of *Les Visionnaires* (Paris, 1963), Introduction, pp. lxx–lxxiv. This lists the numerous editions and performances to 1695. Professor Hall (pp. xxx ff.), agreeing with Lancaster, rejects the explanation given by A. Adam (*Histoire de la littérature française au XVIIe siècle*, I, p. 561) that the play was ordered by Richelieu who dictated its peculiar structure.

Mockery of literary styles and fashions, on which the play depends, focuses particularly on Amidor. He goes into a Dionysian frenzy of 'inspiration' which terrifies Artabaze:

> AMIDOR Je sors des antres noirs du Mont Parnassien
> Où le fils poil-doré du grand Saturnien
> Dans l'esprit forge-vers plante le Dithyrambe,
> L'Épode, l'Antistrophe, et le tragique Iambe.
> ARTABAZE Quel prodige est-ce ci? je suis saisi d'horreur.
> AMIDOR Profane, éloigne-toi, j'entre dans ma fureur.
> Iach, Iach, Évoé.
> ARTABAZE   La rage le possède:
> Contre les furieux la fuite est le remède. [*Exit*]
> AMIDOR Que de descriptions montent en mon cerveau,
> Ainsi que les vapeurs d'un fumeux vin nouveau!
> Sus donc, représentons une fête Bacchique,
> Un orage, un beau temps, par un vers héroïque
> Plein de mots ampoulés, d'Épithètes puissants,
> Et surtout évitons les termes languissants . . .
>   (I. ii and iii)

He jokingly provides Filidan with a *contre-blason* ('Le coral de ses yeux et l'azur de sa bouche', etc.) which still sends the impressionable lover into an ecstasy of admiration. For the supposedly wealthy Phalante, after searching through his pockets and finding several poems of various types, he produces a *Plainte à Cassandre*. It parodies the kind of learned neoplatonic poetry written by Pontus de Tyard, a member of Ronsard's group:

> Doncques rigoureuse Cassandre,
> Tes yeux entre-doux et hagards
> Par l'optique de leurs regards
> Me vont pulvériser en cendre.
> Toutefois parmi ces ardeurs
> Tes hétéroclites froideurs
> Causent une antipéristase:
> Ainsi mourant, ne mourant pas,
> Je me sens ravir en extase
> Entre la vie et le trépas.
> . . . Chante donc la Palinodie,

> Cher Paradoxe de mes sens,
> Et des symptomes que je sens
> Débrouille l'Encyclopédie.
> Ainsi les célestes Brandons
> Versent sur ton chef mille dons
> En lignes perpendiculaires;
> Et devant ton terme fatal,
> Cent révolutions solaires
> Éclairent sur ton vertical.[1]

Phalante is delighted. This is just what he wants to impress his mistress. The poet's professionalism adds a final sarcastic touch. He remarks as he exits:

> Je m'en vais cependant méditer un Poëme.[2]
> Ces vers valent cent francs, à vingt francs le couplet.

(III. iv)

All the literary parody expressed through Amidor is of sixteenth-century poets: Ronsard and other members of the Pléiade group and the garrulous Gascon Du Bartas, author of *Les Semaines*. Desmarets says as much in his introductory *Argument*, which describes Amidor as 'un poète bizarre, sectateur passionné des poètes français qui vivaient avant ce siècle'. They would appear to have been easy targets, representing old styles long discarded. But evidently they had not been by provincial-minded poets and this play should be seen in the context of the stylistic revolution which occurred in the 1630s (and against which burlesque was to some extent a reaction[3]). It aimed at reforming the language of poetry on Malherbian lines, rejecting oddities and

---

[1] Cf. Pontus de Tyard's seriously meant poem *Disgrâce*:

> La haute Idée à mon univers mère,
> Si hautement de nul jamais comprise,
> M'est à présent ténébreuse Chimère.
>
> ... Le clair Soleil par la ligne écliptique
> De son devoir mes yeux plus n'illumine,
> Mais, puisque pis ne peut, se fait oblique, etc.
>
> (*Erreurs amoureuses*, 1549)

[2] Not a general term, as later, but a particular category of poetry, though ill-defined. 'Couplet' in the next line means 'stanza'.

[3] But a cautious one, not directly challenging the 'classical' standards of serious literature. Nearly all its products carried in their titles or sub-titles the words *burlesque*, *comique*, *travesti*, or *ridicule*, as though to show that they were intended only for amusement.

hyperbole in favour of a more restrained and rational diction. At the same time a related battle was being fought by the same body of critics to purge serious drama of its picturesque excesses and enthrone the 'rules' which governed what became known as classical tragedy. As a member of the newly founded Académie Française, Desmarets was actively engaged in this movement, which made his comedy topical at the time, though obscure for the common herd, whose tastes he despised.

Perhaps more surprising was the long-lasting popularity of *Les Visionnaires*. It was intended, says Desmarets in his interesting *Argument*, for an élite of *honnêtes gens* who could appreciate its cultured humour, in other words its literary in-jokes. But if the point of some of these has been lost with the passage of the years there was evidently enough in the general sweep of the play and the exuberant absurdity of its characters to make it still laughable beyond the time of Molière and, in places, even today. It is ironical that a comedy written to condemn excess should have lived on because of its possession of just that quality.

※◎⊙◎※

The unfeasibility of writing really personal literary satire is illustrated by *La Comédie des Académistes*, of which the first manuscript draft no doubt belonged to the same year as *Les Visionnaires*. It cites all the members of the Académie by name, mocks them as persons and as writers and ridicules their mistaken efforts to reform the language. It must have been written with inside knowledge of the Parisian literary world and at least partly by Saint-Évremond, in whose works a revised version was printed in 1705. By then Saint-Évremond was dead, having gone into exile long before for political reasons and become an esteemed member of London society. An earlier edition (anonymous) was published around 1650. It is most unlikely that the play was ever acted, for reasons made clear in a letter written to Guez de Balzac by Chapelain, the unsmiling leader of the Académie, on 28 June 1638:

> Some idle fellow has had the idea of amusing the street-porters [*crocheteurs*: the same word is used by Desmarets and others to typify the vulgar mob] at the expense of our literary senate, for he does not amuse *les honnêtes gens*. He has composed a wretched farce in which we all figure up to the Chancellor [Séguier] himself,

which has caused the play to be suppressed, because whoever admitted to be the author has been threatened with a trip to the Bastille. Seriously, it is a feeble piece of clowning which does us no harm.[1]

The main conclusion to be drawn is that if burlesque dared to sharpen into satire of establishment figures the police were called in to suppress it.

❧❀❧

Nothing of the kind could ever have threatened Thomas Corneille's *Le Berger extravagant*, an innocuous burlesque of pastoral produced as late as 1652. It was based on Sorel's similarly entitled novel of 1628, when pastoral was still very much alive. This died out in the 1640s, but in the 1650s there was a brief revival to which T. Corneille's skit is related. Like Sorel, the dramatist takes as his protagonist a man as deluded as any of the Visionnaires, whose weak mind was distorted at an early age by reading *L'Astrée*. He seemed to be recovering when 'last winter', as his cousin Adrian explains, he saw *Amarillis* at the theatre (evidently Tristan L'Hermite's pastoral) and his folly redoubled. He leaves Paris for the country, dressed as a shepherd with crook and sheep and followed by his friends also in stage-shepherd costume or disguised as nymphs, tree-goddesses, a magician and a river-god. Their object is partly to humour and perhaps cure him, partly to tease him with various tricks while conducting their own serious love affairs in the background. Finally he believes he has been changed into a woodland tree and is persuaded to be transplanted to a more convenient site in the grounds of the neighbouring château where his friends are staying.

This was certainly burlesque in intention, as the several references to literary works and the outmoded love-language of the mock shepherd go to prove. But it is weakened by the incredibility of the main character, surrounded as he is by others who are sane without exception. The necessary atmosphere of fantasy is not created. All we have is the leg-pulling of a character who is 'extravagant' enough in his thoughts and actions but, for burlesque, not nearly enough in his words. The idea, as treated, cannot sustain a five-act play.

---

[1] Quoted by H. C. Lancaster, *History*, II, p. 295.

MOLIÈRE: LIFE AND THEATRICAL CAREER

Family – the Illustre Théâtre –
provincial travels and return to Paris –
Les Précieuses ridicules – *establishing a position but*
failing in tragedy – L'École des femmes – *Molière's*
marriage – the Comic War – La Critique – L'Impromptu –
the campaign of Tartuffe – *productions of*
Dom Juan, Le Misanthrope *and other*
plays to 1671 – Les Femmes savantes *and*
Le Malade imaginaire – *death and dispersal of company –*
foundation of the Comédie Française

❦

Molière, the stage-name taken by Jean-Baptiste Poquelin, was born in January 1622, sixteen years after Pierre Corneille and twelve after Scarron. He belonged to a family of comfortably placed Parisian tradesmen – the middle bourgeoisie – who were able to send him to the 'top' Collège de Clermont, a Jesuit-run school whose pupils were drawn from both the middle class and the aristocracy. Afterwards he may well have studied law and qualified for the bar, though definite proof is lacking. His father Jean Poquelin was a *tapissier*, a trade which included the provision not only of tapestry but of other hangings and draperies and even of furniture in that heavily upholstered age. The business-basis was a shop, but Jean Poquelin also held a Court appointment. He was *tapissier et valet de chambre ordinaire du roi*. Besides supplying the royal household with goods, his duties required his attendance at Court to help make the king's bed. At this level, with the access it gave to the inmost tabernacle, the title of valet was far from pejorative. These *valets de chambre* were ranked as squires and had under-valets themselves. When Molière was fifteen his father secured for him the succession of his post at Court which Molière renounced six years later, in January 1643.[1]

He had decided to become an actor and joined up with a group of professionals dominated by the Béjart family and including Madeleine Béjart,[2] an actress four years older than himself. The troupe attempted to establish themselves in Paris under the name of the Illustre Théâtre but failed after two years, having contracted heavy debts. In 1645 they left for a long Odyssey in the provinces which lasted for thirteen years. Molière had already become the acknowledged leader of the company; Madeleine Béjart, one can say with near certainty, was his mistress; other actresses and actors left and joined them, and they performed principally in the south and south-east, to judge by the surviving evidence. Gathering hard-won experience as an actor and manager, Molière also began writing his first plays, Italian-derived farces.

In the summer of 1658 the company were at Rouen, where they met Pierre Corneille who had withdrawn temporarily from the Parisian theatre but was to return to it in the following year and embark on his second period of playwriting. Molière's ambition was to obtain a permanent footing in the capital, virtually for the first time, since the precarious Illustre Théâtre had long been forgotten, and this new venture was thoroughly planned and prepared. One cannot suppose that his father's connections with the Court in quite a different capacity served Molière in any direct way, but it might be that the family experience gave him added insight into the system of wire-pulling. His task was not easy because there did not seem to be much room in the capital for a fourth theatre besides the Hôtel de Bourgogne, the Marais and the Italians. But before leaving Rouen he secured the patronage of the king's brother 'Monsieur', later Duke of Orléans, and with his backing gave a first performance before the Court in the guard-hall of the Louvre. The main attraction was Corneille's eight-year-old tragedy *Nicomède*, followed by *Le Docteur amoureux*, no doubt a rather crude little farce, never printed, written by Molière and

---

[1] He reassumed the title in April 1660, near the beginning of his triumphant return to Paris, and held it until his death. In the interval it had passed to his younger brother Jean, probably on their father's retirement in 1654. This brother died in 1660.

[2] The nominal head of the family was her mother Marie Béjart, generally known after widowhood by her maiden name of Marie Hervé. She played minor parts, while Madeleine was a considerable actress and an outstanding personality.

in which he played the traditional part of the comic doctor. Louis XIV was so delighted that he gave immediate orders for the new company to be installed in the Palais Bourbon, a royal building near the Louvre containing a theatre hall which was to be shared with the Italian players of the *commedia dell'arte*, the two companies using it on alternate days. Molière had arrived. Some two years later (January 1661) he was transferred to a better theatre in the Palais Royal, originally built by Richelieu. He remained there for the rest of his life, again sharing with the Italians.[1]

During his first year in Paris he produced old tragedies by P. Corneille, Du Ryer (*Scévole* and *Alcionée*) and Tristan L' Hermite (*La Mariane* and *La Mort de Chrispe*). Among comedies he gave several performances of Scarron's *Don Japhet* (once before the king), *Jodelet maître* and *L'Héritier ridicule*; of Desmarets's *Les Visionnaires* and of Corneille's *Le Menteur*. He presented two five-act comedies in verse of his own, *L'Étourdi* and *Le Dépit amoureux*, written earlier and first performed in the provinces.[2] Both contained a strong element of farce. La Grange also mentions 'deux petites comédies' or genuine short farces, *Gros René écolier* and *Le Médecin volant*, given at the Louvre on 18 April 1659 for the king. These were probably also by Molière (the first has not survived) and may well have figured earlier in the travelling company's repertory.

But Molière's fully personal triumph came just over a year after his arrival in Paris when his company presented *Les Précieuses ridicules* on 18 November 1659. This short comedy was a mixture of ingredients already found in Scarron and Desmarets, refurbished by a new and skilful hand. There was a bluntly sensible bourgeois father, two silly girls whose heads had been turned by novel-reading and their desire to

---

[1] Much of the familiar factual information given in this chapter is based on the Preface to the first almost complete edition of Molière's works (1682), written principally or wholly by the actor La Grange, and on La Grange's invaluable *Registre*. La Grange joined the company at Easter 1659 and remained with it until his death in 1692, after it had become part of the Comédie Française. He began writing up the *Registre* several years after Molière's death in 1673, so that it is not in itself the day-to-day record that it appears and his memory of earlier events has been proved to be sometimes at fault. But he evidently based the *Registre* on account-books or notebooks which he had kept throughout his career and in which the figures of receipts and payments to the actors of the troupe must have been accurate. On the whole, all the corrections suggested by other sources are relatively minor and bear mainly on dates.

[2] According to the Preface of 1682, in 1653 (but more probably 1655) and 1656 respectively.

D

follow the latest Parisian trends, and two valets impersonating their masters and being finally shown up and beaten, to the humiliation of the girls who had taken them for genuine men of fashion. Molière's talent showed most conspicuously in the exaggeratedly *galant* and 'metaphorized' language, which had only recently been styled *précieux*,[1] which he put in his characters' mouths. This was literary and social parody of a high order mingled with a modicum of farce. The valets invite the women to inspect their honourable war-wounds (a neat adaptation of the *fanfaron* tradition), one begins to unbutton his trousers but is stopped, both are finally undressed to their underclothes on the stage, but the coarse remarks are few and their wooing is not burlesquely rustic as in Scarron. On the contrary, the humour lies in the attempted elegance of their talk and of course in that of the girls. Molière had succeeded in mocking fashionable refinement by pushing it to the point of affectation. He himself played one of the valets, Mascarille, a character-name he had already used in *L'Étourdi*. The second valet, Jodelet, had a much more subdued part, perhaps because Molière wished to take the lead, perhaps also for health reasons. There are references in the play to Jodelet's pallor and to his recovery from an illness, and he was to die only a few months later.

It is possible that the first script of *Les Précieuses* was broader than the printed version and was amended for this reason and because it gave offence to influential members of the real salons. This would explain the unusual gap of two weeks between the first performance of the play and the second, after which it was acted very frequently and lucratively for months to come.

❧

Molière's next four plays seem to have provoked no controversies. They reveal a dramatist still feeling his way with a new public already more than half won over but of whose responses he could not be sure. The short *Sganarelle ou le Cocu imaginaire* (May 1660) was a lightly written farce with reminiscences of Scarron. *Dom Garcie de Navarre ou le Prince jaloux* (February 1661) was a *comédie héroïque*, the name by then usually given to romantic tragicomedies. It was Molière's only

---

[1] The first printed example of the term *précieuses* appeared in the *Nouvelle Histoire du temps* (1654) by François d'Aubignac, who seems to have invented it.

contribution to this semi-serious genre[1] and a complete failure. In the successful *L'École des maris* (June 1661) he wrote a three-act comedy with a love intrigue and a strong farcical part for Sganarelle, acted by himself. *Les Fâcheux* was commissioned by the *surintendant* Foucquet and performed at his château of Vaux-le-Vicomte on 19 August 1661. This short and amusing *comédie-ballet* was the first of its kind. It caricatured various social types and each act terminated in a ballet linked to the central theme. A few days after its first performance Foucquet, a potential non-royal patron of enormous wealth, fell spectacularly from power, but Molière was not involved in the crash. Louis XIV took over the entertainment (which Foucquet had originally given in his honour) and had it performed at Fontainebleau on 25 August. During the winter Molière produced it in Paris with much success.

This short phase established him both with Parisian audiences and with patrons, whose different tastes he generally managed to reconcile. It marked also his virtual rejection as a writer and actor of non-comedy. There was not only the failure of *Dom Garcie*, but his company acted fewer tragedies than during their first year. There was a brief run of new tragedies[2] in November–December 1662 which may have represented a last effort but more probably the fact that he had run dry of other plays to produce. His public accepted and loved him in farce. His tendency now was to convert this into comedy of a more sophisticated kind.

꧁ꕥ꧂

This led to his most important play to that date, *L'École des femmes*. First produced on 26 December 1662, it developed the earlier *École des maris*. Its chief character is the middle-aged Arnolphe, who brings up a girl believed to be an orphan with the sole aim of making her his submissively dependent wife. Ignorant but not stupid, Agnès is

---

[1] He approaches it, but no more, in *La Princesse d'Élide*, composed to fit into the festivities at Versailles in May 1664. (See below, pp. 95–6.) Called a *comédie galante* and with intermezzi of ballet and music, it was as much a spectacle as a play, adapted probably in haste from Moreto's *El desdén con el desdén* with a substantial part for Molière as the *gracioso*. Using pastoral conventions, it glorifies love, but is best regarded as an entertainment frothed up for a special occasion.

[2] The *Arsace* of de Prade (six performances only) and the *Tonaxare*, or *Oropaste*, of Boyer (fifteen performances). So far as is known, neither was ever revived.

instinctively attracted by a young man who appears and finally wins her, to the discomfiture of the daddy-figure. Much of the humour stems from the girl's innocence, touching in places, which causes her to reveal her newly awakened feelings to Arnolphe himself. The young lover also reports the progress of his love affair to Arnolphe, not knowing who he is and taking him for an ally. Arnolphe can be made ridiculous but he is not wholly so. He is an over-prudent man whose calculations, humanly mistaken and ruthlessly selfish, recoil on his own head. And he falls in love with his ward as she grows up, a development he had not foreseen. There were lines in the comedy which offended the pious and the prudish and farce in the pair of rustic servants, but no more than this. To end his play Molière used the machinery of the unexpected real fathers who appear and unite the young lovers, their son and daughter respectively.

The play was highly successful and occasioned a famous controversy which brought publicity but did no lasting damage. Among the attacks on Molière were personal smears which he disdained to answer. The lowest was the innuendo that in Arnolphe he had depicted himself and in Agnès his young wife who, it was even insinuated, was his own daughter. Ten months earlier (20 February 1662) Molière had married. He was then forty and his bride, Armande Béjart, nineteen or twenty. Her birth certificate has not been found, but their marriage certificate has. Molière, who signed J.-B. Poquelin, had as witnesses his father and brother-in-law, indicating a complete reconciliation with his family, if there had ever been a serious split.[1] Armande had Marie Hervé, described on the certificate as her mother, and Louis and Madeleine Béjart, described as her brother and sister.[2]

There have been volumes of speculation about this apparently conclusive evidence. Since Armande was some twenty-six years younger than Madeleine it has been argued that she was her illegitimate daughter, passed off as her sister. Since Madeleine is credited with

[1] Some biographers have naturally made much of the supposed conflict between the solid bourgeois father and his wild actor son, but there is no proof whatever of this. The few surviving documents concern financial arrangements made at various dates and bearing mainly on Molière's share in the inheritance of his mother, who died when he was ten.

[2] First published by Beffara in *Dissertation sur J.-B. Poquelin de Molière* and reproduced in nearly all the serious biographies. La Grange, noting the marriage in his *Registre*, dates it 14 February, but seems to have been out by six days. There could, however, have been a celebration party, with the legal marriage in the following week.

several lovers this would be entirely possible without implicating Molière as the father. If Marie Hervé (Marie Béjart, see p. 86, footnote 2) was the mother of both women, Armande would have been born when she was about fifty, an unusual but not impossibly late age. All that seems to matter is that Armande was with the troupe from infancy, grew up and in time became an excellent actress, and Molière married her. Their relationship can have only remotely resembled that portrayed in the play. One can only guess Madeleine's feelings, and 'guess' is the word. Either she accepted the situation with bitter melancholy, realizing that her attractions had waned since the distant days of the Illustre Théâtre, and witnessed Armande's marriage as an act of heroic renunciation worthy of stage drama; or she had long lost interest in Molière as a man and did not care either way; or she was delighted to see the family influence over him prolonged by her daughter or a young sister whom she had come to regard as a daughter. These various interpretations depend on personal relationships of which nothing definite is known and which are best left to the romanced biographies. The earliest was Grimarest's *Vie de Molière* (1705), written by a man born in 1659 who could have collected much near-contemporary testimony and gossip. For that reason he cannot be ignored, though he is often unreliable.

It is known that Madeleine remained a member of the company until her death in December 1671, acting the parts of *suivante* or procuress (e.g. Frosine in *L'Avare*). Armande became one of Molière's star actresses, admired for her beauty. There was a marital rift in 1667, caused, it was alleged, by Armande's infidelities and lasting some four years until it was healed over. A biographical interpretation sees Molière as the Alceste of *Le Misanthrope* (1666) and Armande as the perversely attractive coquette Célimène (the parts were acted by these two). But one need not follow this literally. Every artist or writer takes hints from life and develops them imaginatively into something which may bear no resemblance at all to the factual circumstances.

None of these personal considerations provoked the 'Comic War' which broke out round *L'École des femmes*. The cause was Molière's rise to favour and the jealousy of his rivals. In the summer of 1662 the company had been summoned to Saint-Germain and had performed

on three days in May and thirteen in June. They had received 1500
livres for the first visit and 14,000 for the second.[1] Noting the second
figure in his *Registre*, La Grange implies that it should have been
15,000 since the company now had fifteen members – a rearrangement
consequent on Molière's marriage to Armande. He also notes that the
actors of the Hôtel de Bourgogne were present, showing 'much
jealousy' and sponsored by the queen mother, Anne of Austria. But
her influence was on the wane, since the young Louis XIV had now
decided to rule absolutely in his own person. Molière was not only
in the money, he had the right backing.

The main interest of the Comic War lies in the two short plays
which Molière wrote to defend his own work and attack his critics.[2]
In *La Critique de l'École des femmes*, produced in June 1663 and diplo-
matically dedicated to the queen mother when published in August,
Molière showed a supreme self-confidence, verging on insolence,

[1] A modern valuation of the seventeenth-century livre or franc is difficult
because of inflation and variations in living-styles. Some 'necessities' have disappeared, some 'luxuries' have become 'necessities'. In his list of expenses for the
thirteen-day visit to Saint-Germain La Grange details 6 livres for four musicians
(*violons*), 11 livres for candles, and one livre for a supper (*collation*) for the
company. An overall approximate value for the livre would be £2 or $5 today
(1975), which would give the company about £28,000 or $70,000 for the whole
visit, less expenses.

[2] The principal stages of the Comic War as they have survived in print were:
L'École des femmes, December 1662; criticism of the play by the young literary
journalist Donneau de Visé in his periodical *Les Nouvelles nouvelles*, February
1663; Molière's *Critique*, produced June 1663 but written, according to the Preface
of *L'École des femmes*, very soon after the première of that comedy, say January
1663; de Visé's *Zélinde ou la Véritable Critique de l'École des femmes et la Critique
de la Critique*, a play replying to Molière's *Critique*, as its cumbersome title
shows, published July–August 1663, perhaps not acted: a play by Edme Boursault,
another young writer, entitled *Le Portrait du peintre ou la Contre-critique de
l'École des femmes*, acted at the Hôtel de Bourgogne September or October 1663;
Molière's *L'Impromptu de Versailles*, a reply to Boursault written in a week and
acted probably on 19 October 1663; de Visé again, with *La Réponse à l'Impromptu
de Versailles ou la Vengeance des marquis*, claimed to have been written in one-
and-a-half days and acted at the Hôtel de Bourgogne, probably November 1663;
the future gazette-writer Robinet's *Panégyrique de l'École des femmes*, a prose
dialogue, hardly for acting, which discussed the play in an unfavourable sense,
published December 1663; *L'Impromptu de l'Hôtel de Condé*, acted at the Hôtel de
Bourgogne in December 1663 and the Hôtel's most open reply to Molière,
written by Montfleury *fils*, son of the famous actor whom Molière had mocked
in *L'Impromptu*. This virtually ended the Comic War, though there were later
echoes in such works as Boulanger de Chalussay's *Élomire hypocondre ou les
Médecins vengés*, a venomous personal attack on Molière in general, not published
till 1670.

towards social groups which disapproved of him. He presents a discussion of his play by a cross-section of characters. An affected *précieuse* is disgusted by the coarseness of certain expressions in *L'École des femmes*. She is told, rather disingenuously, that the 'obscenity' is in her own mind. A ridiculous marquis, snobbish and very stupid, is derided. Molière played this part, one can imagine with what gusto. From then on the *petit marquis*, portrayed as a fashionable idiot, became a type-character for him. In *L'Impromptu* he went so far as to say that 'today the marquis is the comic of comedy' and has replaced the old 'valet bouffon' in making audiences laugh. To rub the point in he is called a 'Turlupin'. Scarron of course had his 'marquis ridicule' but this was a rustic eccentric who would touch no nerves in contemporary Parisian society. People of quality are blamed for their habit of 'always judging and speaking dogmatically of things they know nothing about', whether in the theatre, painting or music. The vanity of authors and their intrigues, with their 'ligues offensives et défensives', are not spared either.

Against this Molière sets the judgement of the pit, so despised by the snobs, and of the Court. The first is guided by *le bon sens* in its applause and its laughter, without necessarily knowing anything of the critical rules. (It was this same *bon sens* or *sens commun* which had enabled Corneille to write his first comedy and move towards realism.) The Court, in spite of a certain ridiculous element (the marquis) is the true centre of good taste and sound judgements – those of normally cultivated people with experience of the world, untouched by pedantry.

Sitting confidently on his two thrones, so disparate in appearance yet in practice undoubtedly the pedestals of his whole career, Molière was no brash untutored comic puffed up by popularity. He knows the 'rules' of the dramatic theorists, seems to have read Aristotle and Horace, and comparing comedy with tragedy, suggests that it is a more difficult art. He examines his own *École des femmes* from angles worthy of some of his later explicators, though with greater brevity. Proud certainly of its material success, he can also supply a critical appreciation.

❧

L'Impromptu de Versailles was a somewhat lighter playlet, provoked by Boursault's *Le Portrait du peintre*, bearing more on the art of the actor than of the playwright. Its subject is a rehearsal – or an attempted rehearsal because it is constantly interrupted by *fâcheux* – which puts his company on the stage under their own names. Molière's social audacity now reaches to the king. Kings demand instant obedience (they are rehearsing for a command performance), whatever the difficulties. 'We must never consider our own convenience. We are only there to please them, and when they command something from us, it's up to us to take quick advantage of the mood they are in.' Thus the actor-manager resigned to organizing a royal entertainment at very short notice, but also a mild joke which he no doubt knew Louis could take and which points to an easy relationship. Any sting it might have is removed by the understanding attitude of the king when he arrives and allows them to put off their new play (never particularized) to another occasion.

Interesting light is thrown on Molière's married life and, in spite of our suspicion of biographical interpretations, this rings so true that it must reflect personal experience. Though it shows that the honeymoon period is over it is not particularly cutting. Molière, having delivered his views on royal commands, urges the company to get on with the rehearsal. 'How can we,' asks Madeleine, who speaks as his equal throughout this play, 'when we haven't learnt our parts?' 'You will learn them,' replies Molière. 'And if not, can't you improvise as you go along?' Armande breaks in: 'Shall I tell you what? You ought to write a comedy where you play all the parts yourself.'

MOLIÈRE Taisez-vous, ma femme, vous êtes une bête.
ARMANDE Grand merci, monsieur mon mari. Voilà ce que c'est: le mariage change bien les gens, et vous ne m'auriez pas dit cela il y a dix-huit mois.
MOLIÈRE Taisez-vous, je vous prie.
ARMANDE C'est une chose étrange qu'une petite cérémonie soit capable de nous ôter toutes nos belles qualités, et qu'un mari et un galant regardent la même personne avec des yeux si différents.
MOLIÈRE Que de discours!
ARMANDE [*Set going and from a quite understandable feminine point of view*] Ma foi, si je faisais une comédie, je la ferais sur ce sujet. Je justifierais les femmes de bien des choses dont on les accuse, et je ferais craindre aux maris la différence

qu'il y a de leurs manières brusques aux civilités des galants.

MOLIÈRE Ay! laissons cela. Il n'est pas question de causer maintenant. Nous avons autre chose à faire. (Sc. 1)

Before one sides wholly with Armande it should not be forgotten that Molière wrote the words.

A subtle professional distinction between the acting of comedy and of tragedy leads to the main substance of the play: the ridiculing by name of some of the Hôtel de Bourgogne actors. Foremost was Montfleury, immensely fat and declaiming all his lines overemphatically, whether the sense warranted it or not. Molière wanted naturalness, but it is clear from his own failures in tragedy that for this genre he was far in advance of his time and the contemporary public was wedded to the grandiloquent style.[1]

He dismissed the Hôtel's new author Boursault with withering contempt, affecting to be unsure of his name. Let the Hôtel mirror my plays if they like, he says, if it brings them prosperity and profit. 'They do need it, and I shall be delighted to make some contribution to their maintenance.'

Molière declared his refusal to take any further part in the controversy so long as it was limited to his professional qualities and mannerisms as author and actor. But there were other matters which he would ask them kindly not to touch. In other words, his private life was his own.

꧁꧂

In the following summer (May 1664) Molière was called to Versailles to take part in *Les Plaisirs de l'île enchantée*. These week-long festivities at the château whose enlargement had recently begun but which was still far from being the grandiose seat of government which it became in the late seventies were given in honour of the queen mother and of the reigning queen Marie-Thérèse. But indirectly they were also a compliment to Louis XIV's modest young mistress, Louise de La Vallière. The king, with half the nobles of his realm, took an active part in the pageants, ballets and displays of horsemanship, winning

---

[1] Four years later (November 1667) Montfleury suffered a stroke of which he died, after declaiming the last act of Racine's *Andromaque*.

the principal prizes to the admiring surprise of his courtiers. In this ostentatious display of costumes, caracoling, music, dancing and splendid meals, Molière's company posed and recited in various mythological roles and acted several plays. They gave *Les Fâcheux* (whose original patron, Foucquet, was now serving the third year of his life prison-sentence), *Le Mariage forcé*, a newer *comédie-ballet*, and the hurriedly written *comédie galante*, *La Princesse d'Élide*, which could provide an elegantly sentimental background for Louis's new romance.[1] Into the general framework of these entertainments they inserted a very different comedy, *Le Tartuffe*.

This satire on religious hypocrisy and its over-simple victims contains a development of certain ideas already germinating in *L'École des femmes*, where Arnolphe reminds Agnès of the 'boiling cauldrons of hell' which await unfaithful wives,[2] and goes on to tell her to study carefully *Les Maximes du mariage ou les devoirs de la femme mariée* which he produces from his pocket. Generally reminiscent of the Ten Commandments though more numerous (Agnès is interrupted when beginning to read out the eleventh), and of the Catechism, the *Maximes* appear to be a deliberate parody of St Gregory of Nazianzen's *Préceptes de mariage envoyés à Olympias*, translated by the prolific Desmarets de Saint-Sorlin. Thus in 1662 Molière was already turning his attention to perverted religion, in addition to the other perversions or exaggerations he had mocked so far. The fact that he was working on *Tartuffe* was known before its first production and a powerful section of religious opinion had begun to show its concern. The king enjoyed the performance but immediately after, supposedly at the instance of the queen mother and her pious advisers, banned further public productions of the play without condemning Molière. He may well have approved of the comedy but on this issue was not prepared to defy the *dévots* and possibly the Church itself.

The line between sincere religion and religiosity is extremely difficult – some would say impossible – to draw. The second may also be sincere on its particular level, but when it is combined with materialistic calculations it can justifiably be called hypocrisy, the name Molière gave it. Even this, however, cannot establish a clear distinction

---

[1] See above, p. 89, footnote 1.
[2]   ... il est aux enfers des chaudières bouillantes
      Où l'on plonge à jamais les femmes mal vivantes.
      Ce que je vous dis là ne sont pas des chansons ...
                                                        (III. ii)

(and it may be questioned whether Molière really meant it to), and, while some highly placed prelates accepted it, others, for the most part less eminent and more stupid, felt that the whole of religion as they conceived it was under attack. A fanatical parish priest petitioned the king with a demand that Molière be burnt at the stake (this was still done at that date) as a foretaste of the hell-fire which awaited his soul. Some great and influential figures showed their approval. The papal nuncio Cardinal Chigi allowed Molière to read the play to him in August 1664. The king's brother Monsieur commanded a private performance in September and the Prince de Condé in November of the same year and again a year later, but the ban on public performances was not lifted.

It seems certain that the play acted in *Les Plaisirs de l'île enchantée* was not the same as the five-act version which alone has come down to us. La Grange wrote in his *Registre* that at Versailles the troupe performed 'trois actes de *Tartuffe* qui étaient les trois premiers'. At some time between then and 1669, and no doubt considerably earlier, the play was rewritten in five acts, the fifth ending with the direct intervention of Louis XIV to rescue the family of the dupe Orgon from the clutches of the religious imposter. In the earliest version the king's intervention could hardly have figured and the play may have ended with the triumph of Tartuffe.

This brief outline of matters which have provoked volumes of controversy, still partly inconclusive, is almost enough for our present purposes. But one relevant question remains unanswered. Was the first acted *Tartuffe* a complete comedy or only part of an unfinished play or performance? La Grange's entry quoted above clearly suggests the second alternative, and a second entry does the same. For the command visit to Monsieur in late September 1664 he notes that the troupe acted various plays, 'et les trois premiers actes de *Tartuffe*'. Those who hold that the original play was complete in script and in performance (whether in three acts or five) have observed that La Grange wrote up his *Registre* long after the events he recorded, by which time his memory of detail was confused.[1] Yet in this instance his wording is quite unambiguous. Why should he bother in two separate entries to say 'the first three acts' if that unusual feature had not stuck in his mind? The normal alternatives would have been to give no description or to write 'comédie en trois actes'.

[1] See above, p. 87, footnote 1.

Supposing that his plain statement was correct, what was the explanation? That Molière had not had time to finish writing; that his original ending was too daring to be risked before such audiences; that, at Versailles, a section of his audience protested; or simply that the play was cut short to give way to supper or some other diversion? It must be said that none of the last three hypotheses is based on any surviving hint, but none is altogether implausible. Meanwhile the whole question is still debated or, at the least, debatable.

In August 1665 the king replaced the Duke of Orléans as the patron of Molière's company, allocating them a subsidy of 6000 livres a year. In spite of this clear sign of general approval, *Tartuffe* was still not authorized. After three years of vain petitioning, Molière produced it in his own theatre on 5 August 1667. This version, sometimes known as *Panulphe*, does not seem to have differed basically from the text finally printed and was definitely in five acts. It has been reconstructed from various hints and from a description in the anonymous *Lettre sur la comédie de l'Imposteur*, published two weeks after the performance.[1] Immediately after this single performance a ban was clapped on the play by Guillaume de Lamoignon, President of the Parlement de Paris – the equivalent of a Lord Chief Justice – who had authority to do so in the absence of the king on a military campaign. On 11 August the Archbishop of Paris forbade the faithful to act, read, or hear the play on pain of excommunication. Molière took nothing lying down. Two days after Lamoignon's ban La Grange and another actor were despatched post-haste to complain to Louis, who was engaged in the siege of Lille. They were received sympathetically amid the cannon-balls and brought back a half-satisfactory answer. On his return to Paris the king would have the play examined and they would act it. The journey cost the company 1000 livres in cash and, since they gave no performances during their comrades' absence, a loss of all receipts over some eight weeks, admittedly in a slack season.

For *Tartuffe* there was another wait of nearly eighteen months until it was at last produced with royal authorization on 5 February 1669, with Molière playing Orgon and Du Croisy Tartuffe. It was a triumph for Molière in every way and a huge financial success. The first-day receipts of 2860 livres are the highest recorded in the whole of La Grange's *Registre*. In the eight and a half weeks of its main first run,

---

[1] The *Lettre* seems to have been written by a well-informed supporter of Molière, perhaps de Visé, quite possibly with his collaboration.

playing three days a week and with five private performances, it grossed the exceptional sum of over 40,000 livres. Most of the public must have agreed with Molière or, if not, were ready to pay to be scandalized.

The long delay had not inhibited other productions. In February 1665 he produced *Dom Juan*, an extraordinary play if taken out of its theatrical context and as much out of line with his previous work as Corneille's *Illusion comique*, though with much more serious inferences. Molière took the story over from other French playwrights and was no doubt influenced also by the players of the *commedia dell'arte* who acted their version of it a little before his. What he made of this strange mixture of romance, scepticism, primitive theology and farce is left to the next chapter but, apart from other passages, his treatment of hypocrisy, more open even than in *Tartuffe*, was flagrantly offensive to the devout. His hero cynically feigns piety in order to elude his plain moral obligations. After a successful opening month Molière dropped the play, no doubt under pressure and not wanting to have a second conflict on his hands. His *Dom Juan* was never acted again in his lifetime, nor was it printed. It might be said to contain more dynamite than *Tartuffe*. After its author's death it was replaced by a milder version in verse composed by Thomas Corneille and acted frequently.

In the *Dom Juan* period Molière was already working on *Le Misanthrope*, produced in June 1666. This brilliant social comedy, the height of his achievement and indeed of the whole comic drama of the century, reflected without much caricature the Parisian manners of the time and showed how thoroughly Molière had come to understand his contemporary world. But the character of the Misanthrope and also, it might be added, of the 'coquette' Célimène, can take this play close to tragedy as later understood. Here again a fuller consideration of it is left to the next chapter.

Around and after *Le Misanthrope* Molière was composing more lightweight plays for the Court, typically with openings for ballet and Lully's music. This book is not about Louis XIV, but his taste in theatre seems to have bridged a strange combination of belly-laughs and quite delicate ballet. Eclectic is perhaps the kindest word. Molière could always oblige and went on doing so almost till the end. But he seems to have criticized rather than obliged in *Amphitryon* (January 1668), a play performed at Court but not ordered for it. This story of Jupiter who came down to sleep with a mortal woman while tricking her well-loved husband had no reference, Moliéristes have assured us, to Louis XIV's relationship with his new mistress Madame de Montespan and her discarded spouse, and it would indeed have been an egregious blunder to suggest an open parallel. Yet it was a strange choice of subject if no contemporary application whatever was in Molière's mind.[1] It was his first adaptation of Plautus, through Rotrou's *Les Sosies*, and Molière drew again on Plautus for his next notable play, *L'Avare*, produced in the same year (September 1668). This caricature of bourgeois manners failed when first produced on the Parisian stage,[2] though it has amply compensated for it since.

After the authorization of Tartuffe, Molière wrote an entirely joyous three-acter, *Monsieur de Pourceaugnac*, mocking a rustic notable in Scarron's manner (as did the later very short *Comtesse d'Escarbagnas* of 1671). But this play is eclipsed by the best of his *comédies-ballets* to that date, *Le Bourgeois Gentilhomme*. In one sense this portrait of a Parisian merchant obsessed by self-improvement is an ingenious variation of Scarron's *Marquis ridicule* theme. Monsieur Jourdain is not a country bumpkin, but compared to the more cultivated characters he shows a loutish side and in their milieu is a provincial, socially if not geographically. His difficulties with wording and elegant speech in the scene with the *Maître de philosophie* (II. iv), the mock Turkish of Acts IV and V, and the final *ballet des nations* introducing Gascon, Swiss, Spanish and Italian, show an awareness of the comic possibilities of language again reminiscent of Scarron.

❦

This might have been enough. Established more strongly than ever at Court with slight pinpricks from Lully who was securing a monopoly not only of opera but of all musical entertainment, secure in the commercial theatre of Paris, Molière had risen in some twelve years to heights unequalled by any other theatrical personality of the century. He was supreme as an impresario and an actor in his particular line. As a playwright he had proved his very varied capabilities and some time before, in what might be considered his greatest period (1664–6), had

[1] *Amphitryon* was in part a machine-play. Mentioning other machine-plays of about the same date, including one with a similar subject, Lancaster attributes Molière's choice to competitive causes (*History*, III, pp. 512–13).

[2] Nine performances from 9 September to 7 October 1668, grossing 4325 livres, then five unremunerative performances in 1669.

written the three plays which transcend comedy. But had he stopped in 1671 we should have been without two comedies which rank among his best.

Les Femmes savantes, produced in his Paris theatre in March 1672, picked up the idea of *Les Précieuses ridicules* and expanded it into a full-length satire on the rather different salons of the seventies. The women, early bluestockings, have heard of Descartes and Epicurus and have 'philosophical' interests foreshadowing the salons of the next century. Linguistic and literary questions nevertheless predominate and the affectations of contemporary literature and its authors are caricatured in much greater detail than in *Les Précieuses*. The play is not a return to an old theme by an author growing short of ideas, but a new invention which has grown vigorously out of it.

The same can be said of *Le Malade imaginaire*. Molière had written at least three short farces on doctors, utilizing the physician-pedant of the *commedia dell'arte*. He now returned to the charge with the farcical medical men of *Le Malade*, but transformed the whole theme by making their deluded patient his central character. The theme in fact is less the peculiarities of inadequate doctors than illness as an obsession, as religion can be shown to be in *Tartuffe*.

The play ended with a burlesque ceremony in dog-Latin in which the patient himself is inducted into the medical faculty, and with the death of Molière, acting the principal part, a few hours after the fourth performance (17 February 1673). Almost immediately his empire began to break up. Some of his actors joined the Hôtel de Bourgogne. A royal order dispossessed the others of their theatre in favour of Lully and merged them with the Théâtre du Marais. The combined company maintained itself for seven years in a building in the Faubourg Saint-Germain known as the Théâtre Guénégaud.[1] In 1680 the actors of the Hôtel de Bourgogne were ordered to leave their own theatre and join them there and all this talent constituted the new Comédie Française. It was a brilliant combination certainly, but as the only authorized theatre in Paris it lacked the stimulus of competition and suffered the handicaps inseparable from official supervision and patronage.

---

[1] The Italian comedians were squeezed into it also until, in 1680, they were given the Hôtel de Bourgogne. For later developments, see below, pp. 168-9.

MOLIÈRE'S COMEDY

*Problem of classifications – burlesque
and literary parody:* Les Femmes savantes –
verbal luxuriance in Monsieur de Pourceaugnac *and
elsewhere – Molière's defence of comedy – reform through
mockery – distinction between comic and tragic 'hero' – realism
and fantasy – muted satire –* Le Bourgeois Gentilhomme –
George Dandin, *a bitter farce? – satire in three great plays –*
Tartuffe, *outline – hypocrisy a side-issue – religion itself
attacked – the Compagnie du Saint-Sacrement –* Dom Juan *and its
antecedents – attack on religion pressed home – scene of the
'poor man' –* Dom Juan *as the classic seducer –* Le Misanthrope –
*problems posed by character of Alceste – precedents in Molière's
work – hardly a 'personnage ridicule' – Alceste and Célimène –
the dénouement – the question of inconsistency –
Molière as satirist – theory of the classical
norm: a partial explanation*

In the course of his career described in the previous chapter Molière not only dominated French comic drama, he established it. That is not to say that there was nothing before him or that he did not owe a great deal to his predecessors and contemporaries, particularly Scarron and the Italians, but he gave standing and direction to a genre which would otherwise have remained secondary to tragedy and tragicomedy. Only a man of the theatre who at the same time was a brilliant dramatist could have done so at that point in history.

Materially this is so evident that it hardly needs pointing out, but it is much more difficult to define the kind of comedy that Molière established, or even wrote. A classification of his plays can be only partially helpful. There are farces such as *L'Amour médecin, Sganarelle ou le Cocu imaginaire, Le Médecin malgré lui, Monsieur de Pourceaugnac* and *Les Fourberies de Scapin;* these can be clearly distinguished from a great comedy primarily of character such as *Le Misanthrope*; there is a different sort of comedy of character, such as *L'Avare*, *Le Bourgeois Gentilhomme* or *Le Malade imaginaire*, in which the protagonist is more exaggeratedly a type; *Les Précieuses ridicules* and *Les Femmes savantes* can be called comedies of manners, but the comedies of character might be put in this class also, depending on the significance attached to a social background which is clearly drawn in. Lastly there are 'entertainments' featuring music and ballet, though it is only possible to cite one short sketch, *Le Sicilien ou l'Amour peintre*, and the 'tragédie-ballet' *Psyche*, written in collaboration, as wholly pure examples. Elsewhere the dancing and singing in the so-called *comédies-ballets* are incidental in varying degrees.[1]

It will be seen that any rigorous scheme of classification under these headings collapses almost before it has been framed. Strictly applied, it covers only a few extreme cases and virtually none of the more important plays. Certainly there are several different kinds of comedy in Molière but few are typified by any single play. They occur in mixed form almost throughout and the most that critics, producers and actors have done since has been to decide which element to stress in their interpretations. This is understandable and indeed essential if Molière's comedy is to remain alive. In producing and acting his own plays Molière knew what effects he wanted to obtain, but he could not guess the reactions of future readers and theatre audiences, any more than could Shakespeare. Though one may protest at what seem to be wanton distortions in either critical interpretation or staging, new views of his work should never be ruled out as a matter of general principle.

Rather than attempt a definitive classification of the plays here, it would be more pertinent to consider certain features of several of them – which in some cases will enable us to decide which predominates.

❦

Though Molière wrote no fully burlesque comedy, burlesque elements, fringing literary parody, occur expectedly enough in *Les Précieuses ridicules* and *Les Femmes savantes*. In the first, as already pointed out,

---

[1] The following are described as *comédies-ballets* or nearly so in the early editions: *La Princesse d'Élide* ('comédie mêlée de danse et de musique'), *Monsieur de Pourceaugnac*, *Le Bourgeois Gentilhomme*, *Le Malade imaginaire* ('comédie mêlée de musique et de danses'). *Les Fâcheux* could be described similarly.

novel-reading is at the root of the girls' over-romantic view of love.[1] The phraseology derived from it and further refined in the fashionable salons is made to appear ridiculous by the still further distortions, mainly of Molière's invention, which it acquires in the mouths of Magdelon and Cathos. *Les Femmes savantes* is a more substantial contribution to literary parody. The novels themselves are now going out of date as subjects of satire, but their romantic love ethic still persists in the mind of Bélise, the heroine's elderly aunt. Continuing the line of Hespérie in Desmarets's *Les Visionnaires*, she imagines that all men fall in love with her. When told by her sceptical brother that various men she names ignore or even abuse her, she claims that this is either through a delicate regard for her modesty or else due to frustrated passion. Reminded that two of them have married, she replies that it is from despair of winning her:

> BÉLISE C'est par un désespoir où j'ai réduit leurs feux.
> ARISTE Ma foi, ma chère sœur, *vision* toute claire. [our italics]
> CHRYSALE [her other brother] De ces chimères-là vous devez vous défaire.
> BÉLISE Ah, chimères! Ce sont chimères, dit-on!
> Chimères, moi? Vraiment, chimères est fort bon!
> Je me réjouis fort de chimères, mes frères,
> Et je ne savais pas que j'eusse des chimères. [*Exit*]
> CHRYSALE Notre sœur est folle, oui.

(II. iii–iv)

Bélise is the craziest of the three Learned Ladies, an almost farcical figure of fun. By a comic misunderstanding, which is entirely hers, she imagines that the young lover's approach to her niece is intended for herself. But in their obsession with 'educated' language, philosophy and science, her sister-in-law Philaminte and her other niece Armande are hardly less absurd. In the big scene in which the poet Trissotin reads his verses to them (III. ii), they are in ecstasies of admiration almost before he has begun and constantly interrupt him to register their delight. He reads his sonnet on a princess's illness, 'metaphorized' as the admission of a hostile guest into her 'rich apartment' or body:

> TRISSOTIN *Votre prudence est endormie*
> *De traiter magnifiquement*

1 See above, pp. 87–8.

Et de loger superbement
Votre plus cruelle ennemie.

ARMANDE *Prudence endormie!*

BÉLISE *Loger son ennemie!*

PHILAMINTE *Superbement, et magnifiquement!*

TRISSOTIN *Faites-la sortir, quoi qu'on die,*
De votre riche appartement,
Où cette ingrate insolemment
Attaque votre belle vie.

BÉLISE Ah! tout doux, laissez-moi, de grâce, respirer.

ARMANDE Donnez-nous, s'il vous plaît, le loisir d'admirer.

PHILAMINTE On se sent, à ces vers, jusques au fond de l'âme
Couler je ne sais quoi qui fait que l'on se pâme.

ARMANDE *Faites-la sortir, quoi qu'on die,*
De votre riche appartement.
Que *riche appartement* est là joliment dit!
Et que la métaphore est mise avec esprit!

For a few moments they admire and explicate the unfinished sonnet.
Then:

ARMANDE Ah! s'il vous plaît, encore une fois, *quoi qu'on die.*

TRISSOTIN *Faites-la sortir, quoi qu'on die,*

PHILAMINTE, ARMANDE, BÉLISE [*together*] *Quoi qu'on die!*

TRISSOTIN *De votre riche appartement,*

PHILAMINTE, ARMANDE, BÉLISE *Riche appartement!*

TRISSOTIN *Où cette ingrate insolemment*

PHILAMINTE, ARMANDE, BÉLISE Cette *ingrate* de fièvre!

TRISSOTIN *Attaque votre belle vie.*

PHILAMINTE *Votre belle vie!*

ARMANDE, BÉLISE Ah!

TRISSOTIN *Quoi! sans respecter votre rang,*
Elle se prend à votre sang,

PHILAMINTE, ARMANDE, BÉLISE Ah!

TRISSOTIN *Et nuit et jour vous fait outrage!*
Si vous la conduisez aux bains,
Sans la marchander davantage
Noyez-la de vos propres mains.

PHILAMINTE On n'en peut plus.

BÉLISE On pâme.

ARMANDE   On se meurt de plaisir.
PHILAMINTE De mille doux frissons vous vous sentez saisir.[1]
  ARMANDE *Si vous la conduisez aux bains,*
    BÉLISE *Sans la marchander davantage,*
PHILAMINTE *Noyez-la de vos propres mains.*
           De vos propres mains, là, noyez-la dans les bains . . .

One's first reaction to this is that Molière has really overdone the
idiocy of his characters and of the verses they are raving over. Funny
perhaps but extravagant beyond reality. But one then finds that this
sonnet and the even sillier epigram which Trissotin goes on to read
were not invented by the dramatist but already existed in the works of
the minor poet Cotin.[2] To create an effect of burlesque parody, all
that Molière had to do was to know them and quote them. So it may be
that his swooning females were not completely out of this world
either. Yet he carries his irony to the limit of the plausible when, in the
remainder of the scene, he causes these particular women to insist on
the equality of the sexes in taste, intelligence and learning. They are
planning the formation of an *académie,* originally mooted in Plato's
Republic but not adequately worked out there, which will discuss
'physics, grammar, history, poetry, morals and politics'. Their rules of
language reform are almost complete already and they will soon be
recognized as the sovereign judges of literature.

So far as it mocks literary models and artificially 'correct' speech
(the servant Martine is sacked for her excruciatingly uneducated
language) this part of *Les Femmes savantes* can be assimilated to
burlesque, though sharper and on the whole subtler than in Scarron.
But important elements in the play are not burlesque. There is a real
danger that Henriette, the 'natural' and domestically inclined sister of
Armande, who seeks fulfilment in life through 'un mari, des enfants,
un ménage', will be forced to marry the unspeakable Trissotin. The
plot interest of this is considerable. Her father Chrysale is a *bon
bourgeois* like Gorgibus of *Les Précieuses* with the same no-nonsense
outlook, but he introduces a new comic factor. In spite of his brave
resolutions to wear the trousers he can never stand up to his wife and

---

[1] The traditional 'shiver up the spine', sometimes said to be the effect of true
poetry. It is a physical fact and shows an emotive response to the work of art, of
which the irreverent Molière was aware. For similar reactions (swooning and
giddiness) treated burlesquely by Scarron and Saint-Amant, see above, p. 65.
[2] *Œuvres galantes en prose et en vers* (1663).

each time deflates or prevaricates before her. He grumbles at length about the disorder his comfortable household is in because of the women's addiction to books and learning and puts the antifeminist point of view with great plainness:

> Il n'est pas bien honnête, et pour beaucoup de causes,
> Qu'une femme étudie et sache tant de choses.
> Former aux bonnes mœurs l'esprit de ses enfants,
> Faire aller son ménage, avoir l'œil sur ses gens,
> Et régler la dépense avec économie
> Doit être son étude et sa philosophie.

(II. vii)

This is more than his daughter Henriette claimed and is not the voice of *le bon sens*, which is represented by his brother Ariste. His blunt male backlash is as extreme in its way as the pedantic refinement of his wife and is intended to point up the contrast. In short Chrysale is presented as a comic character in words and acts and in his own line, which can hardly be related to anything in the burlesque conception. If one were obliged, in quiz-fashion, to name a single 'target' for *Les Femmes savantes*, one might reply succinctly that it was phoney culture. But, as has just been seen, this would not satisfactorily characterize the play as a whole, since it is also a comedy of manners merging into character.

A second feature of seventeenth-century burlesque was verbal exuberance. Unlike Scarron, Molière was not given to inventing new words, but he exploits to the full the possibilities of loquacity and jargon wherever they are appropriate. The most striking example is in his doctors, derived from the pedant-physicians of the *commedia dell'arte* and developed to almost frightening proportions in those days when medical ignorance was a public menace to health. They run from the crude mock-doctor of *Le Médecin volant* (if by Molière) through *L'Amour médecin*, *Le Médecin malgré lui* and *Monsieur de Pourceaugnac* to *Le Malade imaginaire*. In nearly every case their discourse is parodied (and perhaps it scarcely is a parody, any more than was Trissotin's sonnet in *Les Femmes savantes*) with unfailing verve. Witness a short extract from the doctors' consultation in *Monsieur de Pourceaugnac*:

PREMIER MÉDECIN [who has already spoken at some length]
. . . Tout ceci supposé, puisqu'une maladie bien

connue est à demi guérie, car *ignoti nulla est curatio morbi*, il ne vous sera pas difficile de convenir des remèdes que nous devons faire à Monsieur. Premièrement, pour remédier à cette pléthore obturante et à cette cacochymie luxuriante par tout le corps, je suis d'avis qu'il soit phlébotomisé libéralement, c'est-à-dire que les saignées soient fréquentes et plantureuses: en premier lieu de la basilique, puis de la céphalique; et même, si le mal est opiniâtre, de lui ouvrir la veine du front, et que l'ouverture soit large, afin que le gros sang puisse sortir; et en même temps de le purger, désopiler et évacuer par purgatifs propres et convenables, c'est-à-dire par cholagogues, mélanogogues, *et caetera*; et comme la véritable source de tout le mal est ou une humeur crasse et féculente, ou une vapeur noire et grossière qui obscurcit, infecte et salit les esprits animaux, il est à propos ensuite qu'il prenne un bain d'eau pure et nette, avec force petit-lait clair, pour purifier par l'eau la féculence de l'humeur crasse et éclaircir par le lait la noirceur de cette vapeur . . .

(I. viii)

Suffering from no 'dearth of loquacity' the First Doctor continues for a further ten lines and the Second Doctor approves his opinion with comparable verbosity.

Monsieur de Pourceaugnac is the most Scarronesque of Molière's plays, though Molière made many additions of his own. The central idea of a grotesque provincial who comes to the capital to conclude an arranged marriage with a girl who is in love with someone else recalls *Le Marquis ridicule*. Molière's Pourceaugnac is even more gullible and absurd than Scarron's Don Blaize Pol.[1] He is pursued by apothecaries armed with syringes intent on giving him an anal douche; he is persuaded to dress as a woman in order to escape the police and in this guise is accosted as a street-walker by two Swiss tourists; he is confronted by two women both claiming to be his wives and bringing on

---

[1] See pp. 62–4 above.

stage his three supposed children who cluster round him crying, 'Ah, mon papa, mon papa, mon papa!' a joke-situation found in the *commedia dell'arte*. The wives pretend to be from Picardy and Gascony and speak the stage version of the patois or dialects of those regions. Other characters speak with heavy Flemish and Swiss accents and two musicians, dressed as 'médecins grotesques', sing in Italian.[1]

While *Monsieur de Pourceaugnac* is the richest single source of 'verbal fantasy', similar features can be found in several of his other works, notably in the conversation of the peasants in *Dom Juan* (II. i), in the 'Turkish' of *Le Bourgeois Gentilhomme*, and in the Latin induction, called a 'cérémonie burlesque', which ends *Le Malade imaginaire*.

But Molière rarely relies on language in itself to make his audiences laugh. It is supplementary to the characterization, the situation or the theme and, though none of these could be rendered so effectively without it, they already exist in fully recognizable form. Before tracing these basic elements through a further selection of the plays, it is important to consider Molière's own conception of comedy – in short, what he aimed, or said that he aimed, at doing.

Molière's pronouncements on his art that occur outside the plays are few and simple. Unlike Corneille, he wrote no critical examinations and, unlike Racine, no substantial body of prefaces in which a theory is stated or from which it can be deduced. A partial exception and almost the only open statement is in the Preface of *Tartuffe* (published 1669) in which he claims that the use of comedy is to correct men's faults; it has a moral utility. This was the conventional justification of the theatre (not only of comedy) in that age and was the usual defence against the attacks of moralists, particularly religious moralists, who condemned it as harmful. In this case Molière is especially concerned to defend his play on moral grounds and he is repeating at greater length the argument of the *Premier Placet* of August 1664 (his first petition to the king to authorize *Tartuffe*) in which also he singled out hypocrisy as one of the most prevalent and dangerous of 'les vices de mon

---

[1] For a detailed examination of this see R. Garapon, *La Fantaisie verbale et le comique dans le théâtre français* (Paris, 1957), Ch. v, and article by Fausta Garavini in *Revue d'histoire littéraire* (Sept.–Dec. 1972).

siècle'. His reasoning, if not loaded, is at least polemical and it would be hazardous to conclude from this that in writing comedies he saw himself seriously as a reformer. That would suppose an entirely different writer and order of literature. But meanwhile it gave him a respectably relevant argument which he could develop in his own favour as a comic dramatist:

> Les plus beaux traits d'une sérieuse morale sont moins puissants, le plus souvent, que ceux de la satire; et rien ne reprend mieux la plupart des hommes que la peinture de leurs défauts. C'est une grande atteinte aux vices que de les exposer à la risée de tout le monde. On souffre aisément des répréhensions, mais on ne souffre point la raillerie. On veut bien être méchant, mais on ne veut point être ridicule.

Serious rebukes are more bearable than mockery; one does not mind being thought wicked, but one does mind being laughed at. This familiar contention does not always hold good and it can only apply in a relatively tolerant and civilized society in which recourse may be had to a sense of humour. An authoritarian regime can stifle laughter. It speaks well for the Grand Siècle that Molière could voice it with apparent conviction and use it centrally in a *plaidoirie* to which he undoubtedly attached great importance.

The *Tartuffe* preface thus yields a theory, however questionable, on the intention behind comedy (moral improvement and social reform) and the general means by which it is realized (laughter). This is the comic version of Aristotle's tragic catharsis, usually interpreted in the seventeenth century as the purging of any vice by pity and fear. The particular means by which laughter is provoked are discussed in *La Critique de l'École des femmes* which, it will be recalled, was a debate on Molière's controversial play by characters representing various points of view. The reasonable Uranie adopts the theory of the moral purpose and the salutary effect of mockery and insists that the latter, which she freely calls satire, should be kept on a general plane. While this was Molière's special pleading against the suspicion that he was satirizing living personalities – a not unusual suspicion in a century addicted to searching works of literature for 'keys' and one from which he himself cannot be fully cleared[1] – it was also his affirmation

---

[1] The Trissotin of *Les Femmes savantes* is plainly modelled on the poet Cotin (who had attacked Molière) though at the same time he is a type. In

of the necessity of depicting manners and types rather than individuals.

Comedy, Uranie adds, in reply to the poet Lysidas who has just
called it a trivial genre ('bagatelles') in contrast to 'serious plays', is
probably as difficult to write as tragedy. More difficult, continues
Dorante, who voices the balanced judgements of the courtier, and no
doubt Molière's own, because in tragedy you can soar above reality
on the wings of your imagination: 'Lorsque vous peignez des héros,
vous faites ce que vous voulez; ce sont des portraits à plaisir, où l'on
ne cherche point de ressemblance, et vous n'avez qu'à suivre les traits
d'une imagination qui se donne l'essor, et qui souvent laisse le vrai
pour attraper le merveilleux.' But in comedy your characters must be
recognizable as contemporaries: 'Lorsque vous peignez les hommes il
faut peindre d'après nature; on veut que ces portraits ressemblent, et
vous n'avez rien fait si vous n'y faites reconnaître les gens de votre
siècle.'

Molière's insistence on realism or credibility would exclude the
highly fantastic character such as Scarron's Don Japhet, although,
looking at his practice rather than his theory, he does not always avoid
it. It is a question of how far to go. A caricature which does not retain
some features of the original will be ineffective and therefore should
not be wholly ridiculous. In a passage whose significance will be
returned to later, Lysidas remarks that it is inconsistent that Arnolphe,
the 'personnage ridicule' of the play, should behave as an *honnête
homme* in giving money to the young hero. Dorante's reply is: 'Il n'est
pas incompatible qu'une personne soit ridicule en de certaines choses
et honnête homme en d'autres.' Over-exaggeration would destroy
credibility, but on the other hand complete naturalism would not be
funny at all. That would be disastrous in a theory of comedy based on
the necessity of making people laugh and associating laughter entirely
with characterization.[1] A comic dramatist must tread, or rather find,

L'Impromptu de Versailles the actor Montfleury and other members of his
company are brought on the stage with no attempt at disguise.
[1] Characterization was naturally the first concern of a dramatist engaged in
casting and acting his own plays. Situation comes next. His composition of
scenes for comic effect is a matter of situation-cum-character. The overall construction of the play, its 'structure', provides a framework for the scenes and the
activities of the characters. It must be appropriate and reasonably plausible, but
once it is that its practical function has ended. The critic may examine it closely
for whatever it may reveal, and in some cases be justified in doing so, but his

the difficult way between an acceptable distortion and psychological truth and this ultimately explains nearly all the so-called inconsistencies which have been found in Molière's work and which would be better regarded as differences of emphasis.

La Critique insists that laughter is vital (though it is always possible that Molière changed his view later) and contains the famous dictum from the mouth of Dorante: 'Il faut plaisanter, et c'est une étrange enterprise que celle de faire rire les honnêtes gens.'

Strange indeed, since who are *les honnêtes gens* and what makes them laugh? Three reactions to *L'École des femmes*, the primary subject of discussion, are expressed. The over-refined Climène finds it too coarse to be amusing. For the stupid marquis with his earthy sense of humour it is not coarse enough. For Lysidas, the jealous man-of-letters, its jokes fall flat and, doubling as a literary critic versed in the 'rules', he goes on to pick it to pieces on grounds of structure.

Once again, the reply through Dorante is that it has amused *les honnêtes gens*, who are identified with the Court, and what more could or need a practising dramatist say than point to his success with his chosen public? To carry the scrutiny further he would have had to analyse the sense of humour of the seventeenth-century Court – an improbable and perhaps impossible undertaking for a contemporary.

※※※

The comedies that show up the faults of contemporaries are 'satires', Uranie remarks in *La Critique*, and obviously they must be if their 'portraits' are intended to condemn the kind of characters and behaviour they represent. If one does not think of Molière primarily as a satirist it is because the bulk of his work lacks the bitter sharpness of the next century as it appeared in Voltaire and Swift. With them the basis was disgust, they were nauseated by certain aspects of human society. Molière appears more tolerant and his declared aim of depict-

---

approach, like his findings, is alien to the dramatist's preoccupations. Dorante in *La Critique* argues that *L'École des femmes* is constructed according to 'the rules', but he obviously considers that to be secondary and makes the comment, later repeated by Racine, that 'the principal rule is to please'. It is interesting to find that Corneille, an experienced dramatist but not an actor or producer, is much more inclined to discuss theories of construction in his *Discours* and *Examens*.

ing men's faults 'agreeably' promotes the enjoyment factor at the apparent expense of the satirical. One can simply 'enjoy' a Molière play, as most audiences over the past three hundred years have done, without having to ask oneself awkward questions or be disturbed by a sceptical view of the human condition. As enjoyable entertainments on a big scale one would cite four plays all written in the last five years of Molière's life: *L'Avare*, with some reservations, *Les Femmes savantes*, already discussed, *Le Malade imaginaire*, in spite of its subject, and *Le Bourgeois Gentilhomme*.

The last is the most consistently joyous of all his major plays and is typical of that side of his genius on which his main popularity rests. Monsieur Jourdain, his rich merchant with social and cultural ambitions, is highly laughable without being completely grotesque. His foolishness never appears quite incredible and, though it nears that point towards the end of the play, the audience has become progressively attuned and can accept even his initiation as a Mamamouchi as not too fantastic for such a man. He is surrounded by well-tried characters rendered as effectively as ever in this comedy. Madame Jourdain can be traced back to the scolding wife of farce, but here she is a straight-thinking, straight-speaking merchant's spouse who is only lightly caricatured. Her indignation at her husband's follies is amusing but perfectly normal. By her sensible attitude she removes the necessity of providing a *raisonneur* (the 'reasonable' and reasoning character whose principal function is to point out or point up the excesses of the protagonist). This helps to lighten the play, since the *raisonneur* in such plays as *L'École des femmes*, *Tartuffe* and *Le Misanthrope* suggests a moral philosophy which need not be looked for here. The cheeky servant, Nicole, is given full rein and the valet Covielle with whom she pairs is at the top of his form as a deviser of ingenious intrigue. Not in himself a comic character, he has no selfish interests and nothing vicious about him but merely a sense of fun. The lovers are sympathetic and the obstacle to their happiness (Monsieur Jourdain's determination to marry his daughter only to a nobleman) cannot be taken very seriously. Her father's delusion that he is marrying Lucile to the son of the Grand Turk, who in fact is her lover Cléonte in disguise, is never cleared up, so that there is no disillusionment and the play ends gaily on this note. All possible afterthoughts are swept aside by the immediate performance of a ballet. The light treatment of the love theme is established earlier by the humorous misunderstanding between the young lovers and their followers Nicole and Covielle (III. viii–x) which is resolved on the spot, so leaving no persistent complication.

The ridiculous marquis is absent. The aristocracy is represented by Dorimène, a well-bred and sympathetic marquise, and her suitor Dorante. This could have introduced a sinister element, since Dorante is exploiting Monsieur Jourdain's wealth to provide his mistress with entertainment and presents. Monsieur Jourdain believes that he himself is the suitor but any unpleasant taste in this situation is removed by his apparent forgetfulness of his incipient love affair in the excitement of becoming a Mamamouchi, while Dorante ceases to exploit him as soon as the Marquise offers him her hand. The pedant-teacher blossoms in an ingenious updating into the four masters of music, dancing, fencing and philosophy whom Monsieur Jourdain has hired for his social improvement. They discuss and practise their various arts in near-realistic terms and the only plain reminiscence of the old farce is in the scenes in which they quarrel over the respective merits of their professions and end by exchanging blows (II. iii and iv).

In none of this is there any real sting and with the music and ballets (well integrated except for the final one) *Le Bourgeois Gentilhomme* can be taken at its face value as a highly witty romp in five acts.[1] The social significance which could be extracted from it is marginal. It would entail interpreting the play as a sneer at the *nouveau riche* who presumes to climb into the aristocracy. It mirrors the class-conflict, later commentators and particularly post-Marx commentators might argue, but there is little evidence that Molière's contemporaries took it in this way. It is true that it delighted the king and Court, being performed several times before a royal audience in October–November 1670. A good reason for this was that it incorporated the ballets of the new favourite, Lully,[2] and that the king enjoyed the burlesquing of a real Turkish diplomatic mission which had visited him in August. As for the main theme, no doubt the Court was always ready to laugh at the sillier pretensions of the bourgeoisie, but to interpret the play as a

---

[1] Three in the original performance, but there was no essential difference.

[2] Lully played the part of the Muphti or Head Turk, Molière that of Monsieur Jourdain. Madame Jourdain was played by a male actor, Hubert. Molière had already introduced some mock-Turkish into Sc. viii of *Le Sicilien* (1667).

serious rebuke to the social climber is hardly reasonable. On the other side, the play was a great success when produced in Molière's Paris theatre on 23 November 1670. It alternated for over three months with Corneille's *Tite et Bérénice* and continued afterwards to attract substantial audiences drawn largely from the middle class – Parisian merchants and their wives. There is no sign that these were offended by it or thought that it represented a class-conflict that concerned themselves.

This being so, the theory of comedy as an influence for reform breaks down in this instance. *Arrivistes* were common in the Grand Siècle but neither they nor their methods resembled those of Monsieur Jourdain. His portrayal taught no one a lesson, ridiculed no prevalent failing that might be dangerous to society, and can hardly be seen as a corrective. The comedy lies much more in the realm of innocuous burlesque than in that of satire.

༺༼ༀ༽༻

The same cannot be said of Molière's three greatest if less typical plays, *Tartuffe*, *Dom Juan* and *Le Misanthrope*, in which the satire is deep and daring. To them more dubiously might be added a fourth, produced some two years before *Le Bourgeois Gentilhomme*, again initially before the court.

On the face of it *George Dandin* is a farce in three short acts. The protagonist is another kind of social climber, a rich peasant who has married above him and regrets it bitterly. His wife Angélique is about to have an affair with a gallant of her own class. In each of the three acts George Dandin thinks he has caught her out but she turns the tables by various tricks, making him appear in the wrong. Each time her parents are called in and, besides criticizing him for his uncouth language and manners, force him to apologize for his outrageous suspicions of their highborn and virtuous daughter, the last time on his knees. The general theme of the cuckold, or potential cuckold tricked by his wife, was traditional. One important scene is copied from *La Jalousie du Barbouillé*, an early farce probably by Molière himself. A medieval variation of it occurs in Boccaccio (*Decameron*, Day VIII, 4).

The play assumes a social significance which these earlier examples lacked, since Angélique's parents belong to a decayed country nobility who are absurdly proud of their not very distinguished ancestry. Depicted as comic characters, at whom both Court and town could indeed laugh, they have been saved from ruin by the money of their despised son-in-law. The moral of the play is stated didactically in the opening lines:

> Ah, qu'une femme Demoiselle est une étrange affaire, et que mon mariage est une leçon bien parlante à tous les paysans qui veulent s'élever au-dessus de leur condition et s'allier, comme j'ai fait, à la maison d'un gentilhomme. La noblesse de soi est bonne, c'est une chose considérable, assurément; mais elle est accompagnée de tant de mauvaises circonstances qu'il est très bon de ne s'y point frotter. . . . C'est notre bien seul qu'ils épousent et j'aurais mieux fait, tout riche que je suis, de m'allier en bonne et franche paysannerie, que de prendre une femme qui se tient au-dessus de moi . . .

The 'lesson' of *George Dandin* is not to warn against social climbing as such, but against the confrontation of incompatibles which it produces, as a more modern play might warn against mixed marriages of almost any kind. The warning is repeated in other monologues by George Dandin, of unusual earnestness if the play were regarded merely as a farce.

This is not all. George Dandin is not in himself ridiculous to any reasonable audience. He is only made to appear so by characters who are more ridiculous, or are plainly dishonest. What distinguishes him is his resentment of injustice. He knows he is right but is constantly put in the wrong. His final comment is that he might as well go and drown himself:

> Ah! je le quitte [give it up] maintenant, et je n'y vois plus de remède. Lorsqu'on a, comme moi, épousé une femme méchante, le meilleur parti qu'on puisse prendre c'est de s'aller jeter dans l'eau la tête la première.

The emphasis is now back on the traditional classless theme ('épousé une femme méchante') rather than on social inequality, as the full title, *George Dandin ou le Mari confondu*, bears out. It rests on the hopeless dilemma of a character in a situation which he realizes is of his own making and from which the only way out would be suicide. It is of course a tragic dilemma, but without a tragic context. Whatever misery it might bring to the individual, cuckoldry was considered too ignoble to be treated on a tragic level.[1]

George Dandin as we read it today is best described as a black farce or a bitter farce. Whether it was so by accident or design is an open question. Writing over a century later Beaumarchais called it a *drame* and stressed its social significance: 'Au lieu du nom de *George Dandin*, si Molière eût appelé son Drame: *La Sottise des alliances*, il eût porté bien plus de fruit.' (Preface to *Le Mariage de Figaro*.)

The term 'bitter comedy', not invented until the twentieth century, can be applied to the last three plays under consideration.

If *Tartuffe* had ended with the triumph of the impostor, as it has been conjectured that the first version did,[2] it would be bitter unreservedly. This is problematic but even as the play stands the sugar in *Tartuffe*, unlike that in *Le Bourgeois Gentilhomme*, is little more than a top-icing. The religiously inclined Orgon has adopted as his spiritual director the conspicuously pious Tartuffe, whom he first met in the church he attended. Tartuffe's fervent prayers, his breast-beatings, his extreme humility, attracted the attention of the whole congregation and particularly of Orgon, who finally installed him in his own home (I. v). There his righteous criticisms and insistence on unworldliness (though he himself accepts the comforts offered him, particularly good food) antagonize nearly all the family – Orgon's son and daughter, Damis and Mariane, his brother-in-law Cléante, and the servant Dorine. The exception is Orgon's mother, Madame Pernelle, who sweeps out of the house in the memorable opening scene in which she speaks her mind in mother-in-lawish tones on the way the household is run and the behaviour of its members and shows that she is as impressed as her son by the devoutness of Tartuffe.

[1] It has been suggested that several of the love triangles in the tragedies of Corneille and Racine turn on potential cuckoldry or the fear of it. Though true, this is perhaps over-ingenious. The tragic context and consequences dissuade one from saying that Sophonisbe makes Syphax a cuckold by her bigamous marriage to Massinissa, or that Roxane wishes to cuckold Amurat, or that Phèdre Thésée. The word is everything. The approriate word here is 'infidelity'.

[2] Particularly by G. Michaut in *Les Luttes de Molière* (Paris, 1925). For a discussion of the three versions of the play, see J. Cairncross, *Molière bourgeois et libertin* (Paris, 1963). Though Mr Cairncross has a case to make and works partly on hypothetical material, this is a good modern exposition of the question.

This comically blunt character does not reappear until the end of the play (V. iii), after Tartuffe has been unmasked. In spite of her son's protests she refuses to believe for a time that the holy man could be other than he seemed. Her daughter-in-law Elmire is a conciliatory and attractive woman considerably younger than her husband, whose second wife she is. She runs the house without friction with her step-children and treats Tartuffe tactfully until the situation becomes un-bearable. Tartuffe tries to seduce her and it is only by persuading her husband to hide under the table where he can overhear the impostor's advances to her that she opens his eyes (IV. v–vii). He immediately orders Tartuffe out of the house.

This could have been the end of the play – an unmasking and a happy ending in the comic tradition. But in the existing version Tartuffe further reveals his true character and his power over his victim. The infatuated Orgon has made him a 'donation', a legal engagement disinheriting his son and assigning all his possessions to Tartuffe. In addition he has entrusted him as his *directeur de conscience* with some politically compromising documents left in his keeping by a friend. Tartuffe does not scruple to use both these weapons. A bailiff appears and orders the family to leave the house, now Tartuffe's, by the next morning. After this Tartuffe returns with a police officer who, he says, has a royal order to arrest Orgon for subversion.

This would give the 'black' ending. But there is a surprise; instead of Orgon, the officer arrests Tartuffe, who was recognized as a wanted crook when he went to inform against his benefactor. This turning of the tables is accompanied by a panegyric of the king, whose all-seeing eye detects impostures and whose generosity moves him to pardon Orgon's political indiscretion in reward for his past services to the crown (mentioned incidentally in an earlier act). The dénouement, with the steps that lead immediately up to it, show that Molière could have handled melodrama skilfully enough if that had been his line; but nothing closely resembles it in any of his other plays.

To restore the family unity Damis, previously thrown out of the house for daring to tell his father that Tartuffe is trying to make love to his stepmother, has come back loyally to give what help he can. He is a fiery young man and his immediate suggestion is to cut off Tar-tuffe's ears and then kill him – just the kind of impetuous conduct that his wiser stepmother has been trying to avoid through most of the play. His sister Mariane, whom Orgon had offered in marriage to

MOLIÈRE'S COMEDY

MOLIÈRE'S COMEDY 119
Tartuffe as part of his total submission to him, will marry instead a
lover of her choice. Orgon's offer of his daughter has been somewhat
muffled by Tartuffe's pursuit of Elmire[1] but it parallels exactly similar
situations, though on different registers, in *Le Bourgeois Gentilhomme*,
Les Femmes savantes and *Le Malade imaginaire*. In all these a deluded
parent tries to force an attractive daughter into a marriage with a
detestable or ridiculous character whom the parent admires.

It will be noticed that this outline could yield a perfectly viable play
that was not comic. The main comic elements are provided by Madame
Pernelle, a minor character, by the servant Dorine, who is prominent
and active but could be equally so without being funny, and by the
infatuated Orgon himself. Orgon could be represented as much less
absurd without losing his gullibility (and the significance of this will be
returned to). We would then have a domestic-social drama of the type
popular in the eighteenth century, in which the unity of the family is
preserved by the defeat and expulsion of an interloper.[2] It could much
more easily become a *drame* than the *George Dandin* which Beaumarchais considered as one. While the parallel indicates the serious
basis of *Tartuffe* in comparison with most of Molière's other comedies,
the fact that it is not a *drame* and that it is highly unlikely that Molière
would or could have written such a play has considerably more
significance. The 'message' of *Tartuffe*, centring on the characterization of Orgon, is different. Both the internal evidence and Molière's
long campaign to have the play produced show the importance he
attached to it.

What was this 'message'? That hypocrisy is '[un] des plus in-
commodes et plus dangereux [des vices de mon siècle]' says Molière
in his *Premier Placet* and the way to combat it is to expose it to
ridicule (Preface).[3]

This convenient theory is not borne out by the play. In it, hypocrisy
is not ridiculous. Some of Dorine's outspoken remarks and some of
Tartuffe's more blatant references to the will of heaven draw laughs
from an audience conscious of his monstrous self-interest, but the
laughter is shortlived and inclined to be bitter. The character of the

---

[1] But the two things are closely linked for plot purposes. Elmire sees Tartuffe
in private with the idea of persuading him not to press the marriage with Mariane
(III. iii). He dismisses that subject in two lines and launches into a full declaration
of his love for Elmire.
[2] See below, pp. 215–16.
[3] See above, pp. 109–10.

E

hypocrite is not presented as laughable, any more than that of a villain of melodrama. His hypocrisy, to retain the word for the moment, would have paid off or been 'rewarded' if he had not gone one step too far and denounced Orgon to the police, so provoking the royal intervention. The moral of that, hardly intended, is that deception pays so long as you know where to stop. It is not Tartuffe but Orgon, echoed in broader tones by Madame Pernelle to underline his gullibility, who is the 'personnage ridicule' of the play. As various critics have observed, the principal object of laughter is the dupe and not the duper, a feature found in other comedies of Molière's, but nowhere more significant than here. There is no question of Orgon's religious sincerity. It is so extreme that it makes him vulnerable to the grossest deception and blinds him to the human values represented by his family. His 'vice' or failing is to be over-credulous in religion and to trust implicitly a man whom he takes for one of God's ministers:[1] in short, to do what all the great religious moralists, from Pascal downwards, insisted was the first requisite, to 'have faith'. If a clear message emerges from the play, it is here: obsessive religion leads to pernicious results, as do the obsessions with money, social improvement, culture or medicine in other comedies. As a complementary message, religion is for mugs, without distinction between the true and false kinds. The theme of hypocrisy is a red herring.

Molière's enemies were undoubtedly right, whether they analysed his work in this way or reacted instinctively. Molière was a humanist in the modern sense. One cannot doubt this on the evidence of his plays as a whole. One cannot doubt that he was naturally antireligious. What he achieved in *Tartuffe* was to set up the classic portrait of the

[1] It seems that in the earliest performances Tartuffe was dressed as a priest, or in a close approximation to clerical garb. For the single performance of 1667 Molière changed this, as part of a vain attempt to placate the truly devout. His *Second Placet* (the petition sent with La Grange to Louis at the siege of Lille) reveals this, while inadvertently containing signs of Molière's assimilation of 'false' to 'true' religion. Our italics: 'En vain je l'ai produite [ma comédie] sous le titre de *l'Imposteur*, et *déguisé* le personnage sous l'ajustement d'un homme du monde. J'ai beau lui donner un petit chapeau, de grands cheveux, un grand collet, une épée et des dentelles sur tout l'habit, mettre en plusieurs endroits *des adoucissements*, et retrancher avec soin tout ce que j'ai jugé capable de fournir l'ombre d'un prétexte *aux célebres originaux du portrait que je voulais faire*: tout cela n'a de rien servi.' And no wonder. The expedient of dressing the ostensibly austere Tartuffe ('Laurent, serrez ma haire avec ma discipline,' III. ii) as a fashionable man of the world is visibly inappropriate. And however he was costumed for the audience, it makes no difference to Orgon's confidence in his piety.

religious materialist, depicting in one character functioning in one family group all the essential features of the species. Tartuffe is a salesman for salvation, professionally persuasive to consumers on a level at first subliminary; having hooked his fish, he threatens or attacks in the name of a higher spiritual authority any who question his position, careless of the consequences to their human relationships; he preaches austerity while living comfortably himself; he has strong sexual appetites which he manages to justify by an exercise of religious casuistry; he is adept at milking money from his supporters or victims. He cannot be checked on his own ground but only if, by accident or miscalculation, he falls foul of the secular laws.

This portrait in miniature held good for some of the numerous sects and movements that sprang up during the nineteenth century[1] and later and is still recognizable today. Before Molière's time the greedy and lecherous monk was a commonplace of literature, less subtle than Tartuffe, but with similar characteristics. At the other end of the scale the aptly named Princes of the Church, combining power with apparent piety, were influential statesmen and would have their modern equivalents as that or as leaders of big business. None of this was new in Molière's day. He merely gave expression in a dangerously ambitious satire to criticisms which were generally current, but hitherto obscure or fragmentary. His attitude is perfectly comprehensible without attaching him in any strict sense to the *libertins* or freethinkers, the name applied rather broadly to anyone who disregarded or questioned the doctrines of the Church, or to stress the fact that in youth he was probably a pupil of Gassendi, the Epicurean philosopher. Such considerations reinforce the case for his religious scepticism but they are not necessary to explain it. We do not think that Molière was ever a pious little chorister who was converted, or rather deconverted, by personal contacts with atheists.

On the particular issue of *Tartuffe* it seems established that Molière came into conflict with a group known as the Compagnie du Saint-Sacrement, a society of militant Catholics whose activities were largely clandestine. This kind of freemasonry in reverse had been founded in 1629 as a contribution to the Counter-Reformation and numbered influential churchmen and nobles among its members. It acquired in time the support of Anne of Austria, the queen mother.

[1] See e.g. Aldous Huxley's description of some fringe sects in his essay 'Justifications', in *The Olive Tree* (London, 1936).

Among its aims was the suppression of the theatre as a corruptive influence and there is little doubt that it was one of the forces, probably the most active, behind the five-year ban on Tartuffe. President Lamoignon, who intervened immediately after the performance of August 1667, was a member of the Company.[1] When in the 1660s Louis XIV was tightening his grip on the national power, he frowned on this independent pressure-group and this may give a partial explanation of his constant, though at first discreet, support of Molière. Historically and politically this throws extra light on the struggle to produce *Tartuffe*, but it does not contribute much to an interpretation of the play. Nearly all ecclesiastical opinion, including that of the Jansenists to whom the Company was opposed, was anti-theatre and just at this period a particularly violent campaign was being waged against its immorality. Tartuffe the imposter hardly typified the powerful figures who led the Company and, although its humbler members committed various excesses of zeal, they were not notorious for their sexual or financial aberrations. At most some of them begged in the accepted way for their own subsistence or in order to raise money for the Company's charitable works. These bore – like the collections made by other societies – on the relief of prisoners and on foreign missions to infidels. What may be a direct reference to the first of these is Tartuffe's order to his valet:

> Si l'on vient pour me voir, je vais aux prisonniers
> Des aumônes que j'ai partager les deniers.

This provokes the servant Dorine's aside:

> Que d'affectation et de forfanterie!

> (III. ii)

Proselytism and almsgiving, but undertaken in a disinterested spirit, were the main activities the Company's adherents shared with Tartuffe, but their practice of them was certainly not exclusive. The opposition of the Company may well have strengthened Molière's resentment against the interference of religion in human affairs and

---

[1] The first indication of the Company's opposition to *Tartuffe* dated back to April 1664, before the performance at Versailles. The play was evidently known through private readings and the Company's *Annales* already advocated 'working to procure its suppression'. See G. Mongrédien, *Recueil des textes et des documents du XVIIe siècle relatifs à Molière* (Paris, 1965), Vol. I.

even inspired a few touches in his play, but it is hardly justified to attribute his strong general scepticism to this factor alone.[1]

❧

One is always free, though by no means obliged, to detect an allusion to the powerful laymen of the Company in the protagonist of *Dom Juan*, which was Molière's next new production after the first performance of *Tartuffe*. 'Un grand seigneur méchant est une terrible chose', says Sganarelle in the opening scene, and anyone who has seen a production such as Jouvet's in which Dom Juan appeared backed by his two towering strong-arm men can appreciate the force of this.

The legend of Don Juan, which has inspired literally hundreds of works of different kinds,[2] is first found in the Spanish play *El burlador de Sevilla y convidado de piedra* (*The Trickster of Seville and the Stone Guest*), published in 1630 and attributed to Tirso de Molina. This tells the story of an unruly and perverse young nobleman who delights in seducing women and then abandoning them and in tricking their outraged fiancés. It has features of a cloak-and-sword drama on which is imposed a strongly religious moral: 'Repent before it is too late'. Failing to do this Don Juan is dragged down to hell by the mortuary statue of a man he has killed (the Commander), the father of one of his female victims. He is also condemned as an enemy of society because of his infringements of the honour code and his ruthless treatment of the peasant class. He has a servant, Catalinón, who protests and moralizes, but is hardly comic except for his simplicity. The rustics in the play are a community of fisherfolk whom Don Juan meets after a shipwreck. Their depiction is not humorous, but poetic in the vein of pastoral. For them and the other deceived lovers the play ends happily.

As products of two different societies and cultures, the comparison

[1] If one sees the king's intervention which finally saves Orgon as a direct rebuff to the Company, the case might be altered. But it is unnecessary to interpret it in this light, in a theatre where so many happy endings were brought about by a *deus ex machina*.

[2] For a complete account see Gendarme de Bévotte's *La Légende de Don Juan*, 2 vols (Paris, 1911), also his *Le Festin de pierre avant Molière* (Paris, 1907), which gives the texts of the earlier Italian and French plays. For a short outline see my article 'Don Juan' in Cassell's *Encyclopaedia of World Literature*, rev. ed. (London, 1973).

between Tirso's play and Molière's is of great interest, but as a direct influence *El burlador* is unimportant since Molière is unlikely to have known it; it came to him through intermediaries. Transplanted from Spain to Italy, the play lost its moral implications and became near-farcical by the transformation of the valet into an undisguised comic and his promotion to the role of chief character in *El convitato de pietra* of Giacinto Andrea Cicognini, a possible source of the scenario used by the Italian comedians in Paris.[1] Another version by Giliberto, printed in 1652 and now lost, evidently restored Don Juan and some of the more serious elements to prominence. It was translated or adapted as a 'tragicomedy' by two French writers, Dorimon and Claude de Villiers, the Philipin of Scarron's comedies. Both these entitled their plays *Le Festin de pierre ou le Fils criminel* – the subtitle is a reference to Don Juan's defiance of his father; in Molière: 'Ah, mourez le plus tôt que vous pourrez!' (IV. v). Dorimon's play was acted at Lyon in late 1658 and again in Paris in 1661 by the shortlived Compagnie de Mademoiselle (de Montpensier). Printed in 1659, it was also available in that form. Villiers's was written for his company of the Hôtel de Bourgogne and first acted there in 1659.[2]

All these plays conserved the final vengeance of the statue, with the descent into hell. This ending, not out of place in the semi-theological *Burlador* and reminiscent of the old Miracle Plays, might be thought inappropriate in mid-seventeenth-century France, but it seems to have been accepted without question and exploited as a spectacular effect like those of the machine-plays. Both the Hôtel de Bourgogne and the Italians actually introduced an equestrian statue, though whether the horse was a real one and, if so, whether it was persuaded to disappear through a trapdoor is unfortunately not known.

Molière thus had immediately before him the slapstick version of the *commedia dell'arte* players whose theatre he shared and the two recent French versions, similar to each other. Smarting under the ban on *Tartuffe* and intensifying his campaign against 'hypocrisy', he hurriedly[3] wrote what can be considered the most blasphemous play of his time, and indeed of the century.

In *Dom Juan ou le Festin de pierre* Molière put the protagonist's

[1] See above, p. 7.
[2] See Lancaster, *History*, II, p. 638, note 8.
[3] There are various signs of this. One, though not conclusive in itself is that the play is in prose, to which Molière was known to resort when pressed for time. See G. de Bévotte, *La Légende de Don Juan*, I, pp. 96 ff.

name in the title for the first time.[1] The two characters of the seducer and his servant Sganarelle completely dominate the play and all the rest provides background and opportunities for their expressions of opinion and illustrations of Dom Juan's philosophy in action. The underlying though necessary plot is furnished by Dom Juan's relationship with Elvire, a woman he has enticed out of a convent to marry, then deserted. She follows to plead with him, to warn, and finally makes a vain attempt to reform him. Her two brothers who first appear in mid-play (III. iii) pursue him in the cloak-and-sword convention to avenge their sister, but are unsuccessful. Another character, taken over from the previous French versions but unessential to this plot, is Dom Juan's father; he appears in Acts IV and V to remonstrate with him, again vainly. Except for Elvire the only women who come on stage are two peasant girls to both of whom he promises marriage, but no doubt is left of his numerous other intrigues and conquests. The long peasant episode, filling the whole of Act II, exploits the convention of comic rusticity by a sustained use of patois or near-patois. Comic also are Sganarelle's praise of snuff which opens the play, his disguising as a doctor (III. i), and the introduction of the simple merchant Monsieur Dimanche to whom Dom Juan owes money (IV. iii). Not comic but equally incidental to the action is the encounter with the Poor Man (III. ii) which will be returned to. Even the Commander, the instrument of final retribution, is not integrated in the action. He is simply a man whom Dom Juan killed some time previously.[2]

To use relatively modern terms, *Dom Juan* is a discussion play kept moving by a series of incidents, traditional but disparate and sometimes almost irrelevant, and strongly centred on the two main characters. The length of the speeches, unusual in a prose comedy of the time, helps to bear this out. Not inspired by 'verbal exuberance' (except in the first of the peasant scenes, II. i), several are short sermons or anti-sermons, dramatically clumsy, whose main function is to put

[1] The play is always referred to as *Dom Juan*, though it should be *Don*. There was confusion between the Spanish and ecclesiastical titles, both ultimately derived from *Dominus* = Master.

[2] In most other versions, beginning with Tirso's, he is the father of a second woman whom Don Juan seduced. By omitting this character (Doña Ana in *El burlador*, Donna Anna in the opera *Don Giovanni*) Molière removed the Statue's involvement in the plot. It is another sign of his lack of interest in it, except as a framework for his thesis.

over a point of view. The subject of the discussion is religion, contemptuously attacked by Dom Juan and defended by his servant with conspicuous feebleness.

The best though by no means the only illustration of this is in Act III, immediately after the peasant interlude. To escape their pursuers Dom Juan has changed his richly embroidered suit to 'country clothes', while Sganarelle has picked up an old doctor's costume at a pawnbrokers. So attired he has been stopped by several peasants and consulted respectfully on their ailments. He has prescribed various remedies at hazard. It would be funny if they recovered and came to thank me, he says laughingly. Why not? asks Dom Juan. Do you think real doctors know any better? If the patient recovers you are as entitled as they are to take credit for the cure, due really to chance and natural causes.

SGANARELLE Comment, Monsieur, vous êtes aussi impie en médecine?

DOM JUAN C'est une des grandes erreurs qui soit parmi les hommes.

SGANARELLE Quoi! vous ne croyez pas au séné, ni à la casse, ni au vin émétique?

DOM JUAN Et pourquoi veux-tu que j'y croie?

SGANARELLE Vous avez l'âme bien mécréante. Cependant vous voyez depuis un temps que le vin émétique fait bruire ses fuseaux.[1] Ses miracles ont converti les plus incrédules esprits, et il n'y a pas trois semaines que j'en ai vu, moi qui vous parle, un effet merveilleux.

DOM JUAN Et quel?

SGANARELLE Il y avait un homme qui depuis six jours était à l'agonie. On ne savait plus que lui ordonner et tous les remèdes ne faisaient rien. On s'avise à la fin de lui donner de l'émétique.

DOM JUAN Il réchappa, n'est-ce pas?

SGANARELLE Non, il mourut.

DOM JUAN L'effet est admirable.

SGANARELLE Comment! Il y avait six jours entiers qu'il ne pouvait mourir, et cela le fit mourir tout d'un coup. Voulez-vous rien de plus efficace?

[1] 'Is all the rage'. This emetic consisting of wine infused with antimony was prescribed in grave cases, often as a last resort as the subsequent dialogue shows.

The barely concealed analogy between medicine and religion is inescapable. Most of this language would be more applicable to the latter: *impie, croire, l'âme mécréante, ses miracles ont converti les plus incrédules esprits,* with a possible reference to the last sacrament (the *vin émétique*) and to (*grâce*) *efficace.* As the doctors are frauds when they claim to cure physical ills, so are the priests in the spiritual domain.

Short of saying it openly, Molière does everything possible to put the idea across. Since you do not believe in medicine, continues Sganarelle, let's change the subject:

SGANARELLE Je veux savoir un peu vos pensées à fond. Est-il possible que vous ne croyiez point du tout au Ciel?

DOM JUAN Laissons cela.

SGANARELLE C'est-à-dire que non. Et à l'Enfer?

DOM JUAN Eh!

SGANARELLE Tout de même. Et au diable, s'il vous plaît?

DOM JUAN Oui, oui.

SGANARELLE Aussi peu. Ne croyez-vous point l'autre vie?

DOM JUAM [*Laughing*] Ah! ah! ah!

SGANARELLE Voilà un homme que j'aurai bien de la peine à convertir. Et dites-moi un peu, le moine bourru, qu'en croyez-vous, eh?

DOM JUAN La peste soit du fat!

SGANARELLE Et voilà ce que je ne puis souffrir; car il n'y a rien de plus vrai que le moine bourru, et je me ferais pendre pour celui-là.[1] Mais encore faut-il croire quelque chose dans le monde. Qu'est-ce donc que vous croyez?

DOM JUAN Ce que je crois?

SGANARELLE Oui.

DOM JUAN Je crois que deux et deux sont quatre, Sganarelle, et que quatre et quatre sont huit.

SGANARELLE La belle croyance et les beaux articles de foi que voilà! Votre religion, à ce que je vois, c'est donc de l'arithmétique? . . .

Sganarelle goes on to argue from the wonders of creation, and particularly the marvellous mechanism of the human body, which

---

[1] The mention of *le moine bourru* (the bogeyman) was one of the passages censored in the first printed text of 1682.

cannot be explained by science. Demonstrating the way in which the brain directs all the movements of the body, he grows dizzy and falls over, to the vast amusement of the audience.

Molière himself played this part. He entrusted the defence of religion – and this particularly offended the devout – to a buffoon whose heart may have been in the right place but whose brain was not. He was more credulous than Tartuffe's Orgon and more openly absurd. If there is a 'personnage ridicule' in this play (apart from the quite incidental rustic Pierrot) it is he. If there is any trace left of the theory that men's faults and follies can be cured by ridicule, the folly is pious credulity exaggerated to a point where it is seen to be nonsense.

Dom Juan is unimpressed, and even uninterested. In the next well-known scene he carries his scepticism further. The two ask their way of a poor man they meet in a wood, a kind of hermit or pious beggar.[1] After directing them he asks for alms, in gratitude for which he will pray for their prosperity. You must be prosperous yourself, says Dom Juan, if you spend your whole day praying to Heaven. The hermit replies that often he has not even a crust of bread to eat. A diabolical idea occurs to Dom Juan. He takes out a gold coin and dangles it before the hermit: 'You can have this if you will swear [i.e. blaspheme]'. The man refuses: 'No, sir, I would rather die of hunger.' Faced with this rare example of noble conviction in a humble man (or is he another fool like Sganarelle; would martyrdom itself be a folly?) Dom Juan changes his line and utters the much debated words:

Va, va, je te le donne pour l'amour de l'humanité.

This would be entirely appropriate in a humanitarian 'humanist', replacing the 'love of God' with love of his fellow men, and it is always possible that Molière wrote the sentence without premeditation as a link with the immediately following scene (III. iii) in which Dom Juan goes to the help of a man who is being attacked by robbers – and who proves to be a brother of the woman he has seduced. 'Un homme attaqué par trois autres?' he exclaims. 'La partie est trop inégale et je ne dois pas souffrir cette lâcheté.' But this turns out to be a class reaction involving honour – his own honour, as he makes clear – which

---

[1] The name of the 'Poor Man' in the List of Characters, though not in the text, is Francisque, strongly suggesting an allusion to the 'begging monks' of the Franciscan order.

he has always been ready to violate when it suited him. His physical courage is above question and it is on this point alone that his spasmodic responses to the honour code are based. One cannot really credit him with a 'love of humanity' in any genuine sense.

A preferable interpretation of Dom Juan's remark to the hermit is to read it as a prime example of his cynicism, an ironic utterance while throwing the coin to the half-starved beggar and a new way of humiliating him in his faith since the first way has failed. 'Since God cannot help you, just see what man can do,' he implies, but without extending the principle beyond this single situation.[1]

Scoffing at both kinds of law, supernatural and natural, Dom Juan justifies his attitude so far as he feels it necessary, though more often he parries an objection with irony or disdain as though it had no importance. His final crime is to feign religion in response to a long lecture from his father and after he has been visited by the Statue who invites him to sup with him the next day if he dare. He uses the same pretext with Elvire's brother Carlos when pressed to confirm his marriage with her. He would have liked nothing better, replies Dom Juan, but a voice from Heaven has told him that he cannot achieve salvation that way. This hypocrisy is the most abominable crime of all, cries Sganarelle, giving Dom Juan the opportunity for a lengthy tirade on it (V. ii) developing very explicitly the argument of *Tartuffe*. Hypocrisy is a fashionable vice; it enjoys a privileged position; how many, under the cloak of religion, can get away with the most wicked things. He will do the same. At the slightest criticism, 'je ferai le vengeur des intérêts du Ciel et, sous ce prétexte commode, je pousserai mes ennemis, je les accuserai d'impiété et saurai déchaîner contre eux des zélés indiscrets . . .'

So his career almost ends with a false conversion. But the actual end, after his firm refusal to undergo a true one – 'Non, non, il ne sera pas dit, quoi qu'il arrive, que je sois capable de me repentir' (V. v) – is his engulfment in hell-fire with a cry of agony and an impressive burst of stage thunder and lightning. So, it might be said, the sinner is punished,

---

[1] The temptation of the gold coin in return for a blasphemous oath was censored out of the 1682 edition. With it disappeared most of the sting as well as the sense of the scene. The truncated version reads:

LE PAUVRE Je vous assure, Monsieur, que le plus souvent je n'ai pas un morceau de pain à mettre sous les dents.

DOM JUAN Je te le donne pour l'amour de l'humanité. Mais que vois-je là? un homme attaqué par trois autres? [etc.]

overtaken by the most terrible retribution of all, eternal damnation, as in the Spanish original – in which at least he calls at the last minute for confession and absolution, only to be told it is too late.[1]

But that moral lesson is stood on its head in Molière's version. None of his contemporaries seems even to have thought of it. What they saw was a monster of wickedness, defiant to the last, going down to a 'punishment' in which few audiences could have believed in this primitive spectacular form any more than could Molière himself. One recalls his snide reference to 'the boiling cauldrons of hell' in *L'École des femmes*.[2]

Tirso's play has a further scene in which the men and women the Burlador has wronged appear before the king, the temporal judge, and are justified and compensated while their deceiver is condemned. Molière compresses this excellent and obvious moral into a few lines spoken by the comic Sganarelle and, just in case anyone should be tempted to take it seriously, adds that trivial whine about his lost wages, which for him is the worst result of his master's damnation. His complaint was suppressed by the censor, but Molière wrote it. It is as though Wagner had reappeared in the last scene of *Doctor Faustus* (which leads up to a materially similar dénouement) to complain that his legacy was one or two ducats short. Unlike Faustus, Dom Juan gets away with his sins in words and actions, at the expense of a retribution more suitable to pantomime than to serious drama.

Taking this play as a discussion on religion, one finds that this has two other advocates in addition to its clownish champion. One is Elvire who comes back, all passion spent, to implore him to save his soul by amending his ways and to warn him, as in the Spanish original, that time is short (IV. vi). This convent-conditioned woman is touchingly sincere but she advances no argument (she does not feel the need of one) capable of making the slightest impression on Dom Juan, or indeed on a spectator not already convinced of the truth of her religion. The other advocate is Dom Juan's father, Dom Louis, who identifies, as is often the case, religious and secular morality, the

---

[1] DON JUAN   Deja que llame
               Quien me confiese y absuelva.
DON GONZALO [the Statue] No hay lugar; ya acuerdas tarde.

(Let me call for someone to confess and absolve me. / It's no use; you remember it too late.)

[2] See p. 96 above.

dictates of heaven and the code of his family. His most forceful words
bear on this and anticipate the famous remarks of Beaumarchais's
Figaro,[1] through from the other side of the fence:

> Ah! quelle bassesse est la vôtre! Ne rougissez-vous point de
> mériter si peu votre naissance? Êtes-vous en droit, dites-moi,
> d'en tirer quelque vanité? Et qu'avez-vous fait dans le monde
> pour être gentilhomme? Croyez-vous qu'il suffise d'en porter
> le nom et les armes et que ce nous soit une gloire d'être sorti
> d'un sang noble lorsque nous vivons en infâmes? Non, non, la
> naissance n'est rien où la vertu n'est pas ... Apprenez enfin
> qu'un gentilhomme qui vit mal est un monstre dans la nature,
> que la vertu est le premier titre de noblesse, que je regarde bien
> moins au nom qu'on signe qu'aux actions qu'on fait, et que je
> ferais plus d'état du fils d'un crocheteur qui serait honnête
> homme que du fils d'un monarque qui vivrait comme vous.
>
> (IV. iv)

To this long impassioned homily in which his father has expressed
his most cherished convictions and the not unenlightened philosophy
of the best members of his caste ('noblesse oblige'), Dom Juan's brief
and utterly cold reply is: 'Monsieur, si vous étiez assis, vous en seriez
mieux pour parler.' In more modern terms: 'Do sit down, dad, you'd
be much more comfortable.'

꧁꧂

The character of Dom Juan spills out beyond the polemical discussion
to take on an importance of its own. It is not easy at this date,
after all the developments and variations which the character has
undergone, to see him with the eyes of Molière's generation. He was
only beginning to emerge as a type and might have gone, as the earlier
uncertain treatments indicated, in several different directions: as an
awful warning against impiety, as an antisocial rebel, as a black sheep
in an otherwise honourable family, as an egoistic womanizer like Don
Félix in Scarron's *Jodelet duelliste*,[2] or even as a mere foil or prop for
the contortions of the comic valet. Molière's version helped to fix him

---

[1] See below, pp. 247–8.
[2] See above, pp. 56–7.

as the callous seducer endowed in varying degrees with all the features just mentioned, which is a sufficient explanation of his minor inconsistencies.

His cynical and experienced exploitation of sex is prominent. For him the preliminaries of seduction are a refined pleasure in themselves:

> [My italics] . . . On goûte *une douceur extrême* à réduire par cent hommages le cœur *d'une jeune beauté*, à voir de jour en jour les petits progrès qu'on y fait à combattre par des transports, par des larmes et des soupirs *l'innocente pudeur* d'une âme qui a peine à rendre les armes, à forcer pied à pied *les petites résistances* qu'elle nous oppose, à vaincre les scrupules dont elle se fait un honneur et la mener *doucement* où nous avons envie de la faire venir. Mais lorsqu'on en est maître une fois, il n'y a plus rien à dire ni rien à souhaiter; tout le beau de la passion est fini . . .
>
> (I. ii)

This is a rationalization and refinement of the two almost animal cries of the original Spanish Don Juan: *burlar!* (to trick) and *gozar!* (to enjoy). Enjoyment for Dom Juan requires the stimulus of the calculated approach and the girl's gradual surrender to sensuality, and is quickly exhausted. Another stimulus can be called jealousy, though it is in fact a more complicated conception, approaching voyeurism. Dom Juan recounts how he has come across two young lovers, visibly enthralled by each other and about to marry. Unable to make the slightest impression on the girl, he plans to carry her off by force and hires a boat to do so (this was the cause of his shipwreck). Had he succeeded she would no doubt have screamed and struggled (sadism before the letter), but the main pleasure was not in that:

> Jamais je n'ai vu deux personnes être si contents l'un de l'autre et faire éclater plus d'amour. La tendresse visible de leurs mutuelles ardeurs me donna de l'émotion; j'en fus frappé au cœur et mon amour commença par la jalousie. Oui, je ne pus souffrir d'abord de les voir si bien ensemble; le dépit alarma [awoke] mes désirs et je me figurai un plaisir extrême à pouvoir troubler leur intelligence et rompre cet attachement, dont la délicatesse de mon cœur se tenait offensé . . .
>
> (I. ii)

Another 'delicate pleasure' is offered by Elvire's final attempt to make him repent and save his soul. Her neglected appearance, her obvious distress and her tears have affected him in a very different way than she intended. As soon as she has gone he observes to Sganarelle:

Sais-tu bien que j'ai encore senti quelque peu d'émotion pour elle, que j'ai trouvé de l'agrément dans cette nouveauté bizarre, et que son habit négligé, son air languissant et ses larmes ont réveillé en moi quelques petits restes d'un feu éteint?

(IV. vii)

Molière has already etched in essential features of the character as it was represented until the beginning of the Romantic period. For its correspondences in the *ars amoris* of the eighteenth century one should look less to Mozart's *Don Giovanni* than to such works as the numerous 'licentious' short stories and *Les Liaisons dangereuses* of Laclos, in which the pleasure of destroying the happiness of an innocent young couple is the main theme. One need not go as far as Sade but one can say that Molière in his time was quite aware of the attraction for certain natures of the perversions of simple love and was capable of creating a character who experienced them. His treatment is less physical than psychological. At the very least it extends the range of his characterization.

To the simple question of whether Molière was 'with' Dom Juan or 'against' him there is no simple answer. In the moral argument he gives nearly all the trumps to his hero, who in places is obviously his mouthpiece. Yet he is a thoroughly pernicious man – the only point of several scenes is to demonstrate this. It would be easy to say that Molière was a reasonable *libertin* while Dom Juan is a bad *libertin*, sinning by excess, and to go on from there to draw a distinction between the character and his opinions. But nothing in the play suggests this and we have already seen how little importance can be attached to his final 'condemnation'. There is no *raisonneur*, who could easily have been provided, apart from the inadequate Sganarelle (the beginning of one might be discerned in Dom Louis, but he is too marginal). It is difficult to conclude with any degree of conviction. The best one can say is that the play was probably put together hastily, primarily as a follow-up to *Tartuffe*, that it became, if it was not conceived as, a starting-point for the discussion of wider and deeper issues, and that it is a unique work in the whole of his production. Molière dropped it, almost certainly under pressure, but perhaps also because he realized he had gone too far and was not prepared to fight his critics on this particular ground.

❧

'Character' in *Le Misanthrope*, Molière's next play, is certainly of the first importance. But, although it poses problems, they are of a different kind from those in *Dom Juan*. In this polished and sophisticated social comedy which Molière apparently began writing some two years before its production in June 1666, the main problem has always been the interpretation of the central character, Alceste. He is the Misanthrope of the title and it is noteworthy that the *privilège* of the first edition also gave a subtitle: *ou l'Atrabilaire amoureux*, of which the nearest translation is 'the sour man in love'.[1] This subtitle, though significant, has never been accepted as an adequate description of either the character or the play.

Supposing, to concentrate for the moment on the character and the issues raised by him, one put this in terms of a lawsuit. Would it be Alceste versus Humanity, Alceste versus Society, Alceste versus Corruption, Alceste versus Hypocrisy (social this time, not religious), Alceste versus Conformism, Alceste versus Common Sense, Alceste versus Reality or even – though this would be only a partial issue – Alceste versus Feminine Fickleness? If one managed to isolate and identify the parties to the dispute, which would be the plaintiff and which the defendant? Most important of all, which would win, the audience being the judge?

This nutshell contains all the theories which have been or can be advanced when the subject is approached from this particular angle. The first two acts pose clearly the question of who is in the wrong. There is a strong presumption that it is Alceste, but one cannot be quite sure. He enters in a furious temper with his friend Philinte, a moderate and agreeable man with a strong sense of material realities. What has infuriated him was the sight of Philinte's effusive amiability towards a man they have met in the street and whose name, when

---

[1] Atrabilary: of bilious humour, at once melancholy and censorious.

asked afterwards, he can hardly recall. Such behaviour debases friend-ship, Alceste declares. From this point the argument develops, Philinte protesting that one must observe the outward social conventions, Alceste maintaining that sincerity is all. This was the feature singled out in Wycherley's over-simplified English adaptation *The Plain Dealer* (1676), but it is not the whole of Molière's Alceste. Indignant at Philinte's tolerant attitude, he goes on to insist that one should always speak one's mind about other people's faults, regardless of the consequences. He will take none of the usual steps (such as bribery and wire-pulling) to win a pending lawsuit, since his cause is obviously just. He will have it out with Célimène, the young widow he is in love with, and 'purge her of the faults of this age'. If you do that, remarks Philinte, it will be quite a lot. He mortally offends a fatuous courtier, Oronte, by picking to pieces a sonnet Oronte has composed and insists on reading to him. This prefigures the reading of Trissotin's sonnet in *Les Femmes savantes*[1] though the dramatic exploitation and effect are quite different.

In Act II he does tackle Célimène on her complaisant reception of other admirers (it seems mutually understood that he has the first place), but her natural response to his uncompromising directness is not at all what he expected. He pours scorn on the two fashionable *petits marquis* who visit her and the malicious gossip in which they encourage her to indulge. The act ends with the appearance of an officer from the Maréchaux, an important conciliatory body set up to settle disputes between gentlemen before they reached the point of the legally forbidden duel. Alceste's reaction to this arbitration machinery is more unyielding than that of a modern trade-union leader. All he need do would be to frame some acceptable apology for his over-hasty comments. But no compromise from him. To this ridiculously petty point, as the others see it, he attaches a whole philosophy of truth and honour. He found the poem bad, said so, and still thinks so. He nevertheless goes with the officer after affirming his determination never to climb down:

> Hors qu'un commandement exprès du Roi me vienne
> De trouver bons les vers dont on se met en peine,
> Je soutiendrai toujours, morbleu! qu'ils sont mauvais.
>
> (II. vi)

[1] See above, pp. 104–6.

Molière himself has seen fit to indicate the genealogy of Alceste, though not the whole of it. Near the beginning of *Le Misanthrope* (I. i) Philinte observes:

> Ce chagrin philosophe est un peu trop sauvage,
> Je ris des noirs accès où je vous envisage,
> Et crois voir en nous deux, sous mêmes soins nourris,[1]
> Ces deux frères que peint *L'École des maris*.

Alceste immediately dismisses this as a poor joke:

> Mon Dieu, laissons là vos comparaisons fades.

Incidentally this is not the kind of self-advertisement practised by Corneille when in two of his comedies he referred to previous ones.[2] The implication is that, whereas *L'École des maris* was a play, this situation is 'real'. If the audience do not accept this they are at least reminded that it is 'more real'.

L'École des maris concerned two brothers who have brought up two girls as wards, one of them extremely tolerant and the other over-strictly. The first, Ariste (he has the same name as the 'reasonable' brother in *Les Femmes savantes*), criticizes his brother for his curmudgeonly and old-fashioned attitudes:

> Cette farouche humeur, dont la sévérité
> Fuit toutes les douceurs de la société,
> A tous vos procédés inspire un air bizarre,
> Et jusques à l'habit, vous rend chez vous barbare.
>
> (I. i)

There are parallels in *Le Misanthrope* for almost every word of this. Even Alceste's dress is soberly unfashionable and he is distinguished in Célimène's final unflattering portrait of him as 'l'homme aux rubans verts' (V. iv). With bitter sarcasm he criticizes to Célimène the overdressed appearance of the *petit marquis* Clitandre:

> Vous êtes-vous rendue, avec tout le beau monde,
> Au mérite éclatant de sa perruque blonde?
> Sont-ce ses grands canons qui vous le font aimer?
> L'amas de ses rubans a-t-il su vous charmer?
>
> (II. i)

---

[1] They were evidently foster-brothers, or if not that, had been brought up under the same roof.

[2] To *Mélite* in *La Veuve* (III. iii) and more naturally to *Le Menteur* and Jodelet's part in it in *La Suite du Menteur* (I. iii).

At greater length the short-haired brother in *L'École des maris* described ironically the costume of the young fops (*jeunes muguets*). Would you like me to look like them, he asks, and

> M'obliger à porter de ces petits chapeaux
> Qui laissent éventer leurs débiles cerveaux,
> Et de ces blonds cheveux de qui la vaste enflure
> Des visages humains offusque la figure?
> ... De ces souliers mignons, de rubans revêtus,
> Qui vous font ressembler à des pigeons pattus?
> Et de ces grands canons où, comme en des entraves,
> On met tous les matins ses deux jambes esclaves?

To which Ariste replies, as Philinte might have done:

> Toujours au plus grand nombre on doit s'accommoder,
> Et jamais il ne faut se faire regarder.
> *L'un et l'autre excès choque*, et tout homme bien sage
> Doit faire des habits ainsi que du langage,
> N'y rien trop affecter et sans empressement
> Suivre ce que l'usage y fait de changement.[1]

He agrees that some go too far in their attempts to outrun fashion, but in general it is better to be foolish with the majority than wise in a minority of one:

> Il vaut mieux souffrir d'être au nombre des fous
> Que du sage parti se voir seul contre tous.
>
> (I. i)

The uncompromising brother is called Sganarelle, the name which Molière gave to some of the more farcical characters which he played himself, the last being the goodhearted clown of *Dom Juan*. In *L'École des maris* he was a ninety per cent ridiculous figure[2] who was blinded by his obstinate malice and neatly tricked because of it. In the development of this play in *L'École des femmes*, the character is no longer Sganarelle but Arnolphe, a part also taken by Molière, but whose

---

[1] I.e. in clothes as in language follow the changes in fashion, but not too precipitately.

[2] Not absolutely ridiculous because in his final speech (III. viii), essentially a diatribe against the perfidy of women, he remarks of the girl who has eluded him, 'J'aurais pour elle au feu mis la main que voilà', so foreshadowing Arnolphe's reactions.

serious implications are more visible – so much so that it has been possible to see him as a partly tragic figure. To look at him only through Molière's eyes, it should be recalled that the discussion of the character in *La Critique de L'École des femmes* contained the statement that 'Il n'est pas incompatible qu'une personne soit ridicule en de certaines choses et honnête homme en d'autres'.[1]

In assessing *Le Misanthrope* it must also be recalled that Molière repeated in it several situations and numerous identical or nearly identical lines already used in *Dom Garcie de Navarre*,[2] the *comédie héroïque* on which he seems to have set such store as his lone experiment in near-tragic drama. *Dom Garcie* was anterior to the two *Écoles* and the clearest line of development, assuming that the dates of production reflect the dates of composition, is from the almost farcical Sganarelle through the comic but not farcical Arnolphe to the questionably comic Alceste, with a throwback when elaborating this character to the *comédie héroïque* of 1661.

This furnishes a typical example of Molière's working methods and of the complicated yet logical interrelationships between characters in his various plays. Yet it might not help a producer or actor who had to decide on the interpretation of Alceste in the one play of *Le Misanthrope*. These have to put over something which makes immediate sense in the theatre to an audience not composed of students of Molière's drama as a whole. In a comedy of character the focus should be clear at a relatively early stage and by the end of Act I, or at latest of Act II, it would have been possible to establish Alceste as the 'personnage ridicule'. This might seem to have been achieved, not only by his excessive stubbornness and brusque language and behaviour, but by the comments of Philinte, all in the opening scene.[3]

[1] See above, p. 111. Also pp. 89–90 for other comments on the play.
[2] See particularly H. C. Lancaster, *History*, II, pp. 654–5.
[3] My italics:

> Mais encor, dites-moi, *quelle bizarrerie* . . .
>
> Il est bien des endroits où la pleine franchise
> Deviendrait *ridicule* . . .
>
> Un si grand courroux contre les mœurs du temps
> *Vous tourne en ridicule* auprès de bien des gens.
> *On se rirait de vous*, Alceste, tout de bon,
> Si l'on vous entendait parler de la façon.

This last is about his lawsuit, but Alceste replies:

> Tant pis pour qui rirait.

Philinte, however, is his friend and the tenor of his remarks is not so much 'You are ridiculous' as 'Don't make yourself ridiculous'. Célimène in her annoyance (II. i and the following scenes) is hardly capable of making the distinction, while for the other characters Alceste is laughable in himself. But these characters themselves, the absurdly self-satisfied Oronte, the fatuously vain *petits marquis*, and even the prude Arsinoé, are 'personnages ridicules' also, though minor ones. When they laugh at him, Alceste has his reply:

> Les rieurs sont pour vous, Madame, c'est tout dire,
> Et vous pouvez pousser contre moi la satire.

This says everything, particularly if extended beyond its context. It is reinforced by Alceste's protest a moment before he exits to follow the officer at the end of Act II:

> Par la sangbleu![1] Messieurs, je ne croyais pas être
> Si plaisant que je suis.

So at this point we are still not fixed on the character, or rather the image of the character which a producer should offer to the audience. It is still necessary to see what happens afterwards.

❧❧❧

In Alceste's contempt for 'the whole human race' (I. i), the weak point is his love for Célimène. He knows it is unreasonable and he is not blind to the faults of this young widow of twenty, but he finds her attractions stronger. With this physical-cum-emotional attraction goes an unspoken idealization of women, a natural complement to his idealization of men. They ought to be perfect and when they are not he feels let down, which explains his misanthropy. But this reading of the character is not extrapolated by Molière. It belongs essentially to the Romantic assumptions of the nineteenth century and in the seventeenth century to tragedy, tragicomedy and the novels (the importance of *vertu*). All that Alceste can say is:

> Je confesse mon faible, elle a l'art de me plaire;
> J'ai beau voir ses défauts et j'ai beau l'en blâmer,
> En dépit qu'on en ait, elle se fait aimer.

[1] Alceste's oaths, old-fashioned and uncourtly like some of his other language and his sober dress, are part of his psychological make-up.

Near at hand is Célimène's sweet-natured and 'virtuous' cousin Éliante who admires Alceste and would be a much more suitable match for him, as Philinte points out. Alceste fully admits this, but ...

> Il est vrai: ma raison me le dit chaque jour;
> Mais la raison n'est pas ce qui règle l'amour.
>
> (I. i)

In Acts III and IV the main interest turns to Alceste's relations with Célimène. After the two marquis, chatting together, have made it fairly plain that Célimène has encouraged both of them, Célimène is visited by the prudish Arsinoé, a new character whose outspokenness, though based on truth, is sheer mischief-mongering inspired by jealousy and malice. She has come, she says, to warn the young widow of the scandalous rumours which are circulating about her conduct – of which, of course, she does not believe half – and advise her to be more prudent. Célimène retorts on a highly personal level, accusing Arsinoé in effect of hypocrisy, and goes out leaving her outraged visitor to await her coach. Before this arrives Alceste enters. Flattered by Arsinoé and warned that Célimène is deceiving him, he at first refuses to believe her. 'But I have proof,' she says, 'which I will show you if you will see me home.'[1]

Act IV contains Alceste's explosion against Célimène, provoked by an affectionate letter she had written to his despised enemy Oronte of all people (this was Arsinoé's 'proof'). But before this there is a revelatory conversation between the reasonable Philinte and Éliante. It informs us that Alceste's 'bizarre' quarrel with Oronte over the sonnet has been patched up. At first Alceste would not yield an inch, but at last he found a formula which contained the utmost he could concede. He sincerely wished he could have found Oronte's sonnet better:

> Monsieur, je suis fâché d'être si difficile;
> Et pour l'amour de vous je voudrais de bon cœur
> Avoir trouvé tantôt votre sonnet meilleur.

[1] There are perceptible resemblances between this and Scarron's *L'Héritier ridicule*, particularly in the hostility of the two women and the cattiness of their exchanges (Act IV), as pointed out above, pp. 60-1. But the farcical elements are not in Molière and it need hardly be said that his treatment is considerably more sophisticated.

Upon which the Marshals, no doubt heaving a sigh of relief, caused the two to embrace and hurriedly declared the matter closed.

Hearing this, Éliante characterizes Alceste from a new angle:

> Dans ses façons d'agir il est fort singulier;
> Mais j'en fais, je l'avoue, un cas particulier,
> Et la sincérité dont son âme se pique
> A quelque chose en soi de noble et d'héroïque.
> C'est une vertu rare au siècle d'aujourd'hui
> Et je la voudrais voir partout comme chez lui.
>
> (IV. i)

Far from finding Alceste's bluntness ridiculous, she calls it sincerity and describes it as a noble and heroic virtue which she wishes were commoner in the world today. The significance of this is not greatly diminished by the revelation that she has a soft spot for Alceste and would be ready to marry him if – but only if – the apparently incompatible union with Célimène fell through.

This is immediately put to the test in the most tactless way possible. Reeling under the disclosure of the letter to Oronte, Alceste enters, crying in the language of the tragicomedy:

> Ah! tout est ruiné;
> Je suis, je suis trahi, je suis assassiné!
> Célimène . . . Eût-on pu croire cette nouvelle?
> Célimène me trompe et n'est qu'une infidèle.[1]

She has behaved abominably, he insists, and now I appeal to you to avenge me:

ÉLIANTE Moi, vous venger! Comment?

ALCESTE   En recevant mon cœur.
> Acceptez-le, Madame, au lieu de l'infidèle:
> C'est par là que je puis prendre vengeance d'elle,
> *Et je la veux punir* par les sincères vœux,
> Par le profond amour, les soins respectueux,

---

[1] Cf.

DOM GARCIE   Ah! tout est ruiné:
> Je suis, je suis trahi, je suis assassiné;
> Un homme . . . Sans mourir te le puis-je dire?
> Un homme dans les bras de l'infidèle Elvire!
> (*Dom Garcie de Navarre*, IV. vii)

> Les devoirs empressés et l'assidu service
> Dont ce cœur va vous faire un ardent sacrifice.

Firmly but kindly Éliante does not accept a heart offered her for such reasons and remarks that Alceste's anger will probable cool in the presence of his beloved Célimène. Alceste is certain that it will not. She is coming now:

> La voici. Mon courroux redouble à cette approche.

The next scene (IV. iii) is one of the finest that Molière ever wrote. Its tone is set by the opening lines:

> ALCESTE [aside]   O Ciel! de mes transports puis-je être le maître?
> CÉLIMÈNE [aside]   Ouais![1]

Alceste begins by expressing his heroic indignation in the appropriate style:

> Ce n'était pas en vain que s'alarmait ma flamme.
> Par de fréquents soupçons qu'on trouvait odieux
> Je cherchais le malheur qu'ont rencontré mes yeux,
> Et, malgré tous vos soins et votre adresse à feindre,
> Mon astre me disait ce que j'avais à craindre.

Célimène affects surprise. Have you gone mad? she asks, in an ordinary social tone:

> D'où vient donc, je vous prie, un tel emportement?
> Avez-vous, dites-moi, perdu le jugement?

When Alceste shows her the incriminating letter, she immediately admits that it is hers but feigns innocence. Why does he think it was for Oronte, or for any other man?

> Mais si c'est une femme à qui va ce billet,
> En quoi vous blesse-t-il? et qu'a-t-il de coupable?

This is too much for Alceste to swallow in that non-lesbian world. He will read it her to see how she can explain the passionate terms she has used. From that point Célimène passes from defence to attack and Alceste from indignation to pleading. She will not explain, she replies. What right has Alceste to question her? Metaphorically, he is at once

---

[1] 'Oh dear!'

half on his knees. He begs her to convince him that the letter could have been written to a woman. No, says Célimène, tightening her hand on the whip, of course it was for Oronte, I like and admire him. Take that as you please, but above all stop pestering me.

Seeing clearly through her game, Alceste nevertheless offers a compromise such as he would never have suggested over the sonnet. At least make some excuse, he says, and I will do my utmost to believe it (my italics):

> Efforcez-vous ici de *paraître* fidèle,
> Et je m'efforcerai, moi, de vous *croire* telle.

Me, be hypocritical to please you? asks Célimène in a quite natural (for the character) yet deeply ironical reversal of values. You do not 'merit' my love if you are mad enough to suggest such a thing:

> Allez, vous êtes fou dans vos transports jaloux
> Et ne méritez pas l'amour qu'on a pour vous.

(She is still using this bait, and one finds later that it is not merely bait either.)

> Je voudrais bien savoir qui pourrait me contraindre
> A descendre pour vous *aux bassesses de feindre*,
> Et pourquoi, si mon cœur penchait d'autre côté,
> Je ne le dirait pas *avec sincérité*.

Alceste's moral universe is swimming around him. He is perfectly aware of her duplicity which she calls sincerity but he cannot break free. Finally he gives what for him appears the ultimate proof of his love. He wishes that she were unlovable, reduced to misery, of obscure birth with no inherited rank or wealth, so that *he* could rescue her from this situation by the 'outstanding sacrifice' of his heart to her,

> Et que j'eusse la joie et la gloire en ce jour
> De vous voir *tenir tout* des mains de mon amour.

Célimène's reply is exactly what might be expected:

> C'est me vouloir du bien d'une étrange manière!
> Me préserve le Ciel que vous ayez matière!

The scene ends with this and with the entry of Alceste's lackey to tell him that something disastrous has happened. He is comically muddled about what it is, but thinks it has to do with the lawsuit and insists that instant flight is necessary to escape arrest.

In Act V the storm-clouds gather, though not over Alceste, whose lost lawsuit gives him the opportunity for a last diatribe against corruption but whose consequences are not quite as grave as his lackey supposed. He has not been arrested and Philinte reminds him that he can appeal, but Alceste rejects this. It is final proof

> De la méchanceté des hommes de notre âge.
> Ce sont vingt mille francs qu'il m'en pourra coûter;
> Mais pour vingt mille francs j'aurai droit de pester
> Contre l'iniquité de la nature humaine
> Et de nourrir pour elle une immortelle haine.
>
> (V. i)

This links up with his strictures of Acts I and II and is no less violent. But in the meantime things have happened which could modify our opinion of him. He may have a good case after all. The unmasking of Célimène supports that. Challenged to choose definitely between him and Oronte she still prevaricates, refusing to be pinned down, and in the final scene which brings on stage all the main characters, including the two *petits marquis*, she is shown up as a thoroughly frivolous woman. She has played with all her admirers and letters she has written to them in which she criticizes the others are produced and read. Each in turn takes final leave of her, except Alceste. She admits that she has wronged him – though not the others – and apologizes for it. He is ready to forgive her and marry her, provided she will agree to a plan which has been maturing in his mind since the news of his lost lawsuit. He has determined to flee all human society and withdraw to his 'désert' or wilderness. Will she go with him? If she loves him as he loves her, what should the rest of the world matter?

The prospect of spending the rest of her life alone with Alceste in some remote country spot (characteristically, he is not specific) appals Célimène, but she is sincere in recognizing the nobility of the offer, merely saying that such things are above her level (my italics):

> La solitude effraie une âme de vingt ans;
> Je ne sens point la mienne *assez grande*, *assez forte*
> Pour me résoudre à prendre un dessein de la sorte.

She is not speaking ironically since she goes on to offer her hand to Alceste, but in more normal circumstances. Alceste, absolute and idealistic to the last, turns down this half-measure contemptuously:

> Puisque vous n'êtes point en des liens si doux [marriage]
> Pour trouver tout en moi, comme moi tout en vous,
> Allez, je vous refuse . . .

and the two part for good.

So the subtitle of 'l'atrabilaire amoureux' has relevance after all. The Alceste–Célimène relationship provides the main substance of the plot and, besides this, is essential to the Misanthrope's characterization. As we have said, his irrational passion is his weak spot as a man, but it makes him credible and removes him from the field of the 'personnage ridicule'. In all his other dealings he is a man of high principles which he applies to petty examples: the sonnet, affected foppery in dress and manners, the lawsuit. These are not worthy of his resoundingly righteous indignation and the incongruity can be exploited comically and in several passages is. But even when he seems to have made a complete fool of himself reservations occur. There are his own comments: 'Messieurs, je ne croyais pas être si plaisant que je suis'. There is Éliante's defence of him: 'Et la sincérité dont son âme se pique / A quelque chose en soi de noble et héroïque.' And Philinte, in spite of his remonstrances and the snubs he receives, stands by him loyally throughout. If he laughs at all it is not at the man but at his conduct on particular occasions, and then with the object of persuading him to change it.

Molière might have eliminated or reduced these reservations by angling all this differently, but nothing of the kind could be done with the Célimène relationship. Célimène is in the wrong. Though wonderfully characterized and fully 'understandable' she cannot be represented as a sympathetic character. Alceste's approaches are clumsy and counterproductive because based on a misconception of the nature of love and this 'object of love' in particular. The misconception is highly dramatic but certainly not laughable. To make it appear so the whole play would have to be taken to pieces and reassembled on different lines, perhaps by a Scarron or a Desmarets. In short, the Misanthrope *per se* could be conceived as a fully comic character, the Misanthrope in love could not. An actor's problem is where to strike the balance, in the context naturally of the reactions of the other characters and their presentation.

This has given rise to the different interpretations of the part. Those which depict a man in deadly earnest who gets carried away by his convictions into some 'very peculiar' (in Éliante's words, 'fort singulier') words and acts but not follies – one has only to compare the 'follies' of some of Molière's other great characters – seem the most satisfactory.

The text shows that the problem is solvable and the character of Alceste consistent, and there is a strong pragmatic argument to support this. It is not that Molière painted himself in Alceste and his wife Armande in the flirtatious Célimène. Biographical commentators have played with this theory without getting much further. The real reason is theatrical. Molière himself acted the lead in this play which he seems to have been working on for at least two years. Had he nevertheless found difficulties in interpreting the character it is inconceivable that he would not have altered his text in performance and left us with a different version from that published in December 1666, six months after the première. So one has only to discover what Molière's interpretation was. 'Only' is the tantalizing word, since there is little surviving contemporary critical comment, though what there is indicates that no one was perplexed by Alceste's portrayal.[1] The play was at first a reasonable but not conspicuous success, though there may have been extraneous reasons for this. All one can say is that Alceste evidently made sense on the stage for both Molière and his audiences.

The predominance of this character tends to obscure other qualities of the play. It can be approached as a collection of portraits – and this typifies much of Molière and his conception of comedy – but the

---

[1] In his notice of 12 June 1666 the gazette-writer Robinet praised the comedy's high tone, stylistic and moral. He saw in Alceste a worthy reformist critic of the faults of the age ('. . . dans son noble emportement / Le vice est l'objet de sa haine, / Et nullement la race humaine, / Comme elle était à ce Timon / Dont l'histoire a gardé le nom . . .'). But having praised the moralizer he has little to say about the character, except to suggest that he was confused, apparently by love, and impelled to change his life completely: 'Chacun voit donc là sa peinture, / Mais de qui tous les traits censeurs, / Le rendant confus de ses mœurs, / Le piquent de la belle envie / De mener toute une autre vie . . .' (See P. Mélèse, Le Théâtre et le public (Paris, 1934), pp. 257–8, for the complete quotation.)

The appreciative Lettre sur la comédie du 'Misanthrope' (in which Molière may have collaborated and which he approved sufficiently to print as an introduction to the first edition of the play) examines the character of Alceste and concludes: 'Pour ce qui regarde le Misanthrope, on peut dire qu'il soutient son caractère jusques au bout.' Also: 'Voilà ce que je pense de la comédie du Misanthrope amoureux, que je trouve d'autant plus admirable que le héros en est le plaisant sans être trop ridicule.'

portraits are not isolated or static, as they were in the early *comédie-ballet* of *Les Fâcheux*. They merge into and modify each other, giving movement and the element of 'surprise'.[1] This is the difference between the experienced dramatist and Desmarets in *Les Visionnaires* or a moralist-observer such as La Bruyère. Even when Molière's 'portraits' are presented as set-pieces, as they are in the scenes illustrating Célimène's malicious wit (II. iv and V. iv), they are closely linked to the action.

The overall portrait is of a society represented by the group who meet in Célimène's salon and which is well above the merchant bourgeoisie. Implicit in the background are associations with the Court and with other milieux of high standing, legal or financial. It is against this that Alceste pits himself and, to return to the hypothetical lawsuit mentioned on p. 134 above, one would decide that the parties are Alceste versus Society, to which he would attach most of the other 'vices' listed, except Common Sense and Reality. There is little doubt that Alceste is the plaintiff, though he need not have been. He could have avoided a confrontation, just as he could have avoided it in his dispute with Oronte in the play. Alceste loses, though he could appeal. He is unlikely to. Just as he rejected Philinte's suggestion of an appeal in the play, one cannot see him responding to the same Philinte's hint of a compromise or climb-down in the two closing lines addressed to Éliante:

> Allons, Madame, allons employer toute chose
> Pour rompre le dessein que son cœur se propose.

So the comedy ends on a deliberately faint question-mark.[2] Just possibly Alceste might be dissuaded from retiring to his 'desert'. One does not know, one is not supposed to. Molière wrote no sequel to *Le Misanthrope*, nor any other play which might be construed as one. He left it at that.

⚜

[1] Mentioned by Molière as an attraction of comedy in one of his rare comments: 'Éraste: Comme aux comédies, il est bon de vous laisser le plaisir de la surprise' (*Monsieur de Pourceaugnac*, I. i). This bears on the situational effect.

[2] The Comédie Française traditionally omits these lines in performance, bringing down the curtain on Alceste's declared intention to

> ... chercher sur la terre un endroit écarté
> Où d'être homme d'honneur on ait la liberté.

This ending is clearer-cut, but hardly justified.

The last three plays examined throw fuller light on Molière as a satirist. To be effective, particularly on the stage, satire must come into the open. Its object must be identified and its absurdity or harmfulness clearly shown. This was done for religion in its contemporary forms in *Tartuffe* and *Dom Juan*. It was done elsewhere for medicine though, since the deficiencies of doctors were so widely derided in the seventeenth century, Molière was not treading here on such delicate ground. As for contemporary society, classes of it are satirized in various plays, but in the test-case of *Le Misanthrope*, in which Molière could have challenged society at the highest level below the king, including for once the Court, and in places appears to do so, the issue, as we have seen, remains doubtful. Whether through prudence or temperament, Molière did not press this particular attack.

Except for religion and medicine the satirical elements are diffused through his plays and not carried to the bitter conclusions demanded by unequivocal satire. There are satirical implications in *Alice in Wonderland*, but lying so far beneath the surface that one could never class that work as a satire. At the other extreme George Orwell's 'children's story' *Animal Farm* is an unqualified satire. Molière's comedies lie somewhere between the two.

Always ambivalence, always compromise? some impatient reader might ask. He could be answered, in rather outdated terms, by invoking the theory of the classical norm. According to this, reason (e.g. Descartes) and moderation (but e.g. who?) were the ruling principles of seventeenth-century thought and resulted in a laudable and valid view of human nature negatively defined as the avoidance of excess. Contemporaries themselves used this argument, but examples of practice have been hard to find. In the drama alone Corneille, Scarron, Racine and Italianate spectacle all present exceptions. Among the major writers only Boileau seems to support the theory (he was an open satirist) and then Molière, whom he much admired. Molière takes his stand firmly on the 'normal' level and from there lashes out in all directions at any departures from it. There is something to be said for this even today. It can be used to explain his stance if a neatly coherent explanation on general lines is required. But a second look at all his grotesque and eccentric characters and situations and a reminder of the imaginative invention which enabled him to create them cause one to entertain serious doubts. It is true that he often introduced the *raisonneur*, the character who preaches moderation and common sense (Philinte in *Le Misanthrope*, Cléante in *Tartuffe*, Béralde in *Le Malade imaginaire*, and several others), but it would be hazardous to conclude that he always expresses Molière's point of view. Adopting that simple interpretation, how could Molière speak through both Philinte and Alceste?[1] The *raisonneur* certainly has a dramatic function He underlines the craziness of the other characters to whom he serves as a foil. He makes it even clearer that they are 'personnages ridicules' incarnating reprehensible failings and one can broadly concede this interpretation of him while not overlooking the half-developed *raisonneur* Sganarelle of *Dom Juan*, who has a ridiculous side of his own.

So one can laboriously construct a 'philosophy' for Molière, but add at once that this line of approach is unrewarding and misdirected. It is not his 'philosophy' but his 'psychology', expressed in terms of drama precisely through the eccentric but still recognizable characters, that supplies the life and interest of his plays. Whittle down such characters and little remains but some sensible advice.

The examinations we have made of particular plays should make further generalizations less necessary and indicate the variety of Molière's production and the principal qualities of his work. If this had to be defined in one sentence, one would call it comedy of character inextricably associated with comedy of manners, rendered according to a largely inherited technique but made original by an extraordinary sense of the comic possibilities of non-exuberant language.

A complete list of Molière plays will be found on pp. 275-6.

---

[1] Like any other good dramatist or novelist he could of course 'be' both, and for that matter all the other characters as well, by the usual exercise of a creative imagination. But this is a psychological process having nothing to do with the external question of his opinion on misanthropy.

THE SHADOW OF
MOLIÈRE

Plays contemporary with Molière's:
Racine's Les Plaideurs, *Quinault's* La Mère
coquette, *T. Corneille's* Le Baron d'Albrikac – *comic*
aunts and the suivante *Lisette – the Hôtel de Bourgogne actor-*
dramatists – Montfleury fils – *Hauteroche and* Crispin médecin –
rise of one-act comedy – contemporary realism and rusticity –
Baron's plays – Brueys and Palaprat: Le Grondeur –
Boursault: Le Mercure galant – *his* Ésope
plays and attempted innovation

The period covered in this chapter runs from the 1660s to the early
1690s. Though lively enough it produced only a few outstanding
comedies apart from Molière's. The first that will be described were
written in Molière's lifetime and show less dependence on his example
than many produced after his death in 1673. These latter, to make a
broad generalization, represent either attempts to continue or renew
him or embryonic features of a new comedy whose full emergence is
not apparent until the turn of the century.

Around the dates of *Le Misanthrope* and *Tartuffe* three disparate
comedies appeared, of which easily the best was Racine's *Les Plaideurs*
(November 1668). This hilarious three-act satire on the Parisian legal
world was at first a failure, but soon established its popularity and for
over 200 years was acted more frequently at the Comédie Française
than all but three of Molière's plays and any of Racine's tragedies.[1]

The conventional pair of young lovers who obtain consent to their
marriage by a trick belonged to the general French tradition and are
far too familiar, both before and after Racine, to be described as a

[1] See Lancaster, *History*, III, p. 807.

specific borrowing. In any case their main function is to provide a plot which allows the appearance of the divertingly grotesque characters: Perrin Dandin, the judge so obsessed with judging that he has to be restrained from doing so in the middle of the night and pushed back into his house when he tries to escape through a window; the equally obsessed litigants, the bourgeois Chicaneau and the Countess; and the minor legal officers, Petit-Jean, the *portier* or usher, always ready for a bribe, and l'Intimé, the secretary acting as counsel for the defence. These two are exaggeratedly loquacious in the manner of Scarron who may well have furnished suggestions to Racine, as did Rabelais in providing two of the character-names. In any case *Les Plaideurs* belongs to the burlesque tradition for its verbal exuberance and wit as well as for its farcical elements. Besides the antics of Perrin Dandin there is the memorable scene (III. iii) in which puppies are brought into court to persuade the judge to deal mercifully with their father, accused of stealing a capon. They forget themselves in the judge's lap:

L'INTIMÉ	Venez, famille désolée . . .
	Nous sommes orphelins; rendez-nous notre père,
	Notre père, par qui nous fûmes engendrés,
	Notre père, qui nous . . .
DANDIN	Tirez, tirez, tirez.
L'INTIMÉ	Notre père, messieurs . . .
DANDIN	Tirez donc. Quels vacarmes!
	Ils ont pissé partout.
L'INTIMÉ	Monsieur, voyez nos larmes.

Racine, who had just written *Andromaque* and was establishing himself as a leading tragic dramatist, seems to have been slightly embarrassed by his lone venture into broad comedy. He was experimenting, he says in the *Au lecteur*, with an adaptation of *The Wasps* of Aristophanes and, though Aristophanes was not considered a highly respectable author, at least he was a Greek. The adaptation, in spite of taking situations and speeches from Aristophanes' farce, was a very free one. The manners and characters were entirely French. Racine says that the germ of the play was a scenario he intended to write for the Italian comedians but dropped when the actor Scaramouche, who presumably had ordered it, left Paris for a time. This was an odd thing for Racine to have done but, true or not, it gave an additional excuse

F

for the farcical features. Urged on by his friends, some of whom took a hand themselves in the composition, continues Racine, he soon completed a full-length comedy for the regular stage. This explanation, not unparalleled in the seventeenth century when an author wished to disclaim full responsibility for a scabrous or dubious work, was meant to suggest a collective improvisation round a cheerful dinner-table but could never account for so master-minded a comedy as *Les Plaideurs*.

So Racine joined, at a rather late date, the principal exponents of the burlesque, going like Aristophanes – to quote again the *Au lecteur* – 'au-delà du vraisemblable' and indulging in fantasy which Molière, at least in theory if not always in practice, had felt it desirable to avoid. Otherwise the characters would not be recognized as projections of contemporary society and there would be no moral lesson. Another non-Molièresque feature of *Les Plaideurs* was the portrayal of ridiculous legal types. Though found in some earlier minor comedies they had not figured among Molière's great eccentrics, but only in such secondary parts as Monsieur Loyal of *Tartuffe*. They became increasingly important in later comedy.

The comedy of intrigue persisted in Quinault's *La Mère coquette* (1665) and Thomas Corneille's *Le Baron d'Albrikac* (1667). Both approach romantic comedy in the importance attached to the relationship of two young lovers and their final marriage, but the second is more humorous than sentimental and a good example of the tendency to exploit romantic situations for comic effect. Quinault's play, generally considered the best of his four comedies,[1] imitated a play of the same title by de Visé. It includes a lovers' misunderstanding provoked by an intriguing serving-maid, a conceited and cowardly marquis closer to the old *fanfaron* than to Molière's ultra-fashionable Court types, but above all a woman who is jealous of her own daughter and wishes to marry her young admirer whom she thinks she attracts. This situation, new at that date, is paralleled by the infatuation of the young hero's elderly father for the daughter whom *he* intends to marry in place of his son. (Cf. Molière's later *L'Avare*, 1668.) There is

[1] See pp. 45–6 above for his comedy *Les Rivales*.

some mockery of his age, his sexual vigour and his cough, as with Harpagon.

Old men incongruously in love were already too frequent in comedy to be remarkable. One could add to Harpagon, among others, Arnolphe of *L'École des femmes* and Géraste of P. Corneille's *La Suivante*, as well as the archetypal Pantalone of the *commedia dell'arte*. But the 'coquettish mother' of indeterminate age was novel, or relatively so. In Thomas Corneille's *Le Baron d'Albrikac* she is an aunt, so acquiring less serious connotations (aunts being traditionally funnier than mothers), and the desirable girl whom she tries to keep in the background is her niece. The resulting situations are fully developed by the younger Corneille in a manner that made this play a model for later comedies, in which amorous aunts, usually wealthy, abound. The valet's exclamation, 'O le fâcheux dragon qu'une tante éternelle!' could serve as an epigraph for several of them.

By the end of the century 'La Tante', with no personal name, had become a type-character as immediately recognizable to audiences as 'La Coquette'. The main humour in *Le Baron d'Albrikac* arises from the attempts of the hero to approach the niece, which he can only do by pretending to be in love with the aunt, who nearly captures him. Complications caused by stratagems desperately invented to get him off the hook come thick and fast, as might be expected in Thomas Corneille. The servants are prominent. The *suivante*, Lisette, is impudent and ironically wise. She is one of the first of the *suivantes* of that name, which appears so often in later comedies that one loses count.[1] She might also be called a type-character except, as will be seen, that she does vary and evolve. The valet Philipin, the actor who had succeeded Jodelet in Scarron's comedies, has a subdued part in this one. His old function is assumed by another valet, La Montagne, impersonating the provincial Baron d'Albrikac and conducting a mock wooing of the aunt. The real Baron never appears but it is understood that he will arrive later and marry the aunt for her money. There is no unmasking in the actual play, which ends on a satisfactorily cheerful note. Obviously it owes much to Scarron as well as to its more immediate source, Moreto's *La tía y la sobrina*. It is notable for keeping

[1] There was one much earlier and apparently isolated Lisette in Du Ryer's *Les Vendanges de Suresne* (c. 1633). She was a country-bred *suivante* with the chief characteristics of her namesakes. Scarron also had a Lisette in *Le Marquis ridicule* (1655) and Molière in *L'Amour médecin* (1665).

alive these two traditions, the Scarronesque and the Spanish, and for its effective utilization of typical comic resources which recur throughout the century.

❦

These plays, including Racine's, were produced by the Hôtel de Bourgogne, competing with Molière at the height of his success. Most of the other comic drama, at least until 1680, was similarly motivated. Much of it was the work of actors belonging to the troupe of the Hôtel: Champmeslé, the elder Poisson, Brécourt, Hauteroche, while Antoine de Montfleury (1639–85), the son of the tragedian whom Molière mocked in *L'Impromptu de Versailles*, belonged wholly to the Hôtel through his family ties though he did not act himself. His *Impromptu de l'Hôtel de Condé* has already been referred to.[1] Apart from that he wrote two five-act comedies with Spanish settings but Molièresque titles, *L'École des jaloux* (*c.* 1662) and *L'École des filles* (*c.* 1665). His *Le Gentilhomme de la Beauce* (1670) was inspired by *Monsieur de Pourceaugnac* and *La Fille capitaine* (1671) partly by *Le Bourgeois Gentilhomme*. However, his most successful play, *La Femme juge et partie* (1668), was quite independent of Molière. It concerns a husband who wrongly suspects his wife of infidelity and maroons her on a desert island from which she returns after various adventures disguised as a man with authority to have him tortured and executed for his crime. In the end she reveals herself and forgives him. This play, based on a much earlier work by Lope de Vega, was another example of a Spanish romantic *comedia* – almost a tragicomedy – adapted in a comic direction by the husband's fear of cuckoldry and his craven attitude when threatened by his returned wife. It is still not particularly laughable and the dialogue is undistinguished.

As for Hauteroche (*c.* 1630–1707), the most notable of the Hôtel de Bourgogne group, he wrote several plays reminiscent of Molière, including the three-act *Crispin médecin* (1670), which contains a comic doctor and a valet whose well-meant efforts land him in serious trouble. This innocuous play, in which most of the characters are 'nice people', was included in the repertory of the Comédie Française and constantly performed well into the nineteenth century. It must have owed its popularity to the scene in which Crispin, surprised in the doctor's house, pretends to be a corpse and is threatened with

[1] See p. 92 above, footnote 2 on the Comic War.

dissection until the doctor is called away just in time. The comic
potentialities of supposed death were explored also in Hauteroche's
next play, *Le Deuil* (1672), a cheerful little one-acter in which a son
pretends that his father has died and tries to collect money as his heir.
The father turns up and is taken for a ghost by the other characters.
This idea was another borrowing from Molière, an expansion of a
similar situation in *L'Étourdi*, Act II.

The most interesting development from the 1660s on, attributable
particularly to Hauteroche and his companion playwrights, was the
rise of the one-act comedy. It was usually performed as a sweetener
after a full-length tragedy or tragicomedy to send the audience home
in a cheerful mood. Molière had practised it too, but it was not dominant in his work as a whole. In stage practice it can be explained by the
inability of his shorter-winded rivals to compete with him in full-
length comedy and equally by the fact that they specialized in tragedy
in any case and chiefly needed a supply of light curtain-entertainments.
Some of these were crude farces, a return to an older tradition, or a
continuation of it when one remembers that the Italian comedians
were still doing the same thing in their ever-popular performances.
Others had more serious merits and can be characterized as compressed
comedies built round a single situation. Some of these one-acters are
almost half as long as the regular five-act comedies.

They are notable for their realism. Though the characters may be
caricatured on conventional lines, the plays are firmly anchored to
contemporary life and manners. Some echo topical events and are
anecdotic in their treatment of them, so once again recalling the farces
of the 1620s. Many have settings of the kind pioneered by Pierre
Corneille in *La Galerie du Palais*, extending now to country locations
such as farms and inns. Rustic characters grow in number and importance. Usually there is a link with the capital which permits a laughable
contrast with the more sophisticated Parisian visitors. The country
nobility are ridiculed, just as in Molière's *Monsieur de Pourceaugnac*
and *La Comtesse d'Escarbagnas*. The peasants speak rustic or stage-
rustic French as in *Dom Juan* – it seems impossible to get away from
Molière – and this, together with the occasional Swiss or regional
accent, becomes an important element in the comic convention. Two
early examples are Brécourt's *Noce de village* (1666) and Hauteroche's
Le Deuil, which takes place on a farm. Later, to anticipate the next
chapter, it will be used effectively by Dancourt, who begins to turn

the tables in a few plays by making his provincials cleverer and more sympathetic than his Parisians, so faintly initiating the eighteenth-century fashion of rusticity and the revival of lighthearted pastoral. But rusticity for the Hôtel de Bourgogne dramatists was still un-reservedly comic and played a necessary part in their success in estab-lishing local settings and local colour as accepted features of the comic stage. Whether Parisian or provincial their numerous farces and sketches were very much of the moment. This was the cause both of their immediate popularity and of their later neglect. They can still be read with enjoyment – those that were printed – but lack durable qualities. On a general view they were transitional in form and content but, taken as a whole, present nearly all the features that would re-appear in the work of more substantial playwrights.

In this respect they went beyond Molière more markedly than the five-act plays also written in this period in a conscious attempt to renew him. He was regarded first and foremost as a master of the big comedy of character, but the difficulty was that he appeared to have exhausted the range of great eccentrics round whom a substantial play could be built. Who could be placed beside his Arnolphe, his Hypo-crite, his Alceste, his Harpagon, his Monsieur Jourdain, his Argan, his Learned Ladies? The problem was summed up in the Prologue of Dufresny's *Le Négligent* (1692): 'Molière a bien gâté le théâtre. Si l'on donne dans son goût, "Bon," dit la critique, "cela est pillé, c'est Molière tout pur." S'en écarte-t-on un peu, "Oh! ce n'est pas là Molière." '

One could neither escape from Molière nor improve on him, though attempts to do so were made in the 1680s by Michel Baron (1653–1729) who had joined Molière's company three years before his death, then quickly transferred to the Hôtel de Bourgogne. There and in the Comédie Française he became a star actor in both tragic and comic parts. His five-act *L'Homme à bonne fortune* (1686) has for its hero the male counterpart of the coquette. He attracts women easily and plays upon their feelings, but is not specially interested in their money, as was the increasingly common chevalier type. Vain about his appear-ance, he dresses ultra-fashionably, using perfume and make-up. He resembles the 'fop' of English Restoration comedy, or the dandy of a later age. But though socially interesting and conceived on more serious lines than the *petit marquis*, he does not equal the great gro-tesques. Neither does the contrasted hero of *Le Jaloux* (1687), an aggressively masculine type who suffers from a pathological jealousy which ruins his love affairs. Here again, the character is not sufficiently striking to raise him above the numerous other jealous husbands or lovers of comedy. Between these plays Baron produced *La Coquette et la Fausse Prude*, a portrayal of two familiar types which Molière had rendered better in *Le Misanthrope*.

The search for some new eccentricity had however begun, encouraged by the publication in 1688 of La Bruyère's *Les Caractères*, revised and expanded through six subsequent editions until the last in 1694. But, though generally influential, La Bruyère did not in the end provide any central model for stage comedy, the media being too different (a partial exception was Regnard's *Le Distrait* (1697), a weak play). Before Regnard but after Baron there was an early sustained attempt to dramatize a new type-character in *Le Grondeur* (1691), written in collaboration by Brueys and Palaprat.[1]

The protagonist, incidentally a doctor, is a confirmed grumbler and scolder. Nothing pleases him. As 'le plus bourru des hommes' he is a distant cousin of the Misanthrope, on a lower and plainly ridiculous level. He is surrounded by all the familiar devices and characters: a lovers' intrigue which misleads him into agreeing to marriage contracts for his son and daughter, a resourceful *soubrette* (Cathau) and valet (L'Olive) and a reasonable and reasoning brother called Ariste. The newest and to modern eyes the most interesting development in the play is his treatment of his younger son, at once humanly plausible and a reflection of contemporary conditions. Invariably scolded by his father, the fifteen-year-old Brillon perseveres under his tutor and produces a faultless piece of work which he shows proudly to his parent. Even this is criticized, upon which Brillon violently tears up his books and runs away from home. It is feared that the missing boy has been snapped up by a recruiting-officer and enrolled as a drummer in a regiment about to depart for Madagascar. His father, who is fond of him but unable to show it, is said to be in danger of being forcibly recruited himself if he tries to recover him. The regiment needs a doctor. 'And they are even recruiting girls to take with them' says

---

[1] David Augustin de Brueys (1640–1723) and Jean Palaprat (c. 1650–1721) were two lawyers from south-western France who rose to favour together and obtained lucrative offices or pensions. They wrote a number of plays, separately or in collaboration, all unremarkable except for *Le Grondeur* and *L'Avocat Patelin* (1706).

Cathau when it is suggested that she should go and plead with the military. This is in fact a ploy invented by the servants. Brillon has been found and is safe in the house of his uncle Ariste.

The episode contributes to the general liveliness of the play, which was received with enthusiasm. But as a comedy of character it still does not match any of Molière's. The abnormality of the Grumbler is not sufficiently incongruous,[1] neither is the play constructed basically round it. What Molière made to appear so easy was not so in other hands.

✽✽✽

The most noteworthy experiments in a new form of comedy were made by Edme Boursault (1638–1710) who had no close professional involvement in the theatre, which accounts both for his several failures when he wrote for it and for his relative originality. He was a typical man-of-letters who could turn his hand to the novel and short story and to literary journalism in general. While secretary to the Duchess of Angoulême he provided his patron with a 'gazette en vers burlesques' which never reached publication. He was part of the Parisian literary scene and his plays are 'literary' also, in subject and inspiration. As a playwright he began under the shadow of Molière. Though it is uncertain whether his first play, Le Médecin volant (1661), was an imitation of Molière's farce of the same name or of a common Italian model,[2]

---

[1] The question of comic types is discussed in the play itself:

M. GRICHARD [le Grondeur]   Je ne suis, je pense, ni fourbe, ni avare, ni menteur, ni babillard, comme vous …

ARISTE   Il est vrai, vois n'avez aucun de ces vices qu'on a joués jusqu'à présent sur le théâtre et qui frappent les yeux de tout le monde; mais vous en avez un qui empoisonne toute la douceur de la vie et qui peut-être est plus incommode dans la société que tous les autres … on n'a jamais un seul moment de repos avec ceux que leur malheureux tempérament portent à être toujours fâchés …
(I. vii)

This passage, clinched by the use of tempérament in the last sentence, suggests a conception of character resembling that of Ben Jonson's much older Comedy of Humours in England. It has been argued convincingly that in subtitling Le Misanthrope 'l'Atrabilaire amoureux' Molière was influenced by the theory of the four humours, in this case black bile or melancholy, but went beyond this essentially medical interpretation. See G. Couton's Notice to Le Misanthrope in Œuvres complètes, II (Paris, 1971), p. 125.

[2] For a discussion of this see Lancaster, History, III, p. 683.

there is no question that his next, *Le Portrait du peintre* (1663) was a mildly satirical echo of *La Critique de l'École des femmes*, hurriedly composed as a contribution to the Comic War. In 1669 he tried to attack Boileau in another one-act play, *La Satire des Satires*, but the satirist obtained an injunction which prevented it reaching the stage. For the next fourteen years Boursault wrote nothing for the theatre except an unsuccessful tragedy originally entitled *La Princesse de Clèves* and it was not until 1683 that the Comédie Française performed the first and most amusing – though not the best-known – of his three major plays. The title under which it is usually known, *Le Mercure galant*, was at first changed to *La Comédie sans titre*, apparently because *Le Mercure*'s editor, Donneau de Visé, objected to the use of his paper's name for a play which he supposed would attack it. But in the event it contained nothing uncomplimentary.

It is a *pièce à tiroirs*, like Desmarets's *Les Visionnaires* or Molière's *Les Fâcheux*, in which the meagre story provides the frame for a number of different characters and scenes. The hero Dorante wishes to marry the daughter of an infatuated admirer of *Le Mercure galant* and to achieve this is lent the luxurious apartment (which also serves as an office) of his cousin Licidas, the editor. Dorante is allowed to impersonate him and his valet Merlin is turned into a kind of secretary. They have a variety of visitors of the kind who might approach a newspaper office in most periods. A woman demands the correction of a gossip item unfavourable to herself, others bring compositions of their own which they hope to have printed or come seeking publicity for various ends. The chief of these is a crooked tax-collector who wants a good write-up to help clear his name but is sent packing. An old seaman has a true-life story which he is sure would sell a thousand copies of the paper to his fellow veterans if printed. Several years earlier he fought in the battle in which the great Dutch Admiral De Ruyter died – and he personally was responsible since he brought the match which fired the cannon which killed the famous man. Merlin is there to deal with him. He does so in an unexpected way which would be appreciated by any who had wrestled with the minor complexities of French grammar.

LA RISSOLE [the seaman] ... Lui mort, les Hollandais souffrirent
        bien des mals:
        On fit couler à fond les deux vice-amirals.

MERLIN Il faut dire des maux, vice-amiraux; c'est l'ordre.
LA RISSOLE Les vice-amiraux donc, ne pouvant plus nous mordre,
    Nos coups aux ennemis furent des coups fataux.
    Nous gagnâmes sur eux quatre combats navaux.
MERLIN Il faut dire fatals et navals, c'est la règle.
LA RISSOLE Les Hollandais, réduits à des biscuits de seigle,
    Ayant connu qu'en nombre ils étaient inégals,
    Firent prendre la fuite aux vaisseaux principals.
MERLIN Il faut dire inégaux, principaux, c'est le terme.
LA RISSOLE Enfin, après cela nous fûmes à Palerme.
    Les bourgeois à l'envi nous firent des régaux;
    Les huit jours qu'on y fut furent huit carnavaux.
MERLIN Il faut dire régals et carnavals.
LA RISSOLE   Oh, dame!
    M'interrompre à tous coups c'est me chiffonner l'âme,
    Franchement.
MERLIN   Parlez bien. On ne dit point navaux,
    Ni fataux, ni régaux, non plus que carnavaux.
    Vouloir parler ainsi c'est faire une sottise.
LA RISSOLE Eh mordié, comment donc voulez-vous que je dise?
    Si vous me reprenez lorsque je dis des mals,
    Inégals, principals, et des vice-amirals,
    Lorsqu'un moment après, pour mieux me faire entendre,
    Je dis fataux, navaux, devez-vous me reprendre?
    J'enrage de bon cœur quand je trouve un trigaud
    Qui souffle tout ensemble et le froid et le chaud.
MERLIN J'ai la raison pour moi qui me fait vous reprendre,
    Et je vais clairement vous le faire comprendre.
    Al est un singulier dont le pluriel fait *aux*:
    On dit: C'est *mon égal*, et ce sont *mes égaux*.
    Par conséquent on voit que cette règle seule . . .
LA RISSOLE J'ai des démangeaisons de te casser la gueule.
MERLIN Vous?
LA RISSOLE   Oui, palsandié, moi; je n'aime point du tout
    Qu'on me berce d'un conte à dormir tout debout.
    Lorsqu'on veut me railler je donne sur la face . . .

Having failed to sell his story to *Le Mercure*, La Rissole exits angrily on the words:

Adieu, pays.[1] C'est moi qu'on nomme La Rissole.
Ces bras te deviendront ou fatals ou fataux.
MERLIN Adieu, guerrier fameux par des combats navaux.

(IV. vii)

This and other less sustained examples in Boursault's plays are in the tradition of Scarron, who also named a valet Merlin in *Le Marquis ridicule*, whereas names such as Crispin were usual in Boursault's time. But while the concern with words and the humorous effects to be extracted from them are a prominent feature of Boursault, not unexpected in an author so dependent on literary parody and imitation, this hardly justifies describing his comedies as a whole as burlesque. Their interest lies rather in the depiction of manners incarnated in characters assembled without much structural connection – collections in fact of 'portraits' presented with a minimum of dramatic linking; in that and in the innovation in form attempted in his next and most successful play.

Only an amateur playwright could have conceived *Ésope à la ville* (1690), originally entitled *Les Fables d'Ésope*. The frame, more prominent than in *Le Mercure galant*, is provided by the visit of Aesop, the trusted counsellor and representative of King Croesus, to Léarque, a provincial governor who wishes to give him his daughter Euphrosine in marriage. An ugly hunchback possessed of a beautiful mind, Aesop is repugnant to Euphrosine who is in love with the young and personable Agénor. The girl has an outspoken confidante who insults the physically repulsive Aesop to his face. In the end he supports the marriage with Agénor and the arrangement, accepted by Léarque, satisfies the romantic requirements.[2]

Into this serviceable frame Boursault inserts the main substance and novelty of his play. His Aesop goes about the kingdom giving good advice in the form of fables, which he finds are more readily accepted than 'la vérité toute nue' or plain admonitions. He recites no less than fourteen in the course of the play, the majority imitated from La Fontaine, the others more original. They are invariably effective, opening the eyes of his hearers to the reality or untenability of their

---

[1] 'Compatriot'.
[2] In all this there is a distant reminiscence of Corneille's tragedy *Polyeucte*, in which a provincial governor forced his daughter into a political marriage against the original dictates of her heart. Boursault's character-name Léarque is very uncommon, perhaps unique, in the drama of the century. It resembles Néarque, the name of Polyeucte's martyred friend.

positions. He is consulted by a number of characters seeking justice, favours or useful advice, and deals with them equitably according to their merits. Their requests are typical of the French society of the time (the Greek setting is a mere convention), with a strong emphasis on legal and financial corruption, particularly in local government but deriving ultimately from the central power. Other problems submitted to the sage are different or more personal. A woman comes to complain that her fifteen-year-old daughter has run away with a man, leaving her a note, but loses sympathy when it transpires that she has done the same thing herself in the past – three times. A genealogist offers to provide Aesop, an emancipated slave, with a distinguished pedigree. Two actors invite him to attend their theatre at a performance at which his presence will be advertised in advance. Aesop refuses the shared publicity but offers to come to their next performance in an hour's time, which will be too short to attract a larger audience. He comments on the lack of novelty in the current theatre:

> ÉSOPE Donnez-vous au public force pièces nouvelles?
> PREMIER COMÉDIEN Tous les mois.
> ÉSOPE   Ou du moins qu'on fait passer
> pour telles.
> Depuis neuf ou dix ans, et cela n'est pas beau,
> Vos nouveautés, dit-on, n'ont plus rien de
> nouveau.
>
> (V. iv)

The play was a considerable success, so much so that eleven years later it was followed by a sequel, *Ésope à la cour* (1701), also containing numerous fables and written on a more serious note. At first not very successful, its popularity grew in later years, no doubt in accordance with the moralizing vein in eighteenth-century comedy. That this vein should have appeared as early as the 1690s is slightly surprising, but the vogue of La Fontaine's *Fables* (1668–94) which it reflected indicates that even then it was not an isolated trend. In the theatre, however, it could hardly be expressed in the form Boursault gave it. He was in fact moving towards a kind of openly didactic comedy which had been dead in France since the sixteenth-century *moralités*. At his date that conception was unrevivable and his two Aesop plays are remembered more as interesting curiosities than as significant contributions to dramatic technique.

THE CYNICAL GENERATION: DANCOURT, REGNARD, DUFRESNY, LESAGE

End-of-century materialism – absence of true satire – continuing abortive search for great type-characters – development of secondary characters: the coquette, the suivante, *the* femme d'intrigue, *the rogue-valet, the chevalier – the Italian players and their expulsion – the Théâtre de la Foire –* comédie-vaudeville *and* opéra-comique *– Dancourt:* Le Chevalier à la mode, Les Bourgeoises à la mode *– Vanbrugh's English adaptations –* Les Bourgeoises de qualité *– Dancourt's short comedies – Regnard:* Le Distrait, Le Joueur *and gambling theme – Racinian echoes –* Le Légataire universel *– Regnard's lived experience – Dufresny: short plays –* Le Double Veuvage *– Lesage:* Arlequin roi de Serendib, Crispin rival de son maître *–* Turcaret *– satirical depiction of the financier – opposition to the play*

Louis XIV was a long time dying. Literally six days, but as an effective and successful ruler at least twenty-five years. Two lengthy wars, the War of the League of Augsburg (1688–97) and the still more exhausting War of the Spanish Succession (1701–13), rallied all Western Europe against France and milked the country's wealth, still based primarily on agriculture, into notoriously leaky buckets. Ostentation, financial corruption in both the public and private sectors (though the two were so interlocked that no clear distinction could be drawn) and the abdication of responsibility by potential sub-leaders traceable back to the policy of concentration of power in the crown begun long before by Richelieu, combined to erode the national economy. The confident times in which Molière wrote, when most Frenchmen knew their social place or thought they did, were succeeded by a free-for-all in which class distinctions were increasingly blurred and money, diminishing in real value year by year, was openly seen as the key to eminence.

Comedy came to reflect an acquisitive society, nakedly materialistic and an excellent field for adventurers of several kinds and both sexes. It did not analyse the deeper long-term issues – that was hardly its function – but it mirrored their effects in plays of a lively realism more pointed and witty than the comedies of Pierre Corneille. Romance, requiring some idealization of love and woman, was completely out. The most pointed example of this is in Dufresny's *Le Double Veuvage* (1702) which will be returned to later, but a few lines can be quoted now as an illustration. Two young lovers, the sentimentally inclined Dorante and the highly practical Thérèse, are discussing their prospective marriage:

THÉRÈSE Il faut tirer de l'argent de ma tante, c'est l'essentiel.

DORANTE L'essentiel est de savoir si nous nous convenons l'un à l'autre.

THÉRÈSE Belle demande! A l'humeur près, nous nous convenons à merveille, et je vous corrigerai de vos bizarreries.

We have dated the rise of materialism and its emergence in dramatic comedy to the 1690s because it was in that decade and the following one that most of the plays that typified it were written, though Dancourt began a few years earlier. Earlier still there were already signs of changes in an established class system, based ultimately on approximately definable income groups. Rare though they are, they do suggest that flaws in the socio-economic fabric were perceptible a considerable time before most historians record them or can find them a satisfactory cause.

Without invoking Molière's *Bourgeois Gentilhomme* or his *George Dandin* which, so far as they have a social significance, warn *against* departures from the class system, there had been clearer examples of the prescience of playwrights. Some of the most notable occurred in Hauteroche, that interesting secondary dramatist who appears to be facing both ways. In *Le Deuil* the crafty young hero observed:

Il est vrai qu'aujourd'hui
Passât-on en vertu les vieux héros de Rome,

Si on n'a de l'argent on n'est pas honnête homme.
Il en faut *pour paraître*.[1]

His valet continues:

Aussi, pour en avoir,
Il n'est ressort honteux qu'on ne fasse mouvoir.
Lois, justice, équité, pudeur, vertu sévère:
Partout, au plus offrant on n'attend que l'enchère,
Et je ne sache point d'honneur si bien placé
Dont on ne vienne à bout dès qu'on a financé.

These might be dismissed as the commonplaces of platitudinous scepticism, but the tone and period in which they were uttered (1672) give them added significance. Law and order, justice, equity, modesty in women, austere virtue in women and men, honour, are all on offer to the highest bidder in return for 'finance'. These were the qualities on which the whole ethos of tragedy and tragicomedy from Corneille to Quinault had been built and which the comic spirit now openly called in question. In a sense it had always done so through parody and imitation on a frivolous level, but rarely in such direct and comprehensive terms.

The same tendency appeared more fugitively in other dramatists of the 1670s and 1680s. Boursault, it will be recalled, had a fraudulent tax-official in *Le Mercure galant* of 1683, but it was left for his two *Ésopes* of 1690 and 1701 to emphasize materialistic corruption and condemn it. Not till then did it provide the main and almost exclusive theme of comedy.

The more important dramatists considered in this chapter do not, however, condemn the corrupt world they portray. Unlike their successors, they make few moral judgements, even implicitly, but depict contemporary society with an easy acceptance evidently shared by their audiences. Satire, supposing a basis of moral indignation, is either absent or innocuous. One recalls La Bruyère's penetrating statement: 'A man born Christian and French finds that he is restricted in satire; the great subjects are forbidden him.' The great subjects for La Bruyère were religion and politics. When Molière had dared to touch the first he was in deep trouble. He never touched the

---

[1] 'To make an impression' (my italics). The idea of ostentatious wealth.

second nor probably wanted to. In an absolute regime serious political satire must ultimately criticize the Crown, under which the whole nation is organized, and so will involve the concept of patriotism. This was what La Bruyère meant by 'a man born French'.

Such fundamental themes were ignored by the *fin de siècle* comic dramatists. Whatever deductions may be drawn from it now, their mild satire was either unintentional or did not offend their contemporaries. It bore on minor quirks of manners and character and leaves an impression of the A-Joneses laughing at the B-Joneses, without much malice. It might indeed be questioned whether these playwrights should be called cynical at all, though they certainly appear so from a later point of view. But the kind of cynicism which implies dislike and withdrawal was not theirs. They seemingly enjoyed the society they lived in, expecting nothing different, and wrote of what they perceived with great verve and wit.

Molière's influence was still alive, still bearing principally on the obsessive search for new type-characters mentioned in the previous chapter. None of major importance was created, with one exception, in spite of numerous titles testifying (as had *Le Grondeur*) to the dramatists' intentions but not to their achievement. This was not only because Molière had almost exhausted the possibilities but because the image of society was changing and the nature of comedy with it. The era of great men was over until Napoleon's day and this extended to great funny men. As in tragedy and tragicomedy the outstanding individual was no longer in fashion. This applied equally to the heroic and the antiheroic, to the outstandingly admirable and the outstandingly absurd (also to the outstandingly wicked and the outstandingly passionate who had figured in Cornelian and Racinian tragedy). Comedy responded to the social levelling of the period by presenting, *nolens volens*, collections of scaled-down characters distinguishable from each other but roughly equal in importance. The interplay of interests incarnated in persons became the dominant feature of comic drama and made it largely a comedy of intrigue. But it differed from earlier comedies of intrigue (Rotrou, Quinault, some of Thomas Corneille) by its contemporary realism and, if one must resort to categories, can be described equally well as a comedy of manners.

There were innovations in character, but they were not radical. The older types were developed rather than transformed. Coquettes became more frequent, in some instances deliberately exploiting their charm for social and financial purposes.[1] Attractively innocent young girls were less in evidence. If Dufresny's Thérèse mentioned above was an extreme case of the opposite, there were plenty of other sophisticated young women who knew what they wanted and how to get it at least as well as Corneille's female characters of the 1630s.[2] If ignorant, they nearly always had a worldly-wise *suivante* to instruct them. The *suivante* in fact becomes a kind of second mother, guiding her protégée towards what she believes to be her best chance of happiness. She takes on some of the functions of the old nurse, but is entirely different in her youthful and up-to-date personality.

The *femme d'intrigue*, also originally related to the nurse, grows in importance and activity. No longer or not primarily a procuress, she is often a *marchande de toilette*, dealing in dresses, fashion accessories and jewels. With the entry this gives her to wealthy households, she can arrange loans for extravagant or desperate wives. Sometimes she can provide them from her own resources, having amassed a considerable fortune.

The valet continues his progress. Hardly ever a buffoon, he is not always a permanent valet in this fluid society. He serves a master as long as it suits him but is much more independent than the crafty slaves of Roman comedy or even than Molière's Sganarelle. He is turning into an adventurer who may reach high status or may be hanged for fraud or robbery. He becomes the rogue or *picaro* of Lesage and the literature of Spain, in which country social confusion had set in earlier.

Court characters are often dubious. Their titles may be phoney,

---

[1] It seems fair to say that Molière's Célimène did not do this. She had 'arrived' anyway. Her coquetry was a game which turned against her. The materialistic 'coquette' had a descendant in the 'vamp' of interwar Hollywood films.

[2] They also have analogies with the New Woman of exactly two centuries later, as depicted by Shaw in e.g. *Mrs Warren's Profession*. The practical no-nonsense English New Woman, or rather the image of her, succeeded the image of the sheltered domesticated girl and wife of the Victorian Era just as her French counterpart had shown signs of doing at the end of the Grand Siècle. In France, however, the time was not yet ripe for a progress towards financial and political independence and she was pulled back to femininity. The good businesswomen of the eighteenth century either had to work undercover or exert their influence as courtesans. A further partial parallel which also illustrates the difference is that while the Victorian Mrs Warren had used her business sense as a successful brothel-keeper, her university-educated daughter could exercise her talents openly as an expert accountant.

their birth plebeian. The marquis is not usually absurd as he was in Molière, though there are a few exceptions. He is eclipsed now by the chevalier, a fashionable fortune-hunter particularly interested in wealthy aunts and widows.[1] Sometimes he is an army officer or pretends to be. Other characters from military life occasionally appear, reflecting the influence of the end-of-century wars. They are not the boastful *fanfarons* of earlier comedy, but gallant young soldiers genuinely attractive to women.

The invasion of comedy by crooked financiers and tax-officials, already noted above, is now ubiquitous. With them go lawyers, who almost entirely replace physicians both as frauds and objects of mockery. Medicine is not much satirized, either because the subject has worn thin or because it is acquiring greater credibility and attracting fewer charlatans. Religion is left severely alone, mainly through prudence but also no doubt because of some loss of interest in it. The great age of rationalism is just round the corner. One or two worldly young abbés appear in the plays, but they are not the kind of characters who compromise the Church or were closely associated with it in the public mind.

Changes in the form and style of comic drama become apparent, atrributable partly to material conditions in the theatre. The merger of 1680 had given the Comédie Française a monopoly of tragedies and 'regular' comedies performed in French. Only the Italians were excepted and in order to swell their audiences they began towards 1690, if not earlier, to act plays written partly or wholly in French. They thus provided an alternative market for native playwrights and an opportunity for freer and bolder drama than the State theatre could produce. Though they performed some full-length plays their speciality was still the short farce with *commedia dell'arte* characters comparable in other respects to the Comédie Française farces described above on pp. 155-6, but generally even broader and more personally abusive. This eventually got them into trouble and in the

---

[1] In real life, 'Chevalier' was the title given to the younger son of a noble family who would not inherit the main fortune and so tended to seek advancement by other means. From this evolved the expression 'chevalier d'industrie' ('homme qui vit d'expédients', Dict. Larousse).

summer of 1697 they were banned definitively from Paris,[1] but not before they had influenced important dramatists of the 1690s and the attitude of the Comédie Française itself.

The Italians were not to return as an organized troupe until 1716, when they were reinstated in the permissive atmosphere of the Regency and embarked on a long period of brilliant success. But individual actors remained in Paris and took part in the Théâtre de la Foire which for a time succeeded the Comédie Italienne as irregular theatre.

The fairs had always had their sideshows – acrobats, tightrope dancers, puppets and *farceurs* of the line of Turlupin – but in the early eighteenth century their performances became more ambitious. At the two big fairs of Saint-Germain (February to Easter) and Saint-Laurent (July to September) substantial stages were set up and spectators were charged prices comparable to those of the Comédie Française. This theatre defended itself by obtaining a ban on spoken dialogue by the *forains* which would have limited them to mime and knockabout. The ingenious fair-actors riposted by writing dialogue on banners of various sizes, held up for the audience to read. They also resorted to song, since there was no rule against this. The words of the songs, on well-known airs, were displayed like the dialogue to audiences, who joined in enthusiastically. So was born the *comédie-vaudeville*, a successor and development of Molière's *comédie-ballet*, which soon changed its name to *opéra-comique*. In this the influence of the official Opera, established in 1674 when Lully acquired the Palais Royal after Molière's death, was considerable. The vogue of opera spread to the lighter entertainments of the fairs, which often echoed or parodied it on a popular level. For a few years (*c.* 1719–20) comic opera was suppressed through the efforts not of the State Opera but of the Comédie Française. It recommenced in 1721 and prospered

---

[1] Their crowning indiscretion, which is believed to have determined the expulsion after several previous complaints about their 'indecency', appears to have been the performance of a comedy entitled *La Fausse Prude*, attacking Madame de Maintenon. This at least was the explanation given by Madame de Maintenon's enemy, 'Liselotte', Duchess of Orléans, in a celebrated letter: '. . . They were said to have taken off the old baboon in the funniest way. I wish I had seen the play, but I didn't go in case the old girl told the king that I had started the whole thing to play a joke on her.'

Other contemporaries explained the abrupt expulsion similarly. See particularly P. Mélèse, *Le Théâtre et le public*, pp. 51 ff.

independently for another forty years until it was merged with the Italians.[1]

Meanwhile the Comédie Française itself had felt its influence as well as that of the Italians. Its short comedies from the 1690s on often contained songs or ended with songs and dancing, as in Dancourt and Regnard. These little plays reflected the same social scene as the more ambitious comedies, but on a more carefree note. It is difficult to read cynicism into them, let alone bitterness. Their theme is well summed up in the *Divertissement* which ends Dancourt's *Les Bourgeoises de qualité* (1700), itself a short three-act play originally entitled *La Fête au village*:

> Que la fin de ce siècle est belle
> Pour quiconque a bonne moisson,
> De bon vin, maîtresse fidèle,
> Et des pistoles à foison!

❦

Unlike the other three dramatists considered in this chapter, Florent Carton Dancourt (1661–1725) remained faithful to the Comédie Française throughout his career. He had joined the 'family' of the company, becoming an actor in it after his marriage to Thérèse Le Noir, the daughter of La Thorillière, an old member of Molière's company who had passed in 1680 to the Théâtre Français. Even more esteemed as a dramatist in his day than Regnard, he lost ground to him later, though undeservedly. He wrote prolifically and well.

He composed some fifty plays, long and short, first making his mark in 1687 with *Le Chevalier à la mode*, a five-act comedy often considered to be his best and most important play. It concerns the rich widow of a businessman, Madame Patin, who desires to climb into aristocratic society. She has an uninspiring suitor, Monsieur Migaud, who is a lawyer and accountant, but when advised to accept him by her maid Lisette, she objects that it would hardly alter her

---

[1] For a full account of the Théâtre de la Foire, see H. C. Lancaster, *Sunset*, Ch. xix. For the best short contemporary account see the Preface to *Le Théâtre de la Foire* (1721–37), a collection of pieces chosen by Lesage and d'Orneval, who wrote many of them themselves. This can be read conveniently in *Théâtre du 18e siècle*, Vol. I, ed. J. Truchet (Paris, 1972).

status. Rather than marry Migaud, 'I would just as soon go on being Madame Patin.'

LISETTE Oh, il y a bien de la différence. Le nom de Migaud est un nom de robe, et celui de Patin n'est qu'un nom de financier.

MME PATIN Robe ou finance, tout m'est égal; et depuis huit jours je me suis résolue d'avoir un nom de cour, et de ceux qui emplissent le plus la bouche.

(I. iii)

Her ambition has been baited by the Chevalier de Villefontaine, an adventurer who is playing three women at the same time. His best catch financially would be Madame Patin, the unsophisticated bourgeoise, but he keeps in reserve the Baronne, a genuine and formidable aristocrat of indeterminate age, who buys him a new coach and horses. The third fish is young Lucile, whom he meets in the evenings in the Tuileries. Neither of them knows the other's identity, but Lucile is Madame Patin's niece; she also hopes to marry into the aristocracy. In this skilfully constructed play the suspense interest is sustained until the final scenes when the aunt and the niece, after the Baronne, realize that the same man has been pursuing all of them. Unmasked, the Chevalier takes his discomfiture philosophically. He will go back to the Baronne and persuade her to subsidize him until something better turns up.

Le Chevalier à la mode is a light and lively comedy, not more hilarious than the plays, say, of Noël Coward. The servants Crispin and Lisette make drily cynical remarks about their employers and the upper class in general, but are neither corrupt nor laughable in themselves. Reviewing the play in *Le Mercure galant*, de Visé wrote: 'On y voit des peintures vives et naturelles de beaucoup de choses qui se passent tous les jours dans le monde.'[1] The only somewhat fantastic character is the Baronne, whose role is secondary. She has some basis in reality but can hardly have been an everyday phenomenon. Characteristically she is engaged in a lawsuit (cf. Racine's *Les Plaideurs* and, as mirrored in comedy, a high proportion of the country nobility). Crispin warns the Chevalier against deceiving her because she can shoot hares as well as any man and might come after him with her gun.

[1] *Mercure galant*, October 1687. Quoted by P. Mélèse, *Répertoire analytique*, p. 184.

She arrives at Madame Patin's with a pair of swords and challenges her to a duel. When Madame Patin orders her lackeys to throw her out she exits exclaiming: 'Elle veut devenir femme de qualité et elle n'oserait tirer l'épée!'

Apart from this masculine female eccentric this social comedy uses no other types or situations which would have not have been familiar to contemporary audiences. As for a moral lesson, none is attempted.

Neither is it in Dancourt's second major play, *Les Bourgeoises à la mode*, another five-act comedy produced five years later (1692). Though rather less successful than *Le Chevalier à la mode*, it is a finer play and the classic example of its kind and period. The basis on which it is built, novel in this form in French comedy, is the relationship of two young wives, Angélique and Araminte, married to two elderly pillars of the law, M. Simon, a notary, and M. Griffard, a *commissaire* or police commissioner. They find their husbands dull and over-careful with money, an obstacle to their wishes to lead a less bourgeois social life. The husbands fall in love with each other's wives – secretly, they think, but both wives are aware of it and exchange confidences with some amusement. If they cannot obtain funds direct from their own husbands they will loyally pass on whatever money the other's husband gives them; and as hopeful lovers the lawyers are generous enough.

Around this situation is woven a plot involving other characters. Intermediaries are required. One of them is Frontin, an *intrigant* ready for any dubious work if there is profit in it for himself. Another is the familiar Lisette, Angélique's chambermaid, constantly ready to abet her mistress whom she treats as an equal. The third is Madame Amelin who first appears as a dressmaker presenting a bill for 310 francs owed her by Angélique. She goes on to arrange a loan of 2000 francs on the security of a diamond ring which has an important function in the plot. The Chevalier of this play is a complete fraud. He poses as a courtier, living by gambling and women (which makes him socially acceptable . . .), but he began as a lawyer's clerk in the same office as Frontin until both of them were thrown out. The 'Chevalier' went up in the world while Frontin went down, giving the latter an opportunity for blackmail. The 'Chevalier' is the son of Madame Amelin and is embarrassed to meet her in Angélique's house. He is pursuing neither of the experienced wives but Angélique's young and unsophisticated stepdaughter Mariane. Though his deception is discovered he is finally accepted for her when his common and doting mother offers to buy him an official post for the large sum of 60,000 francs. In discussing this play in somewhat depreciatory terms, H. C. Lancaster asked: 'What future awaits poor Mariane with her dishonest husband?' (*History*, IV, p. 786). The whole point is that such questions of sentiment or morality are not raised in the play and are hardly intended to be.

The social mixture presented through a convincing and ingenious plot gives situations and dialogues not inferior to Molière and in some cases more subtle. The best of them centre on the deceptions of the two wives and the delusions of their husbands. Angélique's Monsieur Simon complains that she goes out too much. She could stay at home and invite a few friends in . . . Araminte, for example. Eventually she adopts his suggestion on a big scale. Instead of going out she will entertain every day. Three days will be devoted to music and three to cards and gambling followed by a lavish supper. The seventh day will be reserved for conversation: 'Nous lirons des ouvrages d'esprit; nous débiterons des nouvelles; nous nous entretiendrons des modes; nous médirons de nos amies; enfin nous emploierons tous les moments de cette journée à des choses purement spirituelles.' (IV. vi.)

To limit the size of these assemblies by keeping unwanted persons out it will be essential to have a door-porter. Monsieur Simon is horrified, not only by the expense and the disruption of his domestic life but by the social unsuitability of a door-porter for a notary's house. His colleagues will think him ridiculous.

Les Bourgeoises à la mode was imitated by Vanbrugh in *The Confederacy* (1705), also entitled *The City Wives' Confederacy*. But this transposition to a London scene, while giving English readers a general idea of its model, is inferior to it and necessarily different in its social atmosphere.[1] With *Le Chevalier à la mode*, the original ensures Dancourt's position as an important comic dramatist, though both

---

[1] Sir John Vanbrugh (1664–1726) spent several years in France and was apparently imprisoned for a time in the Bastille. He also adapted Dancourt's *La Maison de campagne* (*The Country House*, 1705), Boursault's *Ésope à la ville* (*Aesop*, 1697), and made three near-translations of Molière (*The Cuckold in Conceit* from *Le Cocu imaginaire*; *Squire Trelooby* from *Monsieur de Pourceaugnac*; *The Mistake* from *Le Dépit amoureux*). His other plays borrow substantially from contemporary French comedy. Other English Restoration dramatists (Wycherley, Congreve) also borrowed from the French.

plays were written in collaboration with Saint-Yon, the extent of whose contribution is not known.[1]

It should not be confused with Dancourt's *Les Bourgeoises de qualité*, already mentioned on p. 170. Made up of familiar ingredients – a country setting, peasants singing and dancing, a ridiculous lawyer's widow who aspires to marry a Comte who ends up by marrying her niece – that entertaining trifle contained a social feature new for its date. If he obtained control of the widow's fortune, says the Comte, a genuine nobleman, he would use it to go into business and recover his estates:

M. NAQUART [a lawyer]   Un homme de votre qualité dans les affaires!

LE COMTE   Pourquoi non? Les gens d'affaires achètent nos terres, ils usurpent nos titres et nos noms même; quel inconvénient de faire leur métier, pour être quelque jour en état de rentrer dans nos maisons et dans nos charges?

(III. iv)

In the twenty to thirty short comedies that Dancourt wrote, the same kind of characters and situations recur in a variety of topical settings which give added richness and colour. Some are *comédies-vaudeville*, others dispense with song and dance. They avoid the element of broad farce characteristic of earlier comedy and of the Italian-inspired contemporary variety. Subject to correction, there is not a single chamberpot in any of them, but instead a quietly witty commentary on manners. To take a few typical examples, *La Maison de campagne* (1688) presents the dilemma of a Parisian merchant who has bought a large country house which rapidly becomes a white elephant. Longing to be accepted by the local gentry, his wife encourages them to eat and stay there, which they do at ruinous expense to their host. His servant shoots a hunted stag, a crime in the eyes of his hunting-mad neighbours. He gets rid of them by turning his home into an inn – an antici-

---

[1] This minor dramatist (d. 1723) had been secretary to the Duc de Guise. His one notable comedy, *Les Mœurs du temps* (1685), is described by Lancaster (*History*, IV, p. 535) as 'the first French play to give a detailed account of the decay of morals usually associated with the *Régence*, created thirty years later.' But cf. Hauteroche, pp. 164–5 above.

pation of the modern country-house hotel – and charging them for his hospitality. The unwanted house is taken off his hands by a prospective son-in-law rich enough to buy it from him.

The contemporary wars are reflected in *L'Été des coquettes* (1690), whose theme is the absence of suitable men in Paris during the summer campaigning season (they returned each winter). Coquettish Parisiennes have to make do with what is left – a poor little singing-master, a scented young man who has briefly become an abbé to escape conscription, a heavy bourgeois businessman and a chevalier type masquerading as a gallant officer constantly due to leave for the army but never going. He is found out but forgiven and the company all go to dinner, as in Molière's *Critique de l'École des femmes* and Jules Romains's twentieth-century *Monsieur Le Trouhadec saisi par la débauche*. The play is a lightweight version of *Le Chevalier à la mode*.

One comes nearer to military life itself in *Les Curieux de Compiègne* (1698). The war is just over, but the army is encamped at Compiègne, close enough to Paris to be visited easily by the merchants of the capital and their wives, families and mistresses. Their motives range from curiosity, feminine admiration for soldiering ('Ah, la charmante chose, la magnifique chose qu'une armée... Ce mélange de bataillons confus, ces escadrons épars, ces officiers, ces valets, ces vivandiers, ces gens de condition!' Sc. ix), to amorous pursuits. Impecunious officers respond readily. In the background are suggestions of the rougher soldiery, but more prominent are the locals who benefit by the army's proximity. Madame Pinuin lodges officers and arranges marriages and love affairs for a consideration. The peasant Guillaume has turned his farm into a cabaret and sleeping-quarters for warriors off-duty. All this savoury realism is sketched in unobtrusively.

Dancourt had already used the theme of the intermixture of Parisians and locals in his most famous one-acter, *Les Vendanges de Suresnes* (1695).[1] To this village outside Paris, as Suresnes then was, townspeople came to help with the grape-harvest, or simply to enjoy themselves. A merchant, Monsieur Thomasseau, has a house there, with a crafty rustic-spoken gardener, a marriageable daughter and a cousin,

---

[1] The title is nearly identical to that of Du Ryer's *Les Vendanges de Suresne* (c. 1633), a comedy with a love intrigue, a pastoral setting, references to the grape-harvest, and a mixture of Parisian and rustic characters. How closely Dancourt looked back at this sixty-year-old play, different from his own in important respects, is an open question, but he may well have taken some suggestions from it.

Madame Dubuisson, who, like Madame Pinuin, lets lodgings and undertakes more dubious business. She has a friend in Lorange, a good example of the crooked *intrigant*, described as 'le plus habile empoisonneur qu'il y ait à Paris'. In the play he merely buys up Suresnes wine and sells it as champagne. He introduces a rather rare note of farce. As part of the traditional marriage intrigue he disguises himself as a she-dwarf and presently claims to have been seduced by one Vivien, a 'marquis ridicule' and unwanted suitor. There is a plain reminiscence of Scarron in this, particularly in the scene in which Lorange challenges the amazed marquis to deny their past relationship:

> VIVIEN Je ne connais point cette créature-là.
>
> LORANGE Tu ne me connais point, traître? Je te dévisagerai[1] si on me laisse faire.
>
> MME DUBUISSON Eh! Ne vous emportez pas de la sorte.
>
> LORANGE Tu ne me connais pas? N'est-ce pas toi qui m'a mise dans mes meubles?[2] . . . Avant que je connusse ce libertin-là, ma réputation flairait comme baume dans tout le quartier du Palais Royal.
>
> MME DUBUISSON Je vous le disais bien, elle a toujours passé pour une fille fort sage.
>
> LORANGE Si vous saviez, Monsieur, comme il m'a attrapée!
>
> (Sc. xxii)

This burlesque of burlesque fits happily into its context. More suitable marriages are finally arranged and this joyous play culminates in grape-gatherers' songs with a refrain which has become proverbial:

> Défiez-vous de ces coquettes
> Qui n'en veulent qu'à vos écus;
> Sitôt que vous n'en aurez plus,
> *Adieu panniers, vendanges sont faites.*

One year before this the Comédie Française had performed its first play[3] by Jean-François Regnard (1655–1709). *Attendez-moi sous*

---

[1] 'Tear your face off'.
[2] 'Set me up in my house'.
   For Scarron's scene, see pp. 63–4 above.
[3] Except perhaps for a tragedy, *Sapor*, which is lost.

l'orme (1694) also had a proverbial title worked into the final songs.
The setting of this one-act comedy is again rustic – a village in Poitou.
Though it contains a cunning valet, a resourceful Lisette, passing
soldiers who pursue the local girls, and a craze for Parisian hairdresses
sent by mail-order with a book of instructions on how to use them
most effectively, the predominant atmosphere is near to pure pastoral.
Most of the peasants are shepherds and shepherdesses. The old medieval
theme of the lustful knight who tries to detach the village maiden from
her faithful greenwood lover[1] is easily recognizable, though updated.
The knight is now a discharged officer. Told to await a rendezvous
'under that elm' he waits in vain, mocked by shepherds who pass him
singing:

> Attendez-moi sous l'orme,
> Vous attendrez longtemps.

The not so simple rustics emerge triumphant.

With this, the most popular of his short plays, Regnard wrote two
or three others for the Comédie Française and a dozen farces between
1688 and 1696 for the Italians. His main popularity and his longlived
reputation as a second Molière rest, however, on three full-length plays
of which the first two continued the search for a distinctive type-
character. In *Le Joueur* (December 1696) this was an addicted gambler
who promises the girl he loves that he will reform but fails to do so.
In *Le Distrait* (1697) the absentminded young hero confuses the names
of two girls and addresses a love letter to the wrong one. In the end he
goes unpunished, though he has to be reminded about his wedding-
day. His vagueness and lapses of memory give plenty of opportunities
for comic touches, each good for a momentary laugh, but not adding
up to anything substantial. His peculiarity is too innocuous to make
him more than a pleasant young man who might well be a secondary
character in a story by P. G. Wodehouse, but hardly a central figure.
He is not redeemed by the conventional plot and familiar other
characters: a gay unscrupulous chevalier, an elderly widow, a helpful
uncle, and the usual pair of servants, named Carlin and Lisette.

Le Joueur had promised rather more. In its period and after, it was
regarded as an outstanding play and Regnard's best, except for *Le
Légataire universel*. There seemed good reason, in a society preoccupied with gambling, to build a character-comedy round that

[1] Renewed of course in Molière's *Dom Juan*.

theme. This had already appeared, more or less incidentally, in several other plays, in Dancourt's one-act *La Désolation des joueuses* (1687), as part of Angélique's plans for home entertainment in *Les Bourgeoises à la mode*, and elsewhere. Later Dufresny depicts the craze of the national lottery – the poor man's gamble – in *Le Lot supposé* (1715). More significantly, Dufresny complained that in *Le Joueur* Regnard had stolen his idea and got in first. Dufresny's *Le Chevalier joueur* was produced in February 1697 two months after Regnard's comedy and was a complete failure. The two plays, Regnard's in verse and Dufresny's in prose, resemble each other too closely for mere coincidence. On his side Regnard accused Dufresny of plagiarism, but the question of priority has never been definitely resolved. It seems probable that the two authors, who wrote for the same company, sometimes in collaboration, discussed the subject in some detail, then possibly quarrelled and went on independently. Their rivalry at least illustrates the topicality of gambling at that date as a subject for a full-length play.

But it was still gambling rather than the gambler. The hero loses, wins, then goes back to lose again. The rest of the play has to be padded, but this is concealed by brilliant writing, the well-sustained movement and excitement of the plot, and the skilful exploitation of old material sometimes ingeniously varied. The gambler Valère is lectured by his father Géronte: 'Votre train de vie est scandaleux,' etc. Valère promises to reform and pay his debts if, as an afterthought, his father will provide the money (I. vi–viii). The masters of singing and other accomplishments are replaced by a *Maître de trictrac* (backgammon) who comes to offer a course of lessons in cheating at dice. In a potentially pathetic creditor scene a female coachbuilder and a tailor come to request payment of money which they urgently need. They are dismissed with promises after Valère's valet has remarked:

> Oui, nous avons tous deux, par piété profonde,
> Fait vœu de pauvreté: nous renonçons au monde.
>
> (III. vii)

One recognizes the influence of Molière's *Dom Juan*, and conceivably of *Tartuffe*.

There is also a supposed marquis who proves to be the cousin of the *femme d'intrigue* and not of blue blood. He boasts in the manner of the old Gascon *fanfaron*, but that is part of a conscious imitation by him. His only naturally ridiculous feature, a slight one, is his habit of executing a little dance-step when pleased with himself and exclaiming 'Saute, marquis!'[1] This character, acting another character to further his intrigues, is an example of the double-take which should not be overlooked in Regnard. It reappears in the echoes, besides those of Molière, of Corneille and Racine noticeable in the comedy. They were delivered, it would seem, with a wink to experienced theatregoers. Thus Valère, having just lost everything:

> Non, l'enfer en courroux et toutes ses furies
> N'ont jamais exercé de telles barbaries.
> Je te loue, ô destin, de tes coups redoublés!
> Je n'ai plus rien à perdre et tes vœux sont comblés.[2]
>
> (IV. xiii)

And thus Angélique, who hopes to marry him, speaking in near-tragic language to her confidante:

> Ne combats plus, Nérine, une ardeur qui m'enchante:
> Tu prendrais pour l'éteindre une peine impuissante.
> Il est des nœuds formés sous des astres malins
> Qu'on chérit malgré soi. Je cède à mes destins.
>
> (IV. i)

It would be tempting to conclude that *Le Joueur* is a comedy which has turned serious. Angélique is sincerely in love with Valère, through *amour* and not through *raison*, and it is only after he has once again broken his promise to stop gambling that she sadly gives him up. Gambling is an obsession which brings him disaster and in the closing scenes various characters, including his father and the girl, reject him and take their leave, as in Scarron's *Marquis ridicule* and *Le Misanthrope*. But this is not a drama of broken lives and there is absolutely

---

[1] Marivaux echoed this in the curtain line of *Le Jeu de l'amour et du hazard* spoken by Arlequin.

[2] Cf. the final scene in Racine's *Andromaque*:

> Grâce aux dieux, mon malheur passe mon espérance.
> Oui, je te loue, ô ciel, de ta persévérance.
> ... Eh bien, je meurs content et mon sort est rempli.

For other Racinian reminiscences in Regnard and Dufresny see below, pp. 186–7. See also p. 70 for a similar procedure in Scarron.

no moral lesson. The last to take leave is the valet Hector, but he does so in mockery of the others. He is merely going into the next room to fetch a volume of Seneca, whose philosophy soothes his master when read to him. The unrepentant Valère concludes:

> Va, va, consolons-nous, Hector, et quelque jour
> Le jeu m'acquittera des pertes de l'amour.
>
> (V. xii)

What might well have become a *drame bourgeois* at a later date is a comedy and not even a bitter one. Nor should Regnard be accused of mixing two tones or presenting grave issues in over-frivolous terms. One might make that criticism today but it would misrepresent a particular moment in history and in drama. Of this *Le Joueur*, with all the derivative features it contains, is perhaps the most typical expression – highly interesting for that reason if lacking the kind of merits expected in a permanent masterpiece.

Some eleven years later (January 1708) Regnard's third major play, *Le Légataire universel*, was produced. 'Character' is now neglected in favour of a basic and relatively original situation. Géronte, a wealthy invalid, contemplates marrying young Isabelle, but is dissuaded. Isabelle's mother will agree to a more suitable match with Géronte's nephew Éraste provided he is made the old man's sole heir; but Géronte wishes to leave 60,000 francs each to a provincial nephew and niece. The valet Crispin impersonates each in turn and so outrages Géronte by his behaviour that he decides to leave everything to Éraste. Before he can make the will he falls into a *léthargie* or coma and is believed dead. Crispin impersonates him before the notaries and dictates a will leaving the bulk of the fortune to Éraste, though with substantial sums for himself and for Géronte's servant-nurse Lisette, whom he intends to marry. Géronte revives and after some alarms is persuaded that he dictated the will during his *léthargie* and finally lets it stand.

The presumed death awakes echoes of Jonson's *Volpone*, which Regnard would hardly have known, and of Molière's *Le Malade imaginaire*, but with the difference that in both those cases the 'dead man' is playing a trick on his heirs, while in *Le Légataire* the trick is played on him. This reversal of the situation was apparently new. The play is predominantly Crispin's. Much of it is taken up by his three impersonations and he speaks the closing lines. Continuing the tendency already noted in *Le Joueur*, some of his language is mock-tragic. On learning of Géronte's recovery he utters the unmistakably Racinian line:

Et l'avare Achéron lâche encore sa proie![1]

Regnard cannot be said to have added much to the portrait of the resourceful valet-cum-intriguer (like Frontin in Dancourt's *Bourgeoises à la mode*, Crispin was once a lawyer's clerk), but he places this established type firmly in the foreground and reslants the part in a comic direction. It had been intended for Dancourt's father-in-law, La Thorillière, but he fell ill and the part was taken by Paul Poisson, the son of an older Comédie Française actor, to whom some contemporaries attributed the play's success.[2]

Le Légataire universel was Regnard's last play, apart from the short *Critique du Légataire universel*, which picked up Molière's idea for *L'École des femmes*, though it was hardly as pertinent. It may have helped to puff the main play. In the following year Regnard died in his large country house. Unlike Dancourt and the others he had no acting or family connections with the theatre. He belonged to the wealthy bourgeoisie though not the nobility and it would be tempting to describe him as a gentleman-playwright like Vanbrugh and Congreve. But the close relations he formed with actors and other dramatists remove any hint of amateurism. He seems in fact almost myopically professional in his re-use of the day-to-day resources of the theatre, added to his contributions to the Italian players. His independent position could have enabled him to stand back and attempt some bigger play with a stronger sense of perspective. Instead he was content to combine the bits and pieces immediately before him in ingenious entertainments which made his name famous. He wrote his major plays in verse, the shorter ones in prose, differing from Dancourt who used prose invariably, except for the interpolated songs. Then and later both media were equally acceptable in comedy (Marivaux's

[1] Cf. *Phèdre*, l. 625: 'Et l'avare Achéron ne lâche point sa proie.'
[2] As with *Le Joueur*, there is an unclear question of priority. Lesage's *Crispin rival de son maître* (see pp. 188–9 below) was first produced on 15 March 1707, ten months before *Le Légataire*. But it is known that *Le Légataire* was read to the Comédie Française troupe on 24 December 1706 and that shortly after changes were begun to adapt the valet's part to Poisson's style. Except, however, for the prominence of Crispin, the two plays are considerably different.

comedies are all in prose), though it seems probable that the actors preferred verse as easier to memorize.

His posthumous novel *La Provençale* supplies a curious postscript. The romantic love affair in it was invented but the main theme of the story was autobiographically true. In his youth Regnard, a great traveller, was captured by Algerian pirates during a voyage in the Mediterranean. Sold as a slave, he spent eight miserable months in Algiers until released on payment of a large ransom. This was exactly the kind of situation used by French dramatists, including Molière, to explain the providential arrival of some character in the last act. Regnard's return home had no such function and he did not use the device, by then old-fashioned, in his plays. But at least he lived through an experience which might be supposed to belong only to comedy and tragicomedy.

Regnard's contemporary, Charles-Rivière Dufresny (*c.* 1654–1724), wrote plays of the same type for the same theatres with less success, though he had compensations of other kinds. Said to be an illegitimate descendant of Henri IV, he held the Court appointment of *Contrôleur des jardins royaux* and enjoyed royal pensions. He collaborated with Regnard in short plays for the Italians and also competed with him. In their clash over *Le Joueur* and *Le Chevalier joueur* he seems to have been hardly done by. His first play performed by the Comédie Française, *Le Négligent* (1692), may have given Regnard the idea of *Le Distrait*, though the plays are dissimilar. For his part Dufresny followed Regnard with a second *Attendez-moi sous l'orme* (1695), a rustic comedy original except for the title. Dufresny again exemplifies the contemporary casting-about for a new comic character and the failure to find one. Apart from his gambler plays (*La Joueuse* of 1709 was another) he tried to renew Molière with his portrait of a female hypochondriac in *La Malade sans maladie* (1699). His short *L'Esprit de contradiction* (1700) centres on a woman who contradicts compulsively. If anyone says 'no' she is certain to say 'yes' and she is thus tricked into agreeing to her daughter's marriage to the right suitor. This slight little piece works out its premises neatly, but Lancaster's description of it as 'a masterpiece'[1] is certainly over-generous, in spite

[1] *History*, IV, p. 767.

of its great popularity at the time and throughout the eighteenth century. There is more substance in *La Coquette de village ou le Lot supposé* (1715), a three-act comedy which turns, as we have said, on the national lottery and shows a peasant-farmer who is tricked into believing that one of his forty tickets has won him the *gros lot* of 100,000 francs. He is a changed man, swollen with arrogance and ready to buy up the local Baron for whom he has so far worked and go to Paris with his daughter Lisette to cut a dash in the capital. This Lisette, the coquette of the title, has been instructed in man-catching by an older widow and hopes to marry the Baron. Failing him, she would settle for a neighbouring nobleman whom the widow is pursuing, so double-crossing her instructress. The widow puts in almost epigrammatic form their hard-headed approach to love:

> Elle a su lui donner l'amour sans en prendre;
> Elle fait de sang froid le discours le plus tendre,
> Et feint effrontément un timide embarras,
> Pleurs qui vont droit au cœur et qui n'en partent pas.
>
> (III. i)

and to marriage:

> L'amitié sans amour,
> C'est ce qu'il nous convient pour un bon mariage.
> L'amour est inquiet et s'ennuie en ménage.
>
> (III. v)

With the revelation that they have not won the lottery, the peasants' brave new world collapses and the father, in total deflation, exits after exclaiming 'Ouf!' twice. His daughter is reduced to marrying the local tax-collector, who observes:

> Deux fois ouf, en langue muette,
> Valent un oui.
>
> (III. v)

If one had to test the persistent and conscious imitation of Molière by the use of a single word, it would be this. First uttered on the stage by Molière himself in the part of Arnolphe in *L'École des femmes*, it was frequently repeated by other playwrights, usually though not invariably as an exit-word, for characters rendered speechless by some crushing disappointment – in this case more than fifty years after its first use.[1]

La Coquette de village developed certain features of Dufresny's earlier three-act comedy, *Le Double Veuvage* (1702), which deserves remembering as the classic of realism on the married state and sentimental love. The lines quoted above on p. 164 have shown the not abnormally romantic Dorante conversing with the practical Thérèse. After marriage, she has said, we shall get on well enough together and I'll cure you of your odd ways. Dorante has been away for a week and has been particularly hurt to find her, not in the lovelorn state he had expected, but singing and dancing gaily. The scene continues:

DORANTE Je ne suis point bizarre, lorsqu'après des raisonnements solides, je conclus que votre gaieté . . .

THÉRÈSE Oh, ma gaieté, ma gaieté! Je conclus moi que ma gaieté vous doit prouver ma tendresse, et voici comme je raisonne – car vous m'avez appris à faire des raisonnements: vous savez avec quelle frayeur j'ai toujours envisagé le mariage, parce qu'il est triste. Je crains donc le mariage naturellement, je vois qu'on me veut marier avec vous, et je n'en suis pas plus chagrine. Eh bien, être gaie en cette occasion-là, n'est-ce pas vous aimer?

DORANTE C'est ne pas me haïr.

THÉRÈSE Et ne me point fâcher du ton dont vous le prenez là, il me semble que c'est vous aimer assez passablement.

DORANTE Passablement est une expression bien touchante . . . passablement!

THÉRÈSE Oh! je veux que vous me teniez compte de la joie que j'ai.

DORANTE Cette joie serait à sa place si vous étiez sûre que votre mariage réussît. Mais dans la situation où nous sommes, vous devriez trembler; et si vous m'aimiez, on vous verrait comme moi, inquiète, agitée, et dans l'horreur d'une incertitude cruelle, languir, soupirer, gémir . . .

[1] The printed editions of *L'École des femmes* have always given 'Oh!', but there is no question that the word spoken was 'Ouf' nor of the deep impression it made.

[*Enter the Countess, who wishes to help the young couple*]

LA COMTESSE Eh bien, Thérèse, je travaille à vous marier. N'êtes-vous pas ravie?

THÉRÈSE (*contrefaisant Dorante*) Au contraire, Madame, je suis inquiète, agitée, et dans l'horreur d'une incertitude cruelle, je languis, je soupire. (*A Dorante*) Est-ce comme cela qu'on aime, Monsieur?

(I. iii-iv)

Under the mockery of the old-style anguished lover, one can sense the beginnings of the new and lighter love discussions which Marivaux will develop; Thérèse is not really as heartless as she appears. But it is a very timid beginning and the main emphasis of the play runs against the *sensibilité* or tenderheartedness which Dorante alone shows. In a previous conversation with the *suivante* Frosine he had heard it condemned as an undesirable quality in marriage. A *sensible* wife is a vulnerable wife, with the attendant risks of cuckoldry – against which the old Cornelian *vertu* would not always be a sufficient safeguard:

FROSINE Si j'étais homme, je choisirais pour mon repos une femme qui fût toujours gaie, et jamais sensible.

DORANTE Je veux de la sensibilité.

FROSINE J'en voudrais dans une maîtresse, mais dans une épouse ... Hon!

DORANTE C'en est tout l'agrément.

FROSINE C'est un agrément bien dangereux pour un mari.

DORANTE On peut être sensible et avoir de la vertu.

FROSINE La vertu ne rend pas toujours une épouse vertueuse, et j'aimerais mieux une femme qui n'eût point de passions qu'une femme qui les sût vaincre.

(I. i)

If even the young lovers are allowed few illusions the cynicism of the older characters is complete.

The Countess's *Intendant* or steward and his wife detest one another, but dare not break openly because each hopes to inherit the other's personal fortune. On the Countess's initiative each is tricked into believing that the other has died and mourns hypocritically. Their

concealed joy ends abruptly when both find that their partners are still
alive and are obliged to simulate relief and mutual affection:

L'INTENDANT Je revois ma chère femme.

    LA VEUVE Voilà mon cher mari.

(*Ils s'embrassent plusieurs fois et se retournent tous deux de l'autre côté
pour reprendre haleine.*)

L'INTENDANT Aïe!

    LA VEUVE Ouf!

L'INTENDANT (*se retournant vers sa femme avec une seconde grimace de
              joie*) Ma joie est si grande que . . . aïe!

    LA VEUVE Je suis si ravie que . . . ouf!

L'INTENDANT Qu'est-ce donc? votre joie paraît troublée.

    LA VEUVE Cela est vrai, il me vient des moments de colère . . .
              contre Madame la comtesse . . . car enfin, en vous
              faisant croire que j'étais morte, elle vous exposait à
              quelque saisissement . . .

L'INTENDANT Elle se jouait à me faire mourir.

    LA VEUVE Dieu merci, vous avez bon visage, vous paraissez
              avoir une santé . . . je suis outrée . . . contre Madame
              la comtesse.

L'INTENDANT Tout ceci n'a fait que redoubler ma tendresse.

    LA VEUVE Je sens aussi que mon amour . . . Hon! que je hais
              Madame la comtesse!

L'INTENDANT Enfin ceci est un renouvellement d'union.

    LA VEUVE Oui, une espèce de second mariage.

(III. v)

Apart from the question of the inheritance, they have other pressing
motives for wishing their spouses to be dead. The *Intendant* is in love
with young Thérèse, his wife's niece, and his wife with Dorante, her
husband's nephew. Dorante especially is aware of the older woman's
designs on him but tries to fend her off by turning the conversation to
money matters and his projected marriage to Thérèse. This gives a
clear echo on a comic level of the Phèdre–Thésée–Hippolyte situation
in Racine's tragedy. At this point the supposed widow believes her
husband to be dead:

LA VEUVE C'est une chose merveilleuse que la ressemblance dans les
           familles. Vous avez toutes les manières de votre oncle, et
           ses manières me charmaient.

DORANTE Suivant les conseils que je vous ai donnés . . .
LA VEUVE Vous avez son geste, sa démarche, son air de visage;
j'aimais tant votre air de visage!
DORANTE Pensons à terminer.
LA VEUVE Ce qui me charmait encore dans mon époux, c'est votre
douceur, votre esprit, toute votre personne enfin.[1]

(II. xiv)

This realistically heartless play pleased contemporaries and long
continued in the repertory. Its anti-sentimentality was underlined by
the songs and dances interpolated in the acts and the 'espèce d'opéra
en raccourci' which ends it. 'True love' is lightly mocked and widowhood laughed at:

Pleurons, pleurons les malheurs⎱
Chantons, chantons les douceurs⎰du veuvage

There is certainly no moral lesson or intention. The knowing
comments of the servants, bearing principally on 'dissimulation', are a
different matter. In spite of the preoccupation with Molière, this play
among others shows that a kind of comedy new in tone and manner
had after all been evolved. It was not, in the older sense, a comedy of
character, and it helps to demonstrate that Dufresny and his fellow
dramatists were at their best when they broke free from that obsession.

⁂

The main reputation of Alain-René Lesage (1668–1747) rests on his
novels, *Le Diable boiteux* (1707), *Gil Blas* (1715, continued 1724, 1735),
and others with Spanish or pseudo-Spanish subjects. In most of them
the picaresque element is strong. As a dramatist he began with three
unsuccessful adaptations of Spanish cloak-and-sword plays, deriving
the comic scenes in one of them from Scarron, before writing his only
two major plays, *Crispin rival de son maître* (1707) and *Turcaret* (1709).
This completed his dramatic production with the important exception
of the hundred or so farces which he wrote between 1712 and 1735 for
the theatres of the fairs, alone or in collaboration. Many of them were

[1] Cf. Toujours devant mes yeux je crois voir mon époux.
. . . Il avait votre port, vos yeux, votre langage.
Cette noble pudeur colorait son visage . . . etc.
(*Phèdre*, II. v)

sung comedies to comply with the regulations then in force and represented a substantial contribution to the establishment of *opéra-comique*.
They varied in nature but some of the earlier ones had Italian characters testifying to the presence of Italian actors in Paris before they
were allowed to return in 1716 as an official troupe.[1]

A pleasant example is *Arlequin roi de Serendib* (1713), representing a
joyful adventure of Arlequin, shipwrecked on some foreign coast, and
told entirely in songs on well-known airs and a mock coronation in
words conjectured to be pseudo-Greek which, since they were in-
comprehensible, escaped the censor's ban. There are farcical *lazzi*, including an ingenious variation of the old chamberpot joke and an
episode in which Arlequin pulls off the tail of a wolf which comes to
attack him and wields it later as a symbol of authority. The scene-
changes and other effects are spectacular, providing evidence of the
scenic resources of the once simple theatres of the fairs. A family of
bandits with guns appear, troops of priestesses and women of the
seraglio from whom Arlequin is invited to choose. He little knows
that this favoured treatment is a preparation for his sacrifice the next
day to the heathen gods.

The theme is thus a parody of *Iphigenia in Tauris*, though hardly of
Euripides' version. It had been used recently in serious operas and was
quite topical. The sacrificers prove to be old friends of Arlequin's,
Mezzetin and Pierrot, disguised as women. The Grand Vizir lusts for
one of them and is demanding sexual satisfaction 'by tomorrow'. They
recognize Arlequin by his distinctive breeches and all escape on a ship
which has been got ready for the purpose.[2]

While Lesage showed exceptional powers of humorous invention in
his farces, these must be considered marginal in the general history of
comedy. His place in this was assured by his two main regular comedies.

Crispin rival de son maître, consisting of one long act, was unoriginal by that date in most of its characters and situations. The plot
revolves around marriage-dowries, reluctant parents and impersonations, but the valets are moved into the foreground more conspicuously
than in previous comedies and the leading one, Crispin, is a true *pícaro*
and crook. More even than the Frontin of Dancourt's *Les Bourgeoises
à la mode* (see p. 172 above), he is an *homme d'intrigue*, with higher

---

[1] For the background of all this see pp. 168–9 above.
[2] This can be read conveniently with other Fair plays in J. Truchet, *Théâtre du
18e siècle*, Vol. I (Paris, 1972).

ambitions. He first appears after taking a month off for an unsuccessful gambling 'expedition' in the provinces with 'un chevalier de mes amis':

> Que je suis las d'être valet! Ah Crispin, c'est ta faute! Tu as toujours donné dans la bagatelle, tu devrais présentement briller dans la finance . . . Avec l'esprit que j'ai, morbleu, j'aurais déjà fait plus d'une banqueroute.
>
> (Sc. ii)

The old half-comic valet, delighted to receive a purse of a few hundred francs, was not up to this standard. Crispin feels capable of making or losing real fortunes.[1] In collusion with another valet who has just spent seven weeks in prison on suspicion of mugging a foreign businessman, he decides to double-cross his temporary master. Impersonating a rival suitor (the ploy was hardly new), he will win the girl for himself, conclude a marriage contract, and escape before consummation with the dowry of 60,000 francs. This, so far as we know, was new. The plot fails, but the two valets or intriguers are finally forgiven and will be set up in business by the girl's father. If there is any moral here it must be that true financial ability can always be discerned and ought to be encouraged.

In *Turcaret*, Lesage's greatest play, the valet, another Frontin, gets away with his loot and is the only triumphant character, but not the central one. Here at last, after allowing for all the changes in society and drama, is a Molièresque character-comedy with a new protagonist. Monsieur Turcaret is a big-businessman with the wealth and influence which go with that position. His main weakness is his simplicity in human relationships. He is infatuated with the Baronne, a young widow and coquette on whom he showers presents and money, some of which she gives to the Chevalier, an unscrupulous gambler whom she secretly

---

[1] An earlier rebellious valet appears in Regnard's *La Sérénade* (1694). In some of his words he foreshadows Figaro more precisely than any of the other examples. Our italics:

SCAPIN . . . On s'accoquine à servir ces gredins-là [nos maîtres], je ne sais pourquoi. Ils ne paient point de gages, ils querellent, ils rossent quelquefois. *On a plus d'esprit qu'eux, on les fait vivre* . . . *et avec tout cela nous sommes les valets et ils sont les maîtres. Cela n'est pas juste.* Je prétends à l'avenir travailler pour mon compte. Ceci fini, je veux devenir maître à mon tour. (Sc. xii)

This was a short one-act play, Regnard's first, and probably too inconspicuous to be remarked or remembered.

prefers and who is exploiting her. Turcaret is of humble origins and is dazzled by the Baronne's social standing. Unknown to the others he has a wife in the provinces. She turns up in Act V to demand her quarterly allowance which has not been paid. She is a more vindictive Madame Jourdain, while her meeting with her husband after ten years of mutually enjoyed separation is reminiscent of the husband–wife reunion in Dufresny's *Le Double Veuvage*. The Baronne sarcastically offers to reconcile them, to the horror of both.

If there is something of Monsieur Jourdain in Turcaret there is also a little, on a much cruder level, of Alceste. Informed of the Baronne's flirtation with the Chevalier, Turcaret storms in, like Alceste to Célimène, and makes a violent scene. She quickly twists him round and he grovels literally, kneeling before her. He will replace with costlier objects his previous gifts to her, the mirror and porcelain ornaments he has smashed. The scene (II. iii), though certainly inspired by *Le Misanthrope*, has none of Molière's finesse. The turn-round is too rapid and lacks credibility. But then Turcaret is a plainly ridiculous figure, which Alceste was not, and in that case near-farce becomes permissible. After pouring out his money on the slightest hint, Turcaret ends by being taken off to a debtors' prison. He has stood security for a bankrupt and cannot find the considerable sum of 200,000 *écus* (about £1 million in modern money) required.

This is the last of Turcaret, but not of the valet Frontin, who has managed to secrete 40,000 francs entrusted to him as a go-between and will use them to start up in 'business' after marrying Lisette. Lisette (a dubious character herself and not the relatively straight-forward *suivante* of so many other comedies) has given him three years to make a fortune and the play inspires every confidence that with her support he will do so. The curtain falls on his closing line: 'Voilà le règne de Monsieur Turcaret fini; le mien va commencer.'

So members nominally of the servant class, already distinguished by their sharper intelligence and grasp of material values, are now climbing the ladder to financial power. They have a long way to go and in real life will meet more formidable competitors than Turcaret near the top, but in comedy at least their potential has been fully recognized.

Of the play as a play it is only necessary to observe that it uses all the familiar features – the elderly man's infatuation with a younger woman, his social ambitions, his discomfiture, the coquette theme, the tricks of the Chevalier and the so-called servants, the *femme d'intrigue* (Madame Jacob, who proves to be Turcaret's less successful sister), the laughably provincial wife from whom the Chevalier extracts money by pretending love – but combines them effectively to give a comedy which is absorbingly fast-moving after Act I and is distinguished by the wit of the dialogue, based on irony. If it were the only play of its period that one read, it could be taken as a sum of numerous others preceding or approaching it and without which it could hardly have been composed.

There remains the character of Turcaret and the depiction of the semi-fraudulent businessman. He is a financier in the modern sense of the word, skilled in making money grow through a variety of enterprises. Not all are dishonest but they are so intertwined that it is impossible to draw a clear distinction. They rest principally on the provision of loans on interest, arranged through third parties so that Turcaret's name does not appear, and no doubt with rake-offs at different levels. He uses his influence to obtain official posts for his friends and so build an empire to support him in return. He is also literally building a magnificent house on a site he has bought in Paris, of which he quotes the dimensions to the nearest inch (III. iii). His fatuous side shows in his pretensions to artistic and literary taste, which is primitive. Also in over-confidence in his financial position, which leads to his downfall, and above all in his misjudgement of individuals, not only of the Baronne, but of Frontin who is planted on him as a clerk and impresses him by his 'simplicity':

LA BARONNE Monsieur, voilà le garçon que je veux vous donner.
TURCARET Il paraît un peu innocent.
LA BARONNE Que vous vous connaissez bien en physionomie!
TURCARET J'ai le coup d'œil infaillible. Approche, mon ami. Dis-moi un peu, as-tu déjà quelques principes?
FRONTIN Qu'appelez-vous des principes?
TURCARET Des principes de commis: c'est-à-dire, si tu sais comment on peut empêcher les fraudes, ou les favoriser?
FRONTIN Pas encore, Monsieur, mais je sens que j'apprendrai cela fort facilement.

TURCARET Tu sais du moins l'arithmétique? Tu sais faire des
comptes à parties simples?

FRONTIN Oh oui, Monsieur, je sais même faire des parties
doubles ...

TURCARET Quelle ingénuité! Ce garçon-là, Madame, est bien
niais.

LA BARONNE Il se déniaisera dans vos bureaux.

TURCARET Oh qu'oui, Madame, oh qu'oui! D'ailleurs, un bel
esprit n'est pas nécessaire pour faire son chemin. Hors
moi et deux ou trois autres, il n'y a parmi nous que des
génies assez communs. Il suffit d'un certain usage,
d'une routine qu'on ne manque guère d'attraper. Nous
voyons tant de gens! Nous nous étudions à prendre ce
que le monde a de meilleur; voilà toute notre science.

(II. iv)

It seems certain that Lesage's caricature of the financier, apparently
based on inside knowledge or close observation, gave offence. The
Comédie Française hesitated to produce the play and only did so when
ordered to by the Dauphin. It ran for seven successful performances
and was then taken off and not produced again for over twenty years
(1730), when it quickly became a classic. It is supposed that pressure
had been exerted by the financial world, though there is no definite
proof. Lesage hints at it in the short *Critique par le Diable boiteux* which
he wrote to accompany his play. He himself draws the comparison with
Tartuffe and makes the same kind of distinction as Molière. Just as
there are 'vrais dévots', so there are 'honnêtes gens dans les affaires'.
Why should these be offended 'de voir sur la scène un sot, un fripon de
leur corps? Cela ne tombe point dans le général.'

The parallel is over-bold, but the fact that it could be drawn at all
is revealing. It indicates that the place of the Church as a temporal
power dangerous to criticize was being taken by the multifaced god of
finance. The assumption that Lesage had been warned off gains
credence when it is remembered that after *Turcaret* he deserted the
Comédie Française and gave his entire attention to the Foire.

Much more sharply than other contemporary comedies, *Turcaret* was
satirical. Judging by the situations and dialogue, the apparent probing
of a live nerve in society was intentional. Historically this gives the
play, unoriginal in its parts, a special importance in its whole. The

fact that it was successfully built round a character is its other outstanding quality. Turcaret comes near to satisfying Molière's requirement of a 'personnage ridicule' who is not completely incredible, though he is never an 'honnête homme'. For these reasons and its realistic picture of contemporary manners it can be seen as an exceptionally vigorous product of a period of drama inclined to appear ingeniously repetitive and interbred. Comedies echoed comedies and also operas and tragedies, though in forms hardly sustained enough to be called parodic. What burlesque there was was confined to the Italians and the Foire. From this mass of interesting and talented comic writing *Turcaret* stands out, at least a little ahead of any other single comedy of its time.

MARIVAUX

Marivaux's formation and early works –
relations with the Italian company – Arlequin, Silvia –
Arlequin poli par l'amour – *vogue of the fairy-tale – first*
Surprise de l'amour – *second* Surprise de l'amour – le Jeu de l'amour
et du hasard – *Silvia's 'game'* – La Double Inconstance – *a bitter*
comedy? – *Marivaux's conception of love examined – other*
plays and 'philosophical' comedies – feminism

Another objection discussed in Lesage's *Critique de Turcaret* was that all
the characters in the play are wicked (*vicieux*). This could never be said
of Marivaux, whose comedies represent a reaction against cynicism,
materialistic values and the tendency which Lesage had noticed in
himself to 'paint manners too closely' ('peindre les mœurs de trop
près'). The distinguishing marks of Marivaux's comedy are the
fantasy which removes it from the domain of immediate social reality
and a preoccupation with sensibility. Both elements are discreet and
restrained. The exuberance of burlesque is avoided and so is a tragic
intensity of passion. The treatment is delicate and bears on feelings
ignored by Marivaux's immediate predecessors, whose slogan might
well have been MAKE MONEY, NOT LOVE. Marivaux's more fastidious
presentation of love accounts for his lasting popularity, though he
wrote numerous works of other kinds. But interesting though these
are they are marginal to his characteristic contribution to French
comedy.

Pierre Carlet de Chamblain de Marivaux (1688–1763) belonged to a
legal and administrative family. His father became Director of the
Mint in the provincial town of Riom and on his death in 1719 Marivaux
was refused the succession of this post when he applied for it. A year
later he lost all his capital in the bankruptcy of John Law, the
financial wizard on a much vaster scale than Turcaret, whose failure

ruined thousands. It would be possible, though hypothetical, to ascribe the origins of the antimaterialism of his mature comedies to these disappointments or more generally to a reaction against his family's financial background, though a much more positive influence was about to appear.

Before this, however, Marivaux, while studying law in Paris, had been welcomed to the salon of the Marquise de Lambert. Less predominantly literary than the salons of Molière's day, it nevertheless encouraged the discussion of ideas and sentiments in a refined ambience and language to which Marivaux responded readily and which must be counted as a background influence on his written work. He had already begun writing, composing works of miscellaneous kinds in which the germs of his later production can be found. Among them were two novels, two burlesque poems, *Télémaque travesti* and *L'Iliade travestie*, and studies of Parisian manners entitled *Les Caractères*, inspired by La Bruyère. He followed a derivative early comedy, probably never acted, with a tragedy, *La Mort d'Annibal*, produced by the Comédie Française in 1720 and a complete failure.

In the same year he linked up with the newly arrived Italian comedians and began to set out on his true road. Between 1720 and 1740 he wrote, principally for them, over thirty plays. Together with his two mature novels, *La Vie de Mariane* (1731–41) and *Le Paysan parvenu* (1734–5), which revolve largely on manners, these constitute his main work.

When the Italians were reinstated in 1716 they were an entirely different troupe. Their cultured leader Luigi Riccoboni, originally a tragic actor, took the stage name of Lélio. His wife, Elena Balletti, was also a woman of considerable culture who acted under the name of Flaminia or as Colombine. She was soon outdone in popularity by the young Gianneta Benozzi, called Silvia. Equally important for Marivaux was the new Arlequin, Tommaso Vizentini, known as Thomassin. He and Silvia created all the parts bearing their names in Marivaux's comedies, in short most of the notable parts, with Lélio's, except those in *La Seconde Surprise de l'amour*, which was performed by Comédie Française actors.

Just as the previous Italian troupe had performed plays in French, Riccoboni's company soon did the same, switching to the second language as the various actors became more fluent in it. The transition is precisely marked in Autreau's *Le Naufrage au Port-à-l'Anglais*

(25 April 1718) which had scenes in French and Italian and a dialogue between Flaminia and Silvia by way of Prologue:

SILVIA Nous allons parler français; cela me fait trembler.
FLAMINIA Pourquoi trembler? Ce que nous allons jouer n'est pas difficile. C'est une petite pièce légère où il n'y a point de caractères trop marqués, où nous ne représentons que ce que nous sommes à peu près, des Italiennes nouvelles débarquées, où nos fautes de prononciation même nous feront honneur. On croira qu'elles sont faites exprès.

Like Silvia and the rest of the company, Arlequin-Thomassin shed the farcical qualities of his predecessors to create what was virtually a new type-character under the old name. Still athletically agile, he indulged in none of the grosser *lazzi* practised by the Arlequin (Domenico Biancolelli Junior) of Lesage's *Roi de Serendib*. Domenico was adopted by Riccoboni's troupe but ceased to be Arlequin, playing instead the less important part of Trivelin. Thomassin was a small man much shorter than Silvia and played in a black mask. He would not be everyone's idea of a perfect lover, yet he captured the public in his persona on account of his elegance, suppleness and charm. The transformation from the old to the new was illustrated almost symbolically in the one-act *Arlequin poli par l'amour* (October 1720), which contains or foreshadows the main features of Marivaux's later love comedies. It was his second comedy performed by the Italians (the first failed) and his real point of departure.

This Arlequin has been carried off by a fairy (Flaminia) fascinated by his physical beauty but unable to draw any response from him. He is stupidly interested only in food and sleep until he catches sight of a shepherdess (Silvia) and immediately awakens to love and mental acuity. Silvia, until then ignorant of love, awakens to it also. The Fairy, though engaged to marry the enchanter Merlin, is dangerously jealous, but with the help of Merlin's servant Trivelin, Arlequin gains possession of her wand and becomes the master of her and the goblins and spirits she has conjured up. At Silvia's request she is left unpunished and the two innocent lovers are united.

The simple story is unfolded with much mime by Arlequin and with music, dancing and stage effects which allow it to be described as a pastoral fairy play. It is this in several senses. What must certainly have been the immediate source was a fairy-tale by Catherine Durand,

first published in 1702 and which Marivaux follows closely,[1] in spite
of the difference in media. This was near the beginning of the great
vogue of the fairy-tale inaugurated by Charles Perrault's *Histoires ou
contes du temps passé* (1697) and Madame d'Aulnoy's more sophisticated *Les Illustres Fées* (1698). The vogue grew through the eighteenth
century, producing a whole library of tales which combined magic
with romance, apparent naïveté with a courtly style often verging on
preciosity. Many of the themes went back to earlier stories in Italian,
Spanish and French. The theme of the clumsy clown transformed by
love can be connected with the archetypal Beauty and the Beast and its
several variations. Perrault's *Riquet à la houppe* belonged to this family.
It is even possible to attach to it *A Midsummer Night's Dream*, that
fairy play crossed with courtly romantic comedy, though Titania's
love for Bottom cannot transform that realistically rustic creature. The
pastoral novel with its delicate love ethic and its occasional nymphs
and enchantments swells the stream. Among several echoes of it in
Arlequin poli par l'amour there is the scene (xiii) in which Silvia wishes
to summon 'all the shepherds of the village' to her help, but is prevented from moving by the Fairy's spell.

In the French theatre the pastoral play as such had died in the 1640s,
but its spirit was prolonged in the machine-play and then in the opera.
Other precedents relevant to Marivaux were furnished by the 'romanesque' tragedies and tragicomedies of the 1660s, as written by Thomas
Corneille and Quinault. Both these dramatists also wrote for the opera
which kept the fashion of lightly fantastic spectacle vigorously alive
in Marivaux's own time.

No one of these analogues or more or less possible sources should
be singled out to 'explain' Marivaux. But taken together they help to
characterize the cultural climate in which his plays were written and
successfully performed. Though they have delighted later generations,
they were a typical product of one facet of the eighteenth-century mind.

✟✟✟

In the ten years following *Arlequin poli par l'amour* the essential
Marivaux was established. In this period he wrote the two *Surprises de*

---

[1] *Le Prodige d'amour* in *Les Petits Soupers de l'été de l'année de 1699* (1702).
This source was brought to light by Shirley E. Jones, who argued the case for it
convincingly in *French Studies* (October 1965).

l'amour, La Double Inconstance, Le Jeu de l'amour et du hasard, and eight other plays mostly of different types.

The first *Surprise de l'amour* was performed by the Italians in May 1722. This three-act comedy presents three couples, each operating on a different register. It opens with a conversation in the mock-rustic language of comedy between the gardener Pierre and the country-bred servant Jacqueline. He wants to marry her and reproaches her for being too distant. She admits she loves him but her aunt has warned her not to respond too readily: 'L'honneur des filles les empêche de parler.' (She might lose her virginity prematurely, though this is not said in so many words.) Like a hungry man, Pierre's appetite will grow and he will love her more. Having established the theme of the woman's hesitation on the earthiest level this couple fade into the background, to be replaced by the end of Act I by the dominant and cultured couple, Lélio and Silvia. After a disappointment in love, Lélio has retired to the country, hating women and marriage. His neighbour the Comtesse (Silvia) has an equally strong aversion to men for reasons not clearly specified. The two meet and condemn each other's sex in a strongly worded argument (I. vii). It appears to be the beginning of a hate relationship, though of course it is something different. The servants of the two principals form the third couple, midway between them and the rustics. Lélio's valet Arlequin and the Comtesse's *suivante* Colombine (Flaminia) meet and by the middle of Act II have fallen plainly in love with each other in the established comic tradition, though the open mutual declaration is delayed until the first scenes of Act III, when they agree to get married. Colombine's teasing attitude, allied to coquetry and presented as uncomplicated, is mainly responsible for the delay. Some sensuality is suggested, but indirectly, as always where this Arlequin-Thomassin is concerned. (Colombine: 'Tout en badinant cependant, me voilà dans la fantaisie d'être aimée de ce petit corps-là.')

To further their own love the two agree to push their employers into marriage, which after two acts appears by no means inevitable in spite of some progress that has been made. Lélio is the first to realize and admit his love, but he is not sure of the Comtesse's response. He is at once fearful of being refused and humiliated and of shocking her by his bluntness. Her predicament is similar. The personal heart-searchings, so frequent a subject for soliloquy in the tragedy and comedy of the seventeenth century, are now complicated by the attempt to search a second person's heart and are dependent upon it. This was Marivaux's great innovation (though Corneille might be said to have begun it in the different climate of some of his comedies), and the embarrassed conversations to which it leads, with the largely unconscious hints and questions they contain, are the characteristic features of the style which came to be called *marivaudage*. It should not be taken to mean affectation in language or *préciosité*, but a natural diffidence in the love approach expressed in perfectly appropriate terms. Even at the end, after the Comtesse has said impatiently; 'Monsieur Lélio, expliquez-vous, et ne vous attendez pas que je vous devine', and he declares his love fully, she still does not fall into his arms but says, 'confused': 'Ne me demandez rien à présent; reprenez le portrait de votre parente[1] et laissez-moi respirer.' Arlequin and Colombine with Pierre and Jacqueline who are all present take this as conclusive and the original play ended with a peasant *divertissement* containing a suggestive song.

This play, with the hesitations of the principal lovers at its heart and the counterpoints of the more simple couples already establishes Marivaux's method, manner and originality. Other plays offered variations or enrichments of the same theme.

The second *Surprise de l'amour* grew out of the first but was more than a revised version of it. Entirely rewritten, it was sufficiently altered in other respects also to warrant attention as a different play. Part of the difference stems from the fact that it was composed, not for the Italians but for the Comédie Française, which first performed it on 31 December 1727. It was Marivaux's third production there, following the unequivocal failures of *Le Dénouement imprévu* (one act, 1724) and *L'Île de la Raison* (3 acts, September 1727). Because of the change of company and style its immediate reception was lukewarm[2] but its

[1] The portrait of the Comtesse plays an important part in the dénouement. Lélio had found and kept it and, when taxed with this, excused himself by saying it resembled a dead cousin of whom he had been fond.
[2] '... On ne peut pas dire que [*La Surprise*] qu'on joue actuellement sur le Théâtre Français ait été aussi généralement approuvée [que l'autre]; mais on convient que si quelque chose a contribué à en rendre le succès moins éclatant, c'est la nouveauté du genre. Cependant ce même genre, dit-on, a déjà fait fortune sur le Théâtre Italien. D'où vient que les mêmes spectateurs qui lui font un si bon accueil dans un lieu le reçoivent comme étranger dans un autre? C'est sans doute qu'on ne porte pas le même esprit à l'un et à l'autre théâtre. Le genre que Molière a consacré au Théâtre Français est le seul qu'on y cherche ...'
But the discriminating connoisseurs are for Marivaux: 'Toutes les voix se

popularity grew through the eighteenth century and after the merging of the Italians with the Opéra Comique in 1762 it replaced the earlier play altogether on the Parisian stage. The first *Surprise* disappeared from the theatre until its revival in the twentieth century.

In the Comédie Française version the peasant characters disappear altogether. The dominant couple are preserved, the Comtesse becoming the Marquise and Lélio the Chevalier (who has nothing in common with the traditional adventurer). The servant couple are Lisette and Lubin. In their function and relationship they correspond to Colombine and Arlequin, though in the French tradition of the *suivante* Lisette is even more outspoken with her mistress and affectionately attached to her than Colombine was,[1] while Lubin is at once clumsier and more dependent on his master than Arlequin. There are additional parts for the pedant Hortensius, a halfhearted caricature integrated into the plot and dialogue but subsidiary, and the Comte, a rival to the Chevalier for the Marquise's hand.

The factors of jealousy and choice which this important new character introduces distinguish the second *Surprise* from the first and favour a still more complex interplay of sentiment. In this play the avoidance of love by the two leading characters is motivated clearly. The Marquise is mourning a dearly loved husband who died a month after their wedding. The Chevalier has lost his beloved by her forced marriage to another man. He does not blame her and has only tender memories of her, transferred ultimately to the Marquise. Neither harbours bitterness or aversion for the opposite sex, and they come together in a friendly way, deciding to share their melancholy on a footing of *amitié* which gradually develops into *amour*. While the intrusion of the Comte gives an impetus to this process and a dramatic

réunissent à dire que la dernière *Surprise de l'amour* est une pièce parfaitement bien écrite, pleine d'esprit et de sentiments; que c'est *une métaphysique du cœur très délicate* [our ital.], et dans laquelle on est forcé de se reconnaître, quelque prévention qu'on apporte contre le genre. Le sujet est trop simple, dit-on. Soit: mais c'est de cette même simplicité que l'auteur doit tirer une nouvelle gloire, telle que celle que la tragédie de *Bérénice* a acquise à M. Racine . . .' (*Le Mercure de France* (Dec. 1727), quoted in *Théâtre complet de Marivaux*, I. ed. F. Deloffre (Paris, 1968).)
The contrast with Molière's comic style and this early comparison with Racine's 'simplicity' are particularly interesting.
[1] She breaks down and weeps when the Marquise rebukes her for attempting to arrange her marriage with the Chevalier (II. vi). She did this out of affection for her mistress and now she is blamed. This is reminiscent on a lighter level of Phèdre's repudiation of the well-meaning Œnone in Racine's tragedy.

excitement which was not in the first *Surprise*, it does not alter the basic tone. The principal lovers are still hesitant, diffident and inter-dependent, and when at the end the Chevalier's feelings can no longer be concealed, the Marquise still does not bring herself to utter the word *amour*, any more than did the Comtesse in the earlier play. Yet her response in this dramatic convention is clear enough. She blushes and 'forgives' him for loving her:

LE CHEVALIER ... Ah Marquise, que voulez-vous que je devienne?
LA MARQUISE Je rougis, Chevalier, c'est vous répondre.
LE CHEVALIER (*lui baisant la main*) Mon amour pour vous durera autant que ma vie.
LA MARQUISE Je ne vous le pardonne qu'à cette condition-là.
(III. xv)

and later: 'Je ne croyais pas l'amitié si dangereuse.'

To extrapolate the Marivaudian progression in this play, it is: sympathy with *estime* (the salon virtue), affection, love mentionable by the man but not the woman. The next step, sex, is totally unmention-able by either, though the lower characters can hint at it. In a short-lived modern production by René Planchon a large bed was prominent on the stage. Into this the Marquise was supposed to hop with the Comte in a moment of confusion and this brief and unsatisfactory encounter reprojected her towards the Chevalier. Materially impossible in the theatrical conventions of the eighteenth century, this heavy-handed updating also betrayed the spirit and wording of Marivaux's text. It ignored the care which he took to avoid any direct reference to physical love between his main characters and to create instead the *métaphysique du cœur* so named by his contemporaries. Perhaps his was a fairyland, but one has to accept it for what it was.

Probably disappointed by the Comédie Française production, Marivaux returned to the Italians for his most famous play, the finest example of this side of his talent. *Le Jeu de l'amour et du hasard* (3 acts, January 1730) used the by then familiar device of the exchange of roles between master and valet to discourage a love affair or to test it out.[1] But this

[1] As in e.g. Scarron's *Jodelet maître*, Molière's *Précieuses ridicules*, Lesage's *Crispin rival de son maître*.

was too simple for Marivaux. He invented a second exchange, between
the heroine Silvia and her maid Lisette. So the cultivated couple Silvia
and Dorante both think they are attracted by servants, while the
servants, Lisette and Arlequin, believe they are aspiring above their
level when they fall in love. The social implications are not ignored
and do much to complicate the tangled web of sentiment. Its disen-
tanglement between Arlequin and Lisette provides an outstanding
scene of human comedy, not unworthy of Molière. Arlequin, sincerely
in love with Lisette and supposing she is her mistress, comes very
humbly to reveal his identity to her. She also has spoken humbly to
the man whom she takes for his master. There is an exchange of
courtesies – 'You are too modest. You do me too much honour.' –
until at last Arlequin blurts out the truth about himself. He is only a
'soldat d'antichambre' or valet and Dorante is his captain:

LISETTE   Mais voyez ce magot,[1] tenez!
ARLEQUIN   La jolie culbute que je fais là!
LISETTE   Il y a une heure que je lui demande grâce et que je m'épuise
           en humilités pour cet animal-là!
ARLEQUIN   Hélas, Madame, si vous préfériez l'amour à la gloire, je
           vous ferais autant de profit qu'un monsieur.
LISETTE   (riant) Ah! ah! ah! je ne saurais pourtant m'empêcher
           de rire, avec sa gloire, et il n'y a plus que ce parti-là à
           prendre. . . . Va, va, ma gloire te pardonne, elle est de
           bonne composition.
ARLEQUIN   Tout de bon, charitable dame? Ah, que mon amour vous
           promet de reconnaissance!
LISETTE   Touche là, Arlequin; je suis prise pour dupe. Le soldat
           d'antichambre de Monsieur vaut bien la coiffeuse de
           Madame.
ARLEQUIN   La coiffeuse de Madame!
LISETTE   C'est mon capitaine ou l'équivalent.
ARLEQUIN   Masque!
LISETTE   Prends ta revanche.
ARLEQUIN   Mais voyez cette magotte, avec qui depuis une heure
           j'entre en confusion de ma misère!
LISETTE   Venons au fait: m'aimes-tu?

[1] 'Monkey-man'.

ARLEQUIN Pardi oui, en changeant de nom tu n'as pas changé de
     visage . . .

(III. vi)

Lisette has responded to Arlequin by revealing herself almost at
once. With laughter and relief the two accept the new and more natural
situation. Plain *amour* is good enough.

But not for the principal couple in whose more nuanced relationship
the core of the play consists. At the end of Act II Dorante has told
Silvia that he is not the valet but the master, but in spite of her inward
relief ('Allons, j'avais grand besoin que ce fût là Dorante') she has not
dropped her mask of 'Lisette'. Looking for greater triumph or certainty
she wants to provoke the offer of marriage to her servant-persona
which Dorante has not yet made. She enlists the help of her father
Orgon and her brother Mario, who are both aware of the whole
situation and treat her with amused understanding. Her brother is to
pretend to have a liking for her, as Lisette, and so awaken Dorante's
jealousy. She bubbles over with delight at the prospect of succeed-
ing:

SILVIA . . . Dorante et moi, nous sommes destinés l'un à l'autre,
     il doit m'épouser. Si vous saviez combien je lui tiendrai
     compte de ce qu'il fait aujourd'hui pour moi, combien
     mon cœur gardera le souvenir de l'excès de tendresse
     qu'il me montre! Si vous saviez combien tout ceci va
     rendre notre union aimable! Il ne pourra jamais se rappeler
     notre histoire sans m'aimer, je n'y songerai jamais que je
     ne l'aime. [*To her father*] Vous avez fondé notre bonheur
     pour la vie en me laissant faire; c'est un mariage unique;
     c'est une aventure dont le seul récit est attendrissant;
     c'est le coup de hasard le plus singulier, le plus heureux, le
     plus . . .
MARIO (*riant*) Ah! ah! ah! que ton cœur a de caquet, ma sœur,
     quelle éloquence!
M. ORGON Il faut convenir que le régal que tu te donnes est charmant,
     surtout si tu l'achèves [my italics].

There is the rub, for she nearly does not bring it off, the *régal* (treat)
is almost missed. The oversensitive Dorante, believing that there may
really be something between Mario and 'Lisette', decides to leave. In a
razor-edge passage he goes out, comes back, goes out and returns

again, unable to tear himself away. At last the explosion comes. Fired
by a long speech by Silvia, he offers marriage unconditionally to the
supposed *suivante* and, after exclaiming, 'Enfin, j'en suis venue à bout',
she reveals her identity.

There is more in this than Silvia's cry of 'Ah! je vois clair dans mon
cœur' uttered towards the end of the previous act (II. xii), which is
often taken to sum up Marivaux's treatment of love. Certainly the
lover's gradual progress to a full realization of his or her feelings is an
important element in these plays. It is the emergence into full con-
sciousness of confused or embryonic impulses and, since this emergence
is helped by others, particularly the *suivante*, it could be assimilated to
Freudian psychoanalysis in which the 'cure' was effected in the same
way. No such parallel was possible for Marivaux. The midwife simile
was available, but would have been too crude. He had used instead the
less appropriate metaphor of judicial torture which forces the suspected criminal to confess the truth:

COLOMBINE Vous êtes un étrange homme de ne m'avoir pas confié
que vous l'aimiez.

LÉLIO Eh, Colombine, le savais-je?

COLOMBINE . . . Je vous ai donné la question,[1] et vous avez jasé dans
vos souffrances.

(*Première Surprise de l'amour*, III. iv)

Had this been all, *Le Jeu de l'amour et du hasard* could have ended,
with only slight alterations, with Act II, since at this point the protagonists both see clearly into their own hearts. But Silvia still has her game
to play – a more dangerous game than, in her self-confidence, she
thinks – in which she stakes relative happiness for the jackpot of total
happiness. Her behaviour can, and probably should, be explained in
this way, but there is ambiguity in it. She intends to test Dorante and
for him the test is cruel. She wants a 'victory' – for love of course, but
what can that mean but herself? And: 'Il faut *que j'arrache* ma victoire
et non pas qu'il me la donne; je veux un combat entre l'amour et la
raison' (my italics). Her brother comments: 'Cela, c'est l'amour-
propre d'une femme.' At all costs she must try out her power and the
final proof of it gives her a delicious 'pleasure'. She puts it differently
in her last speech, imputing her conduct to pure unselfishness (my
italics): '. . . Vous m'aimez, je n'en saurais douter, mais à votre tour

[1] 'Judicial torture'.

jugez de mes sentiments pour vous, jugez du cas que j'ai fait de votre
cœur *par la délicatesse avec laquelle j'ai tâché de l'acquérir.*'
Perhaps she thinks so, perhaps it is so, but Marivaux cannot have
completely forgotten his Arlequin's words in the first *Surprise de
l'amour*: 'En vérité, c'est pourtant un joli petit animal que cette femme,
un joli petit chat, c'est dommage qu'il ait tant de griffes' (I. ii). And
later in the same scene Lélio pointed out that woman is less a cat than
a tiger who will tear out a man's heart, using the word *arracher* again.
But if there is a streak of tiger in Silvia it is an added attraction.
None of Marivaux's heroines is more spirited, more subtle, more
clandestinely vulnerable than this one, his finest stage creation. She
could hardly have been so outside a play which itself is an ingenious
comedy of intrigue, notable for that reason also.

In many of Marivaux's comedies the theme of love's awakening is
either secondary or absent. In *La Double Inconstance* (1723), his third
important play before *Le Jeu de l'amour et du hasard*, it hardly exists.
Here Silvia is a village maiden whom the Prince (Lélio) has had brought
to Court with her rustic lover Arlequin. He wants to detach her from
Arlequin and win her love, but not by force, and he appears to her
disguised as an attractive Court officer. Arlequin is treated generously,
but ladies of the Court are given the task of winning him away from
his first love, in which the subtle Flaminia succeeds, carefully pretexting
amitié rather than *amour*. Silvia succumbs to the 'officer' before she
knows he is the Prince and the love-switch is rewarded by two happy
marriages to new partners. The situations are straightforward and there
is little opportunity for the Marivaudian love analyses of the other
plays so far considered. The heart-searchings of Silvia and Arlequin
bear less on their own or other characters' feelings than on their
awareness of a moral duty to be faithful to each other. When they find
themselves released from this by learning of their 'double infidelity'
they very cheerfully go to their new loves.
This gay comedy becomes a bitter comedy only if one sees in it the
seduction of two unsophisticated characters, honestly trying to obey
the code of loyalty in love, by two ruthless characters who corrupt
them without their realizing it. This reading of the play is possible and
was followed by Anouilh in his re-creation of it in *La Répétition ou*

l'Amour puni. Though it runs against the dominant tone of the play, some justification for it may be found in Arlequin's two dialogues with the Seigneur or Court lord (II. vii and III. iv). In the second this kind of Rosencrantz is sent by the Prince with *lettres de noblesse* which will raise Arlequin to the aristocracy. He does not want them and with ironically simple arguments counters the Seigneur's attempts to connect them with noble ambition and *gloire.* The official persists:

LE SEIGNEUR Prenez, vous dis-je; ne serez-vous pas bien aise d'être gentilhomme?

ARLEQUIN Eh! je n'en serais ni bien aise ni fâché; c'est suivant la fantaisie qu'on a.

LE SEIGNEUR Vous y trouverez de l'avantage, vous en serez plus respecté et plus craint de vos voisins.

ARLEQUIN J'ai opinion que cela les empêcherait de m'aimer de bon cœur; car quand je respecte les gens, moi, et que je les crains, je ne les aime pas de si bon courage [cœur]; je ne saurais faire tant de choses à la fois.

If, he continues, I had the power to hurt others I might misuse it, like our squire at home who doesn't mind beating people because they cannot hit back. Then, replies the Seigneur, accept for your own protection. 'Mettez-vous en état de faire du mal, et pour cet effet prenez vos lettres de noblesse.' Arlequin does so but suddenly reflects that, besides such comforting privileges, nobility may carry obligations. Does it?

LE SEIGNEUR Elle oblige d'être honnête homme.

ARLEQUIN (*très sérieusement*) Vous aviez donc des exemptions, vous, quand vous avez dit du mal de moi?

LE SEIGNEUR N'y songez plus, un gentilhomme doit être généreux.

ARLEQUIN Généreux et honnête homme! Vertuchoux, ces devoirs-là sont bons! Je les trouve encore plus nobles que mes lettres de noblesse. Et quand on ne s'en acquitte pas, est-on encore gentilhomme?

LE SEIGNEUR Nullement.

ARLEQUIN Est-ce là tout? N'y a-t-il plus d'autre devoir?

LE SEIGNEUR Non. Cependant vous, qui suivant toute apparence, serez favori du Prince, vous aurez un devoir de plus: ce sera de mériter cette faveur par toute la soumission, tout le respect et toute la complaisance possibles. A l'égard du reste, comme je vous ai dit, ayez de la vertu, aimez l'honneur plus que la vie, et vous serez dans l'ordre.

Excellent though this sounds, Arlequin is disturbed by the mention of *honneur*. What exactly does it mean?

LE SEIGNEUR Vous approuverez ce que cela veut dire. C'est qu'il faut se venger d'une injure, ou périr plutôt que de la souffrir.

ARLEQUIN Tout ce que vous m'avez dit n'est donc qu'un coq-à-l'âne, car si je suis obligé d'être généreux il faut que je pardonne aux gens; si je suis obligé d'être méchant, il faut que je les assomme. Comment donc faire pour tuer le monde et le laisser vivre?

LE SEIGNEUR Vous serez généreux et bon, quand on ne vous insultera pas.

ARLEQUIN Je vous entends, il m'est défendu d'être meilleur que les autres; et si je rends le bien pour le mal, je serai donc un homme sans honneur?

An insult, insists the official, can only be wiped out by blood, either your enemy's or your own.

ARLEQUIN Que la tache y reste. Vous parlez du sang comme si c'était l'eau de la rivière. Je vous rend votre paquet de noblesse, mon honneur n'est pas fait pour être noble, il est trop raisonnable pour cela.

This attitude to honour and duelling is the same as that of Scarron's Jodelet.[1] But now the case is argued with devastating logic and, with honour, the other aristocratic virtues and values of the previous age, *générosité*, *honnête homme*, *vertu* itself, are submitted to scrutiny by a 'reasonable' man. This early expression of the egalitarianism and humanitarianism of the new century is primarily an attack on a social order which, in the Voltairean view, simple reason applied with irony should be capable of demolishing. But, as with Voltaire, reason has a moral basis. It rests on the 'natural' integrity of the plain man, uncorrupted by class and religious prejudices. Arlequin thus becomes a

---

[1] See pp. 71-2 above.

type of Noble Savage, a visitor from that other fairyland, Reason's Utopia.

If one integrates the social protest in *La Double Inconstance* with the rest of the play, the whole comedy becomes bitter. Clearsighted on class, Arlequin is duped in love, as is Silvia. They accept their rewards in exchange for their emotional integrity. But though this conclusion can be drawn, it is doubtful whether Marivaux intended it.[1] In love, he seems to say, the end justifies the means and, since his characters achieve happiness, that is all that matters.

❦

Yet one must look more closely at Marivaux's conception of love, even in his most 'innocent' plays and characters. It may appear surprising that this conception, as traditionally understood, should have flourished in a century notable for its hedonism, often extending to the lascivious and sometimes to the pornographic. Surely this is incompatible with the dawning of 'tenderness' in immature hearts often considered as typical of him.

One must discard at once the interpretation at the deepest level, which would remove some of Marivaux's plays from the domain of comedy altogether: that the first love is the only true one and for the woman particularly involves a total commitment which can never be transferred to another person. Therefore, generally at an early age, she must make as sure as possible of her own feelings and the man's before reaching a decision on which her life's happiness will depend. There is no second *jeunesse*, there will be no second chance.

This might be said of the Silvia of *Le Jeu de l'amour*, although even she has other motivations, as has been seen. But it is found nowhere else in Marivaux. The two *Surprises* and *La Double Inconstance* concern second loves and none of his other plays supports the theory.

To jump from the sublime to its opposite, were eighteenth-century audiences titillated by watching the love responses of virtual boys and girls and identifying themselves imaginatively with the same immature personae? Could Silvia be described as an early bunny-girl – there are generally bunnies in fairyland – and bouncy little Arlequin still more plausibly as a bunny-boy? Taking one short step further, could he be

---

[1] At that date. Four years later, having written *L'Île de la Raison*, it would be more probable. See below, p. 212.

compared to some Teenybopper's Delight in a modern pop group, making his appeal to the horrible child that is said to be in all of us? The most obvious objections to this are that no contemporary commentator even hinted at it and that, except in the early *Arlequin poli par l'amour*, Silvia is paired not with Arlequin but with Lélio. Nevertheless the truest response to a play is often subconscious and the element of mock-juvenile eroticism which it is possible to see in Marivaux would take a natural place in the sophisticated sensuality of the period. That it would not be foreign to it, though in a farcical form, is illustrated by the lisping Isabelle of the *parades*,[1] of which the earliest was composed towards 1711. Later, there are the adolescents Chérubin and Fanchette in Beaumarchais's *Le Mariage de Figaro*.

A rather different element can be perceived with more certainty. One recalls Dom Juan's description of the pleasures of seduction.[2] He experiences, he says, 'une douceur extrême' in overcoming 'l'innocente pudeur d'une âme qui a peine à rendre les armes, à forcer pied à pied les petites résistances qu'elle nous oppose, à vaincre les scrupules dont elle se fait un honneur, et à la mener doucement où nous avons envie de la faire venir.' Such lines, taken in themselves, could easily be applied to the Marivaudian approach. The distinction is that Dom Juan is an experienced rake relishing the conquest of 'une jeune beauté' and once he has won her the feast is ended. Marivaux's heroes are different men with different intentions and the women pin them down further by asking: 'You are quite sure you will love me always?', receiving an unqualified 'Yes'. Yet the preliminaries are not completely different. A comparable *ars amoris* is sketched out in the first *Surprise de l'amour* (I. ii), in which the attractions of woman for the male are described by Lélio in a revealing conversation with Arlequin. Man's approach to love, he says, is to follow the rules, as though it were a duty or an obligation: 'Nous avons la marotte d'être délicat parce que cela donne un air plus tendre. Nous faisons l'amour réglément . . .' Woman lacks this premeditation; she lights up spontaneously: 'Une femme ne veut être ni tendre ni délicat, ni fâchée ni bien aise; elle est tout cela sans le savoir, *et cela est charmant*. Regardez-la quand elle aime et qu'elle ne veut pas le dire, morbleu, nos tendresses les plus babillardes approchent-elles de l'amour qui passe à travers son silence?'

[1] See below, pp. 234 and 241.
[2] Quoted on p. 132 above.

Man, continues Lélio, needs the stimulus of 'love and pleasure' before his heart comes to life. But:

... le cœur d'une femme se donne sa secousse à lui-même; il part sur un mot qu'on dit, sur un mot qu'on ne dit pas, sur une contenance. Elle a beau vous avoir dit qu'elle aime; le répète-t-elle, vous l'apprenez toujours, vous ne le saviez pas encore: ici par une impatience, par une froideur, par une imprudence, par une distraction, en baissant les yeux, en les relevant, en sortant de sa place, en y restant; enfin c'est de la jalousie, du calme, de l'inquiétude, de la joie, du babil et du silence de toutes couleurs. Et le moyen de ne pas *s'enivrer du plaisir* que cela donne?

Having described so enthusiastically the delights of watching a woman's involuntary responses, Lélio, having been rebuffed in love, is determined to forgo them. Woman, he concludes, using the tiger metaphor already mentioned, is dangerous and should be avoided altogether. The intoxication is wonderful, but the subsequent letdown too cruel. (Yet, like a chronic addict, he relapses in the end and the rest of the play shows in detail how he does so.)

The emphasis, in this key scene and many other passages in Marivaux, is on *plaisir*, regarded unequivocally as the aim of love. There is equal emphasis on *délicat*, *délicatesse*. The delicate pleasure sought by Marivaux's characters was also sought by Molière's Dom Juan. In the passage quoted on p. 132 he speaks of 'une douceur extrême' but later, when describing the stimuli required to awaken his 'love', he uses identical terms. The visible affection of the two young lovers, said Dom Juan, offended 'la délicatesse de mon cœur'. While the cynicism of the practised seducer cannot be transferred to Lélio, his emotive processes can. Both experience the same kind of pleasure and define it in the same way. Lélio, however, is a more genuinely 'delicate' personality and cannot pursue it like a Don Juan. He looks beyond the momentary satisfaction to a lifetime's pleasure in marriage,[1] assuming that, as in the fairy-tales, they will live happily ever after.

No doubt this is more 'moral' and, as it is worked out in the plays, it leads to the further conclusion, necessarily absent from Don Juanism, that the woman's personality must be respected. More than that, she is

[1] See the next chapter for the assumption of the lasting stability of marriage in the *comédie bourgeoise*.

capable of feeling and demanding the same 'delicate pleasure' as the man. The Silvia of *Le Jeu de l'amour* does this, as we have seen. She and the other heroines only succeed by controlling their spontaneity and playing the game with apparent coolness and reserve. The effort entailed, if we accept Lélio's judgement of feminine nature proved later to be rather naïve, must be very great and shows the value she places, not merely on winning the man but on the delicious process of doing so. The result is a double seduction in which the man is not the dominant figure. At best it leads to a shared pleasure, with equality between both sides, though Silvia's desire for 'victory' leaves room for a certain doubt. There would be none if she were a frivolous or calculating coquette of the kind already established in comedy, but she is not typed as one and this interpretation of the part would obviously be wrong. She is much nearer to the Célidée of Corneille's *Galerie du Palais*.[1] What Marivaux achieved was a 'delicate' balance between the two sexes, weighted slightly in the woman's favour, which no other French dramatist had attempted until then.

What has just been written could be transposed to a more immediately sexual plane and there is no need of beds on the stage to underline the analogy. But just as sexual intercourse was an anticlimax for Dom Juan, so it would be for these characters, who should not be pursued beyond the ending of the play. Their enjoyment of each other is, for want of a better word, psychological, though the psychology is founded, however fastidiously, on sensual implications. One is therefore not justified in seeing Marivaux as the dramatist of innocent immaturity, or in confining him to 'tender sensibility'. He uses the appearance of the first to appeal to the sophisticated audiences of his time and can quite rightly be praised as an analyst of love in the line of Racine,[2] but using comedy as his appropriate medium.

The rest of Marivaux's plays, some thirty in number, add little to his reputation or his contribution to French comedy. Some, such as *Le Prince travesti*, a three-act Spanish-style comedy (1724), *Le Triomphe de l'amour* (three acts, 1732), *Les Serments indiscrets* (five acts, 1732), *L'Heureux Stratagème* (three acts, 1733), and the more realistic *Les Fausses Confidences* (three acts, 1737), are concerned with love manœuvres, impersonations and sometimes switches of partners which throw further light on his main plays but do not equal or closely resemble them.

A comedy of manners can be discerned in such plays as *La Fausse Suivante* (1724) and in the one-act *L'Héritier de village* (1725) which contrasts peasant characters advantageously with Parisian sophisticates and resembles Dufresny's *La Coquette de village*.[1] Here and in a few other comedies Marivaux followed Dufresny or Dancourt, with little originality or success.

A small group of plays is made up of philosophical comedies, using that word in its eighteenth-century sense. In *L'Île des esclaves* (one act, 1725) Arlequin is shipwrecked with his master and other companions on an island inhabited by ex-slaves who turn the tables by oppressing any 'masters' who fall into their hands and condemning them to slavery until they mend their ways. The reformist message in this early example of republicanism is heavily stressed in the dialogue. The more ambitious *L'Île de la Raison ou les Petits Hommes* (three acts, 1727) presents a Utopian community governed entirely by Reason which endows its adherents with impeccable if paradoxical morals. They tower physically above the Europeans who have been cast up there and have shrunk on arrival to a tiny size to match the pettiness of their minds and prejudices. Can these creatures be human? the islanders ask. As one by one they are converted to reasonableness they prove to be so and grow to the same size as their hosts. Marivaux had borrowed an idea from *Gulliver's Travels* (translated in 1727 and immediately popular in France) and developed it quite differently. One convention of his islanders, foreshadowing a tendency noticed in *Le Jeu de l'amour et du hasard*, is that the woman should take the initiative in courtship. As the emotionally weaker sex, she should not be exposed to 'resisting' the man's advances but should 'attack' first and at her own choice. A European character half agrees: 'Dans le fond, en France cela commence à s'établir.'

This feminism, no doubt reflecting the views of Madame de Lambert's salon, seems to have been considerably developed in *La Nouvelle*

---

[1] See above, pp. 183–4. Elsewhere also Marivaux introduces peasant characters using the conventional stage-rustic speech.

Colonie ou la Ligue des femmes (three acts, 1729). The play was never printed but can be reconstructed from a contemporary account in *Le Mercure de France* and a shorter version or variation in one act entitled *La Colonie* (1750). The women, headed by Silvia in the first version, demand liberation from the tyranny and injustice of men and threaten to withhold their love if they do not get it. This is represented as another revolt of the slaves. Finally the women are forced to drop their demands, but not before a vigorous protest has been made.

As drama these plays are negligible and are hardly comedies either. *L'Île des esclaves*, with Arlequin, enjoyed a reasonable success. The next two failed, decisively and deservedly, after a single performance. *La Colonie* was acted only by amateurs. They possess some interest, however, as vehicles for Marivaux's ideas and as proof that he was not as isolated as might appear from the general ideology of his period. His mind was open at a fairly early date to rationalism and other influences of the Enlightenment though, unlike Voltaire, he did not attempt to build a whole drama on them.

It is worth stressing that, much more than Molière, he took feminist claims seriously. The most striking illustration of the change in attitudes is provided by Molière's mockery of the pretensions of Philaminte and her companions in *Les Femmes savantes*.[1]

[1] See above, p. 106.

BOURGEOIS COMEDY: SENTIMENT AND MORALIZATION

Diderot and the drame bourgeois *– the
middle-class family and its values – incipient
tendencies in Marivaux – a transitional playwright, Destouches –*
Le Philosophe marié, Le Glorieux, Le Dissipateur *– comédie larmoyante
and* La Chaussée *– Mélanide, Le Préjugé à la mode, L'École des mères –
Gresset's* Le Méchant *– Voltaire and* Nanine *– parody and
lightness: the* parades, musical comedy *– images
of woman and wealth – Sade's solution*

The main direction which literary comedy was beginning to take in
the 1730s led eventually to its virtual extinction for a time. Although
there was no one turning-point, a significant terminal date was 1757–8,
when Diderot wrote his two plays *Le Fils naturel* and *Le Père de
famille* and prefaced them with his theoretical writings, *Les Entretiens
sur 'Le Fils naturel'* and *Le Discours sur la poésie dramatique*. In these
Diderot, an excellent critic if a feeble dramatist, defined and named
what in one place he called 'la comédie sérieuse' and in another 'le
tragique domestique et bourgeois'. From the second term emerged
the category and the conscious conception of the *drame bourgeois*,[1] a
genre intermediate between high tragedy and entertaining comedy,
based theoretically on contemporary social reality. This kind of *drame*
can make for poor theatre, as it did in Diderot's own plays, but its
historical importance has been immense and its survival powers,
thanks to gifted dramatists (Chekhov's work can certainly be related
to it), have kept it alive until today. For Diderot and his generation

---

[1] The term *tragédie bourgeoise* was already current. Voltaire used it in the
Preface to *Nanine* (1749).

it was moral and sentimental (with an important element of pathos, provoking tears), aiming at naturalness in expression and characterization and, inevitably in that part of eighteenth-century thought typified by Rousseau, exalting nature as the infallible guide to right conduct. What was called 'natural' feeling could result only in good acts.

The key-word in this type of *drame* is *bourgeois*, distinguishing it from the historical *drame* and the horror *drame*, which also began to develop. After the conclusion of Louis XIV's last decades and the Regency, the arrived bourgeoisie began to take over and reconstruct for itself an idea of social morality based on the family. It was not the essentially aristocratic family of the previous century, which in its typical forms was dynastic and sought to increase its influence by marriage alliances regardless of the preferences of individuals and by a cultivation of the Crown and to a lesser degree of the Church as sources of wealth and preferment. The wealth of the middle-class family was such as could be built up in a generation or two by hard-working and successful citizens without the favours of the Court. Genealogy was irrelevant – hence the gradual disappearance in literature of the aristocratic snob, the social climber and the backwoods nobleman, even as objects of mockery. This family was a small, ultimately smug unit (in essentials the 'nuclear family' of today) composed of father and mother, perhaps a couple of children, and a restricted number of close relatives and one or two reliable friends. What bound it together was 'natural' affection between its members and respect for the parents, particularly the father, on whose authority the cohesion of the group was considered to depend. This, together with the stability and permanence of marriage, was an essential part of the image. The moral code was no longer derived either from the caste-code or from the teachings of religion, but was self-made like the family in accordance with the circumstances. It was based, as already indicated, on *vertu*, a word which had lost the austere connotations it possessed in seventeenth-century tragedy, and now, according to the theory of 'natural goodness', conditioned true love and happiness instead of running against them.

For all its defects, which became apparent in the course of time, the eighteenth-century family represented a not unworthy attempt to rebuild society on a foundation of hundreds of these like-minded little groups. In self-defence they rejected both Dom Juan and Turcaret. They looked on the rake and the adventurer as menaces, condemned speculation, including gambling, in favour of caution and 'probity', feared brilliance of any kind, material or intellectual, for the traps it might conceal, and suspected the glitter of Parisian and Court circles for the same reason.

Such was the underlying ethos of the *drame bourgeois*. Dull as a concept, it made for dull theatre, but at first it was sufficiently novel and in tune with the age to appeal to a wide public interested in family relationships, the threats to their security from outside and inside, and the eventually successful resistance of the group.[1]

From the mid-century onwards this kind of play tended to absorb comedy which could only compete by assimilating itself to the *drame* and in so doing lost most of the features which had characterized it until then. The process, however, was a gradual one and it is only by looking back that one detects its slow and often uncertain emergence.[2]

In Marivaux the importance of *sensibilité*, derided in slightly earlier comedy, was already noticeable. In his plays it meant delicate feeling and could even be an aristocratic quality, but in other hands and in the *drame* it easily developed into *sensiblerie*, its debased form. Yet one shades into the other (as had religion and religiosity at the time of *Tartuffe*), and the two were assimilated by the insistence that both sprang from 'the heart', making that the supreme arbiter of human relationships. As will be seen, post-Marivaudian comedy advocates openly a *moralité du cœur*, which Marivaux did not do; in him it is merely implicit. Implicit also is his assumption that marriage is a loving and lasting relationship, though again he does not base a whole family ethos upon it. One can also deduce from his plays that he considered love as 'virtuous' in itself when based on natural impulses and gave it precedence over all other considerations, particularly social. He stopped short of the ultimate step of substituting equality of feeling for equality of rank, but he came near it in *Le Jeu de l'amour et du hasard*, swerving away by the disclosure that the two couples

---

[1] The bourgeois family, with bourgeois values, had of course always existed. Molière alone contains evidence enough. The difference is in the emphasis. Molière's paterfamilias is usually tyrannical or inadequate, his wife often a dragon or an *évaporée*. Even when the group is preserved by the solid good sense of a member or a level-headed friend, this is not the main theme of the comedy. The assumption that it should be and that family unity constitutes the moral of the play provides a new angling – apart from the intrusion of a sentimentality which is never in Molière – which makes the *drame bourgeois* a different genre.

[2] Sedaine's principal play, *Le Philosophe sans le savoir* (1765), was first published as a *comédie*. Only later was it called a *drame*, which defines it better.

Silvia–Dorante and Lisette–Arlequin are in fact social equals.[1] Yet
Dorante believed that his beloved was a servant and was led to propose
marriage to her in that capacity. What was a 'game' (for the audience)
in 1730 could be presented as a real possibility twenty years later.

❧

More clearly than Marivaux, two lesser playwrights bridged the gap
between cynical comedy and the fully sentimental family play. The
earlier, Philippe Néricault Destouches (1680–1754), produced his first
plays shortly after Regnard and Lesage and before Dufresny had entirely finished. He was, and remained, preoccupied by the old search
for a central character who could be labelled according to his dominant
quality and was usually unsympathetic. His early plays, *L'Ingrat*
(1712), *L'Irrésolu* (1713) and *Le Médisant* (1715), exemplify this.
They borrowed from his immediate predecessors but differed by an
incipient tendency to point a moral lesson. Had he stopped there he
would hardly be remembered.

There was a break of some ten years, most of them spent at the
French Embassy in London, where patrons secured him an influential
post. Returning to France in 1725, he continued to enjoy Court
appointments as sinecures, settled comfortably in the country estate he
acquired near Melun (of which town he was Honorary Governor) and
wrote his remaining comedies, three of which are particularly interesting.

The first, a contemporary success, was *Le Philosophe marié ou le
Mari honteux de l'être* (five acts, verse, 1727). It is built round an
extraordinary situation. The 'philosophical' hero Ariste, always
immersed in his books, has contracted a marriage with the virtuous
Mélite, but insists that it should be kept secret, partly because of a
disapproving rich uncle (the hackneyed money consideration which
Destouches took over from other dramatists), and partly because a
'philosopher' should shun marriage for the troubles it brings. If the
truth became known Ariste would lose his reputation for wisdom.
His wife loyally keeps the secret, though both are sorely tried when
her husband's friend, the Marquis, attempts to make love to her, not

[1] It might be objected that he went the whole way in *La Double Inconstance*,
where the prince marries the village maiden and the court-lady Arlequin. But
this belongs to the fairy-tale ethos in which such matches were traditional and had
only tenuous connections with social realities.

knowing that she is married. The situation is spun out over five acts, though it could have been terminated at any point by a frank word from Ariste. In the end he speaks it, the rich uncle is won over, and the Marquis accepts a different match. The implied lesson is that marriage is an excellent thing in spite of 'philosophy' and some conventionally cynical remarks by the *suivante*. Mélite is a paragon of loving obedience. Her *vertu*, consisting of fidelity and submission to her husband in almost unbearable circumstances, is finally rewarded by her open recognition as his wife. She is a type of heroine who will recur and be admired in other plays, though in this play she is not the only kind of woman portrayed. There are still traces of sharpness in her more spirited sister, who continually spars with her suitor and treats him with something near contempt. But in the last scene she also succumbs to marriage, with the defiant words:

> Oui, monstre, il est écrit que je t'épouserai;
> Mon penchant m'y contraint, mais je m'en vengerai.

Her suitor has the reassuring answer:

> Pestez, sans vous contraindre.
> Vous m'aimez, je vous aime, et je n'ai rien à craindre.

Since they are in love, everything will be all right.

This vindication of marriage based on heartfelt love becomes a background feature in *Le Glorieux* (five acts, 1732), Destouches's most outstanding play. Other family ties begin to appear and are given full sentimental due, inseparable from the main theme but subservient to it. It hinges on the 'punishment' and eventual reform of an arrogantly vain young man, the Comte de Tufière. His conceit and presumption are represented as aristocratic in contrast to the simpler manners of other characters. He wishes to marry Isabelle, daughter of the wealthy and plain-speaking bourgeois Lisimon, and does so after he has been taught his lesson, summed up as:

> Il faut se faire aimer; on vient de me convaincre.
> Et je sens que la gloire et la présomption
> N'attirent que la haine et l'indignation.
>
> (V. vi)

To effect his conversion the strictures of old Lisimon have not been enough. A plot has been necessary involving the well-tried devices of hidden identities and recognitions. There is a Lisette in this play who differs from previous Lisettes by her discreet refinement. She is more a companion than a *suivante* to Isabelle. She proves to be the daughter of a shabbily dressed old man called Lycandre who has looked after her from a distance (she was brought up in a convent, an apparent orphan). At the same time she learns that the Comte, for whom she had felt an unexplained affection, is her brother. The recognition gives an absurd but typically touching scene showing Lisette (real name Constance) overwhelmed by joy, emotion and respect. 'Your father', says Lycandre in effect, 'is not far off; you will soon see him.'

LISETTE Sortons, monsieur; je veux embrasser ses genoux
Et mourir de plaisir dans des transports si doux.
LYCANDRE Vois n'irez pas bien loin pour goûter cette joie.
Vous voulez la chercher et le ciel vous l'envoie.
Oui, ma fille, voici ce père malheureux;
Il vous voit, il vous parle, il est devant vos yeux.
LISETTE (*se jetant à ses pieds*) Quoi! c'est vous-même? O ciel!
que mon âme est ravie!
Je goûte le moment le plus doux de ma vie.
LYCANDRE Ma fille, levez-vous. Je connais votre cœur,
Et, je vous l'ai prédit, vous ferez mon bonheur.
Mais hélas, que je crains de revoir votre frère!
LISETTE Mon frère? Et quel est-il?
LYCANDRE   Le comte de Tufière.
LISETTE Je ne sais où j'en suis! Je ne respire plus!
Daignez me soutenir.
LYCANDRE   Qu'il doit être confus
Quand il vous connaîtra!
LISETTE   Moi sa sœur?
LYCANDRE   Oui, ma fille.
LISETTE Sans doute nous sortons de la même famille;
Oui, le comte est mon frère, et dès que je l'ai vu
A travers ses mépris mon cœur l'a reconnu.
De mon faible pour lui je ne suis plus surprise.
(IV. iv)

Lycandre is more than an affectionate paterfamilias. He is a wealthy nobleman who lost his estates and was forced into exile in England by his late wife's 'presumption' which involved him in a duel and political disgrace. He has just been reinstated after an appeal to the king, but his wife's detestable example convinced him of the importance of humility. For this reason he had his daughter brought up in poverty and is determined to correct his over-ambitious son.

The bourgeois or levelling moral is incomplete, since Lisette has turned out to be a rich heiress of noble birth, though it is assumed that she will remain modestly humble. In class terms, the play shows the aristocracy criticizing itself for the arrogance of some of its members. The father-image, perfect in Lycandre, is somewhat tarnished in Lisimon, who is attracted by young Lisette and offers in an early scene to set her up in a house of her own as his mistress (he has a wife who does not appear on the stage). He is nevertheless treated with respect as the father of the second girl, Isabelle.

Le Glorieux is thus a halfway house between the older comedy whose conventions it utilizes and a new kind centred upon the virtuous family. It is certainly not yet a *drame*, but it is hardly a comedy either in any of the accepted senses.

There are more comic features in Destouches's third major play, *Le Dissipateur ou l'Honnête Friponne* (five acts, verse), not produced in Paris until 1753, when it was unsuccessful, but acted in the provinces in 1737.[1] In obedience to Destouches's favourite formula the hero, Cléon, is a wild young man determined on display who throws his money about recklessly in reaction, he explains, against his close-fisted late father, until finally he is brought to heel and 'cured'. The way in which this is done provides the main interest. The woman with whom he is in love, Julie, acting in concert with his uncle Géronte and her own father, the Baron, turns his costly gifts to her to good financial advantage, surreptitiously buys up his estate which he has mortgaged to pay his debts, and finally faces him at the gaming-table and wins the entire remnant of his fortune by her skilful cardplay. But her object in ruining him is only to reform him. When she sees that this is achieved she gives back his whole fortune together with her hand in marriage. This highly businesslike yet tenderhearted woman is a notable and perhaps unique creation. Obviously different from the meek heroines of other comedies, this 'honnête friponne' of the subtitle differs also from the earlier rapacious coquettes, who set out to ruin men out of greed or spite. She manages to reconcile goodness with acquisitiveness, an essentially bourgeois problem which will be

[1] According to the *Répertoire du théâtre français*, Vol. 59 (1813).

returned to later. As to the reform of Cléon, one has only to compare this play with Regnard's *Le Joueur*[1] to see the distance that had been travelled since. In *Le Joueur*, which Destouches would almost certainly have known, the gambler hero loses both his money and the girl who sadly abandons him, but he remains unrepentant. Forced to choose between love and his 'vice', he opts for the second. In the ethos of Destouches such a conclusion would have been unthinkable.

Before it is tamed, however, youthful revolt deals some nasty kicks which greatly enliven the play. Cléon and his companions are more openly disrespectful of crabbed old age, particularly fathers and uncles, than in any other notable play of the century. The *suivante* Finette observes:

> Les lois devraient défendre à ces vieux opulents,
> Qui ne sont bons à rien, de passer soixante ans.
> Mais ces oncles malins sont cloués à la vie.
>
> (III. ii)

Old uncle Géronte defends avarice in specious terms. Having declared:

> Plus on aime l'argent et moins on a de vices,

he goes on to argue that the business of amassing money is a full-time interest in itself. If one admires a fine château or a charming woman it is enough to know that one could buy them if one wished, without actually doing so. All these potentialities are contained in one's coffers,

> ... et par là, l'avarice qu'on blâme
> Est le plaisir des sens et le charme de l'âme.
>
> (III. v)

But this is not so for the exuberant young. They need money only to spend it and their attitude to women is considerably more direct. The Marquis, son of the Baron and a friend of Cléon, observes of a girl:

> ... Parbleu!
> C'est un friand morceau.[2] Quel enjouement! quel feu!
> J'en suis fou.

---

[1] See above, pp. 177–80.
[2] The description of a woman as 'a tasty dish' offended the *bienséances* of polite comedy. Apart from this example I have only come across it in the mouths of valets (e.g. Germon in Voltaire's *Nanine*), from whom coarser speech was acceptable.

One of the brightest passages in the play occurs in III. vii–x. Uncle Géronte has just been persuaded that his nephew has adopted a sober and studious way of life when loud bursts of laughter and conversation are heard in the next room. It is, supposes the deluded Géronte, a gathering of learned men disputing about some philosophical question. At that moment the Marquis totters in drunk, waving a table-napkin, followed by a hilarious crowd of men and women who have come to see why Cléon has left the party and urge him to rejoin them.

Such touches make up the comic content of *Le Dissipateur* and probably explain its lack of success in an increasingly serious age. The spendthrift and his gay companions are shown in the end to be anti-social or false friends, but they have had a good run for their money and have been able to state a by no means outrageous case against the stingy life-style. On the opposite side, Géronte is hardly impressive. Only Julie, baron's daughter though she is and aided by luck and skill at the card-table, emerges as a true champion of bourgeois values. She is constantly praised for her *vertu* but more accurately, in the last line of the play, for her prudence.

As in much other eighteenth-century writing the moral conclusion is obvious, but before reaching it so many immoral characters and situations have appeared that the total effect is questionable, and even the author's intention. It is probable that Destouches was on the side of the angels as he conceived them and that one should take at its face-value this passage from his Preface to *Le Glorieux*:

> ... je crois que l'art dramatique n'est estimable qu'autant qu'il a pour but d'instruire en divertissant. J'ai toujours eu pour maxime incontestable que, quelque amusante que puisse être une comédie, c'est un ouvrage imparfait, et même dangereux, si l'auteur ne s'y propose pas de corriger les mœurs, de tomber sur le ridicule, de décrier le vice, et de mettre la vertu dans un si beau jour qu'elle attire l'estime et la vénération publique ...

This is the old argument in defence of comedy, including Molière's,[1] but with significant changes of emphasis: more insistence on the need to 'instruire' and to 'corriger les mœurs', no mention of satire, none of laughter. A comedy can be 'divertissante' or 'amusante', but almost as subsidiary qualities. On the other hand the positive stress on moral uplift is very strong. This is a recipe for didactic drama and the final

[1] See above, pp. 109–10.

sentence might have been adopted as a slogan by Destouches's immediate successors as they moved towards the *drame*.

The degree of sentimentality in Destouches has already been indicated in the descriptions of his comedies. The moral lessons are conveyed by the stories and rammed home in the concluding lines of the plays. Open moralizations in the form of speeches commenting on virtues and vices are comparatively rare and short. A few there are, notably in *Le Glorieux*, but not so many as to serve as more than a pointer to future developments. Some are cynical, as they were in Regnard and Dufresny. The didactic element in Destouches is therefore moderate, in spite of his declarations. For this again his work can be considered as intermediate between two extremes.

❦

Around the year 1740 the term *comédie larmoyante* was born and applied derisively to the work of Pierre-Claude Nivelle de La Chaussée (1692–1754) who began writing in early middle age with *La Fausse Antipathie* (1733) and composed nine other known plays including one tragedy (*Maximien*, 1738) and ending with *L'École de la jeunesse* in 1749. He may also have written some *parades*, the grossly farcical playlets popular in private houses and in the theatre of the fairs.[1]

'Weepy comedy' either becomes *drame*, shedding its comic elements as it had begun to do in Destouches, or it appears as a debased form of tragedy. The dramatists of the previous century had played for tears in tragedy and tragicomedy. One thinks at once of Racine's *Bérénice*, but there were very numerous other examples. A practical playwright[2] planning a weepy play (which is as difficult as Molière's problem of planning a laughable one) has one constant standby. He takes an appealingly innocent heroine and turns the screw until she begins to scream. In high tragedy she continues to scream till the end. In debased or bourgeois tragedy the screw is loosened and there are

[1] See below, p. 234.
[2] There are signs that La Chaussée was this and not a natural emotionalist, unless he experienced a personal conversion to sentimentality in middle age of which nothing is known. For an illuminating summing-up of his early years see R. Niklaus, *The Eighteenth Century* (1970), pp. 306–7: 'Mingled with the *libertins* . . . Lost fortune in the Law bankruptcy, but was still able to live comfortably . . . Wrote *contes* for the licentious society of the Regency . . . Was a member of the *bande joyeuse* that made the *parade* fashionable . . . Was branded as a *méchant* for his behaviour towards women . . .'

tears of relief and joy. With this the second constant resource is con-
current or associated. The affectionate family group gathers round
her and their tears or those they provoke complete the effect. (In
Racinian and, even more, in Cornelian tragedy, the family are a nest
of hatred and envy and their relationships are the opposite of the
eighteenth-century image.)

Both these resources were used in La Chaussée's typical *Mélanide*
(five acts, verse, 1741). Eighteen years before the play opens the unhappy heroine had been secretly married to her lover, but separated
from him by her parents (these would be 'bad' parents, but they do
not appear and are now dead), and the pair have lost sight of each
other. Mélanide is staying with a friend whose daughter is courted by
a young man believed to be Mélanide's nephew and by a serious
Marquis of mature years. The recognitions unite Mélanide and the
Marquis, who is her long-lost husband, while the young man of course
proves to be their son and marries the friend's daughter. The main
stress is not on this young-love relationship but on that of the father
and his unrecognized son. There is a second father-figure in the young
girl's uncle, who seeks to make everyone happy by persuading them
to behave 'virtuously'.

LE MARQUIS Ne faisons désormais qu'une même famille.
        O ciel, tu me fais voir, en comblant tous mes vœux,
        Que le devoir[1] n'est fait que pour nous rendre heureux.

Mélanide is hardly a comedy, though so styled. It has no comic
situations or characters. We have seen what the marquis has become
and there are no comic servants – in fact no servants at all, except for
an anonymous valet who simply carries messages and announces
callers. There is no attempt at humour, wit or irony, but long and
ponderous speeches in praise of *vertu* and *sensibilité*. At its date
Mélanide was moderately successful.

Before this La Chaussée had concentrated on the marital relationship
alone in *Le Préjugé à la mode* (1735), another verse comedy in five acts
which retained some of the usual comic features in the background.
The 'fashionable prejudice' which is attacked and whose roots were in

---

[1] His 'duty' was to remain faithful to his wife when she is at last discovered and
to give up the young girl, for whom he has conceived a passion. The father–son
rivalry had occurred in other plays, but is made more innocent here because the
identities are concealed.

the previous century is that a man of quality should not be in love with
his wife:

> Cet usage n'est plus que chez la bourgeoisie;
> Mais ailleurs on a fait de l'amour conjugal
> Un parfait ridicule, un travers sans égal.
>
> (I. iv)

Observing this convention the husband, d'Urval, has neglected his
wife in favour of various mistresses but has now fallen passionately
in love with her again. But he dare not show it for fear of ridicule. La
Chaussée obviously borrowed from *Le Philosophe marié* of Destouches[1] but found a different motivation and carried the situation
much further. The husband woos his wife anonymously, sending her
costly presents which she thinks must come from some other admirer,
to her immense distress. This new Patient Griselda conceives it as her
duty to remain faithful to her unfaithful husband and also to conceal
the fact that she is unhappy. She never wavers in her unselfish devotion
to him and is finally rewarded by his open declaration of love. The
anti-marriage faction, represented by two cynical and worldly marquis,
are routed, after being condemned by a goodhearted *suivante*.

This play, probably La Chaussée's best, is near-Marivaudian in
places. D'Urval's concealed wooing of his wife gives an opening for
his attempts to divine her feelings towards him and to confirm his own.
At one point he hesitates between revealing his love and leaving
altogether, as happened in *La Surprise de l'amour*. Towards the end
Constance, still groping for his response, wonders among other
questions whether it is embarrassment (*honte*) which prevents him
from approaching her. She is certain of herself but not of him, but
decides to risk everything and declare her love:

> Qu'il vienne en sûreté, mes bras lui sont ouverts.
>
> (V. v)

This is more than a Marivaux heroine could ever have said, but the
circumstances and assumptions are different.

There is a quite subtle lovers' dialogue between a second couple,
Damon and Sophie, who refuses to commit herself because the example of d'Urval and Constance has disgusted her with marriage. She

---

[1] See pp. 217–18 above.

does not reject Damon but puts him off with a 'Je ne m'engage à rien'
and:

> De plus, je vous défends jusques au mot d'amour.
>
> (III. ii)

But the strongest reminder of Marivaux is voiced by Constance discussing with her father Sophie's reasons for refusing a man she likes:

ARGANT Pourquoi refuse-t-elle un homme qui lui plaît?
CONSTANCE Ce n'est point un refus, c'est de l'incertitude.
> On ne s'engage point sans quelque inquiétude;
> En cela j'aurais tort de la désapprouver.
> Peut-être auparavant elle veut s'éprouver;
> Peut-être qu'elle cherche, autant qu'il est possible,
> A s'assurer du cœur qu'elle a rendu sensible.

The explanation, which admirably defines the motives and reactions of
Marivaux's lovers, is completely lost on the insensitive Argant:

> Voilà bien des façons qui ne servent à rien.
>
> (I. iii)

One other feature, which could have been derived from Marivaux
or elsewhere, appears not in the long-suffering Constance but in the
more spirited Sophie. She claims feminine equality in marriage. Why
must the wife stay lovingly around while the husband is unfaithful?

> Quoi! parce qu'un perfide aura le nom d'époux
> Il pourra me porter les plus sensibles coups,
> Violer tous les jours le serment qui nous lie,
> M'ôter impunément le bonheur de ma vie,
> Sans qu'il me soit permis de réclamer des droits
> Qui devraient être égaux . . . Mais *ils* ont fait les lois.
> Il faut que je ménage un cruel qui me brave;
> Sa femme est sa compagne et non pas son esclave . . .

and later:

> Quoi! les hommes ont-ils d'autres droits que les nôtres?
>
> (I. v)

The protest is not carried to its logical conclusion, as it would be
later, i.e. in the wife's freedom to have lovers also, because the domin-

ant assumption in La Chaussée is that the wife will always remain loving, whatever the husband does, and this is part of her 'virtuous' though very exacting image, containing a new idealization of woman after the long phase of cynicism. But at least the question has been raised.

To complete this outline of La Chaussée it is only necessary to mention his third major play, *L'École des mères* (five acts, verse, 1744), in which there is a wholehearted return to the theme of the family reunion. In this case a relationship and rivalry between mother and daughter (whom she thinks is her niece) replace the father–son relationship of *Le Préjugé à la mode*. But there are fathers too, a meek supposed orphan on whom the pathos centres and a final assemblage which nearly completes the family circle. The reform of a black-sheep son, a nominal Marquis representing the cynical *libertinage* of the Court, is foreshadowed as possible. The admirable moral is: for perfect happiness get your children to love you:

> En aimant ses enfants, c'est soi-même qu'on aime.
> Mais pour jouir d'un sort parfaitement heureux
> Il faut s'en faire aimer de même.

This comedy, written exceptionally in irregular verse, enjoyed great success on first production and later. It is full of vicissitudes and is La Chaussée's strongest vindication of bourgeois morality versus 'fashionable' corruption.

It would be unjust to qualify La Chaussée's work as a whole as *larmoyante*, but contemporaries attached the label to him and it has stuck. He was not unique in devising tearfully emotional scenes, but they are rather more numerous and conspicuous in him than in a Destouches, and their existence narrowly justifies crediting him with the authorship of a new kind of comedy. It matched and was influenced by the novel of the time, in particular Prévost's *Manon Lescaut* (1731) and Richardson's *Pamela or Virtue Rewarded* (1740–1) which Prévost translated. *Pamela* tells the touching story of a humble girl who resists seduction by her upper-class employer and is ultimately rewarded by his offer of marriage. The theme in various guises was familiar in French comedy past, present and to come, yet when La Chaussée himself wrote an adaptation for the Comédie Française, the first performance on 3 December 1743 was interrupted by a riot in the pit and the play had to be withdrawn. This may have been due to La Chaussée's incompetence, but possibly to the fact that not all audiences, particularly at a popular level, had as yet been won over to the enjoyment of virtuous emotionalism.

It is interesting to recall that Scarron, overneglected in favour of Molière, had prophetically burlesqued the *comédie larmoyante* – together with other seriously intended features of eighteenth-century comedy – in *Le Marquis ridicule* of 1655. His weepy scene with its phoney recognition[1] would have been inconceivable a century later on the regular stage, since burlesque had long gone out of fashion there. Only in the underground and fringe *parades* was it possible to mock the self-righteous sentimentality of the age.

Bourgeois comedy persisted, though without tearful scenes, in the only notable play of Louis Gresset (1709–77). Gresset began as a teacher in Jesuit colleges, but was expelled from the order after publishing his poem *Vert-Vert* (1734), which poked mild fun at life in nunneries. He may have written a number of plays, but since he is believed to have destroyed several when he repented and returned to piety, this cannot be said with certainty. His reputation as a comic dramatist rests solely on *Le Méchant* of 1747, yet another character-play with an exciting plot which qualifies it also as a comedy of intrigue. The central character Cléon is a 'bad man' in every sense. He stirs up trouble partly through self-interest, partly through sheer malice. He courts insincerely the mature Florise, then aims at her sweet young daughter Chloé. He is attracted by her uncle's money, but equally and perversely by the charm of her pure simplicity. He misleads his trusting friend, Chloé's true lover, in an attempt to betray him. He poisons other relationships and is ready to use a legal weapon to ruin the uncle-figure Géronte. He is the sum of the wild young men of previous plays, but whereas these had been relatively harmless to others and had usually been reformed, Cléon is considered dangerous until the end and, though unmasked, there is only a faint hint that he might just possibly mend his ways. The character is plausible though unmotivated. His 'badness' is presented as inherently temperamental and never analysed. But pernicious though he is, there is no greatness such as can be found in a Dom Juan. He is bad but not evil, a term

[1] See above, pp. 63–4.

with deeper connotations deriving ultimately from religion. He can be combated and checked by *bonté de cœur* – the comfortable middle-class conviction that human goodness is enough and there is no need to bring in Satan.

He serves also to supply the familiar parable, representing all the anti-bourgeois qualities in an extreme form: sexual promiscuity, contempt of marriage, contempt of the family –

> La parenté m'excède, et ces liens, ces chaînes
> De gens dont on partage ou les torts ou les peines,
> Tour cela préjugés, misères du vieux temps;
> C'est pour le peuple enfin que sont faits les parents.
>
> (II. iii)

– and with that, the corruption of smart society in Paris.

In this unoriginal picture Gresset has added, or at least accentuated, two features. His good family live in the country, not as backwoods gentry nor as exiles in a 'desert', but through choice. Uncle Géronte is immensely proud of his house with its landscaped park and garden. He never tires of showing visitors round them. As Cléon remarks ironically to his friend:

> . . . il faut vous préparer
> À le suivre partout, tout voir, tout admirer,
> Son parc, son potager, ses bois, son avenue.
> Il ne vous fera pas grâce d'une laitue.
>
> (II. vii)

But the country virtues are the true ones. Plainness, honesty, and the back-to-nature movement. The comic rustic has disappeared. Here there are no rustics at all, comic or otherwise, but the wealthy bourgeoisie are preparing to adopt their supposed standards.

With this goes almost necessarily Gresset's condemnation of *esprit*, used as a highly suspect and almost a dirty word. From meaning 'quickness of mind' it has degenerated to 'superficial cleverness', too frequent a source of false and malicious remarks. Wit is no longer a desirable ingredient in the human pudding:

> Ami du bien, de l'ordre, de l'humanité,
> Le *véritable esprit* marche avec la bonté.

... Mon estime toujours marche avec le cœur;
Sans lui l'esprit n'est rien ...

(IV. iv)

The ingenuous young heroine totally lacks *esprit* in any sense of the word. She would like a love match if possible, but her overriding preoccupation is to please her mother by obeying her (I. vi). Presented as a pattern of womanhood, she conforms to Charles Kingsley's 'quiet hint' of the Victorian era:

Be good, sweet maid, and let who can be clever,
    Do lovely things, not dream them, all day long;
And so make Life and Death, and that For Ever,
    One grand sweet song.

The first line has justifiably infuriated several generations of women, but seen in its context, which was also that of the mid-eighteenth century, it becomes more understandable.

There is of course some wit in *Le Méchant*, as in the earlier moral comedies, but it is exclusive to the unpleasant characters and is drowned in the floods of virtuous emotion. Was there no real bite at all in the comedy of the period?

※

If anyone could have placed it there it should have been Voltaire, whose *Candide* (1759) is one of the sharpest peaks of bitter satire in world literature. Yet ten years before this and two years after *Le Méchant* he wrote *Nanine ou le Préjugé vaincu* (1749), which follows the conventions of bourgeois comedy and approaches *drame*. Again there is a country setting, 'le château du comte d'Olban'. The principal characters are the sympathetic Comte, his acid relative the Baronne, who expects him to marry her and so terminate the lawsuits which have divided their two sides of the family, and her reluctant rival Nanine, a humble girl brought up in the Comte's household and distantly patterned on Richardson's Pamela. On account of a misinterpreted letter Nanine is wrongly suspected of having an outside lover (the same suspicion tormented the husband in La Chaussée's *Le Préjugé à la mode* and delayed the reconciliation with his wife). But he is Nanine's father and not her lover and, after his appearance in the last act, she marries the Comte. Other characters are the Comte's mother, the Marquise, a goodhearted valet whose part is mainly functional, and a gardener whose simplicity becomes comic only in one brief scene (II. vi). The Marquise, an over-talkative lady, provides some gentle humour but remains respected as a mother. There is no uncle or *suivante* to shepherd the others towards the happy ending.

Voltaire has not troubled to alter the basic postulates of bourgeois comedy, but has injected them with a seriousness which skirts the tragic. Nanine's dilemma is nearly this. She loves the Comte as much as she admires him but is terrified by the risk of showing it and so degrading him to an unworthy level. Refusing his first offer of marriage, she welcomes the jealous Baronne's plan to consign her to a convent (the refuge, in the tragic mode, of the broken-hearted or over-tempted woman: see e.g. *La Princesse de Clèves*; the decision of Junie in *Britannicus*). Such lines as:

> Délivrez-moi, s'il se peut, de moi-même,
>
> (I. v)

and

> Quoi! l'on [la Baronne] me hait, et je crains d'être aimée!
> Mais moi, mais moi! je me crains encore plus,
>
> (I. v)

together with her short soliloquy on her inner struggle (II. iv), go deeper than conventional sentimentality. To the modest heroine of *Nanine* Voltaire gives a credible psychological motivation which other dramatists had omitted. This sweet maid struggles to be good as the lesser of two evils.

In such a situation 'virtue' must occupy an essential place and it is frequently mentioned and praised, but the emotionalism is restrained and mercifully shortwinded. The play moves fast. Situation follows situation and characters succeed characters with none of the preparatory descriptions that Gresset and others had found necessary. *Nanine* marks the end of the obsession with 'portraits' and so of character-comedy as Voltaire's predecessors had conceived it. It is also a short play, in three acts only, and further shortened and tightened by being written in decasyllables rather than the usual alexandrines. (Prose, as the *drame* illustrates, is the wordiest medium of all.)

The family is present but it is not the warmly affectionate bourgeois

I

group. It is treated in a highly interesting and realistic way, for *Nanine* was first and foremost a social comedy or drama by an author equipped to analyse society with relative objectivity and at the same time to argue a thesis of great general importance. We have left to this late stage his main innovation. His Nanine is the first notable heroine of her line (except Richardson's English Pamela) who does not prove to be of superior birth.[1] Her aristocracy consists in her personal qualities and these in themselves make her a suitable and equal match for the Comte. Her father, when he turns up, remains a commoner, conspicuous for his extreme integrity but materially an old soldier who never achieved promotion for lack of the necessary influences. From the moral point of view, which is dominant, he and she are second to none and all humanity are equal (potentially) in this ethos. The point is made constantly throughout the play.

But Voltaire, with his Parisian background and his aristocratic connections and tastes, could not leave it entirely at that. He knew that the aristocratic family was not yet finished and did not lie down easily. The Baronne, an old-time noblewoman, is heavily sarcastic about the Comte's egalitarian opinions:

> Il faut au moins être bon gentilhomme.
> Un vil savant, un obscur honnête homme
> Serait chez vous, pour un peu de vertu,
> Comme un seigneur avec honneur reçu?

and, guessing he is in love with Nanine:

> Allez, aimez des filles de village,
> Cœur noble et grand; soyez l'heureux rival
> Du magister et du greffier fiscal;[2]
> Soutenez bien l'honneur de votre race.

(I. i)

She is a 'prejudiced' aristocrat who is finally shown up as wrong. But even the Comte's mother, a reasonable if slightly dotty woman, expresses social doubts. She is very fond of Nanine and personally can accept her as a daughter-in-law, but remarks warningly:

[1] Lancaster finds some earlier examples in Dancourt and Dufresny (*History*, IV, pp. 762–4), particularly in the latter's *La Noce interrompue*, whose heroine is a Nanette. But these were plays of a different and lighter type and the aristocracy in them belonged to the impoverished backwoods nobility.

[2] 'The village schoolmaster and the local tax-collector'.

La famille
Étrangement, mon fils, clabaudera.[1]
(III. viii)

and in those moral-pointing final lines she adds:

Que ce jour
Soit des vertus la digne récompense,
Mais sans jamais tirer à conséquence.[2]

Had Voltaire drawn back from the logical conclusion of his egalitarian thesis? There is the story that he had originally intended Nanine to prove to be of noble birth like so many other orphans of romance, but was dissuaded from doing so by a woman admirer.[3] Though worth recording as symptomatic of reactions to the play, the story is most improbable. It would entail a rewriting not only of the recognition scene but of most of the play as it stands. The whole action and the sentiments expressed are so angled towards equality of merit or of 'heart' that if Nanine is not of humble stock they become irrelevant.

So Voltaire had written a bourgeois comedy (there is no other category in which to place it) with a bold thesis tempered by some worldly reservations. He himself, like Racine with *Les Plaideurs*, was inclined to shrug it off. This trifle, as he called it in his first Preface, was not originally intended for the Parisian stage and would not have been printed if an unauthorized edition had not appeared which had to be corrected. He condemns both the *comédie larmoyante* and the *tragédie bourgeoise* but, though he had avoided the first, he had come fairly near to the second. He admits the *comédie attendrissante* or 'touching comedy' and allows *Nanine* to be classed as one. But his main concern in this Preface, which has long been recognized as an ingenious piece of fence-sitting, is to affirm the basic distinction between tragedy and comedy. This was only to be expected from a man who was already famous as a tragic dramatist and could not tolerate, at least in theory, the existence of an intermediate or, as he calls it, a bastard genre.

※ ※ ※

[1] 'Will start some peculiar yapping'. The first sense is of hounds on the wrong trail. Also used figuratively: 'Médire sans motif'.
[2] 'Without making too much of it' or 'Without creating a precedent'.
[3] This is found in the 1823 edition of Voltaire's *Œuvres*. See J. Truchet, *Théâtre du XVIIIe siècle*, I (Paris, 1972), p. 1444.

The sharpness and gaiety banished from the regular theatre of the eighteenth century took refuge in the fringe theatres, where they enjoyed a flourishing if mainly unofficial life. The Italians continued for a time as a recognized company, though after 1740, with the death of Arlequin-Thomassin and the retirement of Silvia, their star began to wane. The Théâtre de la Foire[1] expanded and multiplied into the Théâtre des Boulevards, similar independent ventures on the sites of the old walls of Paris which had been levelled. In all these, gross and irreverent farces continued to be performed. A favourite type acquired the name of *parades*. These had some new stock characters who spoke with a conventional *zézaiement* or lisp and other speech distortions which were a distinguishing mark, but otherwise they were identical to the traditional farce. They parodied the values of serious comedy lightheartedly, as in one of the best-known, *Isabelle grosse par vertu* (1738). This modest unmarried heroine has been pregnant the previous year, but this year she merely pretends to be to avoid an unwanted marriage with the elderly Doctor and preserve what is left of her virginity for her true lover Léandre. Her father questions her:

CASSANDRE Mais dis-moi, ma mie, de qui donc est cet enfant?
ISABELLE Ah, mon père! vous savez ma vertu. N'exigez point un pareil aveu de ma part. Je crains d'en accuser quelqu'un qui n'en serait pas coupable.
CASSANDRE J'ai toujours reconnu de bons principes en toi.

Her lover, who has been absent for ten months, is taken in also. He threatens to kill her father for not having guarded her closely enough, and then to do something else:

ISABELLE Ah, que vous m'alarmez! Et quelle est cette autre chose, mon cher Liandre?
LÉANDRE Cruelle z'Isabelle, c'est de mourir moi-même z'en personne devant vous tout à l'heure.
ISABELLE (*pleurant*) Ah! (*Tous pleurent*) Allez, ingrat, allez, je n'étais grosse que de vous voir.
LÉANDRE Que dites-vous?
ISABELLE Tenez, perfide, voilà toute ma réponse.

She lets fall from under her dress a large basin used to suggest the pregnancy and the tears of all change to joy.

[1] See p. 169 above.

Such mixtures of knockabout,[1] coarse wit and mockery delighted not only popular audiences but wealthy patrons who enjoyed amateur performances at parties in their houses. Some of the authors were writers of eminence, like Regnard and Dufresny before them – even Voltaire composed a *parade* in his younger days[2] – but most preferred to remain anonymous. Like the slightly earlier farce-writers they often included songs in the entertainment and this, as already seen, had been the beginning of *opéra-comique*. The development into light opera or, to use the more modern term which describes it not inappropriately, musical comedy, provided another alternative to bourgeois comedy and *drame*. It was produced in an officially subsidized theatre with an outstanding animator and author, Charles-Simon Favart (1710–92). But attractive though it is and a direct throwback in some respects to Molière's *comédies-ballets*, it must be considered as marginal to the history of literary comedy.

As for this, it will by now be abundantly clear that it exalted simplicity, goodness, domestic affection and family solidarity. Such disruptive influences as rebellious youths with extravagant ideas were successfully checked and made to conform. Of the two deep-seated problems which remained one was woman. Ever since her discovery of sex in the Garden of Eden she had continued to be a disturbingly unpredictable element through centuries of literature. Even in Marivaux's fairyland she was presented as impulsive, though charmingly more than dangerously so. Bourgeois drama found a respectable place for her in its mothers and virtuous girls, while allowing a debate on feminism which revealed the fragility of this solution. Still, partial though it was, it seemed morally acceptable. Money was another matter. A moralist could not honestly square its acquisition with a disinterested love of humanity. The best answer was the vow of poverty taken by some of the religious orders, but this was foreign to the eighteenth-century mind and could not be incorporated in a bourgeois morality which combined comfortable thinking with comfortable living standards. It was left to the Marquis de Sade, not usually regarded as a typical middle-class family man, to find the theoretical solution near the close of the century. His improving *drame*, *Oxtiern*

---

[1] Actors beat each other. The Doctor is covered with flour in a custard-pie routine.
[2] *La Fête de Bélébat* (1725). See J. Scherer, *Théâtre et anti-théâtre au XVIIIe siècle* (Oxford, 1974).

ou les Malheurs du libertinage, ended with the words: 'J'ai fait de mon argent le meilleur usage ... Punir le crime et récompenser la vertu ... que quelqu'un me dise s'il est possible de le placer à un plus haut intérêt!'

So from being the root of all evil money is transformed into the root of good,[1] while at the same time Sade unconsciously indicates how a laudable love of humanity could lead to the more debased 'philanthropy' of the nineteenth century. One gave to help others, but not so much as to impoverish oneself. In the bourgeois scheme of things this is perfectly defensible. The giver, who is usually the father, is responsible for his dependents, and excessive generosity to outsiders would injure them.

[1] For a complete contrast cf. Dom Juan's 'charity' in Molière's play, pp. 128–9 above.

BEAUMARCHAIS

*Beaumarchais's life and career – his
parades and early drames: Eugénie, Les Deux Amis –
Le Barbier de Séville – character of Figaro – Le Mariage de
Figaro – character of Chérubin – the main social challenge –
verbal comedy – drame intrudes through Marceline – delayed
production of Le Mariage – La Mère coupable –
drame and comedy in Beaumarchais*

So, but for one factor, this book might have ended, with serious comedy absorbed into the *drame*, lightweight comedy into comic opera, and farce obscure and timid before the Revolution and the Napoleonic regime. A single author invalidates such a conclusion in two outstanding plays – or at a pinch one, since the first by itself could not have made so deep a mark – combining characteristics of the three types in work which had a new tonality of its own. A personal triumph certainly, that of a highly gifted writer who knew how to reanimate old material, but personal also in the profounder sense that his drama incorporated lived experience together with advanced ideas current in some of his generation.

In considering Molière we have tried to show that his plays are not narrowly autobiographical. Neither is Beaumarchais, 'narrowly'. The character of Figaro is not literally himself but there is a nearer approach to identification than, say, in the case of Jean-Baptiste Poquelin and Alceste. How near is a matter of endless and ultimately inconclusive argument. The best verdict is that Beaumarchais's remarkable career throws so much light on his main creation and the plays in which he appears that its outline is necessary to a fuller understanding of them.

He was born in 1732 as Pierre-Augustin Caron, the son of a Parisian watchmaker with a pious and united family. Different though he was, he never revolted, but cherished his four sisters who had great musical talent like himself. He began by following his father's profession and at the age of twenty-two went to Court to offer some of his products there. They included a miniature watch which he presented to Madame de Pompadour. This marked the beginning of his rise in the world. He bought a minor Court post from an official who was ill and soon died, then married the widow, ten years older than himself (1756). She also died a year later. One might see this as a mirroring of the action or aim of so many rogues of comedy, but it was probably sheer coincidence. Because of a badly drawn marriage contract the young widower did not inherit his wife's modest fortune and had to be content with a small country estate which she owned, from which he took his name of Beaumarchais. The brief marriage had, however, strengthened his connections with the Court and by 1757 he was giving harp lessons to the king's daughters and organizing concerts for which he composed music.[1]

Outside the Court Beaumarchais was welcome in the house of Lenormand d'Étioles, the husband of Madame de Pompadour, who had broken with her completely when she became Louis XV's mistress. For d'Étioles, showing another side of his talent, Beaumarchais composed several *parades* with music which he never published or mentioned himself. They belonged to the established type, with a slightly subtler wit in places. Through this patron he met the powerful financier Pâris-Duverney who recognized his business ability and set him on the road to fortune while requiring services in return. It was no doubt Duverney who sent Beaumarchais on a secret financial mission to Madrid. While there, Beaumarchais was also active on his own account. He ruined a Spanish man-of-letters who had broken his promise to marry one of his sisters, intrigued in high circles, and even procured a French mistress, the Marquise de La Croix (she had been his own), for Charles III. In all this it is again possible to see a reflection of some of the Frontins of comedy, but operating on a far grander scale.

On his return to Paris Beaumarchais had two *drames* produced at the Comédie Française (*Eugénie*, 1767, and *Les Deux Amis*, 1770), contracted a second marriage with a young widow who died suddenly two and a half years later, and lost the favour of the king to whom an

---

[1] To rise in this way, through music lessons and composition, had also been an ambition of Jean-Jacques Rousseau (another watchmaker's son) when he went to Paris some fifteen years earlier. But that unworldly genius was less successful.

enemy (Beaumarchais had plenty by now) had repeated a cutting remark not intended for the royal ear.

In 1770 Pâris-Duverney died and a period of lawsuits began, initiated by a dispute over his will but branching into other matters. There were appeals and counter-appeals and a term of imprisonment for Beaumarchais. He emerged finally victorious in 1778 when he obtained a judgement against Duverney's heir, the Comte de La Blache, who had refused to pay Beaumarchais the 15,000 livres which, according to Duverney's accounts, were owing to him. As persistent as any of the litigants of comedy though more gifted, Beaumarchais had intended in the usual way to bribe the judge Goezman through his wife and secretary. The honest Goezman seized the bigger opportunity of accusing him of attempted corruption. The most memorable result was in the brilliant pamphlets (*Mémoires*) which Beaumarchais published to expose and ridicule the men of law. His later comments on legal justice and his caricature of the judge Brid'oison in *Le Mariage de Figaro* evidently owe something to his personal experience of litigation.

Meanwhile he had been reconciled with Louis XV, succeeded in 1774 by the ill-fated Louis XVI. Both kings sent him as their political agent to England and other countries to buy up pamphlets and compromising correspondence which might injure their regime. Between two missions to London, the main source with Amsterdam of this subversive literature, *Le Barbier de Séville* was produced at the Comédie Française. As a direct consequence Beaumarchais became the founder of a Society of Authors. Querying the accounts of his earnings from *Le Barbier*, he discovered that the national theatre was cheating him. He called together a number of dramatists and other writers and set in motion the process which led to a definite agreement on authors' dramatic royalties confirmed in the *loi sur les droits d'auteur* of 1791. But while working on this he was engaged in a much bigger matter.

In 1775 the American colonies revolted against George III, declaring their independence in July 1776. In December of the first year Beaumarchais sent a memorandum to Louis XVI recommending support of the Americans. How far this was decisive in itself may be questioned, but there is little doubt of his later influence. He formed a company with the French Government's unofficial backing to supply arms to the insurgents in exchange for goods. The fighting of course continued for several years and in 1778, after France's open recognition of Washington's Government, Beaumarchais sent eleven ships of his own company's merchant fleet to assist the American cause.

Beside the noble military figures of Lafayette and Rochambeau, Beaumarchais is forgotten. But his undercover help was no less effective than theirs. When lease-lend was instituted in the 1940s under the Marshall Plan, some American at least might have uttered the words: 'Beaumarchais, here we come.' How far political idealism and love of liberty entered into his support of the American Revolution and how far expediency and commercial considerations is difficult to determine. All that is known is that his personal profits were small or non-existent.[1]

From then until the French Revolution he was engaged in other business enterprises, including the publication of the complete works of Voltaire.[2] He contracted a third marriage with a woman who had long been his mistress, won the long fight to have *Le Mariage de Figaro* produced (written 1775–8), then produced his peculiar opera *Tarare* (1786) and his last play, the *drame* of *La Mère coupable* (1792). This, in which characters from the two Figaro comedies reappear considerably changed, was a failure in its first production by an obscure theatrical company.

When the Revolution came in earnest Beaumarchais tried to adjust to it, unsuccessfully. Wrongly accused of having misappropriated 60,000 rifles ordered from Holland to equip the revolutionary armies, he fled abroad, to England, then Amsterdam and Hamburg, where he lived in poverty. His possessions in France were sequestrated and his family imprisoned for a time. Returning to France under the more

[1] At first Congress, influenced by its agents in Paris, ignored Beaumarchais's claims for payment in money or goods on the pretext that the military aid provided was a free gift from the French Government. This and the Spanish Government had financed him, but the subsidy was much below his actual expenditure on war materials and armed ships. In October 1779, more than three years after Independence, he received bills of exchange for $2\frac{1}{2}$ million francs payable after a further three years and hardly negotiable in Europe at that date. Fourteen years later the USA recognized a debt of $2\frac{1}{4}$ million francs to Beaumarchais, but still wished to deduct 1 million as a voluntary contribution from the French Government. Beaumarchais rejected this offer and so obtained virtually nothing. Finally a payment of 800,000 francs was made to his heirs in 1835, thirty-six years after his death.

See particularly J. Marsan, *Beaumarchais et les affaires d'Amérique* (Paris, 1919).

[2] The Kehl Edition (1783–90), beautifully printed in English Baskerville type on paper which has now faded. This luxury edition was a financial disaster. Only 2000 copies were subscribed out of 15,000 printed. Not many years ago separate volumes could be picked up for $12\frac{1}{2}$p each in London bookshops.

liberal *Directoire*, he was reinstated and honoured on the stage at a new production of *La Mère coupable* by the actors of the Comédie Française. He lived on for another two years, to die at his home of a stroke on 17–18 May 1799, when he was sixty-seven.

꧁꧂

Beaumarchais's *parades* were left in manuscript and only discovered in the 1860s. They belonged, as we have said, to the established type and had the same stock characters. Their flavour can be suggested by a speech by the lisping mock-innocent Isabelle in *Jean Bête à la foire* (Sc. ix): 'Mon cher z'amant, je crois que vous m'en contez un peu, et ce n'est pas bien à vous ni à mon ch'père d'abuser z'avec des contes moraux l'innocence d'une jeunesse nubile comme je puis t'être.' And: 'Queux esprit spirituel que mon Jean Bête! C'est z'une chiclopédie!'

His first two *drames* were average specimens of their class, influenced by Diderot's recent examples and theories.[1] Had another man written them they would be lost in the mass. Their interest lies in the fact that they were Beaumarchais's creations on which he worked long and hard; several plans and different manuscript drafts of each exist. *Eugénie*, produced at the Comédie Française in January 1767, was modified after the first night by its author, already following the tactics he adopted for *Le Barbier de Séville*, and went on to enjoy a reasonable success for a first play. It is an unashamedly weepy drama in which the emotionally tortured heroine is constantly on the point of collapse. The emotion spreads to her well-meaning aunt and eventually to the male characters, who weep also. There is no mother, but great stress is laid throughout on the claims and delights of fatherhood. In contrast there are fast-moving unsentimental scenes, involving quarrels between the men, duels and near-duels. Family honour is in question (the pregnant Eugénie has been deceived by a false marriage) and the play is notable as a meeting-point between the old honour drama of Spanish derivation and the new humanitarian drama in which the virtuous heart is mightier than the sword – as already suggested in Marivaux's *La Double Inconstance*.[2] In giving his final version an English setting and characters (the earlier version had

---

[1] See above, pp. 214–15.
[2] See above, pp. 205–8.

been set in France), Beaumarchais was no doubt following Richardson and, more generally, the fashion of things English so prominent in his century.[1] For Beaumarchais, who had not yet visited London, it was a fashion only.

One manuscript draft of Beaumarchais's second *drame* had been entitled *Le Marchand de Londres*, but it ended up as *Les Deux Amis ou le Négociant de Lyon*, set in provincial France. This again contains a domestic theme revolving round a marriageable daughter, but the main subject of this thoroughly bourgeois play is finance and the generous action of a businessman who places friendship above profit. The failure of the play probably contributed to dissuade Beaumarchais from persisting with *drames*, in which case it was a blessing in disguise.

※☜❀☞※

Le Barbier de Séville was produced by the Comédie Française on 23 February 1775, but its genesis was over two years earlier. It was originally written as an *opéra-comique* for the Italians, who refused it, and then recast as a comedy in the unusual form of four acts and accepted by the Théâtre Français in January 1773. Production was delayed by Beaumarchais's imprisonment and lawsuits, which are reflected only dimly in the play's final version,[2] but during that time he worked on it and expanded it to five acts. After a disastrous opening performance Beaumarchais rapidly pruned it back to four acts and three days later it was performed again with a success which has never varied since.

The basic theme is the old one. The ageing Bartholo, a descendant of Molière's Arnolphe with certain features of the Doctor of the *commedia dell'arte*, intends to marry his ward Rosine whom he guards jealously in his house in Seville. The gallant Comte Almaviva, attracted to her during a visit to Madrid, courts her from the street, then obtains an entry on various pretexts imagined by his follower Figaro.

---

[1] This is a vast topic, with numerous ramifications. To confine it to one theatrical influence, the visits of Garrick to Paris in 1751 and again in 1763–5 made an undoubted impact on Diderot and on French actors and other authors who wrote for them.

[2] E.g. Bartholo (to his valets): 'De la justice! C'est bon entre vous autres misérables, la justice. Je suis votre maitre, moi, pour avoir toujours raison . . . Il n'y aurait qu'à permettre à tous ces faquins-là d'avoir raison, vous verriez bientôt ce que deviendrait l'autorité.' (II. vii.)

The pair eventually marry under the nose of Bartholo, taken in by the traditional trick over a marriage contract. The fifth character, Bazile, Rosine's music-master and Bartholo's stupid ally, is more plainly ridiculous than his leader. This comparatively minor part cannot be attached to any one original, but the scene in which Almaviva presents himself as his pupil sent to give Rosine a singing lesson (III. iv) is a plain borrowing from *Le Malade imaginaire* (II. iii and iv). The Comte's other impersonation of a drunken cavalry officer with a billeting order derives more generally from the early comedies of the century.

Such is the familiar skeleton of *Le Barbier*, subtitled *La Précaution inutile* and so traceable back to a short story of that name by Scarron. But in Beaumarchais's hands it undergoes a transformation. There is first the strong element of *opéra-comique*, with songs and music running through the play from the moment when Figaro appears with his guitar in I. ii. The atmosphere of musical comedy is reinforced by Beaumarchais's detailed descriptions of the old Spanish costumes he prescribes for his actors and by the final spectacular scene assembling all the principal characters and a crowd of police officers and valets carrying torches (unnecessary for the plot; a single legal official with one or two *sergents* would have been enough).

But this is more than *opéra-comique*, in which, as Figaro remarks, 'Ce qui ne vaut pas la peine d'être dit, on le chante' (I. ii). Its difference and originality stem from the character of Figaro, while expanding beyond it. Figaro is an emancipated ex-valet and in that respect resembles the Frontins and Crispins of Dancourt, Regnard and Lesage, but his talents are greater and not confined to an aptitude for business intrigue. While practising as a horse-doctor he became an author, was deprived of his post 'sous prétexte que l'amour des Lettres est incompatible avec l'esprit des affaires' (which could never be said of Beaumarchais himself) and wrote a play which was a resounding failure, as Beaumarchais had done in *Les Deux Amis*. Disgusted by the literary rat-race, he abandoned the pen for the razor and travelled all over Spain as a barber with varied fortunes and a philosophic indifference to bad times:

... accueilli dans une ville, emprisonné dans l'autre, et partout supérieur aux événements; loué par ceux-ci, blâmé par ceux-là; aidant au bon temps, supportant le mauvais; me moquant des

sots, bravant les méchants; riant de ma misère et faisant la barbe
à tout le monde . . .

(I. ii)

Now he is ready to rejoin his old master and help him to carry out his
plans.

Figaro has the salient features of the Spanish *pícaro*[1] and it was not
essential for his creator to have lived in Madrid to be familiar with a
type already established in French literature and drama. What distinguishes Figaro from his partial predecessors, philosophical or
intriguing, is his self-confidence, his independence and his fundamental
sense of justice. Adding to this his talents as a writer and musician one
cannot help recognizing a self-projection into the character of the
author's own personality.

Figaro's self-confidence, rooted in the conviction that inherently he
is as good as any other man, is the basis of the social criticism already
apparent, though muted, in this play. He concedes some respect to the
Comte because of his position and power, but cannot resist some
ironic reflections on his natural qualities. Again in that early scene
(I. ii) which sets the tone, Almaviva remarks:

LE COMTE Tu ne dis pas tout. Je me souviens qu'à mon service tu
étais un assez mauvais sujet.

FIGARO Eh mon Dieu, Monseigneur, c'est qu'on veut que le
pauvre soit sans défaut.

LE COMTE Paresseux, dérangé . . .

FIGARO Aux vertus qu'on exige dans un Domestique, Votre
Excellence connaît-elle beaucoup de Maîtres qui fussent
dignes d'être Valets?

The Comte takes this with a laugh, treating it as a good joke, but
a joke all the same.[2] He is not an evil aristocrat. He has many attrac-

---

[1] This word probably contributed to suggest the name of Figaro. Another
hypothesis is that it derived from Beaumarchais's own family name, *le fils*
(pronounced *fi*) *Caron*. A combination of the two would represent the character
very adequately: 'myself as a *pícaro*'.

[2] Other instances with similar implications are:

LE COMTE [*embracing him*] Ah! Figaro, mon ami, tu seras mon ange, mon dieu
tutélaire.

FIGARO Peste! comme l'utilité a bientôt rapproché les distances!

(I. iv)

and:

tions, including a sense of humour, and hardly notices how Figaro has begun to cut his class down to size. There is none of the open egalitarianism of Voltaire's *Nanine* and very little of the appeal to *sensibilité* and *bonté de cœur* of bourgeois comedy. Something of it is preserved towards the end of the play, when Rosine believes she has been betrayed by her lover. She does not know him as the Comte but as Lindor, a man assumed to be poor and of obscure birth to whom she was ready to give herself out of pure love:

LE COMTE Vous, Rosine! la compagne d'un malheureux! sans fortune, sans naissance!

ROSINE La naissance, la fortune! Laissons là les jeux du hasard, et si vous m'assurez que vos intentions sont pures . . .

(IV. vi)

The Comte is as delighted as any Marivaux character to find that he is loved for himself alone. The misunderstanding about his betrayal of Rosine which arose from a misinterpreted letter is quickly cleared up, his true status is revealed, and the couple fall into each other's arms in an equality of passion and of rank. Rosine has been described in the List of Characters and elsewhere as a girl of noble origin, though this statement is not amplified and there are no unknown parents lurking in the wings.

Most probably Beaumarchais meant this conventional scene to be taken seriously, though it leaves a suspicion of parody. In any case the intrusion of egalitarianism through love is very brief and practically the whole burden of social comment is borne by Figaro – though in this play lightly so.[1]

❧✦❧

In its sequel, *Le Mariage de Figaro*, it is still expressed lightly, except in the hero's famous thousand-word soliloquy in Act V (Scene iii),

---

FIGARO Est-ce qu'un homme comme vous ignore quelque chose [guitar-playing]?

(I. vi)

Cf. also Bartholo's remarks on justice for servants, quoted on p. 242, footnote 2.

[1] *Le Barbier* in its definitive four-act verison, as read now. The five-act script which Beaumarchais pruned contained considerably more irony at the expense of justice and the aristocracy.

but much too conspicuously to escape the most perfunctory notice. Hence the ban on the play which delayed its public performance for nearly three years and will be returned to later. The social criticism is not only in the dialogue but constitutes the essence of the plot.

Three years have passed. The Comte is established with Rosine, now Madame la Comtesse, in his château near Seville where Figaro serves as his personal valet and steward. Figaro is about to marry the Comtesse's chambermaid, the lively but 'virtuous' Suzanne, devoted to him and to her mistress. The Comte has voluntarily renounced the iniquitous *droit de seigneur* which permitted the feudal lord to have the first intercourse with the bride of one of his vassals, but he is not above pursuing the village girls and others. He is, says Beaumarchais in his Preface, 'un jeune seigneur de ce temps-là [old Spain], prodigue, assez galant, même un peu libertin'. Strongly attracted by Suzanne, he is bent on sleeping with her before or after she becomes Figaro's wife, though by consent, not force. Nevertheless he has all the material advantages. They depend on him for their livelihoods and for the dowry which has been promised them. He can only be defeated by the resourcefulness of Figaro, supported by Suzanne and eventually by the Comtesse who impersonates Suzanne in a midnight rendezvous and so disguised wins back her inconstant spouse by a ruse which could have been suggested by La Chaussée's *Le Préjugé à la mode*,[1] the reluctant husband becoming an at least temporarily ardent lover.

The Comtesse has suffered acutely, but she is developed beyond the passively virtuous heroines of earlier comedies. There is a chink in her armour, delicately and subtly represented and psychologically plausible. It involves the page Chérubin, Beaumarchais's most original creation, not even excepting Figaro. The page is thirteen according to Beaumarchais's Preface, an adolescent or rather a pre-adolescent. In three or four years he will be positively dangerous to women, but now he is just awakening to the possibilities of love, confusedly, innocently. He has a romantic adoration for the Comtesse, so high above him that she fills him with timidity. She cannot help being touched by it. She herself would hardly be older than twenty, supposing that she had been seventeen in *Le Barbier de Séville*. There is a moment, to quote Beaumarchais again, when 'her affection for a lovable child, her godson, could become a dangerous liking'.[1] But she stifles her 'goût naissant' to remain faithful to her unfaithful husband. The Comte is not so sure. He suspects Chérubin – or perhaps some other unknown person – of courting his wife and tries to send him away from the château. But the irrepressible Chérubin keeps popping up. There is much hiding in closets, behind armchairs and finally in the garden pavilions, which increases the theatrical excitement. On his own level Chérubin is experimenting with the gardener's daughter, the willing twelve-year-old Fanchette. She is a half-child too, a minor character delineated by a few deft touches. 'Il me prend pour un enfant, mon cousin [Figaro]' she protests and exits hopping (IV. xiv). Soon after she brings two biscuits and an orange which she has begged from the pantry to feed the hungry Chérubin (V. i).[2] Other children come from the village, carrying bouquets for the Comtesse and the bride and creating the atmosphere of a rustic fête, but none begins to approach Chérubin as the representative of an intermediate phase in early life, particularly difficult to have conceived and to render on the stage. The part, noted Beaumarchais, must be played by a pretty woman, since no boy of youthful enough appearance could have interpreted it.

The supposed immorality of this pubescent love, and especially the Comtesse's very tentative response to it, apparently shocked some contemporaries. But there was much greater offence in the dominant theme, only latent in *Le Barbier*. There is the struggle between two males for a desirable woman (Suzanne) and, however elegantly it is fought, however it becomes enmeshed in the intricacies of the rest of the plot and is surrounded with gaiety, spectacle and song, there is no question that it is won by the better man, who is a commoner. This is suggested throughout the play and scored in indelibly in Figaro's great monologue in V. iii, with its key sentences:

Non, Monsieur le Comte, vous ne l'aurez pas . . . vous ne l'aurez pas. Parce que vous êtes un grand seigneur, vous vous croyez un grand génie! . . . noblesse, fortune, un rang, des places, tout cela rend si fier! Qu'avez-vous fait pour tant de biens? Vous vous êtes donné la peine de naître, et rien de plus. Du reste,

[1] This is brought out in an admirable sequence of scenes (II. iii–ix) between the Comtesse, Suzanne and Chérubin.
[2] Fanchette was also the familiar name of Madeleine-Françoise, Beaumarchais's third sister.

homme assez ordinaire! tandis que moi, morbleu, perdu dans la foule obscure, il m'a fallu déployer plus de science et de calculs pour subsister seulement qu'on n'en a mis depuis cent ans à gouverner les Espagnes. Et vous voulez jouter . . .

'And you want to take *me* on . . .' Boldly subversive words even towards the end of the century of Diderot's 'Chiclopédie'. This speech, as already noted, echoes the tirade of Dom Juan's father[1] but has a significantly different slant. Molière's Dom Louis was outraged by his son's dishonourable behaviour and remarked that birth alone did not make him an *honnête homme*. Beaumarchais omits such moral considerations and gets straight down to the personal qualities and abilities of the man. His criticism of the aristocracy is not that it is sometimes crooked, but that it is incompetent.

Apart from the social challenge, both the Figaro plays are outstanding as comic drama. The situational effects are numerous and always handled with mastery.[2] The apt humour and quietly appropriate wit of the dialogue had not been bettered since Molière. Beaumarchais was a true writer with that natural feeling for words which, like music, can be cultivated but not instilled. On occasion he can be exuberant without allowing himself to be carried away:

LE COMTE Tu connais donc ce Tuteur?

FIGARO Comme ma mère.

LE COMTE Quel homme est-ce?

FIGARO C'est un beau gros, court, jeune vieillard, gris pommelé, rusé, rasé, blasé, qui guette et furète et gronde et geint tout à la fois.

(*Barbier de Séville*, I. iv)

The lawsuit in *Le Mariage de Figaro* bears on the precise wording of a document, on a grave accent and ultimately on a comma. At some past date Figaro has borrowed money from one Marceline, a middle-aged servant at the château, and has signed an undertaking to repay it on demand or to marry her; that at least is his interpretation. In the litigation scene, less broad than in Racine's *Les Plaideurs* yet still burlesque, Figaro is pleading against Bartholo before the stuttering

---

[1] See p. 131 above.

[2] A fuller exposition of this, if desired, can be found in J. Scherer, *La Dramaturgie de Beaumarchais* (1954). See also, for the staging, J. Meyer, *Le Mariage de Figaro*, Collection 'Mises en Scène' (Paris, 1953).

judge Brid'oison. The first point at issue is whether the contract stipu-
lates: 'I will return the money *or* marry her', or '*and* marry her'. The
operative word is hidden under an ink-splash. After arguing that it is
et, Bartholo suddenly concedes that it might be *ou*, but goes on to give
it an accent and the sense of *where*:

BARTHOLO Examinons le titre en ce sens. (*Il lit*) *Laquelle somme je
lui rendrai dans ce château* où *je l'épouserai* . . . Ainsi
château où *je l'épouserai*, Messieurs, c'est *château dans
lequel* . . .

FIGARO Point du tout; la phrase est dans le sens de celle-ci: ou
la maladie vous tuera, ou *ce sera le médecin*; ou bien *le
médecin*; c'est incontestable. Autre exemple: ou *vous
n'écrirez rien qui plaise*, ou *les sots vous dénigreront*; ou
bien *les sots*; le sens est clair, car, audit cas, *sots ou
méchants* sont le substantif qui gouverne. Maître Bartholo
croit-il donc que j'aie oublié ma syntaxe? Ainsi, je la
payerai dans ce château, *virgule*, ou je *l'épouserai* . . .

BARTHOLO (*vite*) Sans virgule.

FIGARO (*vite*) Elle y est. C'est *virgule*, Messieurs, *ou bien* je
l'épouserai.

BARTHOLO (*regardant le papier, vite*) Sans virgule, Messieurs.

FIAGRO (*vite*) Elle y était, Messieurs . . .

(*Le Mariage*, III. xv)

But Figaro has neither to repay his debt nor marry Marceline
because in the ensuing scene she proves to be his mother. Searching
wildly for a way out, he claims to be the child of noble parents, stolen
by gipsies while still in his cradle. He cannot for the moment produce
the costly clothes and jewels stolen with him, but has a mark on his
right arm to prove it:

MARCELINE (*se levant vivement*) Une spatule à ton bras droit?

FIGARO D'où savez-vous que je dois l'avoir?

MARCELINE Dieux! C'est lui!

FIGARO Oui, c'est moi.

BARTHOLO (*à Marceline*) Et qui, lui?

MARCELINE (*vivement*) C'est Emmanuel.

BARTHOLO (*à Figaro*) Tu fus enlevé par des Bohémiens?

FIGARO (*exalté*) Tout près d'un château. Bon docteur, si vous me rendez à ma noble famille, mettez un prix à ce service. Des monceaux d'or n'arrêteront pas mes illustres parents.

BARTHOLO (*montrant Marceline*)   Voilà ta mère.

FIGARO . . . nourrice?

BARTHOLO Ta propre mère.

LE COMTE Sa mère!

FIGARO Expliquez-vous.

MARCELINE (*montrant Bartholo*)   Voilà ton père.

FIGARO (*désolé*)   Oh, oh, oh! Ay de moi!

MARCELINE Est-ce que la nature ne te l'a pas dit mille fois?

FIGARO Jamais.

LE COMTE (*à part*)   Sa mère!

BRID'OISON C'est clair, i-il ne l'épousera pas.

(III. xvi)

This obvious send-up of all previous recognition scenes immediately turns from parody to pathos. Marceline, accepted as a well-loved mother-figure by a weeping Figaro (and by Suzanne also, when she learns the truth), launches into an impassioned denunciation of men who seduce helpless girls and then abandon and despise them. Too inexperienced to defend themselves, they are condemned to a lifetime's toil in humble jobs. This economic exploitation of the innocent after their sexual exploitation is forcefully brought out by Beaumarchais near the beginning of the Industrial Revolution (eighty years later Victor Hugo made it one of the main themes of *Les Misérables*), but here it appears out of place. Not unreasonably the Comédie Française omitted it in the early performances, 'craignant qu'un morceau si sévère n'obscurcît la gaieté de l'action'. Yet there is no doubt that Beaumarchais intended it seriously and did not find this fragment of moralizing *drame* incompatible with the rest of the comedy (though he stopped short of making the repugnant Bartholo a conventional father-figure). He insists on it in his Preface and quotes in full the passage which his actors had omitted. This unusual heavyhandedness on his part – for so it still appears – must be accepted. For once the philosophical reformer preaches openly. It was an error which Voltaire, or for that matter Molière, would never have committed.

Taken as a whole, this brilliant play is almost too rich. In a few short pages we have only been able to indicate its main qualities; a complete book would be required to explore them adequately.[1] Other playwrights could have derived several comedies from the same material. Its *opéra-comique* facet gave Mozart's famous opera (1786), produced shortly after the first public performance of the parent work (similarly for *Le Barbier*, already recast by Paesiello in 1780 as an opera, eclipsed later by Rossini's version of 1816). But for immediate contemporaries the subversive facet was uppermost, as the early history of the play shows.

Beaumarchais wrote it during 1775–8 while engaged in his American gun-running and the first phase of his dispute with the Comédie Française over author's rights. The theatre, having given way on that point, accepted *Le Mariage* enthusiastically in September 1781, but it still had to pass the official censorship. During the next two and a half years it was submitted to six different censors appointed by the authorities, some approving, some disapproving. Meanwhile it was being read in salons and at Court and provoking conflicting opinions. Louis XVI's first reaction was that it was too immoral to be licensed, but the admiration and curiosity of others steadily outgrew disapproval and in time the king himself came round. A private performance was given in September 1783 in honour of his brother, the Comte d'Artois, and this persuaded him finally. The public première at the Comédie Française on 27 April 1784 was a tumultuous success – almost a riot – followed by a record run. To obtain this and satisfy his censors Beaumarchais had progressively toned down his original version. He had dropped some outspoken passages and had changed the scene from contemporary France to old Spain. But no one was deceived and quite enough dynamite was left to make this appear a dangerously, or excitingly, revolutionary play. The excitement was shared by the very persons and classes that would be swept away by the real Revolution whose imminence they hardly suspected. Theirs was the attitude of the *vaudeville* with which, except for a ballet, the ambivalent Beaumarchais ended his play, alternatively entitled *La Folle Journée*:

SUZANNE   Si ce gai, ce fol ouvrage,
           Renfermait quelque leçon,
           En faveur du badinage

---

[1] There have been several, e.g. F. Gaiffe, *Le Mariage de Figaro* (Amiens, 1928); R. Jasinski, *Le Mariage de Figaro* (Paris, 1948); A. R. Pugh, *Beaumarchais, Le Mariage de Figaro* (London, 1968).

Faites grâce à la raison.
Ainsi la nature sage
Nous conduit, dans nos désirs,
À son but par des plaisirs.   (*Bis*)

BRID'OISON Or Messieurs, la co-omédie
Que l'on juge en ce-et instant,
Sauf erreur, nous pein-eint la vie
Du bon peuple qui l'entend.
Qu'on l'opprime, il peste, il crie;
Il s'agite en cent fa-açons;
Tout fini-it par des chansons.   (*Bis*)

Yet this was not quite Beaumarchais's final word. In *L'Autre Tartuffe ou la Mère coupable* (1792) he completed what might be regarded as a trilogy on the Figaro group of characters. This was the author's own presentation in his not necessarily objective Preface. The first two plays, he says, were gay, showing respectively 'la turbulente jeunesse' of Almaviva and 'les fautes de son âge viril'. Now, 'par le tableau de sa vieillesse . . . venez vous convaincre que tout homme qui n'est pas né un épouvantable méchant finit toujours par être bon, quand l'âge des passions s'éloigne, et surtout quand il a goûté le bonheur d'être père! C'est le but moral de la pièce . . .'

There is no question that *La Mère coupable* is, as it was described, a *drame*, and a typical example of its class. Almaviva, full of honours and immensely rich, has settled in Paris with his wife whom he considers divorcing under the enlightened new laws which make this legally possible. The Comtesse cannot be described better than in Beaumarchais's words: 'très malheureuse et d'une angélique piété'. She has been like this for the past twenty years for the hidden reason that Chérubin, evidently a few years older than in *Le Mariage*, returned to the Spanish château one night and raped her, apparently with her partial consent.[1] She gave birth to a son and forbade Chérubin ever to see her again. He sacrificed his life in an unnecessary military action.

---

[1] The point is left intentionally obscure, though her long repentance suggests that she was not totally unwilling: 'La surprise nocturne que vous avez osé me faire, dans un château où vous fûtes élevé, dont vous connaissiez les détours; la violence qui s'en est suivie; enfin votre crime – le mien . . .' (II. i.)

BEAUMARCHAIS

Letters stained with tears and blood, which are used in the machinery of the plot, bear witness to this. Their son Léon is brought up as the son of the Comte who dislikes him and has always suspected his paternity, though he has no proof before Act II of *La Mère coupable*. For his part he has introduced into the household young Florestine, known as his ward and god-daughter but in fact his illegitimate child by another woman. The two virtuous young people are in love with each other.

He has also introduced a certain Bégearss, who has served him in his various embassies and enjoys the absolute trust of the whole family – the Comte, the Comtesse, Léon and Florestine. He aims by his intrigues to ruin them, after marrying Florestine with a dowry of 3 million francs from the Comte. This second Tartuffe, taken over openly from Molière, is no longer religious – only the Comtesse is that – but poses as a highly moral man of the new humanist type. Preaching 'l'austère probité' he appears to act from the highest motives and to advise his dupes for their own best interests. The inventive Beaumarchais made him an Irish officer in the Spanish infantry and gave him a name similar to that of a lawyer, Bergasse, who had fallen foul of him over a recent lawsuit. This updating of Molière's relatively subtle character produced a plain villain of *drame* and indeed of melodrama. Bégearss sneers and gloats, 'laughing sardonically' (IV. iv). When unmasked he 'grinds his teeth' and 'shows himself in his true colours: "Ah, I've been tricked, but I shall get my own back" ' (V. vii).

He will not, thanks to the faithful, ingenious Figaro who has opposed him successfully but has lost all his sparkle and is no longer a striking character. With him is Suzanne, still the Comtesse's devoted chambermaid, whose heart is always in the right place but whose wit and liveliness have vanished.

No other parts are carried over and, had these been given different names, a few minor changes would have made *La Mère coupable* viable as an independent play. The social protest has almost disappeared since the case formerly argued by Figaro has been won. The Comte wishes to be called simply 'Monsieur', not 'Monseigneur'. Léon incidentally has a kind of social conscience, but it bears on 'liberty', not 'equality'. He is 'un jeune homme épris de la Liberté, comme toutes les âmes ardentes et neuves'.[1] This is shown in a conversation

[1] Cf. the use of this word, applied to a young man, in Corneille's *La Veuve*: 'C'est un homme tout neuf', meaning 'raw, inexperienced' (see p. 76 above). Here *neuf* has come to mean 'fresh, unspoilt'.

with his supposed father to be a matter of generations more than of
class. Like the thirty-year-old André Chénier, Léon was full of
'enthousiasme' and typical of the numerous young liberals who ended,
like Chénier, under the guillotine.

But at this crucial date Beaumarchais shows remarkable caution in
his sociopolitical attitude, beyond paying lip-service through Léon to
some contemporary republican ideals. He withdraws instead to the
bourgeois drama of the family on which the play centres. The intruder
Bégearss is evicted and father, mother, brother, sister are warmly
cocooned in their self-sufficient group, the last two by being married
in it. To achieve this without incest it is necessary for both to be proved
illegitimate and the products of 'guilty' unions. The morality is im-
perfect, though Beaumarchais was at pains to justify it on both legal
and moral grounds,[1] and a cynic might say that the end justifies the
means.

In a survey of French comedy this highly emotional play in which the
characters weep, kneel, faint and moralize in Richardson's manner
might be omitted or briefly dismissed as an ageing writer's return to
the *drame bourgeois* twenty years after *Les Deux Amis* (in spite of some
aristocratic characters, all three of Beaumarchais's *drames* are bourgeois in conception and sentiment). This is indeed the most satisfactory conclusion, but there can be some doubts and qualifications.
The fact that there are characters who are nominally the same as in the
comedies is of small consequence. One can fully enjoy a major work
while ignoring its disappointing sequel. Rather more relevant is the
light which *La Mère coupable* and Marceline's role in *Le Mariage de
Figaro*[2] throw on each other. *La Mère coupable* would tend to prove
that the sentiments attached to parentage were so strong in Beaumarchais that even in his gay comedy he could not forget them
altogether and that he developed them from there into a wholehearted family drama. If the link seems tenuous one must at least
listen to Beaumarchais himself. In his Preface (*Un Mot sur 'La Mère*

[1] In a letter to a legal critic, Martineau, 2 July 1797. Reproduced in *Beaumarchais, Théâtre complet*, ed. M. Allem and Paul-Courant (Paris, 1957), pp.
699–704.
[2] Marceline is not mentioned in *La Mère coupable*. Presumably she is now dead,
along with Bartholo, Bazile and Brid'oison.

coupable') already quoted from, he observes that he had long planned
the work but had perhaps left it too late. He ought to have written 'cet
ouvrage terrible' in his prime. 'Il m'a tourmenté bien longtemps! Mes
deux comédies espagnoles ne furent faites que pour le préparer . . .'
Perhaps when these words were published, in the first authorized
edition of 1797, Beaumarchais really meant them. Or perhaps he
wished to swell the importance of his latest play. But it is almost impossible to believe that at the dates when he was occupied with *Le
Barbier* and *Le Mariage* the major work which he would have preferred to write was his *drame*, or that in any significant sense the
comedies were a preparation for it. This is best interpreted as special
pleading in which the advocate himself may have come to believe, but
which will not stand a critical scrutiny of the evidence – the plays.
From this Beaumarchais emerges as an unlooked-for master of the
comic genre and a quite ordinary practitioner of the *drame*. If in the
past he had really been tempted to subordinate the first to the second,
what saved him was probably an obsession with the Figaro character,
his other self – for there is still identification:

> Lorsque je fis mes autres pièces, on m'outragea longtemps pour
> avoir osé mettre au théâtre ce jeune Figaro que vous avez aimé
> depuis. J'étais jeune aussi, j'en riais. En vieillissant l'esprit
> s'attriste, le caractère se rembrunit . . .

So with the sobered Figaro and his companions in *La Mère coupable*.
It seems better to write them off as irrelevant to *Le Mariage de Figaro*
and to view that master-work as an edifice complete in itself.

CONCLUSION

*Kinds of comedy – satire and reform –
social significance of comedy – money and class-
distinctions – relationship of sexes – love, marriage, feminism –
some traditional type-characters and their evolution – the Court as
comic material – the major dramatists again – P. Corneille, Scarron,
Molière's pre-eminence, the cynical school, Marivaux,
Beaumarchais – structure of comedy: the 'classical'
conception loosely applied – idiom of comedy:
prose or verse – forms of comedy*

The French comedy described in this book evolved from the farces and scattered experiments of the sixteenth century to a dramatic genre capable of containing within itself features that enriched it almost beyond recognition. There was not of course a constant progression. The peak may be considered to have been reached in Molière's day. Seventy years later the genre was languishing and in the second half of the eighteenth century only Beaumarchais breathed back some temporary life into it.

The difficulty of distinguishing between kinds of comedy has been pointed out in earlier chapters: in so many cases they occur mixed. But it is at least worth recapitulating them, since they often serve to suggest an initial approach to a play. The farce, rude in both senses, depended on physical effects combined with absurd situations and words. Prolonged in the eighteenth-century *parades*, it proved indestructible. Only a few of the major dramatists, such as P. Corneille and Marivaux in his greatest plays, were able to avoid it. Though always described as 'popular' it nevertheless could have an appeal for educated audiences or be easily adapted to appeal to them, then as now.

Burlesque comedy grew out of the verbal humour of farce, exploiting language to obtain its laughs by deliberate manipulations or exaggerations of it. The general atmosphere is one of fantasy as opposed to realism and the response of audiences to fantasy is far from universal, which accounts for its relative rarity in the history of comedy. The heyday of French burlesque was the mid-seventeenth century. Sometimes it involved parody and this continued in a restrained and special form in the echoes of tragedy in such early eighteenth-century playwrights as Regnard and Dufresny.

The comedy of intrigue, in which the plot supplies the primary attraction through its complications and surprises, occurs often, but is most prominent from the 1630s to the 1660s in the works of Rotrou, Quinault and T. Corneille, reflecting Spanish and Italian influences. Intricate plotting is not a monopoly of comedy, though when overdone in 'serious' drama it makes it appear less serious. It becomes difficult to accept surprises which are visibly contrived yet pass muster or are even an asset in comedy.

Romantic comedy usually has this involved plot, with characters whose identities are concealed or falsified. This adds to the complications, resolved typically in endings which can be summed up as true love rewarded. As has been seen, there was little pure romantic comedy in France. What there was was associated with pastoral and the lighter kind of tragicomedy. The names of *comédie héroïque* which Corneille attached to his *Don Sanche d'Aragon* (1649) and of *comédie galante* which Molière attached to his *Princesse d'Élide* (1664) describe plays verging on romantic comedy, but such examples were infrequent. The more sentimental love comedy of the eighteenth century, and not only that of Marivaux, might also be classed as romantic comedy, though very different from the earlier kind.

The comedy of character, whose main resource is to present on the stage one or more outstanding types, usually ridiculous, can occur in an almost pure state. But more often it cuts across the other kinds of comedy and appears in plays as varied as Scarron's *Don Japhet d'Arménie*, Molière's *Le Misanthrope* and *Le Bourgeois Gentilhomme*, and Regnard's *Le Joueur*. It is the most difficult type of comedy to write if it is to be both original and successful, calling for an intuitive understanding of contemporary social attitudes. Why should such a person be unusual or ridiculous at a particular period or be made to appear so? Exaggeration, including burlesque, may be used to heighten the effect, but there has to be some agreed conception of idiosyncrasy to build on.

We have already noticed the close relationship between the comedy of character and the comedy of manners. Except in fantastic comedy (and even there there is some link, though less direct and harder to trace because of the greater imaginative distortion) the eccentric protagonists are shown before a background of manners which they either represent in extreme form or react against. But the depiction of manners can take precedence over the depiction of character. Although in many plays not much is gained by attempting a distinction between the two, some comedies, of which Dancourt and his contemporaries provide the best examples, can fairly be classed as comedies of manners since these are the primary concern.

Satirical comedy is hardly a category of the same sort as the others mentioned so far. Except for the fully romantic kind, comedy nearly always contains some satire; it is a question of degree and of the dramatist's handling of his material. The satirical content in Molière, its presentation and effectiveness, has been discussed in the chapter about him. He did not write the sharpest and starkest form of satire, bitter comedy, except in a very few plays, and even in these the degree of bitterness is a matter of interpretation. There are recurrent satirical features in playwrights from Desmarets and Scarron to those of the early eighteenth century, but they rarely go very deep. At the other extreme Marivaux's principal plays are innocent of satire, except perhaps *La Double Inconstance*. At the end of the century Beaumarchais is exceptionally and fully satirical, yet he presents his satire in such an attractive package that even in him it does not appear predominant. The most open and longest-lived kind of satire is found in the short entertainments running from the early *farceurs* through the Italian comedians to the Théâtre de la Foire and its eighteenth-century ramifications. These depended for their existence on a satirical approach, sometimes attacking personalities, but the quality of the satire was generally low and repetitive from generation to generation. The ultimate development was in the puppet-show. Surprising though it may seem, the conflict between Punch and Judy is a satire on the marital relationship if it has any point at all.

According to Molière and others, the satirizing of manners considered undesirable could lead to their reform. This leads to the category of reformist comedy, openly advocating moral improvement as its principal aim. As illustrated by eighteenth-century bourgeois comedy, satire figures in it, but only as one element among others.

In time it shed its satirical tendencies to concentrate on the emotional appeal to right-thinking men and women. The emphasis shifted from the mockery of abuses to a plain depiction of their effects on innocent characters. This virtually took it outside comedy but gave it a future in drama which was prolonged into the present century. An early stage in the process can be discerned already in Beaumarchais.

French comedy throughout this period was closely related to social conditions and attitudes. The relationship has been frequently pointed out in the preceding chapters and no justification seems necessary, since it is basic. More immediately than other kinds of drama and literature, comedy reflected the contemporary social scene. Designed often, because of its nature, as a distorting mirror, it nevertheless brought into focus features of ordinary life which, particularly in the Grand Siècle, can be found nowhere else except in memoirs and correspondence. The insistence on 'realism' beginning with P. Corneille is constantly stressed by playwrights and critics in their comments on recognizability: 'People *are* like that, that is how they do behave.' While tragedy is considered 'noble' and the novel before the eighteenth century is predominantly idealistic on a somewhat lower plane, comedy must come to terms with everyday reality. That is expected of it and held up as its most valuable quality. Obviously it transcends this in almost every major work but meanwhile, as a necessary by-product, it throws considerable light on the detail of material conditions.

The detail has a strong interest in itself and can also be used to support historical reconstructions and research, but there are broader implications. Comedy, always dependent on some kind of topicality, follows changes in customs and their underlying values. From Scarron to Beaumarchais can be traced the decline of the aristocracy with its caste-code of arrogance and honour. The decline as mirrored in comic drama is spasmodic, but there is no doubt of its long-term effects and the eventual substitution of a bourgeois morality inimical to it. The interest shown around 1700 in money, or more exactly in new ways of acquiring it, marks the beginning of the transformation. At first they are usually represented as discreditable, through such characters as the traditional miser, the crooked valet and *femme d'intrigue*, and the financier culminating in Turcaret. Most of these are undesirables, or at best not entirely respectable. With the realization that money is in the foundations of the risen middle class and can be obtained by honest business methods, it becomes respectable and disappears as a theme, together with its shady exponents, because taken for granted. The emotional attachment to the family, so often noticeable in the 'hardheaded' businessman, takes its place in weepy comedy and *drame*.

After money and its various uses, preoccupations with social standing, the relationship of the sexes and an offshoot in feminism, complete the big outline themes which comedy embodies. The class theme, apart from the polarization between nobility and bourgeoisie, allows of numerous gradations and variations. Attitudes of and towards the legal profession and occasional comparisons with merchants and aristocracy are reflected. This aspect of comedy, however, is dominated, as in the case of medicine, by a more general question, that of the integrity and efficacity of justice. Over more than a hundred years the law and its representatives are almost invariably corrupt or ridiculous, and usually both. Though this was traditional, the tradition could hardly have survived without contemporary acceptance. On the evidence of Racine's Perrin Dandin of 1667 and Beaumarchais's Brid'oison of 1784, the comically tortuous judge was a caricature 'recognizable' in both periods.

The peasantry, which on economic grounds would have furnished the extreme contrast with the nobility, gets rather uncertain treatment. This was natural in a theatre patronized by urban audiences who did not know or much care what life was like outside their own sphere. They appreciated the comic rustic with his picturesquely primitive stage language, always good for a laugh, and came in time to appreciate his shrewdness. A growing awareness of his vigour and resourcefulness emerges in the plays of Dancourt and his generation with their provincial and country settings. After this the comic rustic disappears altogether. There is a trend, though in comedy not a strong one, towards an idealization of country life with its honest simple virtues. While this extends beyond the peasant population, it has implicit connections with their supposed morals and greater realism than that of the old-type pastoral.

As for the relationship of the sexes, it is the main and inexhaustible theme of nearly all fiction. Consideration of it can be confined here to two or three of its principal aspects.

In most seventeenth-century comedy, love as an emotion was taken for granted. A mutual attraction between two compatible characters seemed to require no explanation and had to wait until Marivaux for a subtler analysis. Corneille came nearest in some of his comedies to a realization of its dramatic possibilities. Elsewhere incompatibility and the diverting of attraction from one lover to another were regarded as more promising material. Molière exploits incompatibility in a conventional form in *L'École des femmes* and with far greater sophistication in *Le Misanthrope*, while in *Dom Juan* and *Tartuffe* lust makes a rare appearance in a comic drama which was notably chaste in comparison with that of some other countries and periods. At the end of the century love is treated cynically and often subordinated to materialism, but after Marivaux it is reinstated as a plain emotion. It becomes again a wholly commendable natural impulse at the expense of appearing rather dull.

The social significance of 'love' in itself is not very great. It calls rather for explorations of individual psychology unusual in comedy and perhaps outside its domain. But the consequences are fully social. They affect customs of courtship, inter-male and inter-female rivalry, the suitability of intended matings, the importance attached to fidelity, all of which are necessarily related to the *mores* of the time. Above all, the institution of marriage, almost invariably accepted as the goal of love, is given the same standing, whether more or less idealized, throughout the whole period. It is challenged briefly by the eighteenth-century rakes and coquettes, who are shown up as 'vicious', and by a few frivolous Court fops, while cynical reservations are expressed in such plays as Dufresny's *La Coquette de village* and *Le Double Veuvage*,[1] but these are exceptions to the general rule. There are of course unhappy and uncomfortable marriages, but the institution itself is rarely called in question. Though there are many extramarital unions, all are assumed to be temporary and not one is shown as successful. Their main function is to account for the existence of a child who proves to be other than it seems.

With marriage is bound up the long debate on the status of women. The two poles here are the fully domesticated wife, absorbed in the

[1] See above, pp. 183–7.

running of her household and the care of her husband's material needs, and the woman with cultural and intellectual ambitions (the noblewoman is not brought into this argument; if strongly characterized at all it is on grounds of class rather than of sexism). In the seventeenth century both extremes are derided, the first by double-take through the mouths of overdemanding elderly husbands whose opinions are made ridiculous by exaggeration and who are ridiculous figures in themselves. The second is caricatured in the would-be cultured females whose pretensions are higher than their capacities. Molière provides the best examples of both cases, though they can be found occasionally elsewhere. He is, however, more scathing in his treatment of the *femme savante* than of the home-loving male and when one remembers the influence of the real salons and the respect in which they were held his picture seems slightly false. But the public at large accepted it and this was what mattered most. Molière's personal opinion on the role of woman is of course irrelevant. He had Armande and the other actresses of his troupe to give him a very different view to which he could hardly have been blind. But the image of the right kind of woman projected by his plays as a whole is that of the efficiently practical wife, gifted with human understanding but untouched by intellectualism, of which the best example is the Elmire of *Tartuffe*. This was almost inevitable given the lack of educational opportunities and of any scope whatever for the feminine middle class to employ their talents outside the domestic sphere.

Towards the end of the century the female characters of comedy begin to show that they mean business and are perfectly capable of doing it. They range from the *marchandes de toilette* and Dancourt's local landladies to the ingenious yet uncorrupt heroine of Destouches's *Le Dissipateur*.[1] For a time there was no open feminist movement to accompany these mainly economic changes. Antifeminism expressed in the denigration of women or their assignment to secondary tasks disappeared, but hardly until Marivaux and La Chaussée's *Le Préjugé à la mode* (1735) were explicit protests raised, the second bearing on the equal rights of the two partners in a marriage.[2] Nevertheless the feminist undercurrent ran strongly through the comedies of the 1730s.

Bourgeois comedy and *drame* almost put woman back in her old place. Inevitably so in a family-centred drama, and one could say that

---

[1] See above, pp. 220–1.
[2] See above, p. 226.

man also became confined to the domestic circle. Both were there for the benefit of the little group, and any outside interests they might have were not considered dramatically important except so far as the husband's business activities might affect the group's security. But the result for feminism was to stifle it. The image of woman in the second half of the century is that of the virtuous faithful spouse, to which even Beaumarchais subscribed in his depiction of the Rosine of *La Mère coupable*, spending half a lifetime regretting her single unintentional slip. Morally admirable though this image of woman may be, and from one angle highly complimentary, it does not provide a fertile field for comic treatment. The emergent feminism of the earlier seventeen-hundreds was left for renewal in the social drama of a much later date.

❧❧❧

Type-characters corresponded to social assumptions. A great deal could be learnt from a study of these alone. The basic masks of the *commedia dell'arte*[1] had a long life, in the course of which some disappeared while others evolved. The braggart captain died out after the 1640s, leaving only occasional traces in later French comedy. The modification of the burlesque style told against him in any case, but it can also be concluded that the fire-eating warrior had ceased to be an even remotely topical figure. The doctor, reflecting the general suspicion of medical science and its practitioners and in the same persona a popular aversion to any kind of pedantry, was a laughable figure at least until the 1670s, as in *Le Malade imaginaire* and Haute-roche's *Crispin médecin*. A hundred years later Beaumarchais was able to revive him in the character of Bartholo, but in a rather different form. Bartholo's medical and pedantic features are less important and he is half assimilated to Pantalone, the cunning and vaguely lecherous old man. Only in the farcical *parades* is he retained as the simple conventional type.

The Zanni spill out much beyond their Italian originals. Arlequin is completely transformed from a parasitic servant to a gracefully attractive lover by Marivaux working in concert with Riccoboni's new troupe. Before that he had tended to merge with the other Zanni, Brighella, the two giving a character which need not have been borrowed from the Italians at all or from Spanish comedy. The fortunes

[1] See above, pp. 7–8.

K

of the French valet can in themselves serve as a basis for a whole theory of social changes. Their relevance has been pointed out in various places in this book. The valet's progress follows a roughly continuous rising curve. Towards the beginning he is buffoonish and crafty. He sheds his buffoonery but remains crafty, usually in a good cause: to help sympathetic members of a master-class on whom he depends (the attitude of his counterpart the *suivante* is similar). In the final decades of the Grand Siècle he is branching out on his own. He becomes conscious of being as deserving as his masters and uses his talent for intrigue to further his own interests. His final triumph, signalling a victory for ability over birth, is not in Lesage's *Crispin rival de son maître* and *Turcaret*, though it is proclaimed there, but in Beaumarchais's Figaro. But by that time, though ready to serve as a valet, he has really ceased to be one and is presented on the stage as 'a man like ourselves', irrespective of class, with whom it is possible to identify. His outspoken protests and the contemporary reaction to the plays show of course that the democratic implications had not yet won general acceptance, but the minority view which Figaro represented was powerful as well as prophetic.

Variations in economic and class status are exemplified to a lesser degree by other characters. They accord with the development of the valet and it is unnecessary to stress this again. What is noticeable is the decline of interest in the Court, high in Molière but non-existent in the reign of Louis XV, except to provide an occasional motivation for pernicious behaviour. This can be partly explained by the fact that Molière wrote for the Court as well as for the bourgeoisie while his successors did not, or not directly. There is a material relationship with the question of patronage and the composition of theatre audiences over a long stretch of time, but it hardly accounts for this particular change in audience interest. Apart from a relatively small number of entertainments specially designed for the Court, the theatregoing public over the whole period seems to have been much the same – a cross-section of classes distinguished only by the places they occupied and the prices they paid. The conclusion is that the Court and its types, whether admired or derided, had exhausted their attraction as material for the dramatist.

The exceptional richness of French comedy over exactly one hundred years (1630–1730) can be credited to four major dramatists, to whom can be added a number of less creative but still highly talented secondary playwrights whom some of them partly influenced or inspired. The major figures were also influenced by others and exploited traditions and styles which they did not invent, but their use of these was sufficiently original to transform their borrowings into work which possessed a character of its own. While its derivative features can be singled out, they are not of the first importance. The pattern of French comedy, so far as there was one, will have emerged in general lines from this book, but it would be misleading to draw it in with dogmatic clarity. A more realistic approach is through the great individual playwrights and a brief reconsideration of what they stood for and achieved.

Pierre Corneille was right in claiming that he had launched a new kind of comedy after the crude theatre which preceded him. As found in the first five plays it was social comedy aiming at realism in manners and characterization. These belonged to his contemporary world and were presented through ingenious plots with situational vicissitudes. This distanced them from complete realism, yet such people existed and such things could happen; it was perfectly legitimate and indeed necessary to combine them in a fictional pattern in a production for the stage. His comedies were lively – immensely so – rather than gay. The only question is whether they should be regarded as true comic drama. In his period they were, but on a broader and longer view of the genre they are less so. They contain virtually no laughter. The serious dilemmas confronted and the sombre reactions of some of the characters, particularly in *La Suivante* and *La Place Royale*, skirt the tragic, as does the tone of some of the dialogue. While this can be attributed to contemporary uncertainty as to the nature of comedy, it puts this most interesting body of plays in a special class not paralleled elsewhere.

After them, *L'Illusion comique* is made amusing by the character of Matamore, introduced almost gratuitously into this mixed play, and by little else, but it justifies its title by the surprise elements in the plot and the unexpected happy ending. When a few years later Corneille wrote *Le Menteur* he had perfected the comic intrigue and in this polished and witty play set up a model for that kind of comedy.

The comedies of Scarron were based on absurdity – a joyful absurdity maintained in situations, characters and dialogue. Realism is entirely subordinated to fantastic humour. The luxuriance of the language has already been pointed out and it accords entirely with the other elements in the plays. The verbally comic is in the tradition of Rabelais, though partly refined and seasoned with seventeenth-century wit. As examples of the burlesque writing of the 1640s these comedies have never been surpassed. Their comparative neglect since is attributable in part to the exclusion of most of them from the repertory of the Comédie Française, but much more to the fact that this kind of humour is appreciated only by a minority. For many it appears too silly or not coarse enough. Scarron's burlesque epics had these defects, but in his comedies he got the mixture just right. It was good enough for Molière in some of his most successful scenes and frequently re-appears in later dramatists. But all these used it more selectively, tempering Scarron's reckless exuberance with other comic effects, usually more sophisticated. Nevertheless his influence as a comic dramatist, quite apart from the influence of his short stories, persisted from Molière to Beaumarchais. It deserves fuller recognition than it has had so far.

Molière represented the zenith of comic drama, not only in his own time and place but for a very long time after. To remove him would be to tear out its heart – how thoroughly will have become so apparent in previous chapters that an attempt to sum up his genius and variety again in a few lines would be superfluous. The hyperbolical praise which has been lavished on him is unilluminating, while the critical considerations which justify it have been very extensively explored. If there is always something new to be said about Molière it is not necessarily important or even relevant. Certain partial questions still await solution, but a radically new interpretation seems impossible without distortion. No doubt his modern reputation has suffered from over-familiarity, the price of long-recognized excellence. Comparisons between his thirty-odd plays can, however, still prove very rewarding, as can comparisons with other comic dramatists whom he influenced.

This influence was inescapable and after his death in 1673 threatened to freeze French comedy in conventional postures. Departures from the Molière tradition (as in Boursault) were isolated and mainly unsuccessful experiments. Attempts to continue or renew it were not often fruitful, though gradually they contributed to the formation of a new comedy which emerged in the last two or three decades of Louis XIV's reign.

In considering the comedies of the 'cynical generation' it is at last possible to speak of a 'school' of dramatists. Of Dancourt, Regnard, Dufresny and Lesage, no one individual stands out conspicuously above the others, though Dancourt was the earliest in the field by a few years, the most prolific (if Lesage's contributions to the Théâtre de la Foire are discounted) and in our opinion the most gifted. He was particularly successful with his short comedies, sometimes with songs and dances. Between them this group produced a body of comedy which collectively was the most brilliant in Europe. It is essentially a comedy of manners, dramatizing these with a totally unsentimental adult wit and a treatment of the contemporary scene at once realistic and amusing. Its implications might be thought bitter but its tone was not. Like Scarron, this generation has suffered from relative neglect, but its achievements must be ranked high in a survey of French comedy as a whole.

❧

With Marivaux we return to the outstanding individual names. Certainly not cynical, he avoided the opposite excess of sentimentalism by a difficult balancing act of which no one else proved capable. The incipient eighteenth-century regard for 'feeling' appears in his plays as *sensibilité*, a shy, reserved manifestation of feelings allowing for the expression of subtle shades of emotion which, for all their lack of robustness, were far from superficial. His disappointed lovers will not kill themselves, they will simply go away. The fact that finally they do not gives the happy endings habitual in comedy, but celebrated here on a deliberately unmaterialistic and unsexual note. This rendering of love, the main and almost the sole theme, was new in French comedy and made possible by a combination of influences of which the strongest were the requirements and capabilities of the Italian troupe. It is fully typical of only three or four plays among the more than thirty that Marivaux wrote, but these were enough to distinguish him as a master of the sensitive analysis in comedy which before him had been found only in tragedy and tragicomedy and after him had no immediate follow-up. The bourgeois comedy which the eighteenth century went on to produce was loaded with heavy sentiment and the desire to preach moral and social responsibility.

❧❧❧

Beaumarchais inherited all this, but with so much else that he managed to transcend it. *Drame*, farce, *opéra-comique*, burlesque, satire, all participate in his two comedies. One is driven to conclude that it was the accident of personality and lived experience which caused him to combine them in something different. He was not consciously trying to escape from a theatrical tradition and in one sense summed up a whole century of it. But his work cannot rightly be regarded as a synthesis of previous plays, however skilful the blending and palatable the result. What gave it its distinctive flavour was personal, a sufficient explanation of the fact that nothing closely resembling it has been produced since. In their historical context certain features of the Figaro plays can be singled out. They reintroduced gaiety into social comedy. They used comedy to protest against social abuses. On that score they were subtly satirical, generally using satire in cloaked or humorous forms. They embodied the spirit of the pre-Revolution years, at once rebellious, anxious and irresponsible, more faithfully than anything else written for the stage. To achieve this in two plays only may not be enough to make a writer a great comic dramatist, but at least Beaumarchais was a phenomenon suddenly appearing near the end of a dying phase of art.

❧❧❧

Variations in the form and structure, technical and notional, of French comedy over the whole period covered in this book were not fundamental. The 'classical' conception of drama which was being formed in the 1630s preoccupied Corneille when he wrote his comedies of that decade, and later when he looked back on them. He felt that they should abide by the same 'rules' which came to govern regular tragedy and was self-critical when they did not. The most obvious test was observance of the unities of place and time. The first was a matter of staging. A fixed set, designed for only partial changes at most, would decide the question. There the characters met and there the whole action took place. Time was a more elusive factor. Its passage was not definitely marked as it usually was in tragedy, and Corneille's admission that the action of *La Veuve* and *La Galerie du Palais* extended over five days seemed unnecessarily scrupulous. The spirit, however, if not the letter of this unity was observed in nearly all comedy after that date. While there was no insistence on the 24-hour limit, no important comedy supposed a long stretch of time. Characters took part in no actions requiring more than a few days – not even Molière's exceptional Dom Juan. This principle, which had contributed to the concentration of interest on a central situation and its rapid build-up, development and resolution in classical tragedy, was carried over into comedy in a less rigid form but with comparable results. Other 'classical' principles, such as the logical linking of scenes, the rational motivation of entrances and exits, and the insistence on the early appearance of important characters, were generally applied to comedy also. Tartuffe makes his first entrance in Act III, Scene ii, almost halfway through the play, but it has been so thoroughly prepared with all the attendant circumstances that here there is no gratuitous surprise but rather an effectively dramatic fulfilment of anticipation.

Surprise, however, can hardly be eliminated from comedy. As Molière remarked, it is one of its characteristics. In many plays there is an abrupt surprise, foreshadowed by the faintest of clues or sometimes not at all. Among other instances, the most obvious is the arrival of hitherto unknown fathers or uncles in the last act. This was a conventional way of disentangling a plot which could not be unknotted by other means, but it has some dramatic value beyond its utility as a device. Habituated audiences will have anticipated some such solution and their simpler members may well exclaim with self-satisfaction: 'I thought all along that she would turn out to be a duke's daughter'. The unworded 'clue' is then implicit in the characterization.

Surprise is not absent from tragedy either, even in its most purely 'classical' form in Racine, but in comedy it is understandably cultivated as a desirable quality. Nearly always it is controlled and pleasant, unlike the 'shock' of some modern drama.

The idiom of comedy during the seventeenth and eighteenth centuries followed changes in the spoken language, but these were comparatively slight. A major distinction might seem to lie between the use of verse or prose, but this cannot be substantiated. In the earlier years verse was the unquestioned language of all drama, including the comic. It never occurred to Corneille, Scarron and their contemporaries to depart from it. Though advocating more realistically natural dialogue,[1] Corneille remained faithful to the couplet-rhymed alexandrine, varied occasionally by the still more artificial *stance*. With Molière's arrival prose became common in comedy though not at first in the more ambitious type. Its associations with farce tended to confine it to plays of that kind and it was the language of all his farces and near-farces except *Sganarelle ou le Cocu imaginaire*, but including *Les Précieuses ridicules*. He used it also in more delicate productions such as the last four acts of *La Princesse d'Élide*, *Le Sicilien* and *Les Amants magnifiques*, and in four important comedies beginning in 1665 with *Dom Juan*[2] and continuing with *L'Avare*, *Le Bourgeois Gentilhomme* and *Le Malade imaginaire*. Extraneous reasons can be found for some of these cases – usually pressure of time – though not for all. It appears that in his later years Molière showed an increasing preference for prose in any case. Of his last sixteen plays, long or short, from *Dom Juan* on, only four are in verse. They include *Le Misanthrope*, *Amphitryon* in free verse and, after an interval, *Les Femmes savantes*.

From this representative sampling it would be difficult to deduce a comic hierarchy or a tenable theory of the correspondence of the verbal medium with its subject. One feels that the supreme 'classical' comedy of *Le Misanthrope* demands verse, yet had it been written in prose one might not notice it. Would *Tartuffe* lose much in prose and if *Le Bourgeois Gentilhomme* had been in verse would it be a different play? The example of Molière tends to show that the same public and actors were equally receptive to either medium and that the choice lay with the playwright, for reasons not always clear.

It continued to be so long after Molière. Regnard wrote all his main comedies in verse, while his contemporary Dancourt invariably used prose. Dufresny used both with apparent indifference. La Chaussée's bourgeois comedy is in verse, whereas prose would seem more

---

[1] See above, pp. 29–30.
[2] Thomas Corneille's adaptation of this was in verse, like the earlier versions of Dorimon and de Villiers.

appropriate. On the other hand Marivaux wrote all his plays (except for two early failures, one a tragedy, but these show that he could write verse) in prose. Here particularly one might suppose – wrongly – that the stylization of verse, flexibly handled as it could be, would have been a deciding factor in its favour.

After Marivaux and in spite of the contagion of the *drame*, prose still did not oust verse. Almost until the Revolution playwrights were using either for similar types of comedies. There is no apparent discrimination between the two media on grounds of appropriateness. Only the full-bodied burlesque of the first half of the seventeenth century had flourished on verse and had seemed to require it as the language of the exuberant imagination. A Jodelet or a Matamore would sound less outrageous in prose.

As to the outward forms which comedy took, the full-length play, usually in five acts, more rarely in three, with the entire dialogue in spoken words, was always the standard type. The short play, normally in one act, grew in favour after the 1660s and, while never replacing the farce proper, proved capable of conveying more sophisticated humour, though nearly always on a frivolous note. In the 1690s spoken dialogue was combined with songs in the *comédie-vaudeville*, later called the *comédie à ariettes*, and this introduction of music led to its use in full-length plays and to the development of *opéra-comique* as a distinct genre. This was the eighteenth century's most notable innovation in the comic form, though it had a prototype in the *comédie-ballet* of Molière. The songs and dances were sometimes introduced perfunctorily, sometimes well integrated with the action, in which case it becomes permissible to speak of musical comedy. Either kind offered an alternative to the heaviness of the *drame* and helped to keep the comic spirit alive when the other forms were showing signs of exhaustion.

NOTABLE COMEDIES
1552–1784

✤

(A few works of other kinds are shown in brackets to serve as landmarks)

(1532 ff.	Rabelais, *Gargantua* and *Pantagruel*)
(1552–3	Jodelle, *Cléopâtre*, tragedy)
1552 (?)	Jodelle, *L'Eugène*
1561	Grévin, *Les Ébahis*
(1568–83	Garnier, tragedies)
1579	Larivey published first six comedies
1584	O. de Turnèbe, *Les Contents*
(1607–27	H. d'Urfé, *L'Astrée*)
c. 1624	Hardy (?), *Les Ramonneurs*
1629–30	P. Corneille, *Mélite*
1634	P. Corneille, *La Place Royale*
1635–6	P. Corneille, *L'Illusion comique*
c. 1636	Rotrou, *Le Belle Alphrède*
(1637	P. Corneille, *Le Cid*)
1637	Desmarets, *Les Visionnaires*
(1640	P. Corneille, *Horace*)

1643	P. Corneille, *Le Menteur*
1643	Scarron, *Jodelet ou le Maître-Valet*
c. 1645	Rotrou, *La Sœur*
1647	Scarron, *Don Japhet d'Arménie*
1648–9	Scarron, *L'Héritier ridicule*
(1649–53	Madeleine de Scudéry, *Le Grand Cyrus*)
1654	T. L'Hermite, *Le Parasite*
1659–73	Molière's main plays. For complete list see pp. 275–6.
(1666–1711	Boileau, *Satires*)
(1667	Racine, *Andromaque*)
1668	Racine, *Les Plaideurs*
(1668–94	La Fontaine, *Fables*)
(1677	Racine, *Phèdre*)
1683	Boursault, *Le Mercure galant*
1687	Dancourt, *Le Chevalier à la mode*
(1688–94	La Bruyère, *Les Caractères*)
1691	Brueys and Palaprat, *Le Grondeur*
1692	Dancourt, *Les Bourgeoises à la mode*
1696	Regnard, *Le Joueur*
1702	Dufresny, *Le Double Veuvage*
1706	Lesage, *Crispin rival de son maître*
1708	Regnard, *Le Légataire universel*
1709	Lesage, *Turcaret*
(1718–78	Voltaire, tragedies)
1722	Marivaux, *La (Première) Surprise de l'amour*
1727	Marivaux, *La Seconde Surprise de l'amour*
1730	Marivaux, *Le Jeu de l'amour et du hasard*
(1731	Prévost, *Manon Lescaut*)
1732	Destouches, *Le Glorieux*
1735	La Chaussée, *Le Préjugé à la mode*

1747	Gresset, *Le Méchant*
1749	Voltaire, *Nanine*
(1751–80	*L'Encyclopédie*)
(1758	Diderot, *Le Père de famille*)
(1759	Voltaire, *Candide*)
(1762	Rousseau, *Du contrat social*)
1775	Beaumarchais, *Le Barbier de Séville*
1784	Beaumarchais, *Le Mariage de Figaro*

COMPLETE LIST OF
MOLIÈRE'S PLAYS

❧

Dates are of first productions where known

La Jalousie du Barbouillé (attrib.), farce, 1 act. 1660 or earlier.

Le Médecin volant (attrib.), farce, 1 act. 1659 or earlier.

L'Étourdi ou les Contretemps, comedy, 5 acts. 1655 (?).

Le Dépit amoureux, comedy, 5 acts. 1656 (?).

Les Précieuses ridicules, comedy, 1 act. 1659.

Sganarelle ou le Cocu imaginaire, comedy-farce, 1 act. 1660.

Dom Garcie de Navarre ou le Prince jaloux, comédie héroïque, 5 acts. 1661.

L'École des maris, comedy, 3 acts. 1661.

Les Fâcheux, comedy, 3 acts. 1661.

L'École des femmes, comedy, 5 acts. 1662.

La Critique de l'École des femmes, comedy-commentary, 1 act. 1663.

L'Impromptu de Versailles, comedy-commentary, 1 act. 1663.

Le Mariage forcé, comedy to accompany ballet, 1 act. 1664.

La Princesse d'Élide, comédie galante with ballet and music, 5 acts. 1664.

Le Tartuffe ou l'Imposteur, comedy, 5 acts. (1664, 1667) 1669.

Dom Juan ou le Festin de pierre, comedy, 5 acts. 1665.

L'Amour médecin, comedy-farce with ballet, 3 acts. 1665.

Le Misanthrope, comedy, 5 acts. 1666.

Le Médecin malgré lui, comedy-farce, 3 acts. 1666.

Mélicerte, pastoral comedy, 2 acts, unfinished.[1] 1666.

Le Sicilien ou l'Amour peintre, comedy with songs and ballet, 1 act. 1667.

Amphitryon, comedy, 3 acts. 1668.

George Dandin ou le Mari confondu, comedy, 3 acts. 1668.

L'Avare, comedy, 5 acts. 1668.

Monsieur de Pourceaugnac, *comédie-ballet*, 3 acts. 1669.

Les Amants magnifiques, comedy with music and ballet, 5 acts. 1670.

Le Bourgeois Gentilhomme, *comédie-ballet*, 5 acts. 1670.

Psyché (in collaboration with Quinault and P. Corneille), *tragédie-ballet* (near-opera), 5 acts. 1671.

Les Fourberies de Scapin, comedy, 3 acts. 1671.

La Comtesse d'Escarbagnas, comedy, 1 act. 1671.

Les Femmes savantes, comedy, 5 acts. 1672.

Le Malade imaginaire, comedy with music and ballet, 3 acts. 1673.

---

[1] *Mélicerte*, with *Le Sicilien* and *La Pastorale comique* (a short scenario with songs), was composed to order for inclusion in 'Le Ballet des muses', a royal entertainment at Saint-Germain-en-Laye devised by Benserade and repeated several times from December 1666 to February 1667. Molière was unable to complete *Mélicerte* in the short time given him and did not take it up again.

SELECT BIBLIOGRAPHY

❦

GENERAL STUDIES

ADAM, A. *Histoire de la littérature française au XVIIe siècle.* 5 vols. Paris, 1949–56.

ATTINGER, G. *L'Esprit de la commedia dell'arte dans le théâtre français.* Paris, 1950.

DOBRÉE, B. *Restoration Comedy, 1660–1720.* London, 1938.

GAIFFE, G. *Le Drame en France au XVIIIe siècle.* Paris, 1910.

GARAPON, R. *La Fantaisie verbale et le comique dans le théâtre français du Moyen Âge à la fin du XVIIe siècle.* Paris, 1957.

GUICHEMERRE, R. *La Comédie avant Molière, 1640–60.* Paris, 1972.

HERRICK, M. T. *Italian Comedy in the Renaissance.* Urbana, Ill., 1960.

JEFFERY, B. *French Renaissance Comedy, 1552–1630.* Oxford, 1969.

LANCASTER, H. C. *A History of French Dramatic Literature in the Seventeenth Century.* 9 vols. Baltimore, 1929–42.

—— *Sunset, a History of Parisian Drama, 1701–15.* Baltimore, 1945.

LEBÈGUE, R. *Le Théâtre comique en France de Pathelin à Mélite.* Paris, 1972.

LEMAÎTRE, J. *La Comédie après Molière et le théâtre de Dancourt.* 2nd ed. Paris, 1903.

NIKLAUS, R. *A Literary History of France: The Eighteenth Century.* London and New York, 1970.

VALBUENA PRAT, A. *Historia del teatro español.* Barcelona, 1956.

VOLTZ, P. *La Comédie.* Paris, 1964.

THEATRE HISTORY, DRAMATURGY, ACTORS

DEIERKAUF-HOLSBOER, S. W. *Histoire de la mise en scène dans le théâtre français de 1600 à 1673.* Paris, 1960.

—— *Le Théâtre de l'Hôtel de Bourgogne.* 2 vols. Paris, 1968–70.

—— *Le Théâtre du Marais.* 2 vols. Paris, 1954–8.

JOANNIDÈS, A. *La Comédie Française de 1680 à 1920.* Paris, 1921.

LAGRAVE, H. *Le Théâtre et le public à Paris de 1715 à 1750.* Paris, 1972.

LANCASTER, H. C. *The Comédie Française, 1701–1774.* 2 vols. Baltimore, 1951.

—— (ed.) *Le Mémoire de Mahelot, Laurent et autres décorateurs de l'Hôtel de Bourgogne.* Paris, 1920.

LAWRENSON, T. E. *The French Stage in the Seventeenth Century.* Manchester, 1957.

LOUGH, J. *Paris Theatre Audiences in the Seventeenth and Eighteenth Centuries.* London, 1957.

MÉLÈSE, P. *Le Théâtre et le public à Paris sous Louis XIV.* Paris, 1934.

—— *Répertoire analytique des documents contemporains . . . concernant le théâtre à Paris sous Louis XIV.* Paris, 1934. Reprinted with errata. Geneva, 1976.

MONGRÉDIEN, G. *Dictionnaire biographique des comédiens français du XVIIe siècle.* Paris, 1961.

OREGLIA, G. *La Commedia dell'arte.* Stockholm, 1961. Trans. L. F. Edwards. London, 1968.

SCHERER, J. *La Dramaturgie classique en France.* Paris, 1959.

TEXTS BEFORE 1630
Collections

Ancien Théâtre François. Ed. E. L. N. Viollet-le-Duc. 10 vols. Paris, 1854–6. Vols IV–VIII contain Larivey's comedies and others mentioned in Ch. 1.

Le Recueil Trepperel (1612–19). Vol. I (*soties*). Ed. E. Droz. Paris, 1935. Vol. II (*farces*). Ed. E. Droz and H. Lewicka. Paris, 1961.

Individual authors

ANON
Les Ramonneurs. Ed. A. Gill. Paris, 1957.

J.-A. DE BAÏF
Euvres en rime. Ed. C. Marty-Laveaux. 5 vols. Paris, 1881–90. *Le Brave* in Vol. III. *L'Eunuque* in Vol. IV.

R. BELLEAU
Œuvres poétiques. Ed. C. Marty-Laveaux. 2 vols. Paris, 1878. *La Reconnue* in Vol. II.

J. GRÉVIN
Théâtre complet et poésies choisies. Ed. L. Pinvert. Paris, 1922. Contains *La Trésorière* and *Les Ébahis.*

E. JODELLE
L'Eugène. Ed. E. Balmas. Turin, 1955.
—— In *Œuvres complètes.* Vol. II. Ed. E. Balmas. Paris, 1968.

JEAN DE LA TAILLE
Dramatic Works. Ed. K. M. Hall and C. N. Smith. London, 1972.

O. DE TURNÈBE
Les Contents. Ed. N. B. Spector. Paris, 1964.

TEXTS AND STUDIES AFTER 1630

Where good modern editions of plays exist, they have generally been listed in preference to older editions, on grounds of availability. But they cover only part of the field.

Collections

Various multi-volume *répertoires* of plays were published in the eighteenth and early nineteenth centuries. Though not impeccable textually, they contain comedies hardly obtainable elsewhere. Among them:

Théâtre françois, ou Recueil des meilleures pièces de théâtre. 12 vols. Paris, 1737.
Répertoire du théâtre français. 63 vols. Paris, 1813. The section *Théâtre des auteurs de second ordre* (*sic*) begins at Vol. 28. 'Comédies en vers', 35–51. 'Comédies en prose', 52–63.
Répertoire du théâtre français. Ed. C.-B. Petitot. 25 vols. Paris, 1803 and 1817. *Supplément.* 8 vols. Paris, 1819–20.

Le Théâtre de la Foire ou l'Opéra-Comique. Ed. Lesage and d'Orneval. 10 vols. Paris, 1721–37. Contains, among others, Lesage's hundred-odd short plays.

Théâtre des Boulevards ou Recueil des parades. Ed. T.-S. Guellette (?). 3 vols. Paris, 1756.

Le Théâtre-Italien ou le Recueil de toutes les comédies et scènes françaises qui ont été jouées sur le Théâtre-Italien par la troupe des Comédiens du Roi de l'Hôtel de Bourgogne à Paris. Ed. Évariste Gherardi. 6 vols. Paris, 1691. Augmented edition, with music. Paris, 1700.

Nouveau Théâtre Italien. Ed. Luigi Riccoboni. 2 vols. Paris, 1718. Texts in French and Italian.

Théâtre du XVIIe siècle. Ed. J. Scherer. Vol. I. Paris, 1975. Contains Rotrou, *La Belle Alphrède*; two of Tabarin's *Œuvres*.

Théâtre du XVIIIe siècle. Ed. J. Truchet. 2 vols. Paris, 1972–4. Vol. I contains comedies by Lesage (*Crispin rival* and *Turcaret*); Dufresny, *La Coquette de village;* Voltaire, *Nanine;* Piron, *La Métromanie*; N. de La Chaussée, *Mélanide;* Gresset, *Le Méchant;* three Foire plays and three *parades*. Vol. II contains comedies by Favart; Sedaine; Palissot, *Les Philosophes;* Voltaire, *Le Café;* also Diderot, *Le Fils naturel* and *Le Père de famille;* other *drames*, including Sade's *Oxtiern*.

Individual dramatists

Listed alphabetically. Writers of wider range are considered only in their relation to comedy. Editions of single plays, often excellent, are not usually listed when there is a satisfactory collected edition.

MICHEL BARON (1653–1729)
In *Répertoire du théâtre français* (1813). Vol. 37: *L'Andrienne*. Vol. 55: *L'Homme à bonne fortune*. Vol. 56: *La Coquette et la Fausse Prude*.

CARON DE BEAUMARCHAIS (1732–1799)
Théâtre complet. Ed. M. Allem and Paul-Courant. Paris, 1957.
LOMÉNIE, L. DE. *Beaumarchais et son tempts*. 4th ed. Paris, 1879.
LINTILHAC, E.-F. *Beaumarchais et ses œuvres*. Paris, 1887.
SCHERER, J. *La Dramaturgie de Beaumarchais*. Paris, 1954.
POMEAU, R. *Beaumarchais, l'homme et l'œuvre*. Paris, 1956.
VAN TIEGHEM, P. *Beaumarchais par lui-même*. Paris, 1960.

EDME BOURSAULT (1638–1701)
Théâtre du feu Monsieur Boursault. 2 vols. Paris, 1725 and 1746.
Théâtre choisi. Ed. V. Fournel. Paris, 1883.
In *Répertoire du théâtre français* (1813). Vol. 38: *Le Mercure galant, Ésope à la ville, Ésope à la cour.*

DAVID AUGUSTIN DE BRUEYS (1640–1723) and JEAN PALAPRAT (c. 1650–1721)
Œuvres de théâtre de Brueys et Palaprat. Nouvelle édition revue et augmentée. 5 vols. Paris, 1755–6.
Le Grondeur. In *Répertoire du théâtre français* (1813). Vol. 56.

PIERRE CORNEILLE (1606–1684)
Théâtre complet. Vol. I. Ed. G. Couton. Paris, 1971. Contains *Mélite* to *L'Illusion comique.*
Théâtre complet. Vol. I. Ed. P. Lièvre and R. Caillois. Paris, 1957.
Less well documented, but contains all the comedies including *Le Menteur* and its *Suite.*
RIVAILLE, L. *Les Débuts de P. Corneille.* Paris, 1936.
COUTON, G. *Réalisme de Corneille.* Paris, 1953.

THOMAS CORNEILLE (1625–1709)
Œuvres. 9 vols. Paris, 1758.
REYNIER, G. *T. Corneille, sa vie et son théâtre.* Paris, 1892.
COLLINS, D. A. *T. Corneille, Protean Dramatist.* The Hague, 1966.

FLORENT CARTON DANCOURT (1661–1725)
Les Œuvres de Monsieur d'Ancourt. 9 vols. 3rd ed. Paris, 1729.
Théâtre choisi. Ed. F. Sarcey. 5 vols. Paris, 1884.
In *Répertoire du théâtre français* (1813). Vols. 52–5 contain *Le Chevalier à la mode, Les Bourgeoises à la mode, Les Vendanges de Suresnes* and 9 other comedies.
BARTHÉLEMY, C. *La Comédie de Dancourt.* Paris, 1882.
LEMAÎTRE, J. *La Comédie après Molière et le théâtre de Dancourt.* 2nd ed. Paris, 1903.

JEAN DESMARETS DE SAINT-SORLIN (1595–1676)
Les Visionnaires. Ed. H. G. Hall. Paris, 1968.

PHILIPPE NÉRICAULT DESTOUCHES (1680–1754)
Œuvres complètes. 6 vols. Paris, 1822.

In *Répertoire du théâtre français* (1813). Vol. 41: *Le Philosophe marié, Le Dissipateur*. Other plays in Vols. 42 and 59.
In *Théâtre du XVIIIe siècle* (1972). Vol. I: *Le Glorieux*.

CHARLES RIVIÈRE DUFRESNY (1654–1724)
Œuvres. 6 vols. Paris, 1731. *Nouvelle édition corrigée et augmentée.* 4 vols. Paris, 1747.
In *Répertoire du théâtre français* (1813). Vols 39–40: *La Coquette de village* and three other comedies. Vol. 57: *L'Esprit de contradiction.* Vol. 58: *Le Double Veuvage.* In *Théâtre du XVIIIe siècle* (1972). Vol. I: *La Coquette de village.*

JEAN-BAPTISTE LOUIS GRESSET (1709–1777)
Le Méchant. In *Œuvres de Gresset.* Ed. Renouard. 2 vols. Paris, 1811.
—— In *Répertoire du théâtre français* (1813). Vol. 44.
—— In *Théâtre du XVIIIe siècle* (1972). Vol. I.

NOËL LEBRETON, SIEUR DE HAUTEROCHE (1616–1707)
Théâtre. 3 vols. Paris, 1736, 1742 and 1772.
In *Répertoire du théâtre français* (1813). Vol. 35: *Le Deuil.* Vol. 52: *Crispin médecin* and *Le Cocher supposé.*

PIERRE-CLAUDE NIVELLE DE LA CHAUSSÉE (1692–1754)
Œuvres. 5 vols. Paris, 1761–2.
In *Répertoire du théâtre français* (1813). Vol. 43: *Le Préjugé à la mode, Mélanide, L'École des mères, La Gouvernante.*
Mélanide. Ed. W. D. Howarth. London, 1973.
—— In *Théâtre du XVIIIe siècle* (1972). Vol. I.
LANSON, G. *N. de La Chaussée et la comédie larmoyante.* Paris, 1903.

ALAIN RENÉ LESAGE (1668–1747)
In *Théâtre du XVIIIe siècle* (1972). Vol. I: *Crispin rival de son maître, Turcaret* and three Foire plays.
Turcaret. Ed. T. E. Lawrenson. London, 1969.
Short plays in *Le Théâtre de la Foire.* Paris, 1721–37.
SPAZIANI, M. *Il teatro minore di Lesage.* Rome, 1957.

PIERRE CARLET DE CHAMBLAIN DE MARIVAUX (1688–1763)
Théâtre complet. Ed. F. Deloffre. 2 vols. Paris, 1968.
ARLAND, M. *Marivaux,* Paris, 1950.
MCKEE, K. N. *The Theater of Marivaux.* New York, 1958.
GREENE, E. J. H. *Marivaux.* Toronto, 1965.

DELOFFRE, F. *Marivaux et le marivaudage*. Rev. ed. Paris, 1967.

MOLIÈRE (JEAN-BAPTISTE POQUELIN, 1622–1673)
Œuvres complètes. Ed. G. Couton. 2 vols. Paris, 1971. Contains in appendices all the relevant scenes or passages of the works constituting the Comic War listed above on p. 92, note 2; also texts concerning the controversies round *Tartuffe* and *Dom Juan*.
MONGRÉDIEN, G. (ed.) *Recueil des textes et documents du XVIIe siècle relatifs à Molière*. 2 vols. Paris, 1965.
Le Registre de La Grange. Facsimile reproduction. Ed. B. E. and G. P. Young. 2 vols. Paris, 1947.
Molière Mocked. Ed. F. W. Vogler. Chapel Hill, N.C., 1973. Contains *Zélinde, Le Portrait du peintre, Élomire hypocondre*.
MICHAUT, G. *La Jeunesse de Molière, Les Débuts de Molière à Paris, Les Luttes de Molière*. 3 vols. Paris, 1922–5. Standard biography.
ADAM, A. *Histoire de la littérature française au XVIIe siècle*. Vol. IV. Paris, 1952. Contains sound traditional study.
Some recent interpretations:
AUDIBERTI, J. *Molière dramaturge*. Paris, 1954.
GUICHARNAUD, J. *Molière, une aventure théâtrale*. Paris, 1963.
—— (ed.) *Molière, a Collection of Critical Essays*. Englewood Cliffs, N.J., 1964.
GUTWIRTH, M. *Molière ou l'invention comique*. Paris, 1966.
Revue d'histoire littéraire de la France. Special number. Paris, Sept.–Dec. 1972.
Tout sur Molière. Reprint of three special numbers of *Europe*. Paris, 1976.

ANTOINE-JACOB MONTFLEURY (1640–1685)
Théâtre. Paris, 1705.
With Zacharie-Jacob Montfleury (1600–67): *Théâtre de Messieurs de Montfleury, père et fils. Nouvelle édition augmentée*. 3 vols. Paris, 1759.
In *Répertoire du théâtre fra..ais* (1813). Vol. 36: *La Femme juge et partie*.

PHILIPPE QUINAULT (1635–1688)
Théâtre choisi. Ed. V. Fournel. Paris, 1882.
In *Répertoire du théâtre français* (1813). Vol. 36: *La Mère coquette*.

JEAN RACINE (1639–1699)
Œuvres complètes. Ed. R. Picard. 2 vols. Paris, 1951–2.
Les Plaideurs. Ed. J. Fabre. Paris, 1963.

JEAN-FRANÇOIS REGNARD (1655–1709)
Œuvres. Ed. E. Fournier. 2 vols. Paris, 1876.
Le Joueur. Ed. J.–R. Charbonnel. Paris, 1934.
Le Légataire universel. Ed. C.-H. Frèches. Paris, 1965.
CALAME, A. *Regnard, sa vie, son œuvre.* Paris, 1960.

JEAN ROTROU (1609–1650)
Œuvres. Ed. E. L. N. Viollet-le-Duc. 5 vols. Paris, 1820.
In *Théâtre du XVIIe siècle* (1975). Vol. I: *La Belle Alphrède.*
MOREL, J. *Jean Rotrou, dramaturge de l'ambiguïté.* Paris, 1968.

CHARLES DE MARGUETEL DE SAINT-DENIS DE SAINT-
ÉVREMOND (1616–1703)
La Comédie des Académistes. Ed. G. L. van Roosbroeck. New York,
1931.

PAUL SCARRON (1610–1652)
Œuvres. 7 vols. Paris, 1786. Plays in Vol. VI, Fragments in Vol. VII.
Théâtre complet. Ed. E. Fournier. Paris, 1912.
Don Japhet d'Arménie. Ed. R. Garapon. Paris, 1967.
In *Répertoire du théâtre français* (1813). Vol. 35: *Jodelet ou le
maître-valet* and *Don Japhet.*
MORILLOT, P. *Scarron et le genre burlesque.* Paris, 1888.

TRISTAN L'HERMITE (1601–1655)
Le Parasite. Ed. J. Madeleine. Paris, 1934.

VOLTAIRE (FRANÇOIS-MARIE AROUET, 1694–1778)
In *Théâtre du XVIIIe siècle* (1972–4). Vol. I: *Nanine.* Vol. II:
Le Café ou L'Écossaise.

INDEX

*(Page numbers in **bold** type indicate main references to plays)*

❦

Académie Française, 83
Alarcón, J., *La verdad sospechosa*, 26, 40
Alice in Wonderland, 148
Amboise, F. d', *Les Néapolitaines*, 5
American Revolution, the, 240
Anne of Austria, 92, 121
Anouilh, Jean, *La Répétition*, 205
Ariosto, L., 4
Aristophanes, *The Wasps*, 151
Aristotle, 110
Arlequin, *see* type-characters
Aulnoy, Madame d', *Les Illustres Fées*, 197
Autreau, J., *Le Naufrage au Port-à-l'Anglais*, 195–6

Baïf, J.-A. de, *Le Brave*, *L'Eunuque*, 3, 4
Balletti, Elena, 195
Baron, Michel, *La Coquette et la Fausse Prude*, *L'Homme à bonne fortune*, *Le Jaloux*, 156–7
Beaumarchais, P.-A. Caron de
  life and career, 237–41
  and satire, 75, 268
  works: *Le Barbier de Séville*, 239, 241, **242–5**; *Les Deux Amis*, 238, 242; *Eugénie*, 238, **241–2**; *Jean Bête à la foire*, 241; *Le Mariage de Figaro*, 209, 239, **245–52**; *Mémoires*, 239; *La Mère coupable*, 240, 241, **252–5**; *Tarare*, 240
Bedeau, Julien, *see* Jodelet
Béjart family, the, 86, 90, 91

Belleau, R., *La Reconnue*, 3, 4
Benozzi, Gianneta, *see* 'Silvia'
Biancolelli, Catarina, 8
Biancolelli, D., Snr, *Il convitato di pietra*, 7
Biancolelli, D., Jnr, 196
blason, 76
Boccaccio, G., *Decameron*, 4, 46n., 115
Boileau, N., 75, 148
Boursault, Edme: *Ésope à la cour*, *Ésope à la ville*, 161–2, 165; *Le Médecin volant*, 158; *Le Mercure galant*, 159–61, 165; *Le Portrait du peintre*, 92n., 93; *La Princesse de Clèves*, *La Satire des Satires*, 159
Brécourt: *La Feinte Mort de Jodelet*, 54; *La Noce de village*, 155
Brueys, D.-A. de and Palaprat, J.: *L'Avocat Patelin*, 157n.; *Le Grondeur*, 157–8
Bruscambille, 10 and n.
burlesque, 51–2, 74, 256–7

capitano, 7, 73, 78–9. See also *fanfaron*.
Caron, Pierre-Augustin, *see* Beaumarchais
Cervantes: *Don Quijote*, 51–2; *Novelas Ejemplares*, 45, 46
Chalussay, B. de, *Élomire hypocondre*, 92n.
Chapelain, J.: *Lettre à Balzac*, 83; *Lettre à Godeau*, 42n.
Chekov, A., 214; *Three Sisters*, *Uncle Vanya*, 14n.
chevaliers, 168

Cicogni, G. A., *El convitato de pietra*, 124
comedia de figurón, 57
comedia de gracioso, 57, 74
Comédie Française, 25, 26, 53, 101, 147n., 154, 168–70
Comédie Italienne, *see* Italians
comédie à ariettes, 271
comédie attendrissante, 233
comédie-ballet, 89, 103, 235
comédie galante, 89n., 257
comédie héroïque, 88, 138, 257
comédie larmoyante, 223, 227–8, 233
comédie-vaudeville, 169, 271
comedy, 1–2
  'bitter', 117
  'cruel', 2, 21
  'literary', 3, 235
  and love and marriage, 261–2
  and materialism, 164–5
  number of acts, 271
  'reformist', 258–9
  'romantic', 11, 46, 257
  themes of, 260–1
  use of verse or prose, 270–1
comedy of character, 257–8
comedy of intrigue, 152, 166, 257, 265
comedy of manners, 34, 166, 258
'Comic War', the, 91–2
commedia dell'arte, 6–9, 87, 99, 124, 168
commedia erudita, 4, 6, 9, 11
Compagnie de Mademoiselle, *see* theatres
Compagnie du Saint-Sacrement, 121–3
Conte, Valleran le, 10
contre-blason, 76–7, 81
Corneille, Pierre
  comedies: burlesque, 75–6, 77–8; characterization, 34–41; classification of, 41–2; ethical background, 32–3; realism, 29, 31, 34, 265; social background of, 32–3; unities, 42–3
  life, 12–13
  works: *Le Cid*, 13, 24, 33n., 78, 79; *Clitandre*, 13, 24n.; *Discours*, 42; *Don Sanche d'Aragon*, 257; *Examens*, 31, 34, 42; *La Galerie du Palais*, 17–20, 27, 30 ff., 35–7, 42, 155, 211; *Héraclius*, 13n.; *Horace*, 13; *L'Illusion comique*, 13, 24–6, 30, 34; *Medée*, 24;

Mélite, 12–15, 16n., 29, 31, 34, 42; *Le Menteur*, 13, 26–8, 32 f., 40–1, 54, 87; *La Mort de Pompée*, 13; *Nicomède*, 86; *La Place Royale*, 21–4, 26, 31 f., 38–40; *La Suite du Menteur*, 13, 27–8, 33; *La Suivante*, 20–1, 23n., 26, 29, 34–5, 42, 153; *La Veuve*, 16–17, 18, 22, 29, 32, 37n., 42, 75–6
Corneille, Thomas, 49–50; *Ariane*, 57n.; *Le Baron d'Albrikac*, 152–3; *Le Berger extravagant*, 84; *Dom Juan*, 99; *Jodelet Prince*, 54
courtly love, 70–1
Couton, G., *Théâtre complet de Corneille*, 30, 36

Dancourt, Florent: *Les Bourgeoises à la mode*, 172–3; *Les Bourgeoises de qualité*, 170; *Le Chevalier à la mode*, 31n.; *Les Curieux de Compiègne*, 175; *La Désolation des joueuses*, 178; *L'Été des coquettes*, 175; *La Maison de campagne*, 174–5; *Les Vendanges de Suresnes*, 175–6
Desmarets de Saint Sorlin, Jean: *Préceptes de mariage*, 96; *Les Visionnaires*, 40n., 51, 53, 79–83, 87
Destouches, Philippe N.: *Le Dissipateur*, 220–2; *Le Glorieux*, 218–20, 222; *L'Ingrat, L'Irrésolu, Le Médisant*, 217; *Le Philosophe marié*, 217–18, 225
Diderot, D.: *Le Discours sur la poésie dramatique, Les Entretiens sur 'Le Fils naturel', Le Fils naturel, Le Père de famille*, 214
Don Juan, legend of, 123–4
drame, viii, 41, 215, 271
drame bourgeois, 2, 214–15
Du Bartas, G., *Les Semaines*, 82
Dufresny, Charles-Rivière: *Attendez-moi sous l'orme*, 182; *Le Chevalier joueur*, 178–80, 182; *La Coquette de village* (*Le Lot supposé*), 178, 183–4; *Le Double Veuvage*, 164, 184–7; *L'Esprit de contradiction, La Joueuse*, 182; *La Malade sans maladie*, 182; *Le Négligent*, 156, 182; *La Noce interrompue*, 232n.

Durand, Catherine, *Le Prodige d'amour*, 196, 197n.
Du Ryer, P.: *Alcionée*, *Scévole*, 87; *Les Vendanges de Suresne*, 153n., 175n.

esprit, 229–30
Étioles, Lenormand d', 238
Euripides, *Iphigenia in Tauris*, 188

fabliaux, 9
fairy-tale, the, 197
family, the, 215–16
fanfaron, 7, 70, 72, 88, 108. See also *capitano*.
fantasy, 52, 257
farce, 2–3, 9, 86–7, 102–3, 155, 234, 257
Favart, Charles-Simon, 235
feminism, 167 n. 2, 212–13, 262–3
femme d'intrigue, 167
Foucquet, Nicolas, 89
French Revolution, the, 240

galanterie, 70
Garguille, Gaultier, *Chansons*, 10
Garnier, R., *Bradamante*, 15
Gassendi, 121
Gelosi, 6
Gherardi, Évariste, 6–7
Godard, J., *Les Déguisés*, 5
Greek New Comedy, 4
Gresset, L.: *Le Méchant*, *Vert-Vert*, 228–9
Grévin, J.: *Les. Ébahis*, *La Trésorière*, 3, 4
Grimarest, J.-L., *Vie de Molière*, 91
Gros-Guillaume, 9

Hardy, A., 5, 44, 45; *Ariadne ravie*, 57n.; *Gésippe*, 46
Hauteroche, N. L.: *Crispin médecin*, 154; *Le Deuil*, 155, 164–5
honour code, 32–3, 71–4, 206–8
Hôtel de Bourgogne, 9–10, 13, 44, 53, 92, 95, 124, 154, 156
Hugo, Victor, *Les Misérables*, 250
humours, theory of the, 158n.
hyperbole, 52, 77

Illustre Théâtre, *see* theatres
Isabelle grosse par vertu, 234

Italian comedy, 4, 6–9, 45
Italians, the, 168–9, 195, 198, 234

Jansenists, 122
Jodelet, 53–5, 59, 88
Jodelle, E.: *Cléopatre*, *L'Eugène*, *La Rencontre*, 3–5
jongleurs, 9
Jonson, Ben, 158n.; *Volpone*, 180

La Bruyère, J. de, 147, 166–7; *Les Caractères*, 41, 157
La Chaussée, P.-C. de, *L'École de la jeunesse*, *L'École des mères*, 227; *La Fausse Antipathie*, 223; *Maximien*, 223; *Mélanide*, 224; *Le Préjugé à la mode*, 224–6, 230, 246
Laclos, P., *Les Liaisons dangereuses*, 133
La Fontaine: *Fables*, 162; *Le Songe de Vaux*, 79
La Grange, *Registre*, 61n., 87 and n., 90n., 92, 97n.
Lambert, Marquise de, 195, 212
Lambertini, Prospero, 8
Lamoignon, Guillaume de, 98, 122
Lancaster, H. C., ix, 73–4, 173, 182–3
Larivey, Pierre de, 5
Latin comedy, 4, 7, 46
La Vallière, Louise de, 95
Le Capitan ou le Miles gloriosus, 79
Lélio, *see* Riccoboni.
Le Noir, Charles, 13
Le Noir, Thérése, 170
Lesage, Alain-René, 167; *Arlequin roi de Serendib*, 188; *Crispin rival de son maître*, 181n., 187, 188–9; *Critique par le Diable boiteux*, 192; *Le Diable boiteux*, *Gil Blas*, 187; *Turcaret*, 187, 189–93
Lettre sur la comédie de l'Imposteur, 98
L'Hermite, Tristan, *Amarillis*, 45, 84; *La Mariane*, *La Mort de Chrispe*, 87; *Le Parasite*, 79n.
Louis XIV, 87, 92, 95–6, 98 f., 122, 163
Lully, J.-B., 99, 100, 114, 169

Maintenon, Madame de, 52, 169n.
Mareschal, A., 40n.; *Le Railleur*, *Le Véritable Capitan Matamore ou le Fanfaron*, 78

marivaudage, 199
Marivaux, Pierre
  and feminism, 212–13
  and honour, 207
  life, 194–5
  and love, 208–11, 267
  works: *Arlequin poli par l'amour*, 196–7, 209; *Les Caractères*, 195; *La Colonie*, 213; *Le Dénouement imprévu*, 199; *La Double Inconstance*, 198, 217n., 205–8, 209–10; *La Fausse Suivante, Les Fausses Confidences, L'Héritier de village, L'Heureux Stratagème*, 212; *L'Île des esclaves*, 212, 213; *L'Île de la Raison*, 199, 212; *L'Iliade travestie*, 195; *Le Jeu de l'amour et du hasard*, 201–5, 208, 211, 216–17; *La Mort d'Annibal*, 195; *La Nouvelle Colonie*, 212–13; *Le Paysan parvenu*, 195; *Le Prince travesti*, 211; *Les Serments indiscrets*, 212; *Les Surprises de l'amour*, 195, 198–200, 225; *Télémaque travestie*, 195; *Le Triomphe de l'amour*, 211–12; *La Vie de Mariane*, 195
métaphysique du cœur, 201
Miracle Plays, 124
Molière
  features and theories: burlesque, 103, 106; classification of plays, 102–3; his conception of comedy, 109–12; influence, 266–7; literary parody, 103–6; loquacity and jargon, 107; 'Ouf!', use of, 183–4; religious scepticism, 121, 122–3; satire, 112, 148, 166
  and hypocrisy, 96, 99, 109, 119, 124
  life and career, 85–101
  works: *Amphitryon*, 50, 99–100; *L'Amour Médecin*, 102, 107, 153n.; *L'Avare*, 9n., 31n., 91, 100, 103, 113; *Le Bourgeois Gentilhomme*, 50, 100, 103, 109, 113–15; *La Comtesse d'Escarbagnas*, 100, 155; *La Critique de l'École des femmes*, 92–3, 110–12, 138, 159, 183; *Le Dépit amoureux*, 87; *Le Docteur amoureux*, 86–7; *Dom Garcie de Navarre ou le Prince jaloux*, 88, 89, 138; *L'École*

des femmes, 89–93, 96, 137–8, 153; *L'École des maris*, 89, 136–7; *L'Étourdi*, 87; *Les Fâcheux*, 89, 96, 147; *Les Femmes savantes*, 51, 103–7, 113; *Les Fourberies de Scapin*, 102; *George Dandin*, 115–17; *Gros René écolier*, 87; *L'Impromptu de Versailles*, 93–5; (*La Jalousie de Barbouillé*), 115; *Le Malade imaginaire*, 101, 107, 109, 113, 243; *Le Mariage forcé*, 96; *Le Médecin malgré lui*, 102, 107; *Le Médecin volant*, 87, 107; *Le Misanthrope*, 2, 40, 60, 61, 91, 99, 103, 115, 134–47, 190; *Monsieur de Pourceaugnac*, 100, 102, 107–9, 147, 155; *Panulphe*, 98; *Les Précieuses ridicules*, 54, 61n., 68, 87–8, 101, 103; *La Princesse d'Élide*, 89n., 96, 257; *Psyché*, 103; *Sganarelle ou le Cocu imaginaire*, 88, 102; *Le Sicilien ou l'Amour peintre*, 103; *Tartuffe*, 2, 96–9, 110, 117–22, 152, 192
Molina, Tirso de: *El burlador de Sevilla y convidado de piedra*, 123; *No hay peor sordo*, 56
'Monsieur', *see* Orléans, Duke of
Montdory, 13
Montespan, Madame de, 100
Montfleury, A.-J.: *L'École des filles, L'École des jaloux, La Femme juge et partie, La Fille capitaine, Le Gentilhomme de la Beauce*, 154; *L'Impromptu de l'Hôtel de Condé*, 92n.
Montfleury, Z.-J., 95 and n., 111n.
moralités, 9, 162
Moreto: *El desdén con el desdén*, 89; *La tía y la sobrina*, 153
Mozart: *Don Giovanni*, 133; *The Marriage of Figaro*, 251
musical comedy, 235
Mysteries, the, 9

neoplatonic poetry, 81

one-act comedy, the, 155
opéra-comique, 169, 188, 200, 235, 271
Orléans, Duke of, 86, 97
Orwell, George, *Animal Farm*, 148
Ouville, d', *Jodelet astrologue*, 54

Palais Royal, Théâtre du, *see* theatres
Palaprat, Jean, *see* Brueys, David
Pantalone, *see* type-characters
parades, 209, 223, 228, 234–5, 238, 241, 256
Pâris-Duverney, 238, 239
parody, 51, 74–5, 257
Pascal, B., *Lettres provinciales*, 75
pastoral drama, 11, 15, 257
Perrault, Charles: *Histoires ou contes du temps passé, Riquet à la houppe*, 197
Perrin, F., *Les Écoliers*, 5
'Philipin', 54, 59, 153
pièce à tiroirs, 159
Plaisirs de l'île enchantée, 95–6
Planchon, René, 201
Plautus, 4, 7, 45, 46, 66 and n., 100
Pléiade group, the, 3 ff., 82
Poisson, R., 154
Pope Benedict XIV, 8–9
Poquelin, Jean-Baptiste, *see* Molière
précieuses, 88 and n.
préciosité, 68, 70, 199
Prévost Manon Lescaut, 227

Quinault, Philippe: *Comédie sans comédie*, 54; *La Mère coquette*, 152; *Les Rivales*, 45–6

Rabelais, 9; *Gargantua, Pantagruel*, 51–2, 66
Racine, J.: *Andromaque*, 151, 179n.; *Bérénice*, 23, 40, 223; *Brittanicus*, 23; *Phèdre*, 14n.; *Les Plaideurs*, 66, 151–2
raisonneurs, 148–9
Les Ramonneurs, 5
realism, 259; *see also* Corneille, Pierre
Regnard, J.-F.: *Attendez-moi sous l'orme*, 176–7; *Le Distrait*, 157, 177; *Le Joueur*, 177–80, 221; *Le Légataire universel*, 180–1; *La Provençale*, 182; *La Sérénade*, 189n.
Riccoboni, Luigi, 7, 195
Richardson, S., *Pamela*, 227, 230
Romains, Jules, *Monsieur Le Trouhadec saisi par la débauche*, 175
romanesque literature, 77
Ronsard, Pierre de, 81, 82

Rotrou, Jean
influence, 50
type of comedies, 45–6
works: *La Bague de l'oubli*, 20, 24n., 44, 45; *La Belle Alphrède*, 46–9; *Les Captifs*, 46n.; *Célimène*, 45; *Clarice, Cosroès*, 44; *La Diane, Les Deux Pucelles*, 45; *L'Hypocondriaque*, 44; *Les Ménechmes*, 17n., 46n.; *Saint Genest*, 44; *La Sœur*, 44, 50; *Les Sosies*, 46n., 50, 100; *Venceslas*, 44
rusticity, 155–6, 260

Sade, Marquis de, *Oxtiern ou les Malheurs du libertinage*, 235–6
Saint-Évremond, C. de M. de: *La Comédie des Académistes*, 83–4
St Gregory of Nazianzen, *Préceptes de mariage envoyés à Olympias*, 96
Saint-Yon, 174
satire, 51–2, 165–6, 258–9
Scala, Flaminio, 7
Scaramouche, 151
Scarron, Paul
influence of, 266
life, 52
type and style of comedies, 64–5, 66, 68, 70, 74–5
works: *Don Japhet d'Arménie*, 52, 54, 57–8, 61n., 67–8, 87; *L'Écolier de Salamanque, La Fausse Apparence, Le Faux Alexandre, Le Gardien de soi-même*, 53; *L'Héritier ridicule*, 53 f., 59–62, 65–6, 67, 70–1 f.; *Jodelet duelliste*, 53, 56–7, 61n., 69, 72 f., 131; *Jodelet ou le Maître-Valet*, 53, 55–6, 60, 61n., 66, 68–9, 71–2 f., 77; *Le Marquis ridicule*, 53, 61n., 62–4, 70, 108, 153n., 228; *Le Prince Corsaire*, 53; *Le Romain comique*, 9, 52; *Les Trois Dorothées ou Jodelet soufflété*, 53, 56, 72; *Typhon ou la Gigantomachie, Virgile travesti*, 52
Seneca, 3
sensibilité, 216, 224, 267
sensiblerie, 216
Shakespeare, William: *King Lear*, 57; *A Midsummer Night's Dream*, 76, 197; *Romeo and Juliet*, 14n.

Shakespearean fool, the, 74
Shaw, Bernard, *Mrs Warren's Profession*, 167n.
'Silvia', 195–6
soliloquies, 29–30
Solórzano, Castillo, *El Marqués de Cigarral*, 58
Sorel, Charles, *Le Berger extravagant*, 84
soties, 9
soubrettes, 8
Spanish *comedia*, 46, 154
Spanish influences, 24, 26, 45, 53, 56
stances, 71
State Opera, the, 169
stichomythia, 29
suivantes, 54, 153, 167
Swift, Jonathan, *Gulliver's Travels*, 212

Tabarin, 10
Tacitus, 69
Taille, Jean de la: *Les Corrivaux, Le Négromant*, 3, 4
Terence, 4 and n., 45; *The Eunuch*, 5n.
theatres and companies
    Comédie Française, *see under*
    Compagnie de Mademoiselle, 124
    Hôtel de Bourgogne, *see under*
    L'Illustre Théâtre,
    Théâtre du Marais, 13, 53, 54, 79
    Théâtre du Palais Royal, 87, 169
    Théâtre des Boulevards, 234
    Théâtre de la Foire, 169, 234
    Théâtre Guénégaud, 101
    See also *commedia dell'arte* and Italians

'Thomassin', 195, 196, 234
tragédie bourgeoise, 214n., 233
tragicomedy, 2, 15, 50, 165, 257
Troterel, P., *Les Corrivaux, Gillette*, 5
Turlupin, 9, 54, 93
Turnèbe, O. de, *Les Contents*, 5
Tyard, Pontus de, 81
type-characters, 7–9, 93, 153, 166–8, 244, 263–4

unities, the, 42 and n., 49, 268–9
Urfé, Honoré d', *L'Astrée*, 11, 20n., 45, 84

Vanbrugh, Sir John, *The Confederacy*, 173
Vega, Lope de, 45, 46, 154; *Amar sin saber a quien*, 27; *Hermosa Alfreda*, 46n.
verse: decasyllabic, 231; octosyllabic, 4, 52
Villiers, Claude de, 54, 124
Visé, Donneau de, 159: *La Mère coquette*, 152; *La Réponse à l'Impromptu de Versailles, Zélinde*, 92n.
Voltaire: *Candide*, 230; *La Fanatisme ou Mahomet*, 8; *Nanine ou le Préjugé vaincu*, 230–3

Wycherley, William, *The Plain Dealer*, 135

Zanni, 8, 263
zézaiement, 234
Zorilla, Rojas, *Donde hay agravios no hay zelos y amo criado*, 55